D1610383

THE END OF OUTRAGE

The End of Outrage

Post-Famine Adjustment in Rural Ireland

BREANDÁN MAC SUIBHNE

OXFORD

UNIVERSITY PRESS

OXFORD
UNIVERSITY PRESS

Great Clarendon Street, Oxford, OX2 6DP,
United Kingdom

Oxford University Press is a department of the University of Oxford.
It furthers the University's objective of excellence in research, scholarship,
and education by publishing worldwide. Oxford is a registered trade mark of
Oxford University Press in the UK and in certain other countries

First Edition published in 2017

Impression: 1

Published in the United States of America by Oxford University Press
198 Madison Avenue, New York, NY 10016, United States of America

British Library Cataloguing in Publication Data
Data available

Library of Congress Control Number: 2017935047

ISBN 978–0–19–873861–9

Printed and bound by
CPI Group (UK) Ltd, Croydon, CR0 4YY

do Nóra Rose agus Sarah

Acknowledgements

I would not have written this book but for colleagues, in various disciplines, who saw potential in drafts of an essay probing some happenings in a small place 'in the time of the Famine'. And there would not have been a book so soon if Robert Faber had not commissioned it and Cathryn Steele not helped me to finish it. The thoughtful reflections of Oxford University Press's readers made several chapters better and I am deeply grateful to Kerby A. Miller and Cormac Ó Gráda for commenting on substantial sections. I also benefited greatly from discussing some issues with Claire Connolly, Seamus Deane, David Lloyd, Laurence Marley, Lillis Ó Laoire, and Brendan O'Leary. Among others to whom I am indebted are Judy Acaster, Colleen Bain, Steve Ball, Guy Beiner, Hilary Bell, Ciara Breathnach, Mark Bulik, Tom Cannon, Joe Cleary, Róisín Corcoran, Catherine Cox, John Cunningham, Martin Daly, Ciarán Deane, Cormac Deane, Enda Delaney, David Dickson, Jimmy Duffy, Alun Evans, Luke Gibbons, John Gibney, Niall Gillespie, Roy Hamilton, Mary Harris, Julie Kavanagh, Kevin Kenny, Charles McElwee, Steve Macmillan, David W. Miller, David Nally, Willie Nolan, Dónall Ó Baoill, Seán Ó Brógáin, Éamonn Ó Ciardha, Niall Ó Ciosáin, Antaine Ó Donnaile, Kevin O'Neill, Gearóid Ó Tuathaigh, Jim Patterson, Clement Raj, Jane Robson, Frank Shovlin, Stephen Smyrl, Jim Smyth, Elizabeth Stone, Matthew Stout, Nuala Sweeney, Tony Varley, John Waters, Niall Whelehan, and Nicholas Wolf. I had expert guides to the main sources for this study in Aideen Ireland, Niamh McDonnell, Frances McGee, Gregory O'Connor, and Paddy Sarsfield of the National Archives of Ireland; Críostóir Mac Cárthaigh of the National Folkore Collection; Fran Carroll of the National Library of Ireland, and Niamh Brennan of Donegal County Archives, while Siobhán O'Brien of Cheshire Record Office, Chester, Sharon Gothard of Easton Public Libraries, Pennsylvania, and Hazel Nsair of the Anglican Diocese of Melbourne clarified some fine points.

Discussing the politics of post-Famine adjustment with informed people helped me to refine some arguments. Grace Brady hosted two lectures at Quinnipiac University's Great Hunger Museum; Roy Foster invited me to talk to his Irish History group at the University of Oxford; Patrick Joyce arranged for me to participate in a seminar on the Unequal Dead at Cambridge University, and Joe Lee gave me several opportunities to present ideas in New York University. A fellowship in the Moore

Institute at the National University of Ireland, Galway, significantly advanced the project; there, I particularly appreciated the support of Daniel Carey. And thanks too to Louis de Paor and the faculty, staff, and students of the Centre for Irish Studies.

Much is owed to the people of Beagh, most especially my father Patsy Sweeney and Fr John Gallagher. In Ardara, Seamus Gallagher talked to me about shopkeepers and tradesmen, Conall Kennedy about knitting, Malachy Maguire about road-workers, and Lochlann McGill about popular religion. John Breslin provided an architect's plan of his family's public house, Eithne Ní Ghallchobhair supplied copies of folklore materials, and Charlie McHugh gave sage advice. Beyond the town, Vincent McConnell illuminated the life of Moses Ward, the most militant of Ardara's Mollies, Francis Shovlin discussed his native Downstrands, and Richard Wayman took photographs. But the greatest debt is to Kathryn Kozarits, who never ceases to amaze—and who always sleeps well in Beagh.

Sadly, several family members who would have appreciated this history are dead. Among them is one who, after publication, would have said that there was more to it than I knew; another who, out of devilment, would have regretted that there had not been a blacker presentation of some details; and a third who would have closed her eyes, shaken her head, and laughed—my uncles John Joe and James and my aunt Deirdre.

It has been said that a certain type of historian writes 'in the time between the dead and children, between irreparable suffering and hope for the unforeseeable to-come'.[1] Although my own forebears appear in these pages, genealogy's charms are lost on me: this book has been written less to tell Nóra Rose and Sarah whence they came, and more to give them a glimpse of how the world works. And, in a time of widening inequality and environmental collapse, it is with a wish that those two great girls, like the boys and girls who came before them, be persistent and make a difference.

Beagh
February 2017

---

[1] John D. Caputo, 'No Tear Shall be Lost: The History of Prayers and Tears', in David Carr, Thomas R. Flynn, and Rudolf A. Makkreel, eds, *The Ethics of History* (Evanston, IL, 2004), 91–118, 115–16.

Contents

List of Figures

List of Maps

List of Tables

Abbreviations

BH	*Ballyshannon Herald*
BN	*Belfast Newsletter*
CRF	Convict Reference Files
CSF	Census Search Forms
CSORP	Chief Secretary's Office Registered Papers
DCA	Donegal County Archive
DJ	*Derry Journal*
ED	Education Department
FB	Field Book
GRO	General Register Office
GV	Richard Griffith, *General Valuation of Rateable Property... Union of Glenties* (Dublin, 1857), commonly *Griffith's Valuation*
IPSCR	Irish Petty Sessions Court Registers
LJ	*London-Derry Journal*
LSnl	*Londonderry Sentinel*
LStd	*Londonderry Standard*
NAI	National Archives of Ireland
NFCM	National Folklore Collection, Main Collection
NFCS	National Folklore Collection, Schools Collection
NLI	National Library of Ireland
OffP	Official Papers
OP	Outrage Papers
OS	Ordnance Survey
OSFNB	Ordnance Survey Field Name Books
PB	Perambulation Book
PRONI	Public Record Office Northern Ireland
SOC	State of the Country Papers
TAB	Tithe Applotment Book
VO	Valuation Office

Prologue

The Era of Infidelity

Oh, ye Dead! oh, ye Dead! whom we know by the light you give
From your cold gleaming eyes, though you move like men who live,
    Why leave you thus your graves,
    In far off fields and waves,
Where the worm and the sea-bird only know your bed,
    To haunt this spot, where all
    Those eyes that wept your fall,
And the hearts that bewail'd you, like your own, lie dead.

        Thomas Moore, 'Oh, Ye Dead!', *Irish Melodies* (1822)

West Donegal, 31 October 1856. On the dark night of *Oíche Shamhna* the Catholic poor feasted on nuts and apples, and they played games, many of them involving divination. A ring in a piece of barmbrack meant the finder would marry within the year, while a person who found a pea would remain single. Three bowls set in front of a blindfolded young woman determined her spouse: if she placed her hand in one containing clear water, she would get a young man; if the water was dirty, she would get an old man; if the bowl was empty, she would get none. And in nuts set alight near the hearth couples would read their fates: flames that joined foretold a strong union; flames that did not join were an indication that they would separate.

This long night also involved whiskey drinking, mischief, and boisterous fun. Young people sitting in a circle played *Thart-an-Bhróg*, surreptitiously passing a shoe from one to another, and then firing it at an unfortunate in the centre who was hunting for it. Fellows went out robbing cabbages, which they threw at the doors of those robbed, while others carved jack-o'-lanterns from turnips. And then, after they had ducked for apples and all games were played, they brushed the floor, loaded the fire with turf, arranged chairs or creepies (bogwood stools) in front of it, and they went to bed.[1]

---

[1] NFCS 1,048 (Tullymore): 181: 'Superstitions', transcribed, in 1937–8, by Nan Melley (*c.*1923–92) from her father Con (d. 1962) who heard them from his father

That final ritual demands little interpretative effort. The living were welcoming the dead. They were making space for them in that lifeless season when the sun does not rise high above the horizon and the nights are longest and there is no growth; they were deferring to the ancestors when the otherworld comes closest and threatens humankind. In the mid-1850s, then, the people vibrated between two cosmologies, one ancestral or fairy and the other Christian. Central to the non-Christian system were ritualized gatherings around fires or wells, often on dates determined by solar or lunar cycles.[2] Here, near the little towns of Ardara and Glenties, on the night of 23 June, every house had a bonfire, and in some townlands there was one large fire, around which people from all houses gathered, and when the fire had burned out, they would take the cinders and scatter them through the fields of growing crops and they would rub the ashes on their cattle.[3] They called that night *Oíche Fhéile Eoin*, St John's Eve. The following day was the reputed birthdate of John the Baptist, but the festival had no significant Christian dimension. Certainly, no special prayers were said to the Evangelist, and no priest presided. Their *pietas* was, indeed, for older, quieter things.[4] Those bonfires blazed when the day is longest—the summer solstice (midsummer) occurs on 20–2 June— and, if only flickeringly apprehended by those gathered around the crackling bogwood, it was the life-giving power of the sun, not the man who announced the coming of Christ, that they venerated.

Oíche Fhéile Bhríde (1 February), *Bealtaine* (1 May), and *Lúnasa* (1 August) were other sun-defined occasions of festivity. The Catholic poor, in the words of the novelist John McGahern, were going about their 'sensible pagan lives' as they had done 'since the time of the Druids'.[5] And while these people were emphatically Catholic—they prayed *Ár nAthair atá ar Neamh*..., Our Father who art in Heaven... and *'Sé do bheatha Mhuire*..., Hail Mary Full of Grace...—they were remarkably indifferent to the requirements of their Church.[6] Attendance at Sunday mass was an obligation, on pain of mortal sin, upon Catholics, yet in 1834 the parish priests of Ardara and Inishkeel (Glenties) estimated that,

Condy (b. *c*.1850). For a nineteenth-century account of *Samhain*, see Hugh Dorian, *The Outer Edge of Ulster: A Memoir of Social Life in Nineteenth-Century Donegal*, ed. Breandán Mac Suibhne and David Dickson (Dublin, 2000), 262–71.

[2] Gearóid Ó Crualaoich, 'The Merry Wake', in James S. Donnelly, Jr and Kerby A. Miller, eds, *Irish Popular Culture, 1650–1850* (Dublin, 1998), 173–201, 191.

[3] NFCS 1,048 (Tullymore): 198; account by John McHugh, aged 12, Tullycleave, in 1938.

[4] Brian Friel, *Translations* (London, 1980), Act III.

[5] John McGahern, *Memoir* (London, 2005), 211.

[6] On mass attendance, see David W. Miller, 'Landscape and Religious Practice: A Study of Mass Attendance in Pre-Famine Ireland', *Éire-Ireland*, 40/1–2 (2005), 90–106.

respectively, 19.3 and 29.8 per cent of their parishioners were turning up, despite there being then three chapels (Ardara, Glenties, and Fintown) between the two parishes. Fintown's chapel had only just opened, but the towns had boasted purpose-built chapels—not *scáthláin*, shelters—since the 1790s. And across the Gweebarra estuary, in the poorer Rosses, none of four chapels, two dating to the 1780s, had a weekly mass: Dungloe and Lettermacaward each had a single mass every second Sunday, Belcruit had mass on two consecutive Sundays, and Arranmore every third Sunday; here, priests estimated that 25–7 per cent of Catholics attended those services.[7]

There are no hard data on the composition of these congregations. Still, *seanchas*, oral history, about the avarice of priests—there were fees for baptism, marriage, and burial—and the priests themselves having been reared on snug farms or in shops suggest it was the better-off sorts who most frequently attended chapel. It was those sorts too who were more likely to confess and receive communion, which all Catholics were required to do at least once a year, at Easter. Hence, for the typical smallholder, hoking an existence from a few acres of potatoes, their priest married couples and baptized the new-born, administered the last rites to the dying and buried the dead, but chapel and clerically directed devotions did not have a central place in their lives. Moreover, many ostensibly Christian traditions had traces of an older magic. For instance, the cult of the early Christian ascetic, St Conall, was important to the people.[8] Conall's feast falls on 22 May, and between then and 12 September, great numbers would undertake a *turas* or curative pilgrimage to the ruins of a medieval monastic settlement in Inishkeel, a relatively flat and fertile island, about 80 acres in extent, which down to the early nineteenth century was the site of the district's most prestigious burial ground. At Narin, after a spring tide, that is, in the days following a new or full

[7] *First Report of the Commissioners of Public Instruction, Ireland*, HC 1835 (45), xxxiii, 272a–273a, 278a–279a, 280a–283a. Purpose-built chapels had been erected in Ardara and Glenties by 1795. At the time of the survey (1834), Ardara's first chapel had recently (1832) been replaced by a building in the west end of town; see Edward Maguire, *A History of the Diocese of Raphoe*, 2 vols. (Dublin, 1920), i. 478–9; P. J. McGill, *A History of the Parish of Ardara* (Ballyshannon, 1970), 13–23, and Liam Briody, *Glenties and Inniskeel* (Ballyshannon, 1986), 30, 33. In the mid-1830s, there was, in fact, another older chapel in the parish of Ardara, at Mullyvea; however, the parish priest had downgraded or abandoned it and it is not mentioned in his return to the Commissioners; see Ch. 7 of this volume.
[8] Lochlann McGill, *In Conall's Footsteps* (Dingle, 1992), esp. chs. 3–6, explores the cult of Conall. Also see Patrick O'Donnell, 'Inniskeel', *Irish Ecclesiastical Record*, 8 (1887), 781–94, and McGill, *Ardara*, 13–23. On the *turas* in Irish Catholicism, past and present, see Lawrence J. Taylor's fine historical ethnography, *Occasions of Faith: An Anthropology of Irish Catholics* (Dublin, 1995), ch. 2, and Angela Bourke's luminous Introduction to Anna Rackard and Liam O'Callaghan, *Fishstonewater: Holy Wells of Ireland* (Cork, 2001), 7–12.

moon, it is possible to walk dry-shod to 'the island'. On reaching it, pilgrims used to discard their shoes and stockings, if they were wearing any, and to recite a series of fixed prayers as they circled holy wells, sacred stones, and the ruins of medieval churches; the *turas* culminated in the pilgrims passing 'healing stones' around their bodies, in the hopes of alleviating pain or averting illness.[9]

Again, no priest presided and, into the nineteenth century, the most conspicuous figure in the *turas* was a lay-man, the senior member of the Breslin family, who used to stand at *Leaba Chonaill*, Conall's Bed, a rock on which people suffering from back trouble would lie in expectation of a cure, and hold out the *Bearnán*, a simple hand-bell (*c*.700–900 AD) housed in an ornate silver shrine-case (*c*.1400 AD), for the pilgrims to kiss; the bell, it was said, had belonged to Conall. The Breslins had been an 'erenagh' or prebendary family, responsible for the management of ecclesiastical lands, from medieval times to the seventeenth century, when, with the over-throw of the Gaelic order, those lands had passed to the newly established Protestant Church. Still, the enshrined hand-bell had remained in their possession, and, besides taking it to the island when the *turas* was being performed, the head of the family would display it to the sick and the dying. John O'Donovan, who inspected the 'beautiful and elaborately decorated relic' in 1835, was very taken by its representation of the crucifixion, and he imagined Breslin on the island, with the 'elaborately ornamented' shrine, 'exhibiting to the enthusiastic pilgrims, the glittering gems and the symbol of the bloody sacrifice in which the creator of the world drained all his veins of the electric stream that supported his humanity'.[10]

Through the *turas* and the kissing of the *Bearnán*, no less than the various seasonal festivals, the people were keeping faith with their fore-bears, but O'Donovan was cognizant that in west Donegal, and indeed elsewhere in the west of Ireland, many 'venerable old customs' were passing away: 'a different era—the era of infidelity—is fast approaching!', he wrote in 1837.[11] Here, in the townlands north of Ardara that are the

[9] The National Folklore Collection contains many accounts of the *turas*; see e.g. stories collected by the pupils of Kilclooney and Clogher schools in the late 1930s in NFCS 1,048–9. For an account by anthropologist John Henry Hutton, see 'Pilgrimages to the Holy Well and Ruined Church of St. Conal on the Island Inishkeel, Gweebarra Bay, Co. Donegal', *Folklore*, 31/3 (1920), 231–3.
[10] Ardara, 19 Oct. 1835, O'Donovan to Larcom, in *Ordnance Survey Letters, Donegal*, ed. Michael Herity, with a preface by Brian Friel (Dublin, 2000), 100–2.
[11] Roscommon, 29 June 1837, O'Donovan to Larcom, quoted in Gillian M. Doherty, *The Irish Ordnance Survey: History, Culture and Memory* (Dublin, 2004), 137. On O'Donovan's sense of 'tradition' withering, ibid., ch. 6, and Stiofán Ó Cadhla, *Civilizing Ireland: Ordnance Survey, 1824–1842: Ethnography, Cartography, Translation* (Dublin, 2007), 156–63.

main focus of this book, that era of infidelity can be said to have definitively arrived in the last third of the century, when, over much of that area, English replaced Irish as the language of the home, children ceased to hear the old songs and stories, and rituals that had mattered from time immemorial were performed no more. But, in truth, a time of great betrayal had been a long time coming. The dust had settled on the Down Survey (1656–8) by the early 1700s, and, the conquest complete, a transition from an oatmeal- to a potato-based diet—a sudden change, in fact, as potatoes were a 'garden crop' (not a staple food) through the 1600s but, by 1753–4, they constituted the winter diet of the Rosses where, in that season, 'very few' ate any bread[12]—allowed people to marry younger and settle on land that would not yield decent cereals. More households, in turn, meant more families rearing a cow or pig, and, as the district's involvement in the livestock and grain trades increased, markets were also found for herring and salmon, kelp, rabbit-skins, smuggled tobacco, and *poitín*, illicit whiskey, distilled from barley. The pace of demographic expansion was extraordinary: the rectors of Lettermacaward and Templecrone estimated that there were 420 families in the Rosses in 1766; by 1841, the number of families had trebled to 1,274; there was a commensurate increase south of the Gweebarra.[13] And that growth in population was itself a force for cultural change. The cheap fiddle replaced the pipes as the ubiquitous instrument at dances before the end of the 1700s, and families settling permanently on mountain townlands may have contributed to the decline of *buailteachas*, booleying, that is, young people spending the summers on highland pastures herding cattle; notwithstanding some redoubts in the Rosses and south of Ardara, booleying seems to have been significantly curtailed by the early 1800s.[14]

---

[12] A——B——, 'An Account of the Customs, Manners, and Dress of the Inhabitants of the Rosses on the Coast of the County of Donegal, Ireland, in a Letter to the Author', in Joseph C. Walker, *An Historical Essay on the Dress of the Ancient and Modern Irish* (Dublin, 1788), 141–9, 145–6; this letter, dated Dublin, 1788, describes how, in 1753, a Mr N——, possibly one of the Nesbitts of Woodhill (Ardara) or Kilmacreddan (Inver), had accompanied a friend to the district on legal business. The author remarks on women knitting stockings but nobody wearing any, suggesting the stocking trade was already well developed, and notes both men and women were 'excessively fond' of spirits and tobacco.

[13] In 1766 the rectors of Inishkeel and Killybegs estimated that their parishes contained 1,043 families; the 1841 Census returned 3,737 families in those parishes, with Killybegs by then divided into Upper and Lower sections. For the regional context, see Kerby A. Miller and Brian Gurrin, 'The Derry Watershed: Its Religious and Political Demography, 1622–1911', *Field Day Review*, 9 (2013), 38–53.

[14] On *buailteachas*, see McGill, *Ardara*, 75–8, and Mark Gardiner, 'The Role of Transhumance within Rundale', *Ulster Folklife*, 58 (2015), 53–63. On music, see Allen Feldman and Éamonn O'Doherty, *The Northern Fiddler: Music and Musicians of Donegal and Tyrone* (Belfast, 1979) and Caoimhín Mac Aoidh, *Between the Jigs and the Reels: The Donegal Fiddle Tradition* (Manorhamilton, 1994), ch. 2.

Landlords, meanwhile, made efforts at developing their estates, securing patents for fairs and distributing spinning wheels, helping tenants to get spirit licences—here, as on other commercial frontiers, the trading post *cum* drinking shop was the crucial start-up—and promoting the development of towns. In 1760, George Nesbitt (1732–1827) effectively established Ardara at the place where the Owentucker had been bridged in 1723 by securing a patent for four annual fairs and a weekly market; the Hamiltons were forever endeavouring, against all odds, to 'improve' the area around Fintown; and, most dramatically, in the 1780s, the Conynghams, with public money, built a fishing station on the island of Inis Mhic an Doirn, which they duly renamed Rutland after the lord lieutenant who sanctioned the grants.[15] The grand jury, the landlord committee that ran the county, had significantly improved the infrastructure of west Donegal in the mid-1700s—a decent road was first made around the coast of the Rosses in 1758—and, under the Road Act of 1765, it annually allocated funds for roads and bridges, creating, in the process, a cohort of quarrymen and contractors who employed parties of labourers. By 1800, much of west Donegal's modern road network had already taken shape; and it was in need of regular repair, the wages for which work fed labouring families.[16] People who had been familiar with the district in the mid-1700s were now remarking on the extent to which it had changed: a man who had spent 1753–4 in the Rosses found, on his return in 1787, that the people were 'totally altered in their carriage and conduct, their habiliments and habitations, their occupations and manner of living . . . so much improved by their intercourse with others'. Where formerly, he had not seen a man with anything other than a waistcoat and breeches on him, he then met 'spruce young lads fashionably dressed on Sundays, in sattin waistcoats and breeches, with white silk stockings, silver buckles, and ruffled shirts'.[17]

---

[15] McGill, *Conall's Footsteps*, 209, 222–6; Niall Ó Dómhnaill, *Na Glúnta Rosannacha* (Baile Átha Cliath, 1952), 160–3; Pádraig Ua Cnáimhsí, *Idir an Dá Ghaoth: Scéal Mhuintir na Rosann* (Baile Átha Cliath, 1997), 37–46; Wes Forsythe, 'Improving Landlords and Planned Settlements in Eighteenth-Century Ireland: William Burton Conyngham and the Fishing Station on Inis Mhic an Doirn, Co. Donegal', *Proceedings of the Royal Irish Academy*, 112C (2011), 1–32.
[16] William Crawford, 'The Evolution of the Urban Network', in William Nolan, Liam Ronayne, and Mairéad Dunlevy, eds, *Donegal: History and Society* (Dublin, 1995), 381–404. Also see the 1801 grand jury map, by William McCrea of Lifford, DCA, GJ/2/19.
[17] 'An Account', 148. For other perspectives on west Donegal in the mid-1700s, see NAI, Phillips Manuscripts, M. 2,533 William Henry, 'Hints towards a Natural and Topographical History of the Counties Sligoe, Donegal, Fermanagh and Lough Erne . . . 1739', 40–4, and Richard Pococke, *Pococke's Tour in Ireland in 1752*, ed. George T. Stokes (Dublin, 1891), 62–9.

If that particular description gives a false impression of the levels of refinement being generally attained in west Donegal, the demand for agricultural produce ran high in Britain through to Waterloo, drawing more households into the market economy and distributing new commodities more widely. Notwithstanding landlord initiatives, the cattle- and stocking-dealers and egg- and butter-men who travelled the new roads—and, indeed, the tinkers with their 'standings' at fairs—were the point men of commercialization.[18] The men who drew eggs or butter to Derry carried back 'needles, pins, thimbles, and smoothing irons, in short a hardware store on a small scale', and the later wealth of some families, including the McDevitts of Glenties who prospered first in inn-keeping (from the 1700s) and then, most spectacularly, in the stocking trade, had its origins in the horse and cart, if not the ass and creel.[19] Seasonal migration of young adults to the harvest in east Donegal and Scotland, movements well established by 1800, further monetized local economies—payment of rent in kelp, grain, and rabbit-skins or by the working of duty days increasingly gave way to cash transactions—and helped the district to cope with lower agricultural prices after 1815. Derry, meanwhile, had long-established trade-links with Philadelphia that caused its hinterland to be early identified as a labour pool for Pennsylvania's coalmines and canals. In the north-east of that state, anthracite started to be mined in great volume *c*.1820; men from west Donegal were among the first to dig the 'hard coal' and enterprising 'Yankees' were soon coming home for short stays to fetch more broad-shouldered young fellows for the mine patches.[20] By the 1830s, local traders, acting as agents for Glasgow companies, were putting out muslin for poor women to 'sprig' (embroider), and soon other dealers, who had hitherto bought stockings on fair days, would themselves secure contracts with Scottish and English firms and start putting out yarn, keeping women and girls in steady employment. The district, in short, was being fitted into the periphery of the world economy

---

[18] The district's integration into the regional economy can be glimpsed in a report in *LJ*, 8 June 1784, detailing how 'a man of the name of Boyle, who came to this town from Rosses to buy meal, was robbed or defrauded of 153 guineas, his watch and great coat by a fellow who pretended to befriend him in his business in Derry'. The 'unfortunate merchant' did not recover his property.

[19] An egg-man as described in Dorian, *Outer Edge*, 211–12.

[20] E.g. James Cannon, born in 1815 in Rosbeg, was a miner in Summit Hill by 1832. He took US citizenship in 1839 and the following year he returned home. There, he married Rosa (Hugh) McAloon in 1841, and in winter 1844–5 he left again for Pennsylvania, taking his wife and two children with him. They settled in Mauch Chunk, where James mined and Rosa kept Donegal boarders. See the entry on their son, Michael Cannon, an attorney, in *Luzerne Legal Register*, 14 (1885–6), 25–6, and James's obituary in *Hazleton Plain Speaker*, 28 Mar. 1892.

and, between seasonal migration to Scotland, protoindustrialization at home, and the coal and canals its men were digging in industrial America, expectations were rising. A Dublin reporter who visited Ardara attributed significant material improvements to sprigging: 'When the sewed muslin trade was introduced . . . the young girls found that they could not work at it, in their dark and dirty houses, and they insisted on their parents providing chimneys and windows.'[21]

By the time of the Famine, the social structure had changed significantly from that of the mid-eighteenth century. The Protestant proportion of the population had been dwindling for decades—as far back as 1766 the rector of Lettermacaward had decried the 'decay' of its small Protestant community and 'Papists supplanting Protestants in their land'[22]—good farms long tenanted by Protestants were passing to Catholics and a Catholic middle class was growing in size, confidence, and ambition.[23] With the central state now eclipsing the old state of local notables, new opportunities were opening in the administrative apparatus—young men were becoming teachers and clerks, constables and coastguards. But the mass of the people remained mired in poverty. Thomas Ainge Devyr, a native of Donegal town, who travelled the roads of west Donegal buying yarn and selling hardware, before opening a store in Killybegs, used to frequently cross the Gweebarra by ferry:

> Here, I witnessed the boatman's family at their meal of bog potatoes, often without a relish of salt; never with anything better. I saw his children, from five to ten years of age, without any other covering than a piece of ragged flannel pending from the waist, and on one, a child of about three years of age, I never saw a rag of clothing of any kind, although I saw it many times, both in Summer and Winter.

Devyr once spent two days in that boatman's 'hovel' when 'tempestuous water' prevented a crossing, and he shared the family's 'scanty meal of potatoes, that smelled and tasted of the turf on which they grew'; 'nothing better could be procured for money, though several abodes of man were scattered along the bank'.[24] Such families, if well supplied with food and fuel, were living barely above the waterline of despair, and when, in

---

[21] Henry Coulter, *The West of Ireland: Its Existing Condition, and Prospects* (Dublin, 1862), 303–4.

[22] Quoted in J. B. Leslie, *Raphoe Clergy and Parishes* (Enniskillen, 1940), 105.

[23] Miller and Gurrin, 'Derry Watershed', 38–53.

[24] For this description, see Thomas Ainge Devyr's *Our Natural Rights: A Pamphlet for the People, by One of Themselves* (Belfast, 1836); the pamphlet is reproduced in his *Odd Book of the Nineteenth Century; or, 'Chivalry' in Modern Days* (New York, 1882) [Irish and British Section], 112–35.

1830–1 and, again, in 1835–7, poor weather diminished potato crops, there were reports, from priests, ministers, landlords, and coastguards, of deaths from fever and 'actual starvation'; but for government relief efforts, and appeals to charities by priests, significant numbers would likely have perished.[25] Hence, while the Catholic community was understood to be making social advances on the eve of the Famine, by virtue of some people acquiring better land, building businesses, and securing salaried jobs, ragged smallholders and labourers were pushing further onto the bog, up the mountain sides, and into the fishing villages; inequality, within the community, was widening and the cultural ties that bound it were loosening.

If the market was the most assiduous force for change, the relaxation of penal laws in the last third of the eighteenth century had allowed the Catholic Church to assert itself as an arbiter of behaviour. Priests endeavoured to eradicate 'superstition' and regulate conduct at wakes and funerals, patterns, and seasonal festivals. Indeed, in 1835, O'Donovan observed that 'lately' the *turas* to Inishkeel had become an occasion of 'amusement and drinking, so that the RC clergy thought it proper to condemn the practice'.[26] And 'amusement and drinking' were not the only aspects of the *turas* likely to upset priests. The head of the Breslins used to exact a fee from pilgrims who wished to kiss the sacred bell. *Pingin domhsa agus póg don Bhearnán*, A penny for me and a kiss for the *Bearnán*, was the refrain remembered locally.[27] In fact, in 1835, the *Bearnán* was no longer being brought to the island. O'Donovan was told that Conall Mhícheáil of Glengesh, who claimed to be the senior Breslin, had fallen on hard times and, for £6, sold the 1,000-year-old bell and 500-year-old shrine to Major James Ezekiel Nesbitt (1763–1845) of Woodhill, the son of the man who established Ardara; others put the price at 'three young cows and an annuity'. Present at the transaction was James Dombrain (1794–1871), Inspector General of the Coastguard and 'a most intimate friend' of Nesbitt; he had only been appointed to Ireland in late 1819, which dates the sale to the 1820s or early 1830s.[28] It was in the 'most lamentably deaf' Nesbitt's house, that O'Donovan inspected the shrine, but he mixed with people of all classes, and he heard that Conall Mhícheáil's sale of the relic took place 'to the great displeasure of St. Conall and his own

[25] These crises are the subject of extensive correspondence; see e.g. NAI, CSORP 1831/613; 1831/845; 1831/2,183; 1837/5/5–68; NAI, OffP I 1836/318; 1836/131; NLI, MS 13,383 Folders 1, 2, and 4.
[26] Ardara, 18 Oct. 1835, O'Donovan to Larcom, in *Ordnance Survey Letters*, Donegal, 97–9.
[27] McGill, *Ardara*, 17.
[28] McGill, *Conall's Footsteps*, 86. On Dombrain, see Edmond P. Symes, 'Sir James Dombrain and the Coastguard', *Dublin Historical Record*, 56/1 (2003), 56–70.

relatives, who received no part of the money', and who disputed his claim to be the head of the family and his right to dispose of it. 'He will have no luck now', O'Donovan wrote, echoing the disputants, 'because everything got on the devil's back falls under his belly.'[29] Other people said it was not Conall Mhícheáil who sold the *Bearnán*, but a family who had 'got it on loan in the hope that it would cure a sick child'.[30] But sold it was, and the deal may well have been bound up with clerical strictures on the *turas*: the parish priest, Con O'Boyle, was close to the Nesbitts—they had his portrait hanging in Woodhill—and the disposal of the relic that dislodged the Breslins from their centuries-held place in popular devotion consolidated his authority in matters spiritual and, indeed, as a community leader.[31] Strictures on pilgrimages were common in these years.[32] From the last decades of the eighteenth century, priests across Ireland had been deploring the 'disorder' that attended them—and the disorder, of course, owed much to a surge, from mid-century, in the consumption of spirits, and then, in the 1780s and 1790s, when ill-conceived legislation precipitated the collapse of legal distilleries, an extraordinary expansion in the distillation of *poitín*. Later, in the 1810s and 1820s, when priests found themselves contending with evangelical societies, they became more concerned with asserting their responsibility for their flocks. That concern heightened in the 1830s, when the Constabulary (established in 1822 and radically reorganized in 1836) started to police public assemblies, enforce the licensing laws, and make arrests for drunkenness and rioting; in many communities, the priest now took it on himself to get 'his' people to behave. And much as the expansion of the state degraded the landed élite—the Constabulary made it clear to John Barrett, rector of Inishkeel, that they would not be collecting his tithes, ended the Nesbitts' extra-legal collection of tolls from people trading at the Ardara fair, and, in time, prosecuted Galbraith Hamilton of Eden, the local big house, for illicit distillation—the increasingly assertive posture of Catholic clergymen eroded the residual authority of the lineal descendants of the Gaelic élite.[33] In 1802, the parish priest of Inishkeel, Henry

[29] Ardara, 18 Oct. 1835, O'Donovan to Larcom, in *OS Letters*, 97–9.
[30] McGill, *Ardara*, 18 n. 1.
[31] Maguire, *Raphoe*, i. 280–1, discusses O'Boyle's 'cordial friendship' with the Nesbitts; on the portrait, see McGill, *Conall's Footsteps*, 244.
[32] S. J. Connolly, *Priests and People in Pre-Famine Ireland, 1780–1845* (Dublin, 1982), 135–74, esp. 143–4.
[33] On Barrett's attempt to have the police collect tithes in 1822, see NAI, SOC II Box 170, Narin, 15 Apr. 1822, John Barrett to —, and on the authorities' resistance to collecting tolls in Ardara, see, inter alia, NAI, OP 1839/7/9,182 Glenties, 30 Oct. 1839, Hill to Morpeth. Hamilton was fined £75 for possession of 13 gallons of *poitín* in 1867: see NAI, IPSCR Ardara: 12 Nov. 1867; *LJ*, 16 Nov. 1867.

McCullough, remembered as *an Sagart Bán*, the white-haired priest, defied the O'Donnells of Glashagh, who prided themselves on their lineage, and shifted mass from a *scáthlán* at Stranagappog, which convenienced that family, to a place easily accessible to a greater number of people, and in the 1820s or 1830s, the bishop ceased to meet with the diocesan clergy at the O'Donnells' house after the family objected to mass starting before they were seated.[34]

Priests were also then involved in settling disputes between neighbours—in the 1840s, they would do so in courts of arbitration[35]—not least the kin-based faction fights, sometimes involving many hundreds of stick-men on either side, that were a feature of fairs and markets. Boyles and Gallaghers fought in Ardara and Glenties and at Magheramore, a plain west of Sandfield where a great cattle fair was held over several days in October, while Boyles, O'Donnells, and Campbells were the key protagonists in the Rosses.[36] Constabulary officers were typically grateful for the priests' efforts on these occasions, commending individual clergymen in reports to Dublin Castle. However, at the May fair in Dungloe in 1835, James McDevitt, the parish priest, in endeavouring to get a man who had stripped to fight to go home came himself into conflict with the police. McDevitt, who had been drinking earlier in 'the room' of a public house with the rector of Lettermacaward, was dragged scuffling into the barracks, and accused of rescuing a man whom the Constabulary had arrested. An officer quickly released the priest, popularly *an Sagart Rua*, the redheaded priest, lest the warring factions sink their differences and storm the barracks. Foolishly, a sergeant proceeded to outrage the crowd by calling McDevitt a 'drunken hog' or 'drunken dog' or 'drunken ——' as he flung him out the door, and in the ensuing riot—accounts of which varied—the Constabulary fired, killing a man on the street. A sergeant and four constables stood trial for murder; the sergeant was convicted of manslaughter, and the priest—the son of the Glenties innkeeper—was exonerated of any wrongdoing.[37]

If priests' role in maintaining order and acting as interlocutors between young men and the Constabulary made them more important to the people, there were limits to their authority: after all, there were major faction fights in Glenties in the 1820s and the Campbell versus Boyle and

[34] Maguire, *Raphoe*, i. 480–1; J. C. T. MacDonagh, 'Heirs to the O'Donnell Chieftaincy (Part II a): The O'Donnells of Glassagh', *Donegal Annual*, 4/2 (1959), 146–55.
[35] See Ch. 6 in this volume.
[36] McGill, *Ardara*, 66–73.
[37] *LJ*, 4 Aug. 1835. On factions in the Rosses, see NAI, SOC I 2,882/16 Outrages in the County of Donegal... Nov. 1828; NAI, OP 1835/7/42 Guidore, 5 Dec. 1835, Rodden to Stovin; 1836/7/4 Dungloe, 4 Jan. 1836, Taylor to Stovin, and Devyr, *Odd Book* [Irish and British Section], 92–3.

O'Donnell versus Campbell feuds raged in the Rosses through the 1830s, with houses ransacked in some of the most serious battles. Policing and prosecutions—Ardara and Glenties had Constabulary barracks from 1822–3 and Dungloe from 1824—were more important than clerical exhortations in ending the great stick-fights.[38] Moreover, low mass attendance highlights the priests' struggle, in a period of rapid demographic expansion, to get their putative 'hearers' to adopt canonical belief and practice, and it was only with the Famine and the decline of population thereafter that the balance tipped decidedly in their favour. New chapels reduced the distance that people had to travel to Sunday mass, existing chapels were enlarged or replaced, and, while the population fell, there was a sharp increase in the number of priests. For example, in the parishes of Ardara and Inishkeel, where the Catholic population dropped by over one-quarter in the latter half of the century—from 13,219 Catholics in the mid-1830s (religion was not recorded in the 1841 Census) down (26.7 per cent) to 9,701 in 1901—the number of priests roughly doubled from three to four in the decade before the Famine to no fewer than seven in the early twentieth century, changing the priest-to-people ratio from, at best, 1:3,304 in 1841 to 1:1,385 in 1901.[39]

In addition to demographic decline, priests' control of most state-funded elementary schools attended by Catholic children helped to advance their 'civilizing offensive'. Those 'national schools', established here from the late 1830s, greatly augmented the influence of priests, for they hired the masters, and they now had unprecedented access to the young. Children studied catechism in school and, from the early 1850s, the master prepared them for the long-neglected sacraments of confession, communion, and confirmation.[40] Such was the priests' confidence in the first generation to pass through the schools that, having suppressed the drinking and amusement at Inishkeel and displaced the Breslins, they were content for the *turas* that their predecessors had deplored to continue. In the early 1870s, a priest was pleased to report that the island was 'much frequented' by pilgrims.[41] And in 1887, the future cardinal Patrick O'Donnell (1856–1927), who himself belonged to the first generation educated in the national system, could compare the 'devotion and faith' of the 'crowds' who thronged to

---

[38] SOC I 2,622/31 Enniskillen, 31 July 1824, Joyce to D'Arcy. On the Constabulary and faction fighting, see Stanley Palmer, *Police and Protest in England and Ireland, 1780–1850* (Cambridge, 1988), 366–7.

[39] *Irish Catholic Directory* (1920), 175–7. In County Donegal, the Census returned fifty-five Catholic clergymen in 1841 and ninety-eight in 1901.

[40] See Ch. 7 in this volume.

[41] James Stephens, *Illustrated Handbook of the Scenery and Antiquities of Southwest Donegal* (Dublin, 1872), 7.

Inishkeel to the piety of the 'first believers in Christianity'. The pilgrims, according to O'Donnell, were 'possessed of the genuine spirit of Gospel Christians'. And he robustly defended these 'simple, faithful souls' from the charge of 'superstitious observance'.[42] The *turas* was now an acceptable diversion in summer, and one that reinforced the Church's own narrative of endurance; but the real deal was at chapel every Sunday.

The schools that played such a vital role in orienting the people to chapel—and in quietly transforming notions of time and discipline, manners and obedience—were themselves part of an increase in the administrative and coercive capacity of the state in the middle decades of the nineteenth century. By the time of the Famine, the district not only had schoolmasters but also constables, revenue policemen, postmasters, postboys, coastguards, petty sessions clerks, rate collectors, and process servers, all living on wages paid by state agencies. Indeed, O'Donovan, when he anticipated the coming of an era of infidelity, was working on the Ordnance Survey of Ireland, an ambitious project that had commenced in the 1820s and that, here, in west Donegal, was completed in 1835. The new maps conferred official status on particular English spellings of placenames and, while many, if not most, of the approved forms were already in use—some can be found in seventeenth- and eighteenth-century records—others were inventions or errors of the surveyors.[43] For instance, in Beagh—a townland that is central to this book—the name of an ancient road, *Bealach an Ghabhail*, the Road of the Branch or Fork,[44] somehow got transferred to a river which, on maps, is marked Bellanagoal River; the

---

[42] Patrick O'Donnell, 'Inniskeel', *Irish Ecclesiastical Record*, 8 (1887), 781–94, 785.

[43] The representation of the OS in Friel's *Translations* (1980) caused controversy. J. H. Andrews, author of *A Paper Landscape: The Ordnance Survey in Nineteenth-Century Ireland* (Oxford, 1975), catalogued errors: see his 'Notes for a Future Edition of Brian Friel's *Translations*', *Irish Review*, 13 (1992–3), 93–106, and his contribution to J. H. Andrews, Brian Friel, and Kevin Barry, '*Translations* and *A Paper Landscape*: Between Fiction and History', *Crane Bag*, 7/2 (1983), 118–24. Seán Connolly, 'Dreaming History: Brian Friel's *Translations*', *Theatre Ireland*, 13 (1987), 42–4, criticized other aspects of the play, notably its depiction of hedge schools; also see idem, 'Translating History: Brian Friel and the Irish Past', in Alan J. Peacock, ed., *The Achievement of Brian Friel* (Gerrards Cross, 1993), 149–63.

[44] The road is rendered *Bealach na gCúl*, 'the road of the backs', in the transcription, by 13-year-old Mary Theresa Gallagher of Narin, of a story told in 1938 by 81-year-old Mary Harkin (b. 1857) of Summy; see NFCS 1,048 (Kilclooney): 253–4. A river forks at Beagh Bridge and some streams join it further west, and McGill, *Conall's Footsteps*, 187, interprets the last particle of Bella*nagoal* as *an Ghabhail*, of the fork. The road originally cut northwest across Beagh and travellers had to ford the river. After the bridge was built east of the ford in the mid-1700s, the road was rerouted and people travelling to Rosbeg would go through Sandfield and across the Warren. The road's name, however, become associated with the bridge; see the presentment, in 1773, for repairing the road 'between Naran Church and Ballynagole Bridge' in DCA, GJ/1/3. D. O'Donnell, the OS's undependable local guide, suggested the spelling Bellinanoil, but O'Donovan, assuming the original name

name never caught on and the river is today the Beagh River. Likewise, the neighbouring townlands of Ranny and Carn—established divisions in estate and grand jury records—became subdivisions of a townland that the map-makers called Derryness, an archaic name for a place that had long since been divided into two.[45] Children still have to go to school to learn that they live in Derryness, a name used only in official and business corres-pondence and one that has never appeared on a gravestone in Ardara.[46]

Names were the least of the bruises inflicted by the Ordnance Survey on society. Crucially, the Survey spelled the end of vernacular measurement systems: people who had hitherto looked at land in terms of 'cow's grass'—the grass that would keep a cow—would, in time, come to deal in the imperial statute acre. And the maps facilitated the radical reorgan-ization of estates, with landlords quick to use them to replace communal systems of land use that made occupiers, both tenants and subtenants, difficult to control. They also helped constables to complete the first detailed census in 1841, and then, from the mid-1840s, those same constables annually went around making returns of the size of holdings, the acreage under particular crops, and the numbers of cattle, sheep, and fowl in each townland. Most importantly, however, the maps allowed the production of a comprehensive cadastral survey, Griffith's Valuation, here undertaken in 1855–7, that identified all people holding land or buildings and put a value on every acre, rood, and perch, house, barn, and byre. The ideal of individuals paying rates on property—rather than headmen representing groups of land- and householders—could now be realized.[47]

With those mid-century maps, the British state had taken a decisive step towards conquering the opacity of the Irish countryside; all was

---

was *Béal Átha na nGual*, mouth of the ford of the coals, settled on Bellanagoal. NAI, OSFNB, Inishkeel, vi. 242.

[45] In the 1810s, the Conyngham estate identified Ranny and Carn as distinct town-lands, and made no mention of Derryness; this practice continued through the 1850s. See NLI, Conyngham Papers 35,394 (1) Boylagh: Arrears, May 1817; MS 35,394 (2) Rental of . . . Boylagh Estate, for the Year Ending the 1st of May 1856; 35,394 (2) Boylagh Rental for May 1860. Carn, not Derryness, is marked on the grand jury map of 1801, GJ/2/19. An island named Derryness Island by the OS is known locally as 'Dernish'.

[46] O'Donovan understood Derryness, which he encountered in seventeenth-century documents, to be derived from Doire an Easa, 'oakwood of the cataract or waterfall', despite there being no waterfall in the area. Conversely, O'Donnell suggested *Doire-inis*, lit. oakwood-island, which, bizarrely, he translated as 'the pasture by oaks'. Many derivations suggested by O'Donnell are improbable, and some are preposterous; see his suggestions for Beagh, Sandfield, and Summy in OSFNB, Inishkeel, iii. 100–2, 108; viii. 377–9; xi. 21. Tomás Ó Canann, 'Notes on Some Donegal Placenames', *Ainm*, 4 (1989–90), 107–24, 107–13, makes a compelling case for Sandfield having originally been Baile Uí Chanann, later Ballycannon.

[47] On cadastral surveys, see James C. Scott, *Seeing like a State: How Certain Schemes to Improve the Human Condition have Failed* (New Haven, 1998), 46–52.

becoming clearer just as there began to be fewer people to see. Births, deaths, and marriages were recorded from 1864, dogs licensed from 1865, and, at the opening of the new century, the state seemed to see everything: in 1851, there had been 317 Constabulary officers and men (not including 250 revenue officers and police and 128 coastguards) in County Donegal, giving a police-to-people ratio of 1:805—a significant change from 1:2,190 in 1831 (132 officers and men) and 1:1,256 in 1841 (236)—and in 1861 there were 627, giving a ratio of 1:379; by 1901, the Constabulary force had fallen back to 452, but with the continued decline in population, it still produced a similar ratio, 1:385.[48] The Catholic poor themselves, abandoning the old and particular and adopting the new, becoming English-speaking and literate, and keeping holy the Sabbath day, now appeared less exotic to their rulers and capable of further 'improvement', while, paradoxically, the blurring of cultural differences within the broader Catholic community—not least by the removal of the poorest of the poor—had allowed the smallholders of the west of Ireland to stand front and centre in a national opposition that having effectively dispensed with the landlords now aimed to semi-extract the country from the United Kingdom.

THE POLITICS OF POST-FAMINE ADJUSTMENT

In the time of this book, or, more correctly, in the middle third of the nineteenth century, when the key incidents probed in it took place, the 'era of infidelity' anticipated by John O'Donovan was imminent. And central to this book is an act of betrayal, the selfish ploy of a self-serving man, a schoolmaster, Patrick McGlynn, who, in 1856, turned informer on the Molly Maguires, a secret political combination, also known as the Ribbon Society, that from the time of the Famine had been responsible for a wave of offences classified by the state as 'outrages'. Here, a history of his informing, backlit from points over the previous two decades, sheds light on that wave of activity, its origins and outcomes, the meaning and the memory of it. More specifically, it illuminates the *end* of 'outrage', that is, the shifting objectives of those who engaged in it, and also how, after hunger faded and disease abated, tensions emerged in the Molly Maguires when one element sought to curtail such activity, while another sought, unsuccessfully, to expand it. And in that contention, when the opportunities of post-Famine society were coming into view, one glimpses the end,

---

[48] Numbers of police taken from *Return of the Constabulary Police of Ireland...*, HC 1829 (131), xxii. 425, and the Table of Occupation in the 1841–1901 Censuses.

or at least an ebbing, of outrage—in the everyday sense of moral indignation—at the fate of the rural poor. At heart, however, the subject is contention among neighbours—a man who rose from the ashes of a mode of living, those consumed in the conflagration, and those who lost much but not all. And, ultimately, the concern is how the poor themselves came to terms with their loss, that is, how their own indignation at what had been done unto them and their forebears lost malignancy, how their outrage ended.

Among the reasons, some specious, given by McGlynn for his betrayal of the Mollies was a concern to protect a man targeted by them. That man was James Gallagher of Beagh who, over the previous decade, meaning from 1856 back into the Famine, had profited from others' misfortune, and in treating of him, and others in this book, a slight awkwardness arises, for I come from that place.[49] Born in 1969, I belong to the first generation of Beagh people not to enter this world at home but in a thirty-three-bed district hospital (est. 1958) twenty miles away in Dungloe. In the year of my birth, and through the 1970s, direct descendants of six of eight extended families who had held land as tenants in Beagh when McGlynn informed were still there, all working the same patches that their forebears had worked then. The last of the other two families—the 'Morgan Kennedys' and 'Condy Gallaghers'—had only recently passed away. Among the remaining families were descendants of individuals centrally involved in the McGlynn affair, including descendants of James Gallagher. In fact, his great-grandson, Denis Gallagher, the first and, in 1969, the only person in Beagh who owned a car, drove my father to Dungloe after my birth. Nobody else in the townland then possessed any mode of transport other than a heavy pushbike or a donkey and cart, painted in some combination of red, green, orange, or blue. Denis had been in Carn mowing corn with a scythe when my father arrived to ask for a lift to the hospital, and off they set for Dungloe in the Austin Cambridge. Happily, Denis is alive and well, and his extended family and my people, and the other families in Beagh, have all, in living memory, been good neighbours to each other.

The purpose here, then, is most certainly not to channel resentment of a long dead man, nor is it to cause hurt. The living bear no responsibility *for* the dead, and those whose forebears, in their day, had most reason to resent James Gallagher will doubtless find that they themselves have more in common with that man than with their own predecessors—and,

---

[49] In writing of my own place and people, I found Carolyn Kay Steedman, *Landscape for a Good Woman: A Story of Two Lives* (London, 1986) and Patrick Joyce, 'The Journey West', *Field Day Review*, 10 (2014), 62–93, particularly suggestive.

indeed, his neighbours' descendants becoming like him probably damp-ened outrage at his doings, for becoming like him, they must have come to understand him. In that regard, Gallagher may appear to have been ahead of his time, but an alternative understanding, and one pressed in this history, is that he was simply on the side that in time prevailed. Therein lies a reason for writing of events of which the intervening generations talked little, and then only quietly. This story, if sordid, illuminates differences in feeling and understanding, not simply between people in that distant time, but between the long dead and their lineal descendants. And telling this story allows faint outlines of bright futures lost in the mid-nineteenth century to emerge. But the story also points to dark futures averted. And, in that regard, it reveals poor countrypeople—a class too easily and too often imagined as impotent in the face of massive socio-economic change—to have themselves, in small measure but in a moment of significance, combined to moderate the forces remaking their world. Bad as things became, they might have been worse.

Still, there remains James Gallagher and his relationship to his neigh-bours. Primo Levi's *The Drowned and the Saved* (1986) cautions against seeing people who survive gross injustice simply as victims: in a desperate struggle to survive, some people will take advantage of their 'companions in misfortune' and others, for a variety of reasons, will collaborate with the persecutors. For Levi, this is the 'grey zone', the space that separates victims and persecutors—one populated by obscene and pathetic figures, where sometimes, but not always, judgement is impossible.[50] The grey zone of *am an drochshaoil*, the time of the Famine—a phrase that can embrace the years when people adjusted to its effects—is the demimonde of soupers and grabbers, moneylenders and mealmongers, and those among the poor who had a full pot when neighbours starved, and the poorhouse bully who took the biscuit from the weak.[51] Some, though not all, of Gallagher's actions place him in that grey zone, where judgement is, at best, not easy. Yet in a similarly ambivalent position may be found some of his neighbours, who, a few years before the Famine, were themselves not only the beneficiaries of others' misfortune, but complicit in it. Furthermore, notions of the Molly Maguires as white-shirted defenders of the poor oversimplify. Certainly, if the secret society that targeted James Gallagher had first emerged, in west Donegal, in that role in the mid-1840s, by the mid-1850s that protection organization was also function-ing as a protection racket—an evolution which Ribbonism's most astute historian has discerned in earlier decades—and it was developing many of

---

[50] Primo Levi, *The Drowned and the Saved* (New York, 1989 [1986]), 20, 36–69.
[51] See my 'A Jig in the Poorhouse', *Dublin Review of Books* (Apr. 2013), online.

the features of a political machine, albeit one as yet denied direct access to
the levers of power.[52] Hence, if there is no cartoon villain here, there is no
hero. Above all, there is no notion that mid-nineteenth-century injustice
can ever be set right. On the contrary, the starting point is the critic David
Lloyd's potent meditation on redress and memory and revenge, and most
especially his insistence that 'the catastrophic violence of history can be
righted only in relinquishing the desire to set it right, in order instead to
make room for the spectres in whose restlessness the rhythms of another
mode of living speak to us'.[53]

NAMES THAT RING FAMILIAR

James Gallagher, Patrick McGlynn, and other names encountered in this
book ring familiar today around Ardara and Glenties. Yet those names that
ring familiar do not ring true. To the extent that they make the long dead
appear like the living, they obscure the cultural chasms—between state
and society in the past and between that past and this present—across
which this history attempts to recover their experiences and imaginings,
prayers and tears. Most obviously, they are formal English names, and the
rural poor involved in this affair were bilingual, but primarily Irish
speaking; Irish was their first language and that of the home. A man
whose name is given in this book as James would normally have been
addressed as Séamas, Patrick as Pádraig or the common diminutive Pádaí.
These people might also have been further distinguished by reference to
their size, height, or hair colour—Pádraig Mór, Big Patrick or Séamas
Rua, Redhaired James—or maybe their trade or residence. And rather
than being distinguished by a surname, they would often be connected to
their family by mention of their father or mother, and perhaps also a
grandparent: hence, Conall Mhícheáil—Conall son of Michael, the man
alleged to have sold the *Bearnán*.[54]

Customary naming practices survive today in this district, albeit much
diminished since the mid-1900s and, excepting a few Irish-speaking

[52] Tom Garvin, *The Evolution of Irish Nationalist Politics* (Dublin, 1981), 41. Also see
his 'Defenders, Ribbonmen and Others: Underground Political Networks in Pre-Famine
Ireland', *Past and Present*, 96 (1982), 133–55. And Chs. 2 and 5 in this volume.
[53] David Lloyd, 'The Indigent Sublime: Spectres of Irish Hunger', in idem, *Irish
Times: Temporalities of Modernity* (Dublin, 2008), 39–72, 40.
[54] On naming systems, see Robin Fox, *The Tory Islanders: A People on the Celtic Fringe*
(Cambridge, 1978), 31–81. Also see James C. Scott, 'The Production of Legal Identities
Proper to States: The Case of the Permanent Family Surname', in *Decoding Subaltern
Politics: Ideology, Disguise, and Resistance in Agrarian Politics* (Abingdon, 2013), 99–133,
and 'The State's Grip on the Vernacular World', ibid. 96–8.

families, using English-language forms. Knowing the customary names of the people who figure in this book would deepen and enrich it. Those names, and 'the lines that converge upon and diverge from [each] name', would allow the creation of a more 'closely woven web', a clearer representation of 'the network of social relationships into which the individual is inserted'.[55] Certainly, those names would be a reminder that state and society had different ways of seeing. And they would also keep in view the extent to which the documents of state and estate that underpin this history—tithe applotment books (1834), property valuations (1837–9, 1855–6), and a rent roll (1855–6)—wished the very people that they describe into existence. But almost all those customary names are now lost. So, lacking them, this book requires an act of imagination to see the people in these pages as more than shadows cold and wan, that is, to see them for who they were not who they became. It requires the reader to remember that the people knew each other by different names and that, on *Oíche Shamhna*, they set creepies before the fire.

---

[55] Carlo Ginzburg and Carlo Poni, 'The Name and the Game: Unequal Exchange and the Historiographic Marketplace', in Edwin Muir and Guido Ruiggero, eds, *Microhistory and the Lost Peoples of Europe* (Baltimore, 1991), 1–19, 6.

PART I

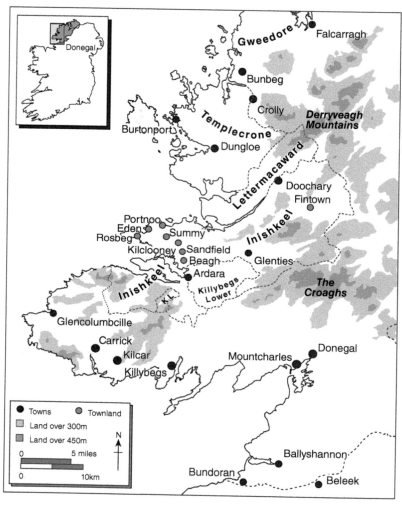

Map 1.1 West Donegal

1

A Letter from Beagh

On one of the first days of April 1856, a letter signed 'Patrick McGlynn, National Teacher, Beigha [sic],[1] Ardara', (Figure 1.1) arrived for Daniel J. Cruise, stipendiary magistrate, at Wood Lodge, a sizeable country house near the one-street village of Mountcharles, County Donegal.[2] Composed in a fluent hand on everyday writing paper, and dated 31 March, the letter made a remarkable offer. If the magistrate would keep his identity a secret and ensure that he was 'rewarded', the writer would enable him to take members of an illegal combination in the act of committing a 'depredation', that is, an offence routinely classified by the authorities as an 'outrage'.[3]

> I dare say you are aware of the distracted state of this country occasioned by a party called Molly Maguires.
>
> I write to inform you that I (by means which I shall not divulge) have a means of ascertaining their movements and that I will inform either you or the police when I become certain that they shall attack a house or some other depredation of the kind. The only means that I see of stopping the career of these villains is by taking them in the act, which I think will not only deter the remainder from such acts in future but restore peace to the country.
>
> Knowing that their connexions are very extensive and that my life would be in imminent danger I shall require to receive the reward which you shall

---

[1] Beagh, the name approved by the OS, had previously been used in grand jury documents and estate papers, including a map (1786); see OSFNB, Inishkeel, vol. 3, 101; vol. 9, 413–14, 437. The variants Beigha and Beyha, which better represent the local pronunciation, continued to appear in official publications; indeed, some documents relating to the national school (est. 1845) use Begha, due to a misreading of Beyha. O'Donovan understood Beagh to be derived from *An Bheitheach*, place of birches; his undependable guide, O'Donnell, suggested it was derived from *beach-ach*, a place of bees, a word pronounced very differently to the townland name.

[2] Alistair Rowan, *North West Ulster: The Counties of Londonderry, Donegal, Fermanagh and Tyrone* (Harmondsworth, 1979), 427, describes Wood Lodge as 'a tiny Regency parsonage: three-bay cottage with central attic glebe. Derelict at the time of writing.' The description lacks context: in 1857, when a typical west Donegal house was valued for taxation purposes at 5s., it was valued at £10 (200s.).

[3] On 'outrage', see W. E. Vaughan, *Landlords and Tenants in Mid-Victorian Ireland* (Oxford, 1994), 138–76.

think reasonable because the information shall cost me both trouble and expense besides the risk of being suspected is great.

But I shall require from you that not only shall this communication be kept secret but that you shall never divulge my name as in any way connected with any proceedings relating to them. I will if rewarded for the risk obtain such information for the authorities as will make them aware when they shall commit the next depredation and let them capture them in the act but that is all.

I will write to you, but I must be certain that it shall never be known who gave the information. Neither will I tell who informed me.

Upon receiving an answer to this I will do all I can to put a stop to their proceedings. Please do not speak to me if you happen to see me in Ardara nor do not make any inquiries of any person. Should you wish to speak [to] me I will see you at any place you please.

I am sorry for writing to such a length.[4]

The 'distracted state of this country' was indeed well known to Cruise, and so too were the Molly Maguires. Since the mid-1840s, 'Molly Maguires' had become a sobriquet for members of the Ribbon Society, an oath-bound secret society, which, from the 1810s, had built a lodge network across much of the northern half of Ireland, physically confronting the ultra-Protestant Orange Order and articulating Catholic nationalist ambition. Or to be more precise, 'Molly Maguires' had been most enthusiastically adopted as a moniker by Ribbonmen in rural areas of west Ulster and north Connacht, among them districts with no history of Ribbon activity, and the appearance of the name from the mid-1840s was coincident not only with a geographic expansion of the Society, but also with a shift in its social composition and the character of its activities, both of which now became more agrarian.[5]

Various stories have been told to explain the name. It was that of a widow evicted from her farm in Antrim, or that of a woman in whose

[4] CSORP 1856/16,473 Beigha, 31 Mar. 1856, McGlynn to Cruise.
[5] Garvin, 'Defenders, Ribbonmen and Others' remains a fine analysis of Ribbonism. Also see Garvin, *Evolution*, 34–43, and Vaughan, *Landlords and Tenants*, 189–202. On the Mollies in Connacht, see Jennifer Kelly, 'Local Memories and Manipulation of the Past in Pre-Famine County Leitrim', in Terence Dooley, ed., *Ireland's Polemical Past: Views of Irish History in Honour of R. V. Comerford* (Dublin, 2010), 51–67. The ethnic, labour, and political troubles in Pennsylvania that culminated in the Molly Maguire trials of 1876–9 are the subject of several studies, notably Wayne G. Broehl, Jr, *The Molly Maguires* (Cambridge, MA, 1964), Kevin Kenny, *Making Sense of the Molly Maguires* (Oxford, 1998), and Mark Bulik, *The Sons of Molly Maguire: The Irish Roots of America's First Labor War* (New York, 2015). Also see George Korson, *Minstrels of the Mine Patch: Songs and Stories of the Anthracite Industry* (Hatboro, 1964 [1938]), ch. 8, and Grace Palladino, *Another Civil War: Labor, Capital, and the State in the Anthracite Regions of Pennsylvania, 1840–68* (Chicago, 1990).

Figure 1.1 Beagh National School

house Ribbonmen met, or, intriguingly, as it hints at internal conflict over a shift in objectives, it was the name of a 'crazy old woman' in Fermanagh who imagined she commanded a great army and, after a schism in the Ribbon Society, it had been given in derision by one group to their rivals.[6] But whatever the origin of the name, the preferred form uttered in predominantly Irish-speaking west Donegal was a double entendre that amplified menace. *Clann Mhailí*, Molly's Children, sounds like *clann mhallaithe*, cursed, infernal clan.

On his appointment to Donegal in 1852, Cruise had quickly formed the opinion that the Ribbon Society (*aka* Molly Maguires) was the 'organized system' behind a wave of 'outrages' in the Glenties–Ardara area in the south-west of the county, the very district from which this letter now purported to have come (Map 1.1). These 'outrages' included attacks on persons and property, midnight arms raids, and intimidation by threatening letters and notices. For instance, at 11.00 p.m. on 2 March 1852, some forty armed men wearing shirts over their clothes, and led by a man in a blue frock or cloak, with a muffler about his ears, marched through the mountain hamlet of Doohary. Standing in his doorway, John Molloy asked if they were mummers, but received no answer. Proceeding

[6] Broehl, *Molly Maguires*, 27–8; Kenny, *Making Sense*, 13–44; Korson, *Minstrels*, 240.

north along the bank of the Gweebarra, the group fired a shot to signal to a party on the other side of the river, and a shot was fired in reply. Later that night, armed men raided the houses of Maurice Cannon of Derrynacarrow Far, and Patrick McKelvey and Thomas Duffy of Befflaght. All three were water bailiffs, living in a remote district near the source of the salmon-rich river. Befflaght, close to Lough Barra, was particularly difficult to approach, no road then running from Doohary to Glendowan. The raiders took guns, powder, and shot, but they did no harm to the bailiffs themselves. Indeed, in Cannon's house, they only spoke one word, which he could not or would not repeat. None of the bailiffs reported the raids, and it was five days before the Constabulary picked up a rumour of what had happened. That same month, some twenty armed men, who had made no effort to disguise themselves, called at night at the house of Patrick McNelis, a comfortable farmer in Sandfield, a townland bordering Beagh. They fired several shots inside the house, and dictated the price at which he was to sell potatoes. Leaving Sandfield, these men went some two miles to Ballymackilduff, where they broke into the house of another farmer, Francis Shovlin, whom they 'slightly carded', that is, scraped his body with paddles embedded with small nails which were used to comb wool. Announcing themselves as 'the Molly Maguires' and 'Sons of Liberty', they fired shots inside the house, and, as had happened in Sandfield, stipulated the price at which potatoes were to be sold.[7]

On some such occasions, the raiders represented themselves as 'Molly's Sons', sent by their mother, to do justice. On others, a man attired as a woman was the leader, who introducing 'herself' as Molly Maguire, demanded redress for wrongs inflicted on 'her' children.[8] John Molloy of Doohary, therefore, might be forgiven for mistaking the Mollies for mummers, for there was something of the theatricality of mumming (and wake games) in their comportment.[9] But a hard man dressed as a widow conveyed menace never conjured by 'Here comes [*sic*] I Jack Straw, / such a man you never saw.' Bursting into a dark house in the dead of night,

[7] OP 1852/7/71 Report of Outrage, Glenties, 7 Mar. 1852; Donegal, 15 Mar. 1852, Montgomery to Under Secretary. See also CSORP 1853/2,493, detailing ten serious 'outrages' in the year to Feb. 1853. 'Sons of Freedom', a name similar to that used in Ballymackilduff, had been adopted by the Dublin Ribbon leader Richard Jones in the late 1830s; see Garvin, 'Defenders, Ribbonmen and Others', 149.

[8] For an incident in Glenfin, when a man dressed as a woman led Mollies, see Ch. 2. And for Cloughaneely Mollies dressing as women for an assassination attempt on a landlord: see CSORP 1860/15,527; NLI, Larcom Papers MS 7,633.

[9] For the Mollies and mumming, see Bulik, *Sons of Molly Maguire*, 37–43, 47–50, 99–103. A man with 'straw on his head down over his shoulders' participated in a raid in Fintown in 1850; see *LJ*, 24 July 1850.

'Molly Maguire' upturned all social and sexual hierarchies. 'Her' very appearance cried havoc.[10]

The raids on the farmers in Sandfield and Ballymackilduff accord with the Mollies' self-representation as protectors of the rural poor. The night visits paid the water bailiffs are more complicated, for there had been a dispute between landlords over the fishery, and there had also been contention when the leader of an extensive faction, who gave employment to bailiffs and fishermen, did not have his lease on a section of it renewed. And the bailiffs were far from wealthy: the raiders had no difficulty entering Cannon's house as 'the door was only laid to, and off the hinges'.[11] At the same time, both the raids on the farmers and those on the bailiffs—like most incidents in which the Mollies were involved in west Donegal—are difficult to relate to the known 'political' objectives of the Ribbon Society, most obviously its professed concern for 'freeing' Ireland. In his first months in Donegal, Cruise himself expressed the view that it was a group 'without any fixed object but which can at once be used for any purpose'.[12] In this assessment, he was echoing local landlords who, conscious of the wider association of the Ribbon Society with ethno-religious contention and some form of nationalism, felt it necessary to impress on officialdom that it was, in fact, the 'organized system' which they faced. 'There is a kind of bastard rib[b]onism prevalent in the district', John Hamilton, owner of small estate at Fintown, wrote in early 1853, 'which has apparently for its object rather association for outrage & plunder with mutual pledges of aid & support, than any thing decidedly of a political or religious character.'[13] It was the Ribbon Society, officials were being told, but not as they knew it. However, those officials had been receiving similar reports from other districts for some years, and they had a clear sense that, with the expansion of the Society in the mid-1840s, it had changed.

Eager to make his mark in Donegal, Cruise had convened a meeting of magistrates in Glenties on 5 February 1853, that successfully petitioned for the Rosses, Glenties, and Ardara to be proclaimed under the Crime and Outrage (Ireland) Act (1847), which severely restricted the right to

---

[10] On cross-dressing in European carnival and protest, see Natalie Zemon Davies, 'Women on Top', in *Society and Culture in Early Modern France* (Stanford, CA, 1975), 124–51.

[11] OP 1852/7/71 Report of Outrage, Glenties, 7 Mar. 1852.

[12] OP 1852/7/434 Glenties, 19 Dec. 1852, Cruise to Wynne.

[13] CSORP 1853/2,493 Donegal, 5 Feb. 1853, Hamilton to Stewart. In the mid-1840s, Hamilton had transferred the Fintown estate to his son, James (1824–1915), but he remained involved in its management. For James's reflections on Ribbonism, see OP 1850/7/163 Donegal, 4 May 1850, James Hamilton to Under Secretary.

bear arms.[14] Under the proclamation, some sixty-six guns, two blunder-busses, six pistols, eight swords, seventy-six bayonets, forty-two barrels, and one stock were surrendered in Ardara barracks by 2 April. Most were probably old yeomanry guns and fowling pieces held by law-abiding farmers, many of whom were Protestant and 'loyal', and their surrender prevented them falling into the hands of the Mollies. An additional seventeen guns and two pistols were given up in Glenties, twelve guns in Letter, thirty-four guns and five pistols in Dungloe, and three guns and two pistols in Bunbeg.[15] Yet the 'outrages' had continued unabated, broiling through the mid-1850s.[16]

These troubles in west Donegal were part of a Famine-raised surge in 'outrage' in the county as a whole, and much of it too the authorities attributed to the machinations of the Ribbon Society. That countywide surge was nationally significant. For instance, the 'establishment' (allocation) of Constabulary for the county was 176, but there were 293 constables serving there in 1852, and 360 by summer 1853; this doubling of the force had been brought about by the repeated drafting of reinforcements to suppress disturbances.[17] Likewise, in 1853–5, the Constabulary offered more rewards (and more reward money) for information on 'outrages' in Donegal than in any other county with the exception of Tipperary, a place long synonymous with agrarian 'outrage'; see Table 1.1.[18] Approaching social unrest, by no means unhelpfully, from the perspective of the Constabulary, historian W. E. Vaughan observes that Donegal was 'one

[14] On the meeting, see CSORP 1853/2,493; for the use of the proclamation, see *Return of the Several Counties and Districts, and Baronies of Counties, in Ireland, Proclaimed under the Provisions of the Crime and Outrage Act...*, HC 1860 (195), lvii. 849.
[15] CSORP 1853/3,134 'County of Donegal, District of Glenties: Arms &c. Given Up to the Constabulary... 2nd April 1852'.
[16] For examples of 'outrages' in Donegal in 1853–5, not all of which are Ribbon-related, see CSORP 1856/17,416 'Return of Rewards Offered through the Constabulary by Placard, during the Years 1853 & 1854'; 'Return of Outrages in which Rewards for Information have been Offered by Constabulary Placards since 1st January to the 17th November 1855'. And for a decade of outrages in north Donegal, see *A Return 'of the Outrages Specially Reported by the Constabulary as Committed within the Barony of Kilmacrenan, County Donegal, during the Last Ten Years'*, HC 1861 (404), lii. 585.
[17] Evidence of Patrick Hobart, County Inspector, in *Select Committee of the House of Lords Appointed to Consider the Consequences of Extending the Functions of the Constabulary in Ireland to the Suppression or Prevention of Illicit Distillation*, HC 1854 (53), 101–13, esp. 108–9. These figures do not include the Revenue Police; there were then some 237 Revenue Police in Donegal, 21% of the national force of 1,090, ibid. 239. Also see the evidence of J. J. Barry, ibid. 26, and OP 1852/7/179 Buncrana, 6 July 1852, Fleming to Naas.
[18] CSORP 1856/17,416 'Total Number of Rewards Offered and Paid in the Years, 1853, 1854, and 1855'. In addition to Constabulary rewards, the authorities posted rewards by 'lord lieutenant's proclamation'; CSORP 1856/17,416, 'Return of Outrages in which Rewards for Information have been Offered by the Lord Lieutenant's Proclamation in the Years, 1853, 1854, and 1855'.

Table 1.1 Constabulary rewards offered in Ireland, 1853–5

County	Number	Sum (£)	Population, 1851	Amount per Capita
King's	78	1,495	112,076	1.33
Donegal	143	2,930	255,158	1.15
Longford	49	935	82,348	1.14
Leitrim	71	1,180	111,897	1.05
Tipperary	161	3,285	331,567	0.99
Westmeath	46	1,060	111,407	0.95
Meath	61	1,247	140,748	0.89
Carlow	29	600	68,078	0.88
Cavan	79	1,370	174,064	0.79
Kildare	36	685	95,723	0.72
Roscommon	61	1,110	173,436	0.64
Londonderry	60	1,120	192,022	0.58
Mayo	94	1,550	274,499	0.56
Galway	102	1,745	321,684	0.54
Louth	24	580	107,662	0.54
Sligo	40	690	128,515	0.54
Down	84	1,650	320,817	0.51
Clare	63	1,030	212,440	0.48
Fermanagh	30	560	116,047	0.48
Kilkenny	38	755	158,748	0.48
Waterford	43	775	164,035	0.47
Limerick	62	1,165	262,132	0.44
Monaghan	28	625	141,823	0.44
Queen's	34	485	111,664	0.43
Wexford	33	580	180,158	0.32
Armagh	26	585	196,084	0.30
Tyrone	41	655	255,661	0.26
Cork	78	1,430	649,308	0.22
Kerry	27	490	238,254	0.21
Antrim	37	733	359,934	0.20
Wicklow	12	185	98,979	0.19
Dublin	9	110	405,147	0.03

Source: CSORP 1856/17,416 'Total Number of Rewards Offered and Paid in the Years, 1853, 1854, and 1855'.

of the worst counties in the country for agrarian crime of all kinds' in the decade after the Famine: 'if the thirty-two counties are ranked according to frequency of agrarian crime, Donegal was eighth in the decade 1851–60'.[19]

Still, within the county, the west stood out as a trouble spot, and, by the mid-1850s, as a particularly recalcitrant centre of Ribbon activity.

[19] W. E. Vaughan, *Sin, Sheep and Scotsmen: John George Adair and the Derryveagh Evictions, 1861* (Belfast, 1983), 25.

In late 1855, little over four months before Cruise's receipt of the
unexpected letter from Beagh, Dublin Castle had systematically assessed
the national, regional, and local state of 'lawless and illegal combinations',
a category that included the Ribbon Society.[20] From this trawl of intelli-
gence, Duncan McGregor, the Inspector General of Constabulary, concluded that the organization remained in existence, with greater or lesser
activity, in the 'whole of Ulster, the northern half of Leinster and the
eastern part of Connaught and of the County Clare', but, in general,
emigration, an improving economy, and better policing had caused it to
go into decline: 'on the whole the system is in less active operation now than
formerly; its decline being chiefly referable to the absence of some of its
promoters, the increased value of agricultural produce, the higher rate of the
wages of labour and in some localities, the vigorous application of the Crime
& Outrage Act, and the increase of Police'. Registering the increasingly
agrarian focus of the Society, McGregor also observed that 'in some parts
a better class of persons are being enrolled: the *name* of Ribbonism being
abandoned, and that of the "Land System" being substituted; while the
members are designated not Ribbonmen but "system men"'.[21]

The situation of the Ribbon Society in Donegal was broadly similar. 'Its
spirit [and] system exist all over this county altho' the offences consequent
thereon have of late diminished', County Inspector John Anderson
reported, giving the suppression of shebeen houses, and a drive against
poitín production as additional factors in its decline. In short, Anderson's
head constables considered the Society to exist but to be 'in abeyance' in
five of the eight Constabulary districts in the county. The exceptions
included two north-eastern districts, both of which had long been heavily
involved in the Ribbon-dominated *poitín* trade, namely, the Carndonagh
District (North Inishowen), where the report was inconclusive on account
of 'greater secrecy' being observed, and the Ramelton District (Fanad and
Downings), where the Constabulary thought it was 'rather on the increase
among the lower class of the Roman Catholic population'. The third was
the Glenties District (Ardara–Crolly), and here, the Head Constable worried that 'its evil consequences are to be apprehended during the winter'.[22]

•

[20] In Nov. 1855, Dublin Castle asked resident magistrates and chief constables across
Ireland if they had detected any 'renewed activity in secret confederacy'; the circular flagged
the likelihood of returned emigrants being involved in such groups. For the substantial file,
see CSORP 1856/11,368.
[21] CSORP 1856/11,368 Dublin, 23 Dec. 1855, McGregor to Larcom.
[22] Anderson's report and those of his officers are summarized in CSORP 1856/11,368
Dublin, 23 Dec. 1855, McGregor to Larcom.

Against the background of this decade-long movement of 'outrage', the letter that Daniel Cruise received in early April 1856, if it proved genuine, would be an opportunity for an ambitious man to make a mark. And, although now in his late fifties, Cruise was ambitious. A Catholic, from a gentry family in Roscommon, where he had a small estate at Ardkeenan, he had been part of the first generation of stipendiary or resident magistrates, that is, paid officials whom, from the mid-1830s, Dublin Castle had deployed to work with the Constabulary in the administration of law and order, a sudden, effective, and often resented superseding of landlords and agents who had served as unsalaried justices of the peace in their own communities.[23] Appointed a stipendiary in 1837, Cruise may have entertained hopes of getting a higher niche in the central bureaucracy and, if he did, a lot now depended on the authenticity of that letter.[24]

Cruise left Wood Lodge for the Castle. There, he showed the letter to Thomas Larcom, the Under Secretary, an immensely capable civil servant who oversaw the entire British civil administration in Ireland.[25] Larcom suggested that Cruise call on Alexander MacDonnell, Commissioner of National Education, the official responsible for some 5,245 schools, to see if he could confirm that the letter had been written by one of his 5,961 teachers.[26] Cruise duly crossed the city to the Education Commission's offices on Marlborough Street. There, after a quick search in his files, MacDonnell confirmed that the handwriting was indeed that of Patrick McGlynn, master of Beagh School, two miles from the two-street town of Ardara (pop. 1851: 651; 1861: 754; 1871: 575). MacDonnell's files would also have shown that McGlynn was a 24-year-old Catholic and a native of Glenties; that he had been appointed to this single-roomed school—'a very excellent thatch house, 24 feet long, by 12 and a half, and 8 in height'[27] (Figure 1.1)—two years earlier on 1 March 1853 (having been dismissed in 1850, after only six months, from a school at Letterbrick in Glenfin[28]); that he had spent some six months in Dublin on

---

[23] For ultra-Protestants, many 'stipendiaries' being Catholics sharpened the sting; see 'Introduction' in Dorian, *Outer Edge*, 15–16; there had been a limited trial of the stipendiary system in the 1810s. For Cruise's obituary, see *Cork Examiner*, 1 Oct. 1870; the GRO gives his age, at death, as 72.

[24] On Cruise's prior appointments, and his first impressions of Donegal, see *Select Committee on Extending the Functions of the Constabulary*, 92–101.

[25] CSORP 1856/16,473 Donegal, 11 June 1856, Cruise to Larcom, provides a narrative of events.

[26] *Twenty-Third Report of the Commissioners of National Education in Ireland, (for the Year 1856), with Appendices, Vol. I*, HC 1858 (2304–I), xx. 202–3.

[27] ED 1/24/112/1–2.

[28] *BN*, 12 Mar. 1857. Although McGlynn claimed to have taught in Letterbrick (est. 1849), he is not mentioned in correspondence on the school, suggesting he may have been a monitor not a teacher. See ED 2/13/20; 2/14/29; 2/50/70; Letterbrick.

a training course in 1854;[29] that he had since attained the level of 'third class' teacher; that he had some sixty-six children on his rolls, and, as was common in rural schools, a daily attendance of about half that number.[30] And further poking may have shown McGlynn to be married; in fact, he and his wife, Catherine, had a daughter, Anne, then aged 11 months, and, in April 1856, Catherine was three months pregnant.[31]

On his return to Donegal, Cruise wrote to McGlynn, asking him to call to see him, as he was unwilling to enter into correspondence on the subject raised in his letter. And so on a day in mid-April, the young schoolmaster crunched up the gravel walks to Wood Lodge. McGlynn, like the majority of people in west Donegal, lived in a small thatched house. It may have been only single-roomed; at most, it had two rooms. With the exception, perhaps, of the priest's house in Lough Hill, outside Ardara, he had probably never set foot in such an expansive and finely furnished private residence as that being rented by Cruise. Built little over ten years earlier on an elevated site looking south over Donegal Bay, Wood Lodge's carpeted hall was large enough for two eight-day clocks, four chairs, a 'beautiful' stained-glass hall lamp, a flower stand—Cruise tended a 'great variety of hothouse plants'—and a hat stand. The drawing room, where McGlynn was likely shown, contained two loungers, two neat and sub-stantial easy chairs, a dozen mahogany chairs, in green damask—with curtains, Brussels carpet, and a hearth rug to match—as well as various tables and cabinets and a Collard and Collard grand square piano. The centre-piece of the dining room was a 'very superior set of Mahogany pillar and claw dinner tables, with centre and two ends', surrounded by twelve chairs and two armchairs. Cruise kept a decent cellar: in 1858, when he auctioned the furniture ('of the first quality and modern style ... superior'), other lots included fourteen dozen of 'old claret, port and sherry wines', and 'a quantity of Guinness's porter in bottle'. The coach-house contained two phaetons, a fly jaunting car, and a gig, and his stables had five well-bred horses, including two brood mares got by well-known stallions.[32]

Here, in unfamiliar comfort, McGlynn heard Cruise agree to the terms offered in his letter of 31 March: if the master enabled the magistrate to

---

[29] *LJ*, 11 Mar. 1857.
[30] ED 2/59/50: Begha [*sic*]; *Twenty-Second Report of the Commissioners of National Education in Ireland, (for the Year 1855), with Appendices*, HC 1856 [2142–I], xxvii, appendix C, 180–1. On the early years of Beyha [*sic*] School, see ED 1/24/112/1–2; ED 2/12/74; ED 2/54/157.
[31] CSORP 1857/6,799 Clontarf, 27 July 1857, Cradock to McGregor, gives the children's ages.
[32] *LJ*, 20 Oct. 1858.

capture Molly Maguires committing an 'outrage', he would receive a reward, and nobody would ever know that he was an informer.[33] And Cruise having accepted those terms, McGlynn returned to Beagh to live among the people whom he had resolved to betray. A few days later, on Sunday 20 April, he sent Cruise, through the mail, a note on a page torn from a copybook. 'Please warn Reilly against talking to me in Ardara', he began, adding, 'Please tell him to lend me some arms. I will give them back when I drop the present pursuit.' 'Reilly' was Hugh Reilly, a Cavan-man, then in his early thirties, who had abandoned agricultural labour in 1845 to join the Constabulary; he was then about a year in Ardara, where he would see out his career.[34] An attack on James Gallagher of Beagh, McGlynn continued, was imminent. It would most likely happen on the night of Tuesday 22 April. He was not yet certain that the Mollies would do anything on that night—'they may do nothing untill the fair of Glenties [12 May] when they get the police away', that is, the Ardara constables on duty in the neighbouring town—but he would let Reilly know for sure on Monday night.

On Monday evening, McGlynn duly met with Reilly. Plans had changed, he told him: there would be no attack on Tuesday. And then on Tuesday, McGlynn again sent Cruise a short note on a page torn from a copybook. Gallagher, a man in his forties, was now to be attacked on Wednesday night, 23 April. 'There is a probability of their gathering and doing nothing', he explained, 'but still they are fully determined upon it. I think they are resolved giving him a most severe beating and he being a man of very delicate constitution it is as likely as not that they would kill him.' On Monday night, he added, he had 'travelled' with Reilly 'the most private rout[e]' to Gallagher's house, 'because I knew there was a likeli-hood of [the Constabulary] meeting [the Mollies] should they take any rout[e] only the one I showed him'.[35]

Cruise received this note on Wednesday 23 April. Gallagher was to be attacked that night. With little time to prepare, he left for Glenties, the district headquarters of the Constabulary, some fifteen miles from Mountcharles. There, he made arrangements with Sub-Inspector John Watkins for a party of police to accompany them, under cover of darkness, to Beagh where they were to lie in ambush at Gallagher's house for the Molly Maguires. Cruise, Watkins, and an unspecified number of

[33] CSORP 1856/16,473 contains eight letters from McGlynn to Cruise, dated 31 Mar.; 20, 22, and 26 Apr.; 4, 7, and 22 May, and 2 June 1856.
[34] Hugh Reilly (1824–88) spent much of his career in Ardara, where he married Bridget Doherty (1840–1938) in 1858; he died there in 1888. The family used the form O'Reilly.
[35] CSORP 1856/16,473 Beigha, 20 Apr. 1856, McGlynn to Cruise; Beigha, 22 Apr. 1856, McGlynn to Cruise.

constables left Glenties at 8.30 p.m. Given that more than twenty Mollies were sometimes reported to be involved in raids, they were unlikely to have taken less than six constables with them. According to Cruise, the party turned off the road to avoid being observed, and then walked 'more than twelve miles through a bog' to Beagh. He exaggerated the distance: whether the police went south, over the Ardara Road, or west, over the Maas Road, before cutting across the bog, the distance would have been closer to eight miles. But it would have felt like twelve miles, for even in daylight the terrain is difficult, and the constables would have been carrying carbines (rifles) and pistols. Moreover, if, as is almost certain, the Constabulary had come over the Ardara Road, they would also have had to traverse the Owenea river. Helpfully, there had been a full moon on the previous Sunday and the night was clear. The weather had also been unseasonably dry through the spring, and land that might otherwise have been waterlogged was now easier to cross than usual. Watkins, a native of Cork, was 27 years of age, and, anticipating an encounter with armed men, the constables whom he picked for the job were likely about his own age, fit, and able. However, Cruise was 58 years old. The 'severity and slavery' of the night march, he later reported, exceeded 'any thing I experienced since I first became a Resident Magistrate, now nearly twenty years'. Arriving in Beagh at 11.30 p.m., the armed party hid on what Cruise termed 'the mountain'—in truth, whin- and heather-covered outcrop—near Gallagher's house, and there they waited for the Mollies. And at 3.30 a.m., when nothing had happened, they slipped away, picking their way back through bog and marsh, as light began to glow over the Croaghs. By 6.30 a.m., the earliest they can have reached Glenties, the sun had risen.[36]

Frustrated, Cruise wrote to the young schoolmaster, expressing disappointment that the ten-hour expedition had been in vain. McGlynn was not perturbed, replying calmly on Saturday 26 April that he was sorry Cruise had been 'disappointed' after making 'such a journey'. However, he should 'rest assured the information was as correct as they [the Mollies] had themselves'. That night, they 'went down strands'—meaning to the area around Kilclooney and Loughfad, about two to three miles north of Beagh, popularly 'Downstrands' (in Irish, Íochtar Tíre, the low country)—to bring up some members for the attack, 'but the committee-man of that part was sick and the fellows of the lower parts would not come wanting him'. They had now postponed the attack until Sunday

---

[36] CSORP 1856/16,473 Donegal, 11 June 1856, Cruise to Larcom. After a protracted period of dry weather which had left the land 'parched', it rained on 10 May, and there were heavy showers on 11–12 May. See *BH*, 16 May 1856.

27 April. 'If the[y] do nothing on Sunday night', he added, 'it is likely it shall not be done this summer.' And he finished by reassuring Cruise that nobody knew that the police had been in Beagh: 'No person heard that you were there [the] last night.'[37]

The Royal Mail delivered on Sundays. McGlynn's letter, like that which had brought the police from Glenties on 23 April, reached Cruise on the day on which the attack was supposed to take place. Now, Cruise sent word to Watkins to proceed to Beagh while he himself went direct to Ardara. Arriving in the town at 10.00 p.m., he met with Reilly, whom McGlynn had also tipped off. Shortly before midnight, Reilly brought Cruise the two miles out to Beagh. Watkins and a party of police were already there, lying in ambush as before. Although they were only 50 yards apart, they would not see each other until shortly before 3.30 a.m. Then, 'when daylight was appearing', they broke cover to return to Glenties. Cruise went with them across the bog; Reilly, presumably, returned directly to Ardara.

Either the magistrate had been fooled twice, or the master had been telling the truth and the Mollies had changed their plans at a late hour. The prize was great—Cruise gave him the benefit of the doubt. However, having been twice notified of attacks on the very day that they were supposed to happen, Cruise now worried that McGlynn might not be able to get word to him in time to interdict a raid. Indeed, it was a serious concern, for his district extended over 100 miles from Gweedore in the north-west to Bundoran in the south-east, and he was sometimes required to substitute for his counterpart in north-east Donegal. It was often late when he arrived back at Wood Lodge, and he sometimes stayed away from home overnight. And so he wrote again to the young man, telling him to also communicate with Watkins in Glenties. The sub-inspector duly got a message from McGlynn, via Reilly, that Gallagher was to be attacked on Thursday 1 May and that night, for the third time in nine days, he took his men across the bog to Beagh. But again, no Mollies appeared, and, at 3.30 a.m., the party slipped silently away.[38]

Now, Cruise's patience started to wear thin. He sent McGlynn a stern letter, remonstrating about wasting police time. McGlynn, having some-how heard that Cruise had gone into Arranmore, an island off the coast, delayed replying until Sunday 4 May. He was unflappable. He had told Reilly to have the police in Beagh as early as possible, he wrote, but the party that left Glenties had come 'rather far over the Ardara road and word was immediately circulated to that effect which prevented [any attack]'.

[37] CSORP 1856/16,473 Beigha, 26 Apr. 1856, McGlynn to Cruise.
[38] CSORP 1856/16,473 Donegal, 11 June 1856, Cruise to Larcom.

And the previous Sunday—27 April, the second occasion the police had
been in Beagh—the Mollies had called off the planned attack on Gallagher
as the night was very clear and 'they had not strangers enough'. 'But Sir',
continued McGlynn, 'I should be well satisfied after missing nine times to
take them on the tenth. I have known them often to gather last winter
without affecting any thing. You may rest perfectly satisfied that the
information I give is correct as they themselves have it.' He was putting
himself at risk, he reminded Cruise, and he threatened to break off
communication unless he was provided with a weapon:

> I cannot however look after any more informations until I get arms. I know
> I should be well paid were they taken but it might be to provide for my
> funeral were I not prepared for a surprise.
> If provided with arms I shall still exert myself but cannot at all be
> responsible for the information that is they may often gather and do nothing.
> But if any thing is done without me giving previous information (in this
> locality) then Sir I may be censured.[39]

On Tuesday 6 May, Cruise received this explanation of the failure to attack
Gallagher on the second (27 April) and third (1 May) nights that the
Constabulary had been in Beagh, and the demand for arms (which he
apparently resisted). Two days later, on Thursday 8 May, Cruise attended
the petty sessions in Ballyshannon, about twenty miles from Wood Lodge.
Arriving home that evening, he found yet another envelope—his sixth—
from the schoolmaster. It contained a note of only two lines, written in haste.
As with previous letters, it announced that Gallagher was to be attacked on
the very night that it was received. A letter from Glenties, that came by the
same post, let Cruise know that, via Reilly, Watkins too had got word from
McGlynn of the imminent attack, and that he would be again taking a party
from Glenties to intercept the Mollies; if he wished to join them, a constable
would be waiting for him in Ardara to accompany him out to Beagh. Cruise,
who had just completed a forty-mile round trip, left for Ardara.[40]

•

On Wednesday 7 May, the day that McGlynn sent that note to Cruise,
an unannounced visitor had called on him—the school inspector, Louis
Harkin. National schools were inspected twice a year, and teachers dreaded
the process as it could result in docked wages or dismissal. In the national
system's early years, some teachers kicked against inspection—locally, in

[39] CSORP 1856/16,473 Beigha, 4 May 1856, McGlynn to Cruise.
[40] CSORP 1856/16,473 Donegal, 11 June 1856, Cruise to Larcom; Beigha, 7 May
1856, McGlynn to Cruise.

1852, James Bradden lost Laconnell School, when he refused to 'be examined, examine a class, or take any part in the school business' while the inspector was present—but the intrusive ordeal, that often saw masters demeaned in front of 'scholars', was unavoidable. It was also becoming more severe, following a parliamentary inquiry in 1854 that exposed considerable 'incompetence' among schoolmasters.[41] Indeed, since then, the inspector in the Derry District, Christopher Graham, had caused the salaries of over thirty-four teachers (mainly in Inishowen) to be withdrawn. This de facto firing of so many teachers caused controversy, with complaints about Graham's severity aired in the press in winter 1855–6.[42] McGlynn's school was in a different district, and Harkin, a Belfast-man who had himself been a teacher, was less abrasive than Graham, but he would have felt the colder wind now blowing from Marlborough Street.[43] In the parish of Ardara, where there were then fifteen national schools, John Campbell had been dismissed from Brackey in 1855 for 'disputing with the people in the locality, neglecting school, and being insolent towards [the] manager', meaning the parish priest, John D. McGarvey,[44] and some other teachers had come close to being fired. Notably, in 1854, John Cunningham, the master of Meenavalley school, had been fined and 'severely admonished' for his 'disrespectful manner and language' to the inspector and told to remove his 'domestic furniture' from the schoolroom and to close off all communication with his 'apartment',[45] and James McAfee, the teacher in the town school attended by Protestant boys, had been warned that if he 'continued to indulge in habits of intemperance' he would not be retained in the service of the Board.[46] Worryingly for McGlynn, in July 1855, he himself had been 'severely' admonished on the 'state' of Beagh; the inspector had judged the supply of books 'inadequate', the accounts 'inaccurate', and the school 'stationary'. Things had improved by December—his accounts were then 'neat and accurate' and the school 'progressing'—but the master had been then reprimanded for the 'backwardness' of the pupils in grammar and geography. And so McGlynn needed a good report.

---

[41] *Report from the Select Committee of the House of Lords, Appointed to Inquire into the Practical Working of the System of National Education in Ireland...* , HC 1854 (525), xv.

[42] *LJ*, 28 Nov. 1855.

[43] Louis Harkin, appointed inspector in 1854, was a son of Hugh Harkin (1791–1854), a teacher, journalist, and leader of Catholic opinion in Belfast. Louis's brother Alexander was a prominent surgeon.

[44] ED 2/13/86: Leckconnel; ED 2/13/88: Drumboighill; ED 2/54/115: Brackey.

[45] ED 2/59/10: Meenavalley.

[46] ED 2/59/6: Ardara (First) Male.

That Wednesday, when Harkin arrived in Beagh, only twenty-one children—eleven boys, with an average age of 9; ten girls, with an average age of 8—were present. It was a number significantly below the usual attendance of thirty-two (twenty boys, twelve girls), which was itself less than half the number (sixty-six) on the roll. However, low and irregular attendance was common in rural schools, and Harkin made no issue of it. Rather, he examined the state of the building, observed McGlynn's teaching—nineteen pupils were working on the first or second books (of a series of five) and two on the third or fourth books—and he reviewed the accounts, jotting down details on official forms. He told McGlynn to get the 'inscription' (the wooden name-board identifying the building as a school) renewed, and to supply a want in books and other supplies. But, importantly, Harkin found the accounts to be 'neat and accurate' and the school to be again 'progressing'.[47] The master should have had a sense of relief that evening. Yet the attack on Gallagher was scheduled for the following night, and Cruise was growing impatient.

•

Cruise reached Ardara at 11.00 p.m. on the night of Thursday 8 May. Watkins, as promised, had a constable waiting to take him out to Beagh. Arriving about 12.30 p.m., they concealed themselves 'in the mountains' beside Gallagher's house. Meanwhile, Watkins had brought a party of police across the bog, and they were lying in ambush as before. And again, nothing happened, and they left at 3.30 a.m. At this stage, Constabulary parties had come across the bog on four separate nights—23–4 April, 27–8 April, 1–2 May, and 8–9 May. Cruise had come with them on the first occasion and joined them on the second and fourth, returning with them to Glenties. Over these fifteen days, the master had revelled in having the magistrate at his beck and call. A swaggering self-assurance is evident in his letters, hinting at a sense of being smarter than those whom he was betraying and an enjoyment of possessing information coveted by the powerful man to whom he was betraying them. Perhaps, his letters point to narcissism. Certainly, some reveal shocking selfishness: he later suggested that his pregnant wife might appear in court as an informer, when that was a step he himself was unwilling to take.[48] Still, as Cruise may have inferred from the very first letter that he received from McGlynn, the self-regarding young man had financial concerns—in fact, he had been prosecuted several times for unpaid debts—and he was

[47] ED 2/59/50: Begha (Beagh).
[48] CSORP 1856/16,473 Beigha, 2 June 1856, McGlynn to Cruise.

worried too about his own safety. His self-confidence, then, had likely never concealed from Cruise a vulnerability that made him malleable. McGlynn, he seems to have grasped, had the essential qualifications of an informer and some desirable, provided, of course, he had prior knowledge of the movements of the Molly Maguires. The magistrate had hitherto indulged him. But now, after the fourth night march, Cruise changed tack. He wrote to McGlynn, telling him to come to Wood Lodge on Friday 23 May.

Friday was a school day. On Thursday, McGlynn went to see the parish priest, McGarvey, the 'patron' and 'manager' of the school, to ask that he be allowed to give the 'scholars' the day off. McGarvey refused to oblige, and McGlynn then wrote to Cruise, asking if they could meet on Saturday 31 May. Cruise replied that he would be at home on Sunday. And so, on 1 June, two months since he had first written to the magistrate, the master arrived at Wood Lodge for the second time. Now, the magistrate rounded on him, accusing him of 'setting me astray and being the cause of unnecessarily harassing me and the men', adding that if he knew as much as he had told him, he must know a good deal more. A heated conversation ensued, during which Cruise may have threatened the young man with legal proceedings. And by the time McGlynn left Wood Lodge, he had agreed to send 'a list of the names of all those implicated stating the different ranks those in command held' and to provide 'evidence in support of the truth of the list'.[49]

Back in Beagh, McGlynn played for time. 'I am making out the list which I promised', he explained to Cruise in a long letter on 2 June, 'and cannot send it so soon as I thought. [B]ecause of me being a stranger here I know no more than twenty myself by name but I know sixty of them by eyesight as it is called, and must get as many names as I can by degrees as enquiry might lead to suspicion[;] however I will have a list of forty by this day week.'[50] Cruise replied in a letter marked 'to remain in the office till called for'. McGlynn had asked that he do so, 'because Sir my wife might open it if I should not be at home'. And he was often away from home, the public houses of Ardara—most especially, John Dorrian's on the main street and Denis Hanlon's opposite the chapel—having a strong draw. Cruise's reply told the master that he should again come to Wood Lodge. On this occasion, 8 June, the magistrate took a soft approach, reassuring him that 'if he made a sworn information before me and that it turned out to be true and was supported by other evidence, and that the parties were

---

[49] CSORP 1856/16,473 Ardara, 22 May 1856, McGlynn to Cruise; Donegal, 11 June 1856, Cruise to Larcom.
[50] CSORP 1856/16,473 Beigha, 2 June 1856, McGlynn to Cruise.

convicted, I would consider it the same as if I had succeeded in arresting them in the commission of the offence which was his first proposition'. McGlynn now swore a lengthy 'information' or statement, and, abandoning his original and oft-repeated insistence that he must not be exposed as an informer, he agreed, if called upon, to testify in court as a crown witness.[51]

McGlynn's 'information' went far beyond the proposed attack on James Gallagher that had absorbed so much of the Constabulary's time over the previous two months. In fact, Gallagher was not even mentioned. Rather, McGlynn revealed himself to be a Ribbonman or Molly Maguire, and he took Cruise into an underworld of secret signs and passwords, for which members paid 6d. every quarter (three months), and meetings in the backrooms of public houses to plot attacks on the Society's enemies. In the course of this 'information', he named over twenty men as members of the group, not only in and around Ardara, but across west Donegal. And he gave a detailed account of the circumstances in which he himself had been made a Molly Maguire. Specifically, he recounted how, in January 1854, when he was about ten months in Beagh, he had been in company, in Hanlon's public house, with Neil Breslin, apparently of Ardara, and William Maxwell, a shoemaker, of Doohill, just outside the town. Breslin asked him if he knew anything about what was going on. McGlynn replied that he did not, and that he did not want to know, and they had left the matter there. Two days later, McGlynn had been again drinking in Ardara, this time with James Melley, then master of Meentinadea School, three miles out the Donegal road.[52] Melley asked if Maxwell and Breslin had spoken to him about 'taking stuff', meaning the signs and passwords of the Ribbon Society. McGlynn said that they had, but he had not taken it. Melley thought that he had been unwise—if the stuff was offered, it was dangerous to refuse it. He himself, he said, had taken it 'out of fear', and only on condition that he would not have to do anything, that is, not be involved in any 'outrage'. McGlynn was prepared to take it on the same terms, and he accepted an offer by Melley to talk to Maxwell on his behalf. The following Sunday, Melley, Maxwell, and McGlynn went after mass to Hanlon's. There, in a backroom, Little John Breslin of Doohill, the master of the Ardara lodge, was sitting with several men, including Big John Breslin of the Point and Neil Breslin. McGlynn sat on a bed beside Little John who produced a prayer book, which he asked the schoolmaster to kiss. Then, in a low voice, he recited an oath to the Holy

---

[51] CSORP 1856/16,473 Information of Patrick McGlynn, School Teacher of Beagh . . . , 8 June 1856.
[52] ED 2/13/62: Meentinadea.

Trinity, which McGlynn was to repeat, with his hands on his breast, swearing 'to assist in every way I could every member of the society, to keep everything secret, to obey the master in all things he would tell me and to know no allegiance to any person unless those connected with that body'. McGlynn then gave a shilling to Breslin, who in turn gave him the passwords for the quarter. Having made him a Ribbonman, Breslin announced that McGlynn, like other national teachers, would not go out at night with 'attacking parties'.[53]

The act of swearing an 'information', as historian W. E. Vaughan observes, 'ignited the blue touch-paper that made the magisterial firework go off with a reassuring bang or fizzle out in dampness and disappointment'.[54] The 'information' sworn in Wood Lodge had the potential to severely disrupt the Ribbon Society in west Donegal: McGlynn having formally accused men of a specific offence—membership of an illegal society—the authorities now had the power to arrest them and compel witnesses to give evidence on oath. Still, despite having sworn that he would appear in court as a crown witness, McGlynn continued to clutch at a hope that he would not have to testify, and that his informing would remain unknown, for Cruise had encouraged him to believe that one or more of those named would also inform, and that the Crown would not need his evidence. To this end, Cruise assured the schoolmaster that when the men were arrested, he too would be taken up, and brought into custody with those whom he had betrayed. That Sunday in Wood Lodge, McGlynn asked Cruise not to act on his information until he heard from him again. However, on McGlynn's leaving Mountcharles for Beagh, Cruise himself left for Glenties barracks. There, he dispatched mounted men to the Constabulary in Fintown, Dungloe, Killybegs, and Carrick, with warrants for arrests to be made at precisely 2.00 a.m. The Glenties Constabulary, meanwhile, were to arrest two townsmen at the same hour. Then, at 9.00 p.m., Cruise and a large party of police left Glenties for Ardara, where, in the barracks on the Front Street, the constables confirmed the townlands and houses in which the wanted men resided. The augmented force was then divided into parties of different sizes, depending on the numbers to be arrested, and sent out at staggered times so that they would all arrive at their destinations at 1.30 a.m. No arrest was to be made before that hour, and all the wanted men were to be taken at or as near it as possible.

The Constabulary was stretched: 'So limited were we as regards men, not having time to assemble a force', Cruise would later remark, 'that I had

---

[53] CSORP 1856/16,473 Information of Patrick McGlynn . . . 8 June 1856.
[54] W. E. Vaughan, *Murder Trials in Ireland, 1836–1914* (Dublin, 2009), 60.

but three men with myself.' Nevertheless, by 3.30 a.m., all the parties that left Ardara had returned to the town with seventeen prisoners, among them Patrick McGlynn. Also in the barracks was Michael Gallagher of Owenteskna, who had been caught the previous day in a still house in Lergynasearhagh; Cruise tried and convicted him on the spot, fining him £6 or to be imprisoned for three months. It is likely that he just wanted him out of the barracks, which was not purpose-built, but a house adapted for the Constabulary. It could not accommodate the large number of police and prisoners now crowded into it, and shortly after 4.00 a.m., Cruise ordered the men march the seven miles to Glenties. There, at 6.30 a.m., they were lodged in the bridewell, where two townsmen were already in custody. Those detained in outlying areas—Carrick (1), Killybegs (1), Fintown (1), and Dungloe (1)—were marched to Glenties with a 'strong escort' that night or the following day, making a total of twenty-three prisoners, including McGlynn.[55]

Among those now in custody were Ribbon leaders from five parishes. Little John Breslin, possibly a linen weaver, and the shoemaker William Maxwell, both of Doohill, were respectively the master and chairman of the Ardara lodge, and James Moore of Loughfad was master for the lower section (Downstrands) of that parish; it was his illness on the first night that the Constabulary came to Beagh that had deterred others in his area from going to attack Gallagher. Neil O'Donnell, a publican cum road contractor, and Patrick Maguire, a carpenter, were the master and chairman of the Glenties lodge.[56] Charles Herroran was master of the Killybegs lodge, while Martin Quigley was the Dungloe master; Quigley was the son of a road contractor who was likely also a shopkeeper or publican.[57] And an even higher ranking member had also been taken—James Gallagher of Fintown, fingered by McGlynn as the delegate for the 'barony of Boylagh and western part of Bannagh', meaning the representative of west Donegal on the Society's county board. In short, the authorities had detained a significant portion of the middle management of the 'organized system' that had been central to the trouble in west Donegal for the previous decade.

---

[55] See e.g. *Belfast Mercury*, 25 June 1856. For Gallagher's conviction, see IPSCR Ardara: 9 June 1856.

[56] DCA, GJ/1/18 'Amount Asked off the County of Donegal at Summer Assizes 1856' returns O'Donnell as having a contract, for two and a half years, to maintain the road from Glenties Workhouse to Letterilly; it paid £9 19s. per annum.

[57] *Northern Whig*, 18 Nov. 1851, notes Francis Quigley, Martin's father, being fined for hiring a car without a licence, which suggests an involvement in trade; in 1856, Francis had a contract to repair roads for two and a half years; the contract was worth £10 per annum. See DCA, GJ/1/18.

Some of these men had long been suspected of membership of the Ribbon Society; certainly, O'Donnell, the Glenties master, was known by his parish priest to be involved, and his landlord knew that Gallagher, the delegate, was a highly placed member.[58] Moreover, the authorities had a good idea of the types who became Ribbonmen, and strikingly, as if McGlynn had merely put sighted quarry within the magistrate's reach, Cruise's correspondence betrays no surprise at any name given to him. Indeed, the social composition of west Donegal lodges, as evidenced by the men now in Glenties Bridewell, would have been familiar to any magistrate who had dealt with Ribbon cases elsewhere—townsmen involved in trade, including respectable or, at least, well-to-do men, filled key leadership positions, while poorer smallholders, artisans, and labourers supplied the base.

Conspicuous among those now in custody, as was common in Ribbon cases, were publicans and the sons of publicans. Again, the father of Quigley, the Dungloe master, was likely a publican-shopkeeper; certainly, O'Donnell, the Glenties master, kept a public house, and from Ardara (Figure 1.2), where there were sixteen public houses, at least one publican—Barney Kelly, a committeeman—was now in custody, while another arrested man, Neil Breslin, may have belonged to a public house in the west end of the town. Two other Ardara publicans or publicans' sons—John Dorrian and James Hanlon—would soon be arrested on Ribbon charges and another publican cum road contractor, Patrick Friel, had been charged with Ribbonism the previous year, meaning that at least a quarter of the town's public houses were now known to the authorities to have Ribbon connections.[59] Road contractors too had long been associated with the Society, and the Dungloe master (Quigley),

[58] When Gallagher was brought to trial in 1857, his landlord, James Hamilton, acknowledged that he had heard that he was a Ribbonman; see Ch. 6. Intriguingly, in Dec. 1852, Hamilton had written to Dublin Castle, explaining that he had been 'trying to get into the working of the Ribbon system' in west Donegal, where it was 'rife and active' and where 'nightly meetings' and 'armed parties' were a 'terror to the well-disposed'. 'I have at last got a man who has been high up in them', he continued, 'and I believe is so still.' This unnamed man had identified the two 'principal men' and described their papers. Hamilton wanted to 'knock up' one of their meetings, and asked how he should proceed. See OP 1852/7/419 Donegal, 5 Dec. 1852, Hamilton to Under Secretary. On his priest's awareness of O'Donnell's involvement, see Ch. 5.

[59] John Sweeney of Ardara, arrested on McGlynn's word, belonged to a family that subsequently acquired a public house and dabbled in politics; one of their number, also John, was a candidate for the Board of Guardians in 1898. That family was related to the Sweeneys of Altnagapple, two of whom were arrested on McGlynn's information, and the family of Matthew Sweeney of Beagh, who was also arrested. On these connections and a late reference to family members being involved in secret society activities, albeit mistaking the Mollies for the Fenians, see *DJ*, 22 Dec. 1950. For Friel's road contracting, see GJ/1/19: Barony of Banagh, Summer Assizes 1857.

Figure 1.2 Ardara, *c.* 1890; courtesy of the National Library of Ireland

Glenties master (O'Donnell), and, in Ardara, John Dorrian or his father, were involved in road contracting in the 1850s and 1860s, either bidding for contracts for which they themselves employed labourers or going security for contractors. And the delegate, James Gallagher of Fintown, was also in that business.[60] Finally, schoolmasters often figured in political groups, and there were now three teachers in custody: Edward Kennedy, master of Crannogeboy, James Melley, formerly master of Meentinadea and now master of Carrick, and the informer, McGlynn.

As regards age, the Ardara master Little John Breslin may have been in his fifties, while Moses Ward (1826–1912) of Brackey, a mason by trade, was about 30 years of age, as too as was the chairman William Maxwell (1825–1905).[61] However, most of the arrested men whose ages are known were in their early to mid-twenties: McGlynn was 24, Dungloe

---

[60] In 1863 'James Gallagher, farmer, Fintown' was fined 10s. and costs at Glenties petty sessions for having 'permitted to remain on the public road at Meenaleenaghan, from 8 to 10 August, between 30 and 40 carts of broken stone not spread'. See IPSCR Glenties: 4 Sept. 1863. Downstrands chairman, James Moore of Loughfad, or a close connection, acted as a surety for a road contractor many years later: see IPSCR Ardara: 14 Dec. 1880, when a man of that name was prosecuted for Joseph Boyle of Ballymackilduff failing to keep a road in repair. He was prosecuted again the following year when Boyle failed to complete another contract, see IPSCR Ardara: 9 Aug. 1881. Also IPSCR Ardara: 11 Mar. 1884.

[61] On Breslin's age, see Ch. 10. Maxwell's age is taken from prison records: NAI, CRF M/36/1857. Ward's age is taken from his 1901 and 1911 census returns, and his tombstone in Ardara; GRO death register identifies him as a mason.

master Martin Quigley (1835–1914), 21, and Ardara committeeman Condy McHugh (b. 1829), 27.[62] Several were married, including Maxwell, McHugh, and the schoolmasters McGlynn and Kennedy. But, not surprisingly, given their ages, many prisoners were single, the sons of house- and landholders not house- or landholders themselves. For example, Con, Jack, and James O'Donnell of Tullycleave were probably the sons of one or other of three householders of that surname in that townland in the mid-1850s; certainly, nobody with their names *and* surnames had property there in those years. Similarly, Matthew Sweeney of Beagh held no land: he was a son of either Myles or Owen Sweeney, both typical west Donegal smallholders, living in houses valued at 5–7 shillings and each holding 15–16 acres, most of it rough pasture, which put them, in terms of acreage, at the bottom of the middle tier of society: 46.4 per cent of holdings in west Donegal comprised less than 15–30 acres, 31.4 per cent comprised more (see Table 1.2). Most of the arrested men known to have held land can also be placed in that same tier or below it. Only Gallagher, the delegate, stands out clearly as a strong farmer/grazier. He held 24 acres 2 roods 25 perches, some of it good land in Fintown—£4 15s. valuation, compared to the £2 valuation on the holdings of Myles and Owen Sweeney—where he was subletting a remarkably good house (10s. valuation) to the Poor Law Union for use as a dispensary; the only other house he held in Fintown was a herd's house, suggesting that he was likely the James Gallagher holding a house (5s. valuation) and just over 50 acres of poorer land (£2 valuation) in the adjacent townland of Loughnambraddan.[63] Still even if only renting in Fintown, the Ribbon delegate was, comparatively, a man of means. He was literate too, as were several other prisoners, including, obviously, the schoolmasters, but also Maxwell, a shoemaker, Ward, a mason, and Little John Breslin, possibly a weaver—and literacy was as yet a very rare attainment for men of their age (30–50). And so there were rich men and poor men, literates and illiterates, prominent townsmen and inconspicuous countrymen now in custody, and Cruise had dealt a formidable blow to the Molly Maguires.

•

[62] Big John Breslin of Shanaghan, named by McGlynn but not arrested for some months, was 24. The ages of Breslin and McHugh are in prison records, CRF G/22/1857; Quigley's age is taken from emigration records and his obituary, McGlynn's from press reports and emigration records; see Ch. 8.

[63] The area and valuation of holdings are taken from *GV*; Beagh was valued in July 1855, the valuations were revised before the end of 1856, and the data were published in Sept. 1857.

Table 1.2 Holdings, 1857: Beagh and Glenties Poor Law Union

Landholder	Valuation (Land and Buildings)	Acreage	Acreage Category in Agricultural Returns	% PLU in Category	% PLU in Lower Categories	% PLU in Higher Categories
James Gallagher	£13 5s.	158a. 1r. 33p.	100–200	4.9	92.5	2.5
John McHugh	£4 10s.	33a. 3r. 30p.	30–50	12.2	68.5	19.2
Condy Gallagher	£2 10s.	30a. 1r. 25p.	30–50	12.2	68.5	19.2
James (Táilliúr) Kennedy	£2 5s.	23a. 3r. 0p.	15–30	22.2	46.4	31.4
Thomas (Táilliúr) Kennedy	£2 5s.	23a. 3r. 0p.	15–30	22.2	46.4	31.4
Patrick Kennedy (Bridge)	£3 5s.	21a. 3r. 25p.	15–30	22.2	46.4	31.4
Patrick (Nancy) Sweeney	£2 5s.	18a. 3r. 30p.	15–30	22.2	46.4	31.4
Owen Sweeney	£2 0s.	16a. 3r. 20p.	15–30	22.2	46.4	31.4
James (Pat) Kennedy	£1 15s.	16a. 2r. 0p.	15–30	22.2	46.4	31.4
Myles Sweeney	£2 0s.	15a. 2r. 30p.	15–30	22.2	46.4	31.4
Cornelius (*aka* Nogher) McHugh	£1 5s.	9a. 0r. 32p.	5–15	32.3	14.0	53.6
Condy McHugh	£1 5s.	9a. 0r. 32p.	5–15	32.3	14.0	53.6
Ellen Callaghan	£0 15s.	2a. 0r. 0p.	1–5	12.4	1.6	85.9

Source: Griffith's Valuation; *Agricultural Statistics of Ireland, for the Year 1857*, HC 1859 [2461], xxvi.

Glenties Bridewell—the high-sounding name of the place where the arrested men were now confined—belied the reality of three steel-doored cells and two dayrooms in the basement of the town courthouse. Erected in 1843, the courthouse was—with Glenties barracks (c.1823–4), national schools (1840), and poorhouse (1845)—an outpost of the more activist state called into being in the decades before the Great Famine. Still, its basement was a poor excuse for a temporary holding centre and several inspectors of prisons had expressed disquiet that it had ever been approved for that purpose. The windows of the cells looked onto the road and the prisoners could easily converse with passers-by, while the yard was surrounded by wall so low that it was 'entirely useless'.[64]

At some stage that morning, Cruise had McGlynn brought up from the bridewell. He now asked him if it was likely that any of the other prisoners would turn informer. McGlynn replied that he was sure that some men would inform. And asked the name of the man who knew most and would be most likely to do so, McGlynn, 'after some consideration', said Condy McHugh of Beagh, whom he had identified in his statement as a committeeman in Ardara. Illiterate and more comfortable speaking Irish than English, McHugh had warmed to the master after his appointment to the school in 1853. It would soon transpire that, after McGlynn had been 'made' a Ribbonman, McHugh had trusted him to fetch weapons from other committeemen in the town and carry messages to Downstrands. They were about the same age, and, at the time of their arrest, they had only recently married, McGlynn probably in 1854 and McHugh in late 1855 or early 1856: McHugh's wife, Catherine Cannon of Doohill, was then about 20 years of age and the couple was, as yet, childless, and it was only after July 1855 that he had built a house on an 18-acre tract which his father had given to himself and his brother Nahor.

Cruise again acted quickly. A little after midday, he had McHugh brought to him, spoke to him about the charge against him—but did not, he would claim, hold out any inducement or threat—and then left him to mull over his situation. A short time later—'inside an hour'— McHugh asked to see him a second time, and there, in the courthouse, he swore an information strongly corroborating McGlynn's and giving a few additional names. And he put his 'mark' to it, committing himself to stand over it in court.[65]

Later that day, Cruise released McGlynn on bail. The rest of the men spent Monday night in Glenties, and the following day, 10 June, Cruise, Watkins, and a force of twenty constables marched them, presumably cuffed or in chains, from Glenties to Donegal. They were held overnight in that town's bridewell—a 'most wretched' building 'unfit for the purpose for which it is assigned'[66]—and, then on Wednesday morning,

---

[64] *Twenty-Eighth Report of the Inspectors-General on the General State of the Prisons of Ireland, 1849; with Appendices*, HC 1850 [1229], xxix. 305, appendix II, 44. In 1823 John Barrett, rector of Inishkeel, twice requested the erection of a barracks in Glenties; see SOC I 2,520/21 Narin, 14 Mar. 1823, Barrett to Gregory; 2,520/30 Narin, 20 June 1823, Barrett to Gregory.

[65] CSORP 1856/16,473 Information of Condy McHugh of Beagh, 9 June 1856. Nahor (sometimes Noher, Nagher, or Nogher) is a diminutive of Conchubhar (Connor or Cornelius).

[66] *Thirty-Fifth Report of the Inspectors-General on the General State of the Prisons of Ireland, 1856*, HC 1857 Session 2 (2,236), xvii, appendix I, 31.

Watkins took them under 'strong escort' to Lifford, where they were to be lodged in the county gaol to await trial at the assizes in the third week of July. In truth, there had been no need to take the arrested men to Donegal. The direct route to the county gaol—Bealach na gCreach, a lonely mountain road, to Glenfin and then good roads through Ballybofey to Lifford—was thirty-seven miles, while that from Glenties to Donegal was eighteen miles and that from Donegal, via Ballybofey, to Lifford a further thirty-two miles. But, for Cruise, the long march was an opportunity to overawe the alienated and impress the loyal in Frosses, Mountcharles, and Donegal.

The march gave the men time to think and talk. En route from Donegal to Lifford, Watkins sent a dispatch back to Cruise letting him know that the prisoners suspected McGlynn and warning him that, if this became known to 'the people', the master's life would be in danger. In truth, it was no wonder that the arrested men suspected the schoolmaster, for McGlynn was different to them. He was a fluent English-speaker, while many of them would have been awkward in the language. He had also achieved a high level of literacy; although some of the arrested men could read and write, others, like McHugh, were illiterate. And most import-antly, while McGlynn's people, in Glenties, would have been known in Ardara, he was, as he told Cruise, a 'stranger' there. Yet he was a stranger who knew a lot about his neighbours. Children's chatter reveals much, and since his appointment to the roadside school three years earlier, he had become privy to secrets in houses in Beagh, Tullycleave, Ranny, Carn, and Sandfield. He was also the person most likely to be called upon by neighbours to read letters from America or to write letters, in which things that few knew were let slip.[67] At the same time, it can scarcely have escaped attention in the post office (Andrew Young's at the top of the Front Street, opposite the church and meeting house), that, over the previous two months, McGlynn had been receiving an unusual number of letters, not least as he had asked Cruise to mark some letters 'to remain in the office till called for'. And the number of letters, in McGlynn's hand, that had been sent to Wood Lodge between 31 March and 2 June (eight in all) may also have been remarked upon.

It is possible, then, that McGlynn had been suspected for some time. It would have been a considerable achievement for six to twelve men to do once undetected and then keep secret what the Glenties Constabulary believed that they had done four times, that is, leave their barracks at night, pick their way through several miles of bog and marsh, lie out into

---

[67] On letter writing and reading, see Dorian, *Outer Edge*, 85–7, 93–5, 230.

the early hours of the morning, and then go back the way that they had come. If nothing else, their arrival after dawn in Glenties might be noticed or one of them might be indiscreet. Significantly, McGlynn himself had told Cruise that on the evening on 1 May, the third occasion on which a police party came from Glenties, the constables had been seen leaving the Ardara Road, and word had been 'circulated' and reached Beagh.[68] And well might word reach Beagh, for once they left the road and crossed the Owenea, it was one of only half a dozen townlands within easy striking distance.

Here, the knowing ones can have had little difficulty ascribing a reason for this curious departure. *Poitín*-making was common in west Donegal, but it was not particularly prevalent around Ardara. In fact, only one person in the entire parish of Ardara is listed in a return of sixty-three known *poitín*-makers in the Glenties Constabulary District (Ardara to Crolly) compiled in late 1854, and that individual, Cormick McDevitt, a 'noted smuggler', lived in Loughderryduff, a townland close to which the Constabulary party passed en route to Beagh.[69] Illicit distillation was still properly the concern of the Revenue Police, which had two officers and eleven men in barracks around Ardara. However, the Constabulary was not uninterested in *poitín*, and with the disbandment of the Revenue Police now imminent, it was becoming more interested in it; hence, the production of that list of *poitín*-makers in late 1854. Consequently, if the Constabulary had been seen to leave the Glenties–Ardara road, as McGlynn claimed, yet did not raid McDevitt, then something strange was afoot. One other possible objective for such a trek would have been enforcing the fishery laws. In townlands west of Ardara, people were 'much disposed to poach' on the Owenea, using gaffs and trammel nets by day and gaffs and torches at night. Protecting the salmon was the business of water bailiffs, employed by the landlords who owned the fishery. Legislation enacted in the 1840s allowed bailiffs to call on the Constabulary for assistance in interdicting poachers. Still, police lying in wait for poachers was, as yet, unprecedented. Moreover, while sizeable salmon are often taken at that time of the year, it was early in the season for many poachers to be 'on the river', particularly when water levels were low after the dry spring.[70] And so, if the police had been seen leaving the

---

[68] CSORP 1856/16,473 Beigha, 4 May 1856, McGlynn to Cruise.
[69] This substantial file, CSORP 1857/2,185, was compiled in late 1854.
[70] See the evidence of waterkeeper William McAfee in *Fourth Annual Report of the Commissioners of Public Works, in re the Fisheries of Ireland*, HC 1846 (713), xxii, appendix II, 174–5, and *LJ*, 24 Dec. 1845.

road on 1 May, then people may have discounted the notion that their target was a man with a net.

Crucially, there is a vague hint in Cruise's reports that the Constabulary may have been seen before 1 May. On 27 April, the second occasion that the Constabulary came to Beagh, there had been an unexplained shot, possibly a signal, heard 'at a considerable distance' as the party lay in ambush near Gallagher's.[71] It is conceivable, therefore, that somebody had noticed something on the very first night that the Constabulary came, or else got wind that they had been there. And it is possible too that the Mollies had then tested those who knew of their original plan—and people from Ardara to Downstrands had known of the first proposed attack on Gallagher—and watched to see if the Constabulary might be brought again. But certainly, if, as McGlynn claimed, constables were noticed leaving the Glenties–Ardara road on 1 May, it seems probable that by the time that the men were arrested in the early hours of 9 June, somebody knew for over a month that something was amiss between the Owenea and Downstrands.

The wonder, then, was not that the arrested men suspected Master McGlynn, but that the magistrate had released him on bail on 9 June, and allowed him to go back to Beagh. Cruise now directed the Constabulary to inform McGlynn that if he apprehended any danger, he was to come with his wife and child to Mountcharles or Donegal, where he would be supported. On 13 June, four days after his release on bail, Watkins and Head Constable Thomas Wiley took Daniel McDevitt's taxi from Glenties to Beagh. The master must have been worried, for he left with them for Ardara. There, at the hotel, the police hired Thomas Maloney's taxi-car to take McGlynn to Mountcharles that night; the taxi cost 12s. 10d.[72] McGlynn spent the night in the barracks and, the following day, he swore a 'further information' for Cruise, giving additional details about the activities of several men mentioned in his first statement and identifying fifteen more Molly Maguires. Some of these men had quit their homes after the first arrests, and not all could be taken, but two publicans, James Hanlon and John Dorrian, were picked up in Ardara, and another schoolmaster in Mountcharles. That schoolmaster, 25-year-old Cormac Gillespie, was a particular target of Cruise. Earlier that year, Ribbonmen had visited a Mountcharles bailiff or farmer named Thomas Cassidy, and he had since received a threatening letter, telling him if he did not 'give satisfaction' (pay money) to the orphans of Patrick M'Call, he would

[71] CSORP 1856/16,473 Donegal, 11 June 1856, Cruise to Larcom.
[72] CSORP 1856/16,473 Mountcharles, 14 June 1856, Further Information of Patrick Glynn [*sic*], Beagha. CSORP 1856/19,443 includes receipts relating to the transport and support of the McGlynns.

receive a second visit. Gillespie had been acquitted the previous December of stealing and selling a pistol, and Cruise was now trying to pin that threatening letter on him. McGlynn's assertion that he knew Gillespie to be a Ribbonman increased the possibility of a conviction.[73]

There may now have been as many as twenty-six alleged Mollies in Lifford, and Cruise was concerned that McGlynn might be 'tampered with', that is, bribed or bullied into retracting his evidence. Specifically, he heard from a 'credible' source, whose name he did not reveal in his reports, that 'a large sum of money would be made up for him by the friends of the prisoners and the Brotherhood generally to send him out of the country'. In Beagh, meanwhile, Catherine McGlynn had been threatened.[74] Worried about her safety, or rather concerned that Ribbonmen might get her to dissuade her husband from testifying, Head Constable Wiley arrived back at her house on the morning of Sunday 15 June. He told her to be ready in two hours as Maloney's taxi was coming to fetch herself and her child.[75]

Catherine McGlynn may have been born and reared in Sandfield, just over the bridge from Beagh. Interviewed by Cruise a month after the arrests, the McGlynns' servant girl, Sally Gallagher, mentioned having been sent one night to her mistress's mother's house to fetch clothes, passing James Gallagher's house on her way back, and Peggy Harkin, Catherine's sister, being in the house on her return.[76] There were then Harkins in Sandfield, but as Peggy Harkin's marital status is not known, Catherine cannot be shown to have been one of them. Clearly, however, she was from the immediate locality, and so it is possible that she was related, perhaps closely related, to men whom her husband's word had sent to Lifford—men who, if convicted of Ribbonism, faced lengthy sentences. But no such connection is known. All that is known is that later that Sunday, having gathered up what she could of the family's belongings, the pregnant woman got onto Maloney's taxi with her year-old daughter and left Beagh. It was a week to the day since her husband had sworn his first information. The McGlynns spent that night and the following one in the barracks in Mountcharles. They were then moved to Donegal and lodged with police protection in Margaret Boyle's boarding house, where they, like the men in the county gaol—including the other 'crown witness', Condy McHugh—awaited the assizes in late July.[77]

[73] *LJ*, 11 Mar. 1857; *LStd*, 12 Mar. 1857; *LSnl*, 13 Mar. 1857. Gillespie's legal troubles are detailed in ED 2/59/74: Glencoagh.
[74] CSORP 1856/16,473 Donegal, 16 June 1856, Cruise to Larcom.
[75] CSORP 1856/19,443 Glenties, 8 Oct. 1856, Wiley to Hobart.
[76] CRF G/22/1857 Informations of Sally Gallagher . . . 8 July 1856.
[77] CSORP 1856/16,473 Donegal, 16 June 1856, Cruise to Larcom; Donegal, 11 June 1856, Cruise to Larcom; for accommodation expenses, see CSORP 1856/19,443.

2

Bastard Ribbonism

Molly Maguire's ubiquity in west Donegal in the mid-1850s would not have been predicted by the authorities a decade earlier, for, while the Ribbon Society was well organized in eastern parts of the county from the early 1810s, the Constabulary believed that it had no presence at all in western districts before 1845.[1] That distribution was consistent with ethno-religious contention having caused the rise of the Society in the first place. In the east of the county, where there was a substantial Protestant population, there was spasmodic friction between lower-class Protestants and Catholics, most especially in Letterkenny–Milford–Fanad and in Donegal Town–Pettigo–Ballyshannon. In contrast, west Donegal was predominantly Catholic with only small pockets of Methodists and Churchmen. Certainly, colonial realities were never far from view. If few in numbers, Protestants—in Irish, *Gaill* (foreigners) or *Albanaigh* (Scotsmen)—were visibly advantaged, most families holding more and better land than most of their Catholic neighbours, and their religion and preferred language were those of the state. Moreover, all the landowners were Protestants, and only they and their agents got appointed to the grand jury (local government) and commission of the peace (bench). In Irish-language song and story, the *Gaeil* (lit. Gaels, fig. Catholics) gave voice to an abiding feeling of oppression. For instance, a lament composed by Eoghan Óg Mac Niallais (*fl.* 1800–20) of Ardara for Donnchadh Ó Baoill—a member of the family that, before the conquest, had dominated the district—asked rhetorically if it were not better for him that he was now dead and buried with his forefathers in Inishkeel than *faoi chosa Gall, faraor, ag díol cíos leo*, under Protestants' feet, alas, paying rent to them.[2] Still, communal relations were, by and large, good. '[T]here is no

---

[1] In 1840, when a suspected Ribbonman was detained for burglary near Glenties, the arresting officer judged that '*to sow the seeds* of Ribbonism . . . was the principal object of his visit to this neighbourhood, *and not being successful* he turned to rob'. See OP 1840/7/ 13,863 Glenties, 19 June 1840, Rodden to McGregor; emphasis added.

[2] Énrí Ó Muirgheasa, ed., *Dhá Chéad de Cheoltaibh Uladh* (Baile Átha Cliath, 1934), 184–5.

bad Party Spirit in it', James Pearson, a Methodist schoolteacher wrote of the Ardara area, in a letter sent to Dublin Castle soliciting relief in 1837; 'we can, and do, go in and out with and render to each other all the offices of friendship and good neighbourhood.'[3] Indeed, a half-century earlier, in 1786, when the first Wesleyan preacher arrived in Ardara, and, for want of 'more suitable accommodation', took a room in a public house, he found that two men drinking together in the bar were the Catholic priest and Protestant minister. Having established the purpose of his visit—they had guessed he was either a commercial traveller or a gauger (revenue official)—the priest, Patrick McNelis, told the young evangelist that he had come to the wrong place: 'You are not wanted here. My friend, the rector, looks after his people, I look after mine, and we get on quietly and nicely together! No one else is wanted.'[4]

By then, the descendants of the pre-conquest élite, if conscious of what had been lost in the shipwreck of the seventeenth century, had long since reconciled themselves to the new captains. Security of tenure and grand jury road contracts, employment as bailiffs, encouragement in business ventures—not least, the establishment of inns in the mid-1700s—and other petty indulgences had coopted key families. Many were connected to Dálaigh na Glaisí, the O'Donnells of Glashagh and Ballinamore, the most important—and most self-important—branch of the old ruling family left in west Ulster. Ruairí Rua Ó Dónaill (1763–1841) rode to hounds with the county gentry and got himself made sub-constable of the barony of Boylagh, a post that brought a whiff of power sufficient to puff his *mórtas Dálaigh* (O'Donnell pride), and a stipend that gave an otherwise middling farmer means to live beyond. In short, the O'Donnells of Glashagh and their connections further west—the McDevitts and Dunlevys of Glenties, O'Donnells and McAloons of Letterilly, Craigs of Kilclooney, and Maloneys of Ardara—had come through the eighteenth century helping to maintain order, and the long involvement of such notables with the establishment militated against trouble at a lower level with what was, locally, a vastly outnumbered Protestant community.[5]

---

[3] CSORP 1837/5/48 Memorial of James Pearson, Ardara, to Earl Mulgrave, Lord Lieutenant; received 17 June 1837. Séamas Ó Grianna (1889–1969) represented inter-denominational relations in the Rosses in his parents' and grandparents' time as without *mioscais* (hatred) but acknowledged tensions over international politics; see *Nuair a Bhí Mé Óg* (Corcaigh, 1979 [1942]), 143–57.

[4] Charles Henry Crookshank, *History of Methodism in Ireland*, 3 vols. (Belfast, 1885), i. *Wesley and his Times*, 411–12.

[5] For O'Donnell's obituary, see *LJ*, 26 Oct. 1841.

Furthermore, if west Donegal Protestants generally were advantaged, they were by no means all better off than their Catholic neighbours. Protestants worked and traded with Catholics, socialized with them— 300 people of 'all persuasions' attended a soirée organized by the town teetotallers in John O'Donnell's of Ardara in December 1841—and suffered with them through hard times: in a famine in 1837, when Pearson, the Methodist schoolmaster, described two sisters dying in each others' arms 'beneath the canopy of heaven' he did not specify whether the unfortunates were Catholic or Protestant.[6] Here, if Churchmen and Methodists tended to be conservative in politics, they held aloof from Orangeism, and some accepted the legitimacy of Catholics' political grievances. Strikingly, when the tithe agitation of the 1830s was winding down, William Barrett, the son of the rector of Inishkeel, chaired a mass meeting at the harvest fair in Glenties, on 12 September 1838—some reports put the attendance at 30,000—at which the main speakers were priests and the rhetoric markedly nationalist. The meeting had been called to protest at the impounding of nine head of cattle belonging to the Glenties priest, Dan Earley, for non-payment of the tithe portion of his rent; under the Tithe Commutation Act of that year, tithe was now collected from landlords not tenants. 'I think it monstrous', Barrett, a lawyer, told the crowd, 'to suppose that the Roman Catholic should be forced to contribute towards the support of a clergyman in whose religion he has no faith, and from the tenets of which he dissents.'[7]

An incident early in the Famine stands out too. In May 1846, when hunger was beginning to bite, three Dublin boats put into the Church Pool at Narin to purchase potatoes at high prices. 'Countrypeople' assembled in great numbers and, over several days, crowds attacked and beat farmers carting potatoes to Portnoo and they stoned the boatmen and coastguards who were deployed to protect their vessels; indeed, they attempted to scuttle one of the boats by cutting its cable. One of the leaders was a man named Scott, either a Protestant or from a Protestant background, who wrested a pistol from a coastguard, and there is no reason to suppose that Catholics, like the McNelises of Sandfield and Shovlins of Ballymackilduff, raided by the Mollies six years later, were not among the potato sellers.[8] Another incident earlier in spring 1846, in nearby Summy, had its roots in brooding sectarian animosity, yet

---

[6] *LJ*, 11 Jan. 1842. CSORP 1837/5/48 Memorial of James Pearson, Ardara, to Earl Mulgrave, Lord Lieutenant; received 17 June 1837.

[7] *LJ*, 25 Sept. 1838. Also see *Sligo Champion*, 22 Sept. 1838; the *Champion*'s owner, Edward Howard Verdon, was one of the few non-clerical speakers at 'the great anti-tithe meeting'.

[8] OP 1846/7/12,225 Glenties, 20 May 1846, Holmes to Lucas.

paradoxically, as it involved a 'mixed marriage', it also marked the limits of such feeling. There, on Sunday 15 February, the corpse of 74-year-old Sam Crummer (b. 1771), a Protestant, was recovered from a lake. The investigating magistrate exaggerated when he reported that the corpse— wrapped in a heavy iron chain attached to a rock nearly four stones in weight—exhibited 'an appearance of atrocious mutilation, which perhaps the records of crime do not exceed'. Still, the old man had met a brutal end. His chest, all his right ribs, and jaw were broken, and his mouth cut, as if by a knife, to his chin. His skull had also been fractured, causing his brains to protrude, and there were cuts and contusions all over his face and body. Crummer had lived with his only son, also Samuel (b. 1815), to whom he had transferred half the family farm when he married. However, when the young man's wife died not long after the birth of their second child, he had converted to Catholicism to marry their servant girl—'greatly to the annoy-ance and against the consent of all his friends'. Accounts vary, but the old man had either resolved to leave the remaining half of his farm to his grandchildren by the first marriage, and not leave 'as much as a shilling' to his son, or he was preparing to transfer the land to a relative. On Old Sam being missed, Young Sam and his wife, Peggy, were suspected by the 'friends' of the murdered man, who, they claimed, had often been heard to say that his son and daughter-in-law had threatened him, telling him 'the lake would be a bed for one of them yet'. The neighbours commenced a search, and tracked blood from the Crummers' door to the lake, where they found the prints of a small bare foot and a large shoe. Dragging the lake with an implement used for cutting seaweed, they soon recovered the battered corpse. Word was sent for the Constabulary, who found bloody straw in a room of the Crummers' house that served as a byre. Here, it was speculated, the 'powerful young man', 6' 2" in height, had knocked his father down and 'broke in his chest with his knees' while his wife was sticking him with a grape or other sharp implement.

The couple had been immediately arrested; 30-year-old Peggy was pregnant, and so their trial was twice postponed. A girl, Catherine, was born in Lifford Gaol in August 1846, and, ultimately, Peggy and Sam were tried for murder in March 1847. The evidence was entirely circum-stantial, they pleaded not guilty, and they were vigorously defended, with the blood found in the house ascribed to a wound made by a smith on the shoulder of a mare; witnesses testified that they had seen the horse bleeding. Still, after deliberating for only forty minutes, the jury convicted them of murder. The judge, Richard Pennefather, assumed the black cap and sentenced them to death. In late April, the lord lieutenant commuted Peggy's sentence to transportation for life—her child died a few days out from Tasmania in May 1848—but Young Sam, 'a stolid, illiterate man', protesting his innocence and alleging that 'some members of his family' were the perpetrators, was sent to the gallows.⁹

Capital punishment was widely seen as barbarous by the mid-nineteenth century, and even the Tory *Londonderry Sentinel*, which embraced the opportunity provided by the hanging of the 'wretched parricide' to deplore 'mixed marriages', was pleased that the crowd which gathered in Lifford to watch it did not exceed 'a thousand persons'. In the condemned ward, Crummer had told the sheriff, the gaol officials, and clergymen that 'the murderers of his father had not been found out yet'. He was said to have 'endeared himself to the jail authorities all of whom were much affected when he took leave of them'. Just after midday, the door to the drop— above the front door of the gaol—gently opened, and out came Crummer, with a white shirt over his clothes and wearing a white death-cap, with a slow but firm step, followed by the hangman dressed in black. 'Gentlemen and ladies', Crummer said, after the rope had been fitted,

> I am going to inform you that I am about to die, and I wish to tell you that I am innocent, and that I never lifted hand or foot to my poor father, nor would I do it, but [newspaper reporter claimed not to have heard the name] of Ardara swore my life away for a little money these hard times. I leave my blessing to my children and all friends, and I forgive all as I hope to get forgiveness myself.

He got a little agitated when the hangman pulled the white cap over his face, saying that he wished 'to see the light of heaven before his departure from this world'. He asked for the governor, who assured him that it was usual to have the face covered. A priest consoled him, patting him repeatedly on the shoulder and talking to him in Irish. Then the bolt was pulled, releasing the trap.¹⁰

•

⁹ For the initial report of the murder, see OP 1846/7/4,673 Glenties, 17 Feb. 1846, Holmes to Lucas. And for press reports, see *BH*, 27 Feb. 1846; *Freeman's Journal*, 23 Feb. 1846. For the trial, see *Vindicator*, 17 Mar. 1847; *BH*, 19 Mar. 1847. Pennefather, when recommending commutation of the death sentence imposed on Peggy Crummer, acknowledged that the evidence against Sam was 'entirely circumstantial'; CRF C/16/1847 Merrion Square, 22 Apr. 1847, Pennefather to ——. NAUK, ADM 101/39/2/3 fo. 17 *Medical Journal of the Hired Ship John Calvin, from 21 December 1847 to 23 May*, notes the death of their child; also see Trevor McClaughlin, *Irish Women in Colonial Australia* (St Leonards, 1998), 38.

¹⁰ A report of the hanging in *LSnl*, 1 May 1847, was widely reproduced in other newspapers. Some liberal papers, including *LJ*, 5 May 1847, excised its remarks on mixed marriage. 'At all events', the *Sentinel* had opined, 'the awful tragedy should teach two lessons, namely, the evil of ill-assorted marriages, and the danger and pernicious results of covetousness. Mixed marriages have been the fruitful source of discord and crime in Ireland yet we find the Romish clergy doing all they can to promote them in order to gain proselytes to their religious system . . .' Also see the account by an 'opponent of capital punishment' in *Northern Whig*, 4 May 1847.

It was during what Sam Crummer called 'these hard times' that the Molly Maguires established themselves where hitherto the Ribbon Society had been known only by repute. In March 1845, coincidentally the month that people kibbed their doomed potatoes, Benjamin Holmes, a resident magistrate based in Glenties, heard from a colleague responsible for north Donegal that Ribbon 'delegates' had entered the county for the purpose of promoting the Society. Holmes himself initially found no evidence to confirm this story, and he was inclined to dismiss it. Certainly, around Glenties, he wrote, there was nothing 'indicative of combination or political secrecy on behalf of the People'. But in Mountcharles, a constable gave him a curious report. He had heard from a 'highly respectable Roman Catholic gentleman', he said, that at mass in Frosses on Sunday 23 February, the curate Daniel Spence had

> read to his flock the Ribbon Oath and other documents which had been put into his hand by a person who did not wish the dissemination of those principles, that five [*sic*] delegates had come into the parish—one from Donegal, one from Ballyshannon, one from Ballintra, one from Pettigo, one from Ballybofey, and one from Strabane—to spread Ribbonism. He warned his hearers against joining the Society as 'it would be the means of putting a stop to Repeal', and cautioned them to keep private what he had said to them.[11]

The curate and then the constable—and now the resident magistrate and Dublin Castle—had detected an effort by what, in Donegal, had been an eastern and urban-centred grouping to reorganize existing lodges and to establish new ones—an effort that may be a sign that the Society, at national or provincial level, was recovering from the arrest and trial, in 1839–40, of its ambitious Dublin leader, Richard Jones.[12] In summer 1845, 'Molly Maguire' started appearing on threatening notices in the old Ribbon heartlands, around Ballyshannon and Ballybofey/Stranorlar, being particularly common in disputes about land. For instance, on the night of 12 July, a landlord, William Young of Mounthall, Killygordon, had a notice posted under his door, and he found another tied to its knocker, both giving him three weeks to get rid of his land steward, and

---

[11] OP 1845/7/4,715 Glenties, 6 Mar. 1845, Holmes to Lucas. For a memoir of Spence, a native of Stranorlar, see Maguire, *Raphoe*, ii. 24–5. On the 'strong Ribbon party' in his hometown, see the evidence of Golding Bird, 20 July 1853, in *Select Committee on Extending the Functions of the Constabulary in Ireland*, 52–3.

[12] Garvin, *Evolution*, 39–43; see too, Desmond McCabe's entry on Jones in *DIB*. The expansion of the Society into west Donegal from winter 1844–5, and the use from that time of the moniker Molly Maguire, is coincident with the development of the Mollies in Leitrim, as traced in Kelly, 'Local Memories', 55 ff.; there, 'the first threatening notice from Molly Maguire . . . appeared in Cashcarrigan in mid-February 1845'.

the steward himself received a similar ultimatum, telling him to quit, or Molly would be back 'for his head'.[13] Further south, near Ballyshannon, James Cassidy, a big farmer (and Catholic) who had rented land in dispute in Coolcolly, received at least two such letters, one warning him not to evict a subtenant, and another instructing him to dismiss a girl who, in defiance of notices telling people not to labour for him, had taken the job of watching his crops:

> James Cassidy if you dont send away this Raskil of a girl that you are in keeping for corrupting, Badness and rascality. This is the second time I sent you notice be not under a Mistake if you dont adhere to my Precepts and send away this adulterating witch from your place remember you shortly will reap the benefit—I dont mean to make remarks about this evil carracter or about many other affairs you need not think you have police or soldiers at your back for if you and her was locked in a chest i'll find you out....
>
> Molly Maguire and Sons...[14]

If the moniker 'Molly Maguire' was new to Donegal in 1845, the posting of such items was well established in the repertoire of popular political action. Since the late eighteenth century, threatening letters and notices, sometimes illustrated with sketches of guns or gallows, coffins or graves, had been received by landlords, agents, and bailiffs in dispute with tenants about rents, by farmers paying low wages to labourers, by forestallers and shopkeepers deemed to be overcharging for goods, and by rectors and tithe proctors, gaugers, and cess collectors. In times of political strife, magistrates, yeomen, and army officers had received them too.[15] Consequently, some local landowners had been nonchalant about 'Molly Maguire', regarding it as just the latest colourful name to be adopted by those who would challenge their authority and rejecting the idea that it had anything to do with the Ribbon Society proper. One told Holmes that 'the name is made use of by residents who may have any sort of prejudice against persons'.[16] However, some threats were made good: Young's steward was attacked and six large stacks of Cassidy's wheat and oats (valued at near £25) were destroyed.[17] And while, in spring 1845, Holmes himself

---

[13] OP 1845/7/15,775 Glenties, 19 July 1845, Holmes to Lucas.

[14] OP 1845/7/15,103 n.p., 12 July 1845, Holmes to Lucas, and 1845/7/18,435 Pettigo, 29 Aug. 1845, Holmes to Lucas, both with copies of the threatening letters.

[15] Vaughan, *Landlords and Tenants*, 150–6; Stephen Gibbon, *Captain Rock, Night Errant: The Threatening Letters of Pre-Famine Ireland* (Dublin, 2004), 9–43. On the writing of threatening notices, see Dorian, *Outer Edge*, 151–6.

[16] OP 1845/7/16,981 Stranorlar, 7 Aug. 1845, Holmes to Lucas.

[17] For the attacks on Cassidy's property, see OP 1845/7/28,285 Glenties, 6 Dec. 1845, Holmes to Lucas; 1846/7/7,273 Memorial of James Cassidy of Ballyshannon..., Farmer

had not countenanced the prospect of the Society organizing in west Donegal, he shortly got a hint that something of a new, more political character was afoot there when, at the harvest fair in Glenties, he purchased *Wonderful Prophecy*, a broadsheet, printed in Belfast, that foretold an Anglo-American war, the downfall of England, and Ireland's 'divided sons' uniting. It was apparently 'much sought after at all the fairs' that autumn.[18] By spring 1846, Molly Maguire was very definitely in Glenties. In mid-February, John McIlheny of Strasallagh found a notice attached to his cowhouse, threatening to card him. In this instance, it was rumoured that McIlheny was 'not acting equitably towards his son who had been married a year or two, and that the son might have had the notice written and posted to bring the father to a fair settlement':

Take Notice

John McElhenny, get the affair between yourself and your son settle in a short time, dont sleep on it or you will have a party of the Molly McGuire some night about your house that will scratch your backs my honest old friend, the journey is to far for my children to go to settle the affairs between you and your son. I dont like to take my oath, but by the City of Dublin if you do not I will give you a hand in the case

Molly McGuire[19]

Over the next few years, the conceit of Molly's sons being brought a long distance to see justice done became common in west Donegal; indeed, as early as 1848, the authorities believed there were several Ribbon lodges in the wider Killybegs area, and that their members were 'well supplied with arms'.[20] Now, across the county, in the dimly lit backrooms of public houses and in barns, woods, and fields, young men were going down on their knees and, by repeating an oath read by a lodge master, they were being 'made' Ribbonmen:

I declare and promise in the name of St Patrick, Patron of this Kingdom that I will keep inviolably all the secrets of this Board, not to leave the society or join any other society, not meaning tradesmen or soldiers. At any of our meetings not to drink to intoxication, nor not to provoke, challenge or fight with any of our Brethren, and if a Brother should be offended or ill-spoken of to aid and assist him with the earliest information. And in dealing to give the preferences to our Brethren so far as circumstances will allow. And that

(received 23 Mar. 1846). And for the attack on Young's steward, see OP 1848/7/32 Copy of the Information of John McGinty of Meenawau . . . , 3 Feb. 1848.

[18] OP 1845/7/20,783 Glenties, 27 Sept. 1845, Holmes to Lucas, enclosing *Wonderful Prophecy* (Belfast: Henry Watson, n.d.).

[19] OP 1846/7/5,739 Glenties, 20 Feb. 1846, Holmes to Lucas, enclosing a copy of the notice.

[20] OP 1848/7/207 Donegal, 26 July 1848, Blake to Redington.

we would not allow or admit anyone of indifferent character into our Society knowing him to be such.

Each quarter, the members would pay the master small sums of money for signs and passwords, by which they could identify their 'brothers'. 'Ireland is in a bad state', a man would say; and a 'brother' hearing it, would answer 'Foreign countries will assist us.' 'May God send a change upon the times' would come the reply, which would in turn elicit the response 'It was never more required.' And the brothers, if instructed by the master, would commit 'outrages', some of which amounted to nothing more serious than the posting of a threatening notice, while others were attacks of shocking brutality, including maiming and murder.[21]

Against the background of high food prices and hunger, epidemic disease and desperate emigration in the mid- to late 1840s, the Society did experience setbacks. Notably, in spring 1848, two informers betrayed fifteen men in Glenfin, the gateway from south-west Donegal to Ballybofey, Strabane, and Derry.[22] Further south, in that same season, another two informers, after converting to Protestantism, implicated some twenty-eight 'brothers', mainly in Ballyshannon, Bundoran, and north Leitrim.[23] Among those named were several men in 'comfortable circumstances'— a publican, a baker, and a teacher—and, most significantly, a well-to-do farmer, William Gettens of Portnason, near Ballyshannon, known since the 1830s to be a Ribbonman, and by then a leading figure in the Society in the province of Ulster.[24] But the intimidation of witnesses precipitated the collapse of the Glenfin and Ballyshannon cases, and 1848 ended with the assassination of a Glenswilly landlord, Dr Samuel Davis, on his own doorstep in Letterkenny, on 22 December, and, a few days later, on St Stephen's Day, an attempt to kill George Wray, agent of the Townawilly estate, by detonating gunpowder buried beneath the chimney of his living room in Ardnamona.[25] Both Davis and Wray had been evicting

---

[21] OP 1848/7/32 Stranorlar, 3 Feb. 1848, Johnston et al. to Somerville, enclosing Copy of the Information of John McGinty of Meenawau . . . , 3 Feb. 1848. Also see 1848/7/44 Raphoe, 15 Feb. 1848, Kirkham to Blake. And see Ch. 1 in this volume, for McGlynn's account of being 'made' a Ribbonman.

[22] OP 1848/7/32 Stranorlar, 3 Feb. 1848, Johnston et al. to Somerville.

[23] OP 1848/7/130 Ballyshannon, 21 Apr. 1848, Blake to Redington; Information of Patrick Mulhern, Ardfarn . . . , 20 Apr. 1848; Information of James Gilloway, Ardfarn . . . , 21 Apr. 1848.

[24] On Gettens's early involvement in the Society, see OP 1839/7/7,672 Ballyshannon, 7 Aug. 1839, Hayden to McGregor; *LJ*, 23 Mar. 1841.

[25] For the investigation into the smuggling, from Scotland, of casks of gunpowder, and their concealment in Townawilly, see OP 1849/7/141, most especially n.p., 26 Apr. 1849, Tierney to Redington, and Information of Hugh Slevin, a Pauper in Donegal Workhouse, 25 Feb. 1849. On the recovery of a cask containing 25lbs of gunpowder on an unoccupied farm, see OP 1849/7/268 Donegal, 15 Sept. 1849, Montgomery to Somerville; Eugene McCafferty, the parish priest, supplied the information leading to the discovery.

tenants for non-payment of rent—'tossing all the houses and wrecking the people', as one pauper in Donegal poorhouse said of Wray[26]—and the attacks were widely credited to Ribbonmen. Within two years, an attack on another landlord caused thirty-two magistrates to petition government to 'exterminate the Ribbon System' by proclaiming several townlands in Glenswilly under the Crime and Outrage (Ireland) Act. By this stage, 'disposable men' (undercover detectives) had been working their way through the county's trouble spots but turning up nothing to seriously compromise the Ribbon Society.[27]

In Donegal generally, then, the Society had emerged from the Famine strengthened or 'ramified' as one landlord put it.[28] And its confidence was apparent. On the afternoon of St Patrick's Day 1850, a procession of 800–1,000 persons—including 'strangers' who arrived in twelve or fourteen cars from Derry—marched from Convoy to Raphoe behind three men wearing green caps and ribbons. It was the first large-scale public display by the Society in Donegal for many years. On coming in sight of a Constabulary party, commanded by the County Inspector, blocking their entry to Raphoe, one of their leaders had raised a cap on a stick, causing most marchers to disperse. Still, some 200 marchers had proceeded towards the town, only dispersing on the Riot Act being read at the Constabulary line. One man was arrested for possession of a pistol and another for drunkenness, but the event passed off without any breach of the peace.[29] The liberal *Londonderry Journal* discerned a 'particularly bad spirit' in this 'Ribbon Assemblage', 'coming as it did, so immediately after the passing of the new act against party processions and the Lord Lieutenant's proclamation forbidding them'—the Party Processions Act had received the royal assent in March—and in a neighbourhood where an Orange procession had been 'put down' by the magistracy on the previous 12 July. In other words, the *Journal* thought it a triumphal, coat-trailing display: 'In truth, the ignorant of both of the extreme factions are alike regardless of the law—equally implacable in their resentments, and, in

[26] OP 1849/7/141 Information of Hugh Slevin..., 25 Feb. 1849.
[27] On detectives in Glenfin, see OP 1851/7/379; in Glenswilly and Buncrana, OP 1851/7/315; 1851/7/343; in Gweedore, OP 1852/7/424 and CSORP 1853/14,778; and for an appeal for a detective to be sent to Fanad, CSORP 1853/10,609. For doubts on their efficacy, see OP 1852/7/419 Donegal, 5 Dec. 1852, Hamilton to Under Secretary; CSORP 1853/3,451 Letterkenny, 15 Apr. 1853, Coulson to Under Secretary. On the wider use of detectives, see Elizabeth Malcolm, 'Investigating the "Machinery of Murder": Irish Detectives and Agrarian Outrages, 1847–70', *New Hibernia Review*, 6/3 (2002), 73–91.
[28] OP 1849/7/11 Rockhill, 2 Jan. 1849, Stewart to Stewart.
[29] OP 1850/7/67 Lifford, 18 Mar. 1850, Montgomery to Redington.

their eagerness to defy and insult, equally prepared to bring disgrace on themselves and their country.'[30]

This renewal and expansion of the Ribbon Society had several sources. In east Donegal, and, in particular around Ballyshannon, it involved a squaring up to the Orange Order, which had been vocal and aggressive during the Famine. More widely, it was a product of a deepening sense among the Catholic poor that the state bore ultimate responsibility for the horrors visited on the country, and a heightened resentment of landlords. As early as September 1847, the *Ballyshannon Herald*—not unfairly dismissed by one liberal as 'a low Orange print'[31]—had grasped the extent to which distress had tightly braided national and class antagonism: 'Social disorganization is nearly complete. The mass of the people are steeped to the lips in poverty . . . Class is divided against class. The proprietors of the soil are generally regarded as oppressors of the cultivators of the soil. Dreadful hatred of England, of her institutions, is widely diffused among the humbler orders in Ireland.'[32] In this context, the Society was providing an organizational home for young men who had concluded, in the words of a song carried in the *Londonderry Journal*, that 'we were struck by the rod of an angry God, / for kissing the chains that bound us'.[33] Most immediately, its lodges offered the prospect of direct action to men energized by communal resistance to the state and landlords, whose collectors had come, from 1848, looking for arrears of rent, rates (taxes for the support of poorhouses, payable by people holding property valued above £4), and cess (taxes that funded the county administration), and not getting those arrears, seizing stock, crops, and other goods, and, for unpaid rent, evicting tenants. Latterly, elections to the boards of guardians that set rates gave the Society realizable 'political' objectives. In the Glenties Union, in March 1850, 'a large party supposed consisting of 300 armed men' traversed contested electoral divisions at night, and called at the houses of rate-payers (voters), swearing them to support the candidate 'approved of by them'. The following March, when there was another election for the Graffy, Glenties, and Glenleheen divisions of the same union and the Constabulary was busy with the census, three officers and sixty-four men of the 35th Regiment of Foot was moved from Ballyshannon to Glenties to preserve the peace, to the 'evident chagrin' of local Ribbon leaders.[34]

[30] *LJ*, 27 Mar. 1850. [31] *LJ*, 26 Feb. 1839. [32] *BH*, 17 Sept. 1847.
[33] 'The Exile', by A. S. W., in *LJ*, 12 June 1850.
[34] OP 1850/7/83 Mountcharles, 20 Mar. 1850, Russell to Conyngham; 1851/7/89 Glenties, 5 Mar. 1851, Stuart to Townsend; Glenties, 15 Mar. 1851, Montgomery to Redington; 1851/7/101 Letterkenny, 22 Mar. 1851, Townsend to McGregor; Glenties, 20 Mar. 1851, Stuart to Townsend. *Fermanagh Mail*, 20 Mar. 1851, thought (wrongly)

A democratic deficit illuminates the intensity that the Ribbon Society brought to these petty contests. In 1851, the population of Boylagh—roughly, Ardara to Crolly—was 21,643 (11,165 female; 10,478 male). Then, a year after the Irish Franchise Act of 1850 had lowered the property qualification for voting in Westminster elections, only thirty-six men in the barony were registered to vote; the Irish electorate now comprised about 10 per cent of adult males, and it would be over a generation before the next major expansion, the 1884 Reform Act, brought it up about 30 per cent.[35] But at least there were elections to Westminster. The most significant local government body was the grand jury, which set local taxes and awarded contracts for road construction and repair that employed many young men, giving it a presence in the lives of the poor. However, it was an appointed agency and, despite some tinkering in the 1880s, it was to remain dominated by a landed clique until its replacement by an elected county council in 1898. Hence, in the 1840s and 1850s, a district's board of guardians was the only representative body to which a significant number of householders could elect people.

AN AMERICAN PACKAGE?

The democratic deficit throws a Constabulary preoccupation, from the late 1840s through the mid-1850s, with returned emigrants—most especially 'disappointed Americans'—into some relief.[36] In these years, before the establishment of the Fenians in 1858, few returned emigrants likely came back as self-conscious agents of sedition. However, all who returned came with firsthand experience of a society with an extraordinary level of political participation—a broad male franchise for federal, state, county, city, and township elections—where politicians courted tavern-keepers, contractors, and other influential figures in the Irish community. For all returned emigrants, but particularly those who had done well in America, re-entry into a colonial society—where, other than the boards of guardians, there was not even a pretence that petty policy bore any

that the troops were required 'probably to prevent an outbreak on the 17th, or Patrick's Day, or to assist in collecting the poor-rate'.

[35] CSORP 1853/1,290: 'A Return of the Number of Parliamentary Voters in the Registry of each Barony in the County of Donegal ... 20th Day of November 1851'.

[36] Officials' concerns about returned emigrants in 1848 are well documented: OP 1848/7/193, Dublin, 8 Aug. 1848, Redington to Fenwick, notes that 'Government are in possession of information stating that a number of Emigrants have returned from America for the purpose of encouraging disaffection.' And for the same concern in the mid-1850s, see CSORP 1856/11,368.

relationship to majority will—was a cold experience. That experience was made colder still by the ubiquity of the Constabulary—there were twice as many policemen in Ireland as in Britain, for instance—and the authorities' regular restriction of civil liberties when faced with unrest: Ireland was no Land of Liberty. And crucially, the Ribbon Society would have been a recognizable entity to 'Yankees', for the Society's American branch, the Ancient Order of Hibernians (AOH)—established in 1836 as St Patrick's Fraternal Society, it changed its name in 1838—had, in the years of the Famine, become the largest fraternal organization of Irish workingmen in the United States.[37] A hypothesis here suggests itself: the very Society that expanded in Ireland in the 1840s—after the Hibernians had come out of the backrooms and into the light in New York, Pennsylvania, and beyond—may itself have been an American parcel. In other words, if the American Hibernians—most especially, the Molly Maguires of north-eastern Pennsylvania—have been conventionally understood to have imported Irish organizational forms and modes of action, it is still possible to regard the Ribbonmen who reorganized in Ireland from the mid-1840s, as having been shaped, in some measure, by the sister organization on the far side of the Atlantic.[38]

Here, at the intersection of return migration, the rise of Hibernianism in America, and the emergence of the Molly Maguires in west Donegal, one family stands out.[39] In 1857, Denis Holland, a Belfast-based republican journalist, toured north and west Donegal, investigating the landlord and state response to a Molly-initiated campaign against Scottish and English sheep-farmers who had leased mountain pasture formerly grazed by smallholders' stock. John Doherty, parish priest of Gweedore and a known associate of suspected Ribbon leaders, brought him out to Meenacladdy.

[37] There is no comprehensive scholarly history of the AOH in Ireland or America. However, see Garvin, *Evolution*, 95–9, 137–40, and A. C. Hepburn, *Catholic Belfast and Nationalist Ireland in the Era of Joe Devlin, 1871–1934* (Oxford, 2008), chs. 4–5; on the US, see Bulik, *Sons of Molly Maguire* and Kenny, *Making Sense*. The connection, if any, between Jones's reorganization of the Ribbon Society and the establishment of the AOH in the US has yet to be fully explored.

[38] Garvin, *Evolution*, 41, argues that 'Rather like an American big-city machine working in reverse, Ribbonism, instead of using patronage to buy activists, succeeded in persuading its activists to contribute sums of money to it.' Garvin here underestimates the extent to which lodges dispensed patronage, not least through influence on road contracting. Similarly, A. C. Murray's dismissal of Ribbonism as 'rural gangsterism', in 'Agrarian Violence and Nationalism in Nineteenth-Century Ireland: The Myth of Ribbonism', *Irish Economic and Social History*, 13 (1986), 56–73, overlooks, inter alia, lodges' interventions in elections and the help they gave members seeking employment. For a critique, see Niall Whelehan, 'Labour and Agrarian Violence in the Irish Midlands', *Saothar*, 37 (2012), 5–17.

[39] The Campbells of Dungloe also had Ribbon involvements in Ireland and Hibernian connections in the US, see Ch. 9 in this volume.

There, they chatted with one of the 'wretched peasants', a man named 'Mihil' (Mícheál), who had a wife and 'three or four' children to support. 'This man when describing the misery of himself and his fellows, amid the desolation of the mountain waste', Holland wrote, 'uttered some exclamations in Irish that sounded like oaths.' Affecting to have thought 'that nothing like an imprecation ever escaped the lips of these simple peasants', the journalist remarked on the man swearing to the priest. Doherty smiled, and said, 'I am afraid Mihil learned to curse a little in America.'[40]

'Mihil' was Mícheál Airt O'Donnell, and he was no 'wretched peasant'.[41] He had left Meenacladdy for America in 1844, and he and his wife had been doing 'tolerably well'. However, he told Holland, 'the immorality and infidelity they had seen around them—and the spectacle of many ignorant and neglected Irish falling away, amid the temptations of vice, from religion and virtue—had frightened him and his poor wife; and they resolved to make every sacrifice and hurry back to Ireland, with all its miseries again, "for fear the childre [*sic*] would lose the religion"'. Arriving home in 1852–3, he again had taken a holding in Meenacladdy, where he now opened a public house, that is, the trade which he had pursued in America, and, as evident from Holland's comments, he spoke his mind.[42] Over the next two decades, Mícheál Airt's nephews, who were Hibernians, were central figures in the Molly Maguire troubles in the 'hard coal' fields of north-eastern Pennsylvania, where they were suspected of involvement in the assassination of mine officials. Indeed, their brother-in-law, Jack Kehoe, a publican and Hibernian master, with ambitions in state politics, was dubbed 'the King of the Mollies' by the press. Kehoe was hanged for murder in 1878. But before that, in the early hours of 10 December 1875, one of Mícheál Airt's nephews, Charles O'Donnell, and a niece, Ellen, were shot and killed in Wiggans Patch, when armed men, understood to have been working for a coal company, raided their house. Eight years later, in 1883, Mícheál Airt's own son, Pádaí (*aka* Pat) (1835–83) came to international attention when, on a ship off the coast of Africa, he shot and killed James Carey, an informer whose evidence had hanged five men for the sensational assassination of the Chief Secretary and Under Secretary in Dublin's Phoenix Park. Carey had been given an alias by government, and

---

[40] Denis Holland, *The Landlord in Donegal: Pictures from the Wilds* (Belfast, n.d. [1858]), 51–2.

[41] 'Mihil' is identified as Mícheál Airt Ó Domhnaill (*aka* Michael O'Donnell) in Dónall P. Ó Baoill, 'Ar Cuireadh Iachall ar Phádraig Ó Dónaill Carey a Scaoileadh?', *Scathlán*, 2 (1983), 16–32.

[42] On the O'Donnells' business acumen, see Cití Nic Giolla Bhríde and Dónall P. Ó Baoill, 'Bunadh Airt Uí Dhonaill', *Scathlán*, 2 (1983), 90–1.

was being relocated to Natal when O'Donnell struck. Convicted of murder, he was hanged at Newgate. It was over a generation since his father, home from America, had looked around Meenacladdy, thought about state and society in Ireland, and raged against the injustice of it all.[43]

POST-FAMINE ADJUSTMENT

If the rise of the Mollies in west Donegal from winter 1844–5 can be connected, in the first instance, to an organizational drive by Ribbon leaders, and then to a spike in popular resentment of the state and landlords in the years of the Famine, it is the blowback from hard choices that poor people made to get themselves through that crisis which best explains the group's recalcitrance in the 1850s. The 1831 Census had returned the population of Donegal as 289,149; by 1841 it had risen to 296,448. Allowing for a falling rate of increase, it might have been expected to reach 302,000 by 1851; in fact, it fell to 255,169.[44] Notwithstanding widespread and deep privation, two related questions confront the historian. First, why was the Great Famine not worse in Donegal? Joel Mokyr has estimated that the excess mortality rate in the county was 10.7/1,000, the ninth lowest rate in the country. The estimated rates for the counties of north Connacht—58.4 in Mayo; 52.1 in Sligo; 49.5 in Roscommon—dwarf it. No less surprisingly, it is the third lowest estimated excess mortality rate in Ulster: the counties with lower rates are Down (6.7) and Derry (5.7). Mokyr's estimates for Armagh, Antrim, and Tyrone are 15/1,000; they are twice as high for Monaghan (28.6) and Fermanagh (29.2), while Cavan had the highest in Ulster (42.7), four times that of Donegal.[45] And second, why did the poorer agricultural districts in the west of the county not lose a larger percentage of their population? The greatest decline in population was in the east of the county, where land is more fertile, while in the west, where in places, like Meenacladdy, the valuation of agricultural land per capita was among the lowest in the country, some electoral divisions actually experienced an increase in population: see Map 2.1.

[43] On the O'Donnells in Pennsylvania, see Ó Baoill, 'Ar Cuireadh Iachall', 28–31; Broehl, *Molly Maguires*, 258–66; Kenny, *Making Sense*, 207–8.

[44] *Return of the Population of the Several Counties in Ireland, as Enumerated in 1831*, HC 1833 (254), xxxi. 1, and *Census of Ireland for the Year 1851. Part. I . . . County Donegal*, HC 1852–53 (1567), xcii. 153.

[45] Joel Mokyr, *Why Ireland Starved: A Quantitative and Analytical History of the Irish Economy, 1800–1850* (Abingdon, 1983), 267: table 9.2, Average Annual Excess Death Rates, 1846–51, by County; the rates quoted here are lower bound estimates.

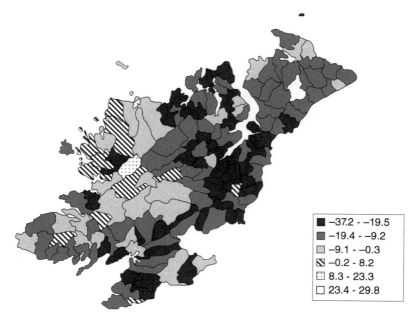

■	−37.2 - −19.5
■	−19.4 - −9.2
▫	−9.1 - −0.3
◨	−0.2 - 8.2
▨	8.3 - 23.3
□	23.4 - 29.8

Map 2.1 Population change, 1841–51: County Donegal
All-Island Research Observatory, Ordnance Survey Ireland Licence EN 0072711

This pattern of depopulation can be explained.[46] In the years before the blight arrived, the majority of households in Donegal depended heavily for sustenance on potatoes which they grew on rented ground and they had a variety of strategies to pay their rent (and rates, cess, and other demands) and to carry themselves from the consumption of the last of the old potatoes through to the new harvest, that is, from no later than mid-June—and much earlier for those with the smallest potato patches—through mid-August, when the lower class generally subsisted on oatmeal. Here, a broad distinction can be drawn between strategies for food acquisition in the east and the west of the county. In east Donegal, the three decades before the Famine had seen the domestic linen industry exposed to direct competition from cotton which, combined with the mechanization of the industry in east Ulster, had undermined the position of weaving households. Unable to replace their fathers at the loom, many

---

[46] On the mistaken idea that west Donegal had uncommonly philanthropic landlords and was not heavily dependent on potatoes, see my '"Bastard Ribbonism": The Molly Maguires, the Uneven Failure of Entitlement and the Politics of Post-Famine Adjustment', in Enda Delaney and Breandán Mac Suibhne, eds, *Ireland's Great Famine and Popular Politics* (New York, 2016), 186–232.

weavers' sons had become cottiers or wage labourers. At the same time, opportunities for women to contribute to household budgets by spinning contracted, while agricultural depression, which favoured a return to pasture, capped the demand for agricultural labour and depressed wages. The result was an impoverished, under-employed substratum of society that ever earlier in the year had to resort to markets for food. And that class suffered immensely when, in 1845–9, wages plummeted and food prices soared.

In contrast, people in west Donegal were not as *directly* dependent on markets for food. The district had never been much involved in linen weaving, and hence the contraction of that sector did not have a major impact on it. Here, knitting of stockings and seasonal migration had become central to household economies in the half-century before the Famine, if not indeed earlier. The price of a pair of stockings was low: in the early 1830s, Neil Hewston, parish priest of Lettermacaward, estimated that a woman or child could only earn between a ha'penny and a penny per week knitting stockings. However, the demand was stable all year round, women of all ages could knit, and pregnancy and nursing interfered little.[47] Moreover, rather than purchasing foodstuffs in *mí an ocrais*, women might receive meal as payment from the merchants for whom they knitted. In fact, merchants routinely exchanged foodstuffs, tobacco, or snuff with knitters, rather than paying them in cash. Knitters—in contrast to fishermen, for example—were a good credit risk. And so too were women with children and adolescents hired on large farms in east Donegal, often for over six months of the year, or whose menfolk and unmarried young women travelled to Scotland to work at the harvest. Responses to a questionnaire distributed to clergymen as part of the Poor Inquiry in the 1830s give an impression of local variations in seasonal migration. The question asked—'What number of labourers are in the habit of leaving their dwellings periodically, to obtain employment, and what proportion of them go to England?'—was awkwardly phrased, and the reference to England, rather than Scotland, likely threw some respondents. Still, per the 1831 Census, the proportions of migrants to 20-year-old males were highest in Lettermacaward (100:472, 21 per cent), Clondahorkey (200:1,470, 13.6 per cent), and Templecrone (200:1,863, 10.7 per cent). Unfortunately, no data were returned for Gweedore, where the rate of seasonal migration was the highest in the county in the late nineteenth century.[48]

---

[47] *Poor Inquiry (Ireland): Appendix (D)...*, HC 1836 (36), xxxi. 305.
[48] *Poor Inquiry (Ireland): Appendix (A) and Supplement*, HC 1835 (369), xxxii. 320, 324. The number of seasonal migrants leaving Lettermacaward (100) given by Hewston,

It appears, then, that in the years of the Famine, lower-class strategies for acquiring food did not collapse as completely in west Donegal as they did in the east of the county, that is, that some stocking merchants—and also sprigging merchants who put out muslin for women to sew—continued to pay women with oatmeal, which they had the capacity to buy in bulk; kelp merchants too were said to have paid their suppliers in meal in these years.[49] At the same time, seasonal migration to the navvy camps and large farms of Scotland took away hungry mouths in the leanest period of the year, and made it easier for those who remained to get 'trust meal', meal on credit, as they would have family members returning with 'Scotch' pounds after the harvest. Certainly, there is evidence of the persistence of knitting and seasonal migration—and the continued operation of associated credit networks—through the worst years of the Famine. For instance, in spring 1847, when William Bennett, a Quaker relief-worker, went into Arranmore, which was then experiencing severe distress, he remarked, 'The feature that struck me most forcibly was, that among this whole population, estimated at 1,500, there was not a single particle of work of any description, that we could see going forward, either inside the cottages, or outside upon the soil, except one old woman knitting.'[50] This old woman intrigues, for she begs the questions, Who had given her the yarn? And what did she get for the stockings? Strikingly too, the years of the Famine witnessed an expansion of the stocking trade in west Donegal to meet growing British demand. Lord George Hill paid out £70 for stockings and socks at his store in Bunbeg in 1844, and by 1854 he was paying £600, a sum almost equal to the rental of his estate.[51] (Hill was a newcomer to the trade, and, if his own account can be credited, he got women to knit who had not knitted before and paid well. Hence, the growth of his trade during the Famine is an indicator that demand was now so great that established merchants in south-west Donegal, the hub of the industry, were having difficulty meeting it with existing business models; there, in Glenties, the years after the Famine saw the McDevitts rapidly eclipse smaller merchants by moving to a putting out system.[52])

---

the priest, is taken to be more accurate than that (20) offered by James Kilpatrick, the rector. For the numbers of 20-year-olds, see *Abstract of the Population Returns, 1831*, HC 1833 (634), xxxix. 246–7.

[49] On kelp, see Cathal Póirtéir, *Glórtha an Ghorta: Béaloideas na Gaeilge agus an Gorta Mór* (Baile Átha Cliath, 1996), 56–7.

[50] William Bennett, *Narrative of a Recent Journey of Six Weeks in Ireland...* (London, 1847), 73.

[51] *Report from the Select Committee on Destitution (Gweedore and Cloughaneely)...*, HC 1857–58 (412), xiii. 24, 75, 285, 292–3, 405–6, 472.

[52] See Ch. 9.

Other factors contributed to west Donegal's relatively clean escape from the Famine. Not least of them was recent experience of localized famine. Repeated weather-related crop failures in the 1830s had both honed domestic coping and adapting strategies, and familiarized community leaders—priests, schoolmasters, shopkeepers—with the workings of both governmental and non-governmental relief agencies. And that experience stood to them: of £100,000 spent by the semi-official British Association for the Relief of Irish Destitution from January to September 1847, £10,379 6s. 11d. was spent on relief in Donegal; only Mayo (£17,510 11s. 4d.) and Cork (£19,506 11s. 9d.) received more money. Cavan, where excess mortality is estimated to have been four times higher than in Donegal, received a quarter of the sum spent there.[53] Furthermore, if most money was spent where the Association's agents travelled in those months and later, it was spent in the west of the county.[54] Likewise, that two prominent members of the Relief Commission either owned (John Pitt Kennedy) or had owned (James Dombrain) property in west Donegal cannot but have helped the district. Finally, that Hill had opened a large store and mill a few years before the Famine was also an unintended asset for a wide area in the worst years: governmental and non-governmental organizations had a place to deposit relief supplies and grind meal. But ultimately, across west Donegal, it was tattie-hoking and knitting *and* the credit networks which they had called into being that mattered most.

•

Glenties Poorhouse was the 'last game of all'[55] for the indigent and the ill, the infirm and the abandoned in a 'poor law union' that comprised the greater part of west Donegal. John Mitchel, the republican writer, who saw it just after its completion, thought its Tudor architecture seemed to mock 'those wretches who still cling to liberty and mud cabins'. To them, 'in their perennial half-starvation', he wrote, it must have appeared 'like a Temple erected to the Fates, or like the fortress of Giant Despair, where-into he draws them one by one, and devours them'.[56] Originally designed

[53] *Report of the British Association for the Relief of the Extreme Distress in Ireland and Scotland with Correspondence of the Agents, Tables, &c. and a List of Subscribers* (London, 1849), 139.

[54] From autumn 1847 through midsummer 1848, some £4,982 of £9,171 granted by the Association to poor law unions in Donegal went to the Glenties Union; ibid., 141. Glenties was the only Union in Donegal in which the Association granted cash for the 'relief of general distress'; ibid. 145.

[55] Dorian, *Outer Edge*, 223, writing about Milford Workhouse.

[56] John Mitchel, *The Last Conquest of Ireland (Perhaps)*, facsimile edition with an Introduction by Patrick Maume (Dublin, 2005 [1861]), 116.

to accommodate 500 'inmates', when completed—and without any add-itions being made—it could house 800, and it had been full, and more than full, at times, in the Famine years.[57] But numbers had fallen as conditions improved from 1849. A week in midsummer, when many people, even in good times, had exhausted their old potatoes, registers the change. There had been 910 people—mainly children under 15 and infirm women—in the poorhouse in the first week of June 1849, 419 in 1850, 280 in 1851, and 285 in 1852, but by 1854 there were only 117, and if the number rose to 153 in 1855, it would never again go that high again in that week; it dipped to 77 in 1856, and hovered around 100 for the rest of the decade.[58]

If 'the Famine', for west Donegal, was, by and large, over by harvest 1849, the immediate legacy of hunger, disease, and high food prices was debt. And, crucially, debt included not only arrears of rent, rates, or cess— that is, money owed landlords and the state—but also monies owed to local lenders. Prominent in this category were mealmongers, to whom the poor, even in good years, resorted for foodstuffs on credit once their potato stocks were exhausted; many of these people were themselves publican-shopkeepers or merchants involved in the butter and egg, sprig-ging or stocking trades, who might accept repayment in cash or kind. At the same time, people reached a variety of arrangements with better-off neighbours to obtain meal or money, often offering stock, goods, or land as collateral.[59] In many instances, debts to smaller local lenders were likely run up in the latter stages of the crisis—1848–9—when landlords and rate and cess collectors started to press their demands. And, ultimately, the debts to these local lenders too fell due, and, not always being paid, there was conflict, particularly when land put up as collateral was lost or when stock was seized as payment. Seán Mac Calbhaigh of Mín an Lig gave meal on credit to people in the mountain districts north of Glenties in *na droch-aimsearaibh*, the bad times, and, in the wake of the Famine, he took legal action against those who failed to repay him, getting court orders to seize property—cattle and sewn muslin or sprigging. A man named Tuathal Ó Gallachóir composed a song, *Seán na Mine* (Seán of

[57] For the figure of 500, see *Return of the Acreable Contents, and Population of the Several Unions in Ireland in 1841; The Number of Workhouses; Number of Inmates Each Workhouse was Constructed to Contain, and the Total Number of Paupers in each on the 27th March 1847*, HC 1847 (397), xlix. 3. Glenties poorhouse was shoddily constructed, see *Report of the Commission for Inquiring into the Execution of the Contracts for Certain Union Workhouses in Ireland*, HC 1844 (562), xxx. 4, 123, 149; one inspector described it as 'excepting Castlederg . . . the worst built workhouse I saw in Ireland' (82).

[58] Calculated from DCA, BG/92/1/4–12 Glenties: Poor Law Union Minutes Books.

[59] See Dorian, *Outer Edge*, 215–17, on people 'borrowing' food in small quantities from neighbours.

the Meal), that excoriated his meanness, imagining him, with his bag on his back, being denied admittance to Heaven.

Nach Seán atá cráidhte fán triofal bheag gránda
A sgab sé mar cháirde ar a' bhaile seo thíos . . .

Isn't it Seán who is bothered about the wee trifle of grain,
That he scattered on trust on the townland below . . .?
'Tis Seán will be in trouble before the Almighty,
For what he did around Glenleheen,
On penniless mountain women.
He took their handkerchiefs (sprigging) for himself,
Hoping to *profit* on them again;
But when he goes to the mountain he will severely regret
That he did not leave the people their cattle.[60]

Tellingly, the parishes of Ardara, Inishkeel, Letter, and Templecrone, where the stocking trade and seasonal migration had caused credit networks to be most widely elaborated before the Famine, formed the district where Molly Maguire 'outrages' were most common in the early to mid-1850s. Here too, one can discern a viciousness—bordering on gratuitous violence—in 1854–5, when property prices climbed out of a trough into which they had been pitched in the Famine. There was an extensive trade in 'good will' or 'tenant right' in these years. A tenant was able to sell his interest in his holding or, indeed, in a portion of it. In the course of the Famine, tenants had divested themselves of land, sometimes entire holdings, in return for food, or else to get cash to purchase food at inflated prices, or to pay rent and rates, or to get an able-bodied young person to Scotland or, if lucky, across the Atlantic. Now, the recovery of land prices left some people feeling cheated, making 'land-grabbers' particular targets of the Mollies.

The spike in prices may also have increased inter-generational tension within families when young men found they could not afford land. In Meenagrillagh, adjacent to Beagh, a campaign of intimidation against James Arle, an old farmer, culminated on the night of 21 October 1855, when a party of twelve to fifteen men came to his house. 'They dragged me out of my bed', he told the Constabulary, 'fired a shot and swore they would blow my brains out; they tied a handkerchief over my eyes, put a rope round my neck, [and] led me naked to a field in front of the house.' Having led him back to the house, they forced him to put out his tongue and threatened to cut it out, then putting him on his knees forced him to swear 'to be good to William Macready and his family, and if I knew any

---

60 Ó Muirgheasa, *Dhá Chéad*, 336–7.

of the party also to say nothing about the affair or they would visit me at another time as this was only a warning'. William Macready, the man blamed for bringing the Mollies to Meenagrillagh, was Arle's son-in-law, who, it was alleged, wanted the farm signed over to him; he too was a Protestant, as was one of his associates, Alexander Burns of Tullymore.[61]

Crucially, if the Mollies were representing themselves as upholding the rights of the poor, they were not themselves all poor men. Patrick Friel, an Ardara publican cum road contractor, was the prime suspect in the attack on Arle and, only six months after that attack, McGlynn's information revealed several other local publicans to be centrally involved in the group. Other incidents too brought well-to-do traders to the authorities' attention. For instance, Edward McGrath was a Glenties publican and egg-dealer, who used to take goods from the town to sell at Derry market.[62] In December 1855, he was stopped and robbed near Raphoe, when he was returning home after disposing of '£53 worth of goods belonging to parties who had taken land for which the tenant right (common in this country) had not been paid by the incoming tenant to the out-goers', that is, he was selling goods for people considered land-grabbers. Suspiciously, however, McGrath had offered no resistance and four car-men accompanying him had offered him no assistance. On investigation, the authorities concluded that 'a plan was formed with the connivance of Ed. McGrath to waylay him and take the money from him, under what is commonly called about Glenties a Glenswilly Decree, that is taking by force what cannot be obtained otherwise'.[63]

If the Ribbon Society had long involved a section of the 'Catholic trading class', as political scientist Tom Garvin phrases it, putting itself 'at the head of what had originally been societies for communal or agrarian defence', the Famine had increased contention within that class in west Donegal, that is, between those deemed to be taking advantage of the poor—most obviously,

[61] CSORP 1855/9,395 Donegal, 5 Nov. 1855, Cruise to Larcom; Information of James Arle, Meenagrillagh, 30 Oct. 1855; Information of James Arle and Jane Adair, Meenagrillagh, 30 Oct. 1855; Information of Jane Adair, Meenagrillagh, 30 Oct. 1855. Also see the informations of his servant boy, Daniel Malloy, and John McConnell of Tullycleave, both of whom encountered his attackers at the Owenea, CRF G/22/1857. Arle was involved in eleven cases at the Ardara petty sessions in 1855–60.
[62] McGrath (1812–87) appeared at Glenties petty sessions on several occasions, being usually described as a publican, but occasionally as a dealer. For instance, on 7 Sept. 1866, his publican's licence was revoked on account of his house 'being riotously and irregularly kept'; it was later restored. On 2 Nov. 1866, he was convicted of being drunk on the street, assaulting a constable in the execution of his duty, and tearing his tunic, and on 16 Aug. 1869, a case against him for refusing to surrender an unlicensed pistol and to close his shop was sent to the Quarter Sessions. See IPSCR Glenties. *Slater's* (1870), 238–9, returns him as a grocer and spirit and porter dealer, while *Slater's* (1881), 348, lists him as an egg dealer.
[63] CSORP 1856/10,193 Buncrana, 3 Dec. 1855, Considine to Larcom.

land-grabbers and mealmongers—and others, prominent among whom were publicans cum road contractors, who espoused a concern for small-holders and gave employment.[64] At the same time, it was also clear by the mid-1850s that protecting her 'children' was no longer Molly Maguire's sole concern: Molly increasingly wanted something for herself. Even before the Famine, Ribbonmen had come to control much of the *poitín* trade in north Donegal, and people involved in other shady enterprises, such as horse dealing, found it beneficial to join.[65] Now, there were also signs of racketeering. In winter 1855–6, Thomas McMurray of Strabane set himself up in Glenties as agent for some Scottish and English butter merchants, purchasing all the butter brought to him at a higher price than that paid by established local shopkeepers. At 8.30 a.m. on 23 April, as he was travelling with two servants from Ballybofey to Glenties, three men stopped him at Clogher. One struck him twice with a stick, and another snapped a pistol in his face, and then robbed him of £29 or £30 in copper and silver and a silver watch valued at £3. The attackers told him to return to Strabane, and not to go to Glenties again.[66] On the same road, at Edeninfagh, men taking cartloads of fish from Teelin to the Laggan were stopped, and their boxes dumped at the side of the road, presumably for not paying protection.[67] Meanwhile, across Donegal, Ribbonmen, by intimidating non-members, ensured their 'brothers'—often publican-shopkeepers who employed labourers to carry out the work—received grand jury contracts for road-construction and repair; the contracts both paid well and secured custom for their houses.[68] And there were public offices filled by Ribbonmen. Most audaciously, William Gettens of Portnason had himself elected poor rate collector in the Ballyshannon Union. Again, Gettens had been known to the authorities since the 1830s to be a Ribbonman: it was an open secret in the

[64] Garvin, *Evolution*, 42.

[65] Two of the Símí Dohertys, a well-known travelling family, who traded horses and, as tinsmiths, crafted and repaired utensils required for *poitín*-making, were exposed as Ribbonmen in Feb. 1857. Cousins, and both named Simon, one was arrested in Dunfanaghy for armed extortion for the Society and the other in Belfast for horse-stealing. See CSORP 1857/1,260 Buncrana, 12 Feb. 1857, Considine to Larcom.

[66] CSORP 1856/14,936: Glenties, 25 Apr. 1856, Watkins to McGregor; Donegal, 13 May 1856, Cruise to Larcom.

[67] Briody, *Glenties and Inniskeel*, 310.

[68] On Ribbonmen and road contracting, see CSORP 1858/14,388 Donegal, 15 May 1858, Harte to Larcom, where the county surveyor assures the Under Secretary that the Society '*directly*' affected the department over which I have controul to the prejudice of the public interest'; he also complains that Robert Russell, agent of the Conyngham estate, publicly supported known Ribbonmen in Glenties when they objected to Harte's refusal to issue a certificate (for payment) to a contractor. For the intimidation of a coach operator to reinstate a dismissed driver, see CSORP 1857/2,964 Derry, 3 Apr. 1857, Hushoff to Larcom, enclosing a copy of a threatening letter signed 'A Son of Molly's' [*sic*].

1850s that he was the 'county delegate' for Donegal and a key figure in the national leadership.[69] But, from 1858, Gettens—who had been several times arrested on the word of informers only to have the cases collapse— was regularly taking people to Ballyshannon petty sessions for non-payment of rates, until, in October 1860, the Board took action against him for withholding monies collected.[70] A farmer cum shebeen-man (he was twice prosecuted in 1855 for selling spirits without a licence in Ballyshannon) cum public official (rate collector), the Ribbon leader was a subscriber to D'Alton's *King James's Irish Army List (1689)* (1855), a reminder, perhaps, that contra his west Donegal 'brothers', the keystone of his politics was anti-Orangeism.[71]

West Donegal lodges flexed their muscle in poor law union elections in the early 1850s, and they were not disinterested in higher politics. There was some rhetoric about freeing Ireland and Ribbonmen understood themselves to be rebels. However, while, by violent retribution, the lodges kept meal-mongers, land-grabbers, and moneylenders in check, there was no grand plan for revolution. A lodge might help a man to recover unpaid wages or get him satisfaction for some grievance relating to land. Indeed, it could get a fellow a job, not least as many masters were themselves road contractors. And it was those 'practical things' not 'great causes' or 'grand ideas' that now concerned the men meeting in the backrooms of public houses.[72]

In his assessment of the Ribbon Society in late 1855, Daniel Cruise, by then three years in Donegal and most familiar with the west and south of the county, had seen land and little more than land, and the backwash of the Famine: 'the greater part . . . if not all' of the Ribbon activity in his district was 'mixed up with the system of tenant right and to regain possession of lands which some of them have been for several years

---

[69] In 1854, when a detective trying to infiltrate a lodge in Liverpool listed four top Ribbonmen in Ireland, including Gettens, the Dublin authorities remarked 'already well known as members of the Ribbon Society'. See marginalia on CSORP 1859/1,959 Metropolitan Police Office, 24 Oct. 1854, Felix O'[Reilly] to Commissioner of Police. The other three were Peter Traynor of Magheramayo, near Dolly's Brae, Castlewellan, County Down; Edward Smyth, from near Clough, County Down, and Owen McNeill, publican, 13 Mary's Market, Belfast. On the prosecution of Gettens for illegally selling spirits, see IPSCR Ballyshannon: 20 Aug. 1855.

[70] IPSCR Ballyshannon: 20 Sept. 1860, as prosecutor, and 4 Oct. 1860, as defendant. For Gettens's work as a rate collector, see DCA, BG/38/1/21 Ballyshannon Poor Law Union Minute Books, 1 May–27 Nov. 1858; BG/38/1/23 Ballyshannon Poor Law Union Minute Books, 14 Jan. 1860–16 Feb. 1861: State of the Workhouse for the Week Ending 11 Aug. 1860.

[71] John D'Alton, ed., *King James's Irish Army List (1689)* (Dublin, 1855), vi.

[72] Phrases taken from Peter Quinn's suggestive discussion of machine politics in 'Local Politics: Irish-American Style', in his *Looking for Jimmy: A Search for Irish America* (Woodstock, 2007), 101–11.

dispossessed of or sold what they call their good will of and which in many instances they seek to regain'. But based in the north-eastern town of Letterkenny and taking a wider view, the County Inspector emphasized the extent to which the lodges' hand reached into all corners of society and economy. The Ribbon Society, he reported, 'has more or less influence in every transaction, from the occupation or letting of land to the enlistment of a recruit for the Militia'.[73]

Both were right. The magistrate had identified the issue that most animated Ribbonmen—or more accurately, the Ribbon base—in the west and the policeman had, no less accurately, discerned the range and scale of their activities, and divined the ambition of their leaders. In that, there is nothing unusual: more than one secret society has been the chrysalis of a political machine. East Donegal's Ribbon lodges had undoubtedly become less involved in 'outrage' by the mid-1850s, but the Constabulary had erred on the side of optimism when they judged them to be 'in abeyance'. To some extent, they were simply finding different ways of doing things and different things to do. And a similar reorientation was under way in western lodges, and the tension that it occasioned was a factor in the writing of the letter that Cruise had received from Beagh in April 1856.

---

[73] CSORP 1856/11,368 Donegal, 27 Dec. 1855, Cruise to Larcom, and Dublin, 23 Dec. 1855, McGregor to Larcom, summarizing Constabulary reports and quoting the County Inspector.

PART II

3

The Last Places Man Created

About ¼ of this townland is under tillage, the rest is bog overlying
granite—the road from Ardara to Narin runs up through the townland, & crosses over Beagh Bridge. The townland does not possess any
remarkable objects—it is divided into Beagh East & Beagh West.

Entry on *Beagh* in Ordnance Survey Field Name Book,
Inishkeel, vol. 3 (1829–35), 101

Beagh lies west of three hills—Tullycleave, Tullymore, and Tullybeg. At
the end of March, the time of year when Patrick McGlynn penned his first
letter to Daniel Cruise, those hills rise green above rust-coloured *caorán*,
lake-dotted bog and heath, stretching four miles from the Owenea to a
fertile swathe in Kilclooney. Beagh also rises, but it scarcely forms a hill
and its scraps of arable amount to little beside the best land in the Tullies.
Here, the good land—south-sloping on the shoreside of the Narin
Road—may have been tilled for centuries. However, much, if not most,
of the rest of it—certainly much of the land cultivated on the bogside of
the road—may only have been broken in the late eighteenth or early
nineteenth century, after a shift in the base-diet from oats—bread and
brachán (stirabout)—to potatoes combined with greater involvement
in the market (the cattle, pig, butter, and egg trades) and with non-
agricultural production (tailoring, sprigging, and, above all, knitting)
and some limited wage labour (for large farmers or road contractors) had
enabled more families to exist on less land and on land of lesser quality.

And so this half-hill comprises some of the last places man created
before the deluge that was the Great Famine. Among them is a forlorn
field, facing north and falling from bog to marsh that drains into the
unmoving blackness of a turf-stained trout stream which rises and falls
with the tide but never seems to flow. Nancy Sweeney, a widow, and her
son, Patrick, were working this particular field when Patrick McGlynn
wrote his first letter to Daniel Cruise. It had been made by the mid-1830s,
but probably not long before then, and not necessarily by a Sweeney.[1]

---

[1] Beagh was surveyed in 1835, and the field can be discerned on OS sheet 73. Nancy
Sweeney is listed as a tenant in Conyngham Papers MS 35,394 (2) Rental of the . . . Boylagh
Estate, for the Year Ending the 1st of May 1856.

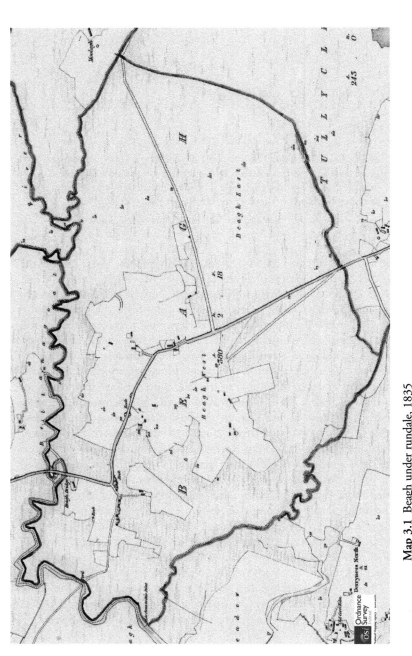

Map 3.1 Beagh under rundale, 1835
Ordnance Survey Ireland Permit No. 9088 © Ordnance Survey Ireland/Government of Ireland

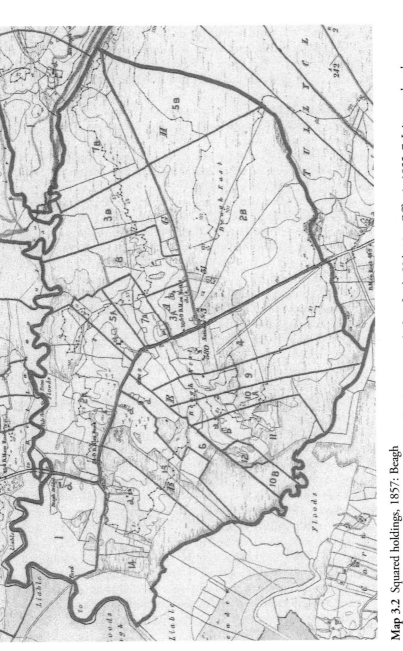

Map 3.2 Squared holdings, 1857: Beagh
This map is the revised Ordnance Survey map of 1847–50 as marked up for the Valuation Office in 1855–7. It is reproduced courtesy of www.askaboutireland.ie

And there were to be later, more desperate efforts at making land, that is, using seaweed and shit to turn patches of half-bog into something on which one could grow potatoes. The most pitiful effort was behind McGlynn's school, where, by the time of the Famine, people were kibbing spuds on a tiny patch of arable manufactured from ground described by a surveyor as 'heathy . . . bog pasture'.[2] John Mitchel, who passed through south-west Donegal in 1845, got it terribly wrong when he said that the inhabitants of the district's 'ragged looking, windowless hovels' had 'gathered themselves from the wastes, and huddled together to keep some life and heat in them'.[3] On the contrary, they were gathering themselves *onto* 'the wastes'; they were trying to feed children where their people had fed cattle.

In the year that Mitchel wrote of the wider district, Beagh was likely supporting about 115–20 people. The 1841 Census had returned 110 people—sixty males and fifty females—living in nineteen houses, and, by 1851, there were twenty-two houses, which *might* suggest the formation of three new households in the intervening years. But, in 1851, four of those houses were empty, and the population had stumbled to 100. It would steady itself in the 1850s, stretch to 109, in seventeen houses, in 1861, but stagger downwards in succeeding decades as less and later marriage and the emigration of the majority of children born of those marriages produced a cultural and demographic rot. By the beginning of the new century, there was roughly half the number of people in half the number of houses that there had been when the blight came on the potatoes, and the state failed society.[4] And still it fell, until, in the mid-1960s, it struck bottom at perhaps as few as thirty-five people, the majority of them elderly, in eight houses. I was the last child brought home to Beagh in that decade when, demographically, it seemed to be tottering to extinction.

A scarifying transformation of the physical and moral-economic landscape of Beagh had coincided with the cresting of its population in the late 1830s and early 1840s, and the first intimation of its collapse in the late 1840s and early 1850s. Two detailed base maps made of the townland in the mid-nineteenth century are extant. The first is an Ordnance Survey map, drawn to a scale of six inches to one statute mile by the Royal Engineers in 1835 (Map 3.1). This map was then revised and contoured in 1847–50 (Map 3.2); buildings that had been demolished since 1835 were erased and buildings that had been since erected were added. Surviving progress reports indicate that this second map was at an advanced

[2] NAI, PB: Donegal, Boylagh, Inishkeel, Beagh, 1855–6: tenement 2B.
[3] Mitchel, *Last Conquest*, 116.   [4] Census of Ireland, 1841–1901.

stage of preparation by the end of 1847.[5] In 1835, when the first map was made, Beagh was held in a distressed form of *rundale*, an infield–outfield system of land use; but within twelve years, by 1847, the townland had been 'divided' into 'squared' farms.[6] And in that great change—from a system that involved communal rights and responsibilities to one of individualized risk—the deep origins of animosity towards James Gallagher may be found, for enabled by the hunger and hardship of the late 1840s and early 1850s, he had thrived in the new 'divided' townland, and he had done so at the expense of his neighbours, and, indeed, at the expense of his own father.

DIVIDED LAND

In rundale's classic form—and there were many variants[7]—people lived in a tight knot of houses and tilled an 'infield'.[8] An embankment or wall set this fertile area off from an 'outfield' on which turf might be cut or livestock grazed in summer. The 'infield' was often not divided by permanent walls or ditches and it was either cultivated, to a greater or lesser extent, collectively or else plots were periodically redistributed among households to ensure that each got a share of land of different

[5] Sheet 73 of the 2nd edition of the Ordnance Survey includes the relevant details: 'Surveyed in 1835...Engraved in 1836...Revised and Contoured in 1847–50...Revisions and Contour Lines Engraved in 1853...'. NAI, OS1/1848/1–2: Progress Reports. On the revision of Donegal, and the difficulty of dating OS sheets, see Andrews, *Paper Landscape*, 209–21, and appendix F. For an earlier (1829) boundary map of the district, see the 'sketch map in four parts' of the section of Inishkeel in the barony of Boylagh, OS36 C72 (1–4); unfortunately, it includes no field markings in Beagh and only a single house, Kennedy's at the bridge. OS surveyors had access to a 1786 townland map of the Conyngham estate. Unfortunately, that map does not appear to be extant. Surveyors produced sketch maps of the estate in the late 1830s when many townlands were squared; a surveyor's map, dated 1839, of 'Dawris, Eden and Ballyhillagh' in PRONI D4,493/2, is one such map; no surveyor's map of Beagh has been found.

[6] In 1855–6, when Beagh was assessed as part of the General Valuation, valuators marked up the 2nd edition OS map to indicate land and houses held by tenants and subtenants. They did not erase features; hence, buildings that had been demolished since 1847 can be seen on the marked-up map, but they cannot be found in either PB: Beagh, 1855–6 or GV.

[7] Arnold Horner, 'Geographers and the Study of Rundale', *Ulster Folklife*, 58 (2015), 13–22. James Anderson, 'Rundale, Agrarian Economy and Agrarian Revolution: Tirhugh, 1715–1855', in Nolan et al., *Donegal*, 447–69, traces the system's decline over a wider area than the title suggests; and see Fox, *Tory Islanders*, 91–2, 123–5, for a late survival. On the cultural world of rundale, see Lloyd, 'The Indigent Sublime', 39–49, and, on its dissolution, see David P. Nally, *Human Encumbrances: Political Violence and the Great Irish Famine* (Notre Dame, IN, 2011), 206–7.

[8] Surveyors often referred to these clusters, which might vary in size from a few to several dozen houses, as 'villages'.

quality. Much to the horror of outsiders—not least officials fixing property taxes, such as tithe or rates—a single holding might comprise several
patches scattered through the infield, and the tenant would have the right
to graze a particular number of cattle on the outfield. Here, within the
arable sections, most physical divisions were of a kind with those described
by John Barrett, rector of the parish of Inishkeel, in the 1820s: 'the usual
enclosure is a bad mound composed partly of stones and partly of sods,
merely to answer for one season. The cattle in winter being permitted to
roam at large, destroying the wretched fences now in use, they must be
consequently made anew each successive spring.'[9] In some places, the
expansion of population caused a second cluster with its own infield and
outfield to be established, operating separately from the original. Indeed,
this cell-like separation seems to have occurred in Beagh, which, in 1804,
had been let in 'two equal parts', Beagh East and Beagh West, presumably
reflecting a popular denomination of the tenancy on the shoreside of the
road *baile thiar* (west townland) and that on the bogside *baile thoir*
(eastern townland).[10]

In Beagh, in 1835, there was one major arable area, set off in places
from the rough pasture by a substantial stone and turf ditch, and bisected
by the Narin Road, the dividing line between the eastern and western
sections. There was then no great knot of houses in the townland. Rather,
there were four groups of three to five houses and these were not particularly tightly packed. There was also an appendage to the bogside section of
this area—that field which would be part of Nancy Sweeney's holding two
decades later. And there were three outlying patches of arable, on all of
which stood houses. Two of these patches—one down by the bridge, and
the other to the south of it—were comparatively sizeable; the third was a
tiny field, a little beyond that which would become Sweeney's and even
further beyond hope. Here, somebody, less out of optimism than an
absence of options, had conjured soil by the mid-1830s, erected a shelter
that might be called a house, and tried to feed a family. Literally, then,
people were breaking the bounds of custom, and moving onto what
Mitchel was to call the 'wastes'. But it was not 'waste' in any meaningful
sense of the word—it was what valuators, in the 1830s and later, called
'bog pasture', indicating that it was being used. Calling such land 'waste'

[9] 'Parish of Inishkeel, County Donegal: Replies of John Barrett to Queries of North
West Farming Society', in Angélique Day and Patrick Williams, eds, *Ordnance Survey
Memoirs of Ireland*, xxxix. *Parishes of County Donegal II, 1835–6: Mid, West and South
Donegal* (Belfast and Dublin, 1997), 67–73, 67.
[10] On the letting of Beagh in 1804, see NAI, VO, FB OL4.2302: Inishkeel No. 2,
compiled in Oct. 1839. Under these leases, the rent on each 'part' was £17; the two parts,
being 'equal', presumably comprised the same cow's grass rather than the same acreage.

was an aspersion on either the landlords who owned it or those tenants and subtenants who rented it. Yet expounded in parliamentary inquiries and improvers' pamphlets from the late eighteenth century, the notion that Ireland contained vast 'wastes'—unbroken by spendthrift landlords who squandered their rents rather than 'improving' their estates, or else overlooked by inherently idle tenants and subtenants content to live in squalor on ever-diminishing potato patches—had become so pervasive in political and economic discourse that even a clear-thinking critic of the establishment like Mitchel could not see through it. Today, earth-moving machines, corrugated plastic pipes, and chemical fertilizer might convert the 'waste' of Beagh into arable, but such agricultural alchemy would require an investment on which one would see no return: it would truly be a waste. In short, the 'waste' remaining in Beagh in the mid-1830s was good for nothing but that for which it had been used until the pressure of population growth *and* the paucity of non-agricultural employment led people to try to cultivate parts of it—rough pasture for cattle and a source of turf, the odd rabbit, or pheasant, and reeds for thatching. Still, a limit was being reached. The most adaptable food known to man—the vegetable with the highest nutritional yield per acre—was being grown on approximately 25 per cent of the arable land with the remainder given over to barley (*c*.15 per cent), oats (*c*.25 per cent), cabbage and turnips (*c*.5 per cent), or else in meadow (*c*.30 per cent).[11] The place was near yielding its nutritional capacity, for although, in theory, more potatoes could be grown, barley and oats were required to pay rent and meet other demands, meadow was needed for the cattle that supplied the family with milk and brought cash at market, and some rotation was necessary to maintain the quality of the arable. And there was precious little arable left to make.

The resources of the wider district were being strained too. For some observers, density of population—and food crises and associated epidemics in 1817, 1820–1, 1831, and 1835–7—was bringing a Malthusian destiny into view. Writing in the 1820s, Barrett, the rector, worried about 'the overabundant population' of Inishkeel. The parish, he argued, was scarcely growing enough crops to feed itself: 'Were it not for the importation of provisions from the province of Connaught, this parish would very frequently be in danger of starving.' Increased migration (permanent and seasonal) might hold starvation at bay, as too might later marriage.

---

[11] This crude estimate is derived from *Census of Ireland, 1851, pt. II, Returns of Agricultural Produce*, HC 1852–53 [1589], xciii. 280. Then, in the electoral division of Dawros, on holdings of 15–30 acres, there were 556 acres under crops: 145 acres (26%) were under oats, 88 acres (15.8%) under barley, 133 acres (23.9%) under potatoes, 22 acres (3.9%) under turnips, 7 acres (1.2%) under cabbage, 2 acres (0.3%) were under flax, and 159 acres (28.5%) of meadow or clover.

However, without a significant expansion of non-agricultural employment, people would be ever more vulnerable. And the prospects of
increased employment were slim: the stocking and sprigging trades, for
instance, were already extensively organized, and, as Barrett pointed out,
while fishing could be 'greatly improved' the key issue here was 'whether,
from the remoteness of this district from towns or a large population, an
adequate reward could be procured for increased exertion'.[12]

One must avoid too dismal an interpretation, most especially the
notion that the particular catastrophe that came to pass was somehow
inevitable. There was nothing inevitable about blight; and, more importantly, the state response to blight might have been more generous and
effective. Nor was the demographic collapse that followed the Famine
inevitable. Indeed, in Gweedore, in the north-west of the county, where
the value of agricultural land per capita in some electoral divisions was far
below that around Ardara and Glenties, a high rate of seasonal migration
allowed the population to increase steadily through the latter half of the
nineteenth century and into the twentieth.[13] Still, across west Donegal,
the signs of strain were clear in the 1830s. People were cultivating land
higher on the hillsides and further into the bog, their holdings were getting
smaller, and the period during which they depended on markets for food
was commencing earlier in the year. 'Nothing can exceed the miserable
appearance of the cottages in Donegal', the poor law commissioner
George Nicholls wrote in 1837, 'or the desolate aspect of a cluster of
these hovels, always teeming with an excessive population.' He had
gone into such cabins, and found the people 'intelligent and communi-
cative, quick to comprehend, and ready to impart what they know'. They
admitted, he wrote,

> that they were too numerous, 'too thick upon the land', and that, as one of
> them declared, 'they were eating each other's heads off'—but what could
> they do? There was no employment for the young people, nor relief for the
> aged, nor means nor opportunity for removing their surplus numbers to
> some more eligible spot. They could only therefore, live on, 'hoping', as they
> said, 'that times might mend, and that their landlords would sooner or later
> do something for them'.[14]

[12] 'Parish of Inishkeel, County Donegal', 69, 73.

[13] On Gweedore, see Breandán Mac Suibhne, 'Agrarian Improvement and Social
Unrest: Lord George Hill and the Gaoth Dobhair Sheep War, 1856–1860', in Nolan
et al., *Donegal*, 547–82, and idem, 'Soggarth Aroon and Gombeen Priest: James MacFadden
of Gaoth Dobhair and Inis Caoil', in Gerard Moran, ed., *Radical Irish Priests* (Dublin, 1998),
146–84, 151–70.

[14] *Second Report of Geo. Nicholls, Esq. . . . on Poor Laws, Ireland*, HC 1837–38 (91),
xxxviii. 12–13.

The poor reposed no great faith in their landlords. Yet those comments ascribed by Nicholls to a smallholder have the ring of truth, that is, the poor themselves were coming to see their own numbers to be making their subsistence precarious. The best estimates have Ireland's population increasing from *c.*2–2.5 million in the mid-1740s to *c.*5 million in 1800 and to *c.*8.5 million in 1845; and the rate of increase was greatest on the bad lands of the west.[15] Hence, it is conceivable that, from the Tullies to Downstrands, people who were old in the 1830s had seen the number of houses in each townland triple or even quadruple in their lifetimes. Traditionally, population was seen in a positive light; a sign that people had the necessities of life, it denoted prosperity, stability, and security.[16] But the diet was getting blander and, after the pummelling of west Donegal in 1831 and 1835–7, it was hard to look to the future with confidence. Well indeed might a poor man conclude that the people were eating each other's heads off.

It was at this point that Beagh and many other townlands in west Donegal were 'divided' into squared farms. Crucially, this development was not a specific response to the perception of an 'overabundant population' nor indeed to the food crisis of 1835–7. Rather, chance (the death of a British monarch) and convention (the life-span of that monarch having been in the terms of leases drawn up in the late eighteenth and early nineteenth century) determined the time of the squaring. And the prime concern of the landlords who ordained it was not checking population growth but making the place, that is, the people, easier to control, the better to extract rents. Squaring was, of course, justified in the language of 'improvement'—rationality, efficiency, and productivity— and the landlords may well have believed it to be a 'better' system that would nurture rugged individualists eager to better themselves.[17] However, it is not clear that it necessarily increased yields. Moreover, if squaring was accompanied by some reclamation, as happened in Beagh, much of the land won from the *caorán* was so poor that it was surrendered to the rushes as soon as the population started to fall. Furthermore, as those who actually worked the land often resisted squaring, clearly they were not all convinced that the change was likely to make their subsistence more secure. Still, for present purposes, the question of productivity is moot. Landlords believed the shift was in their own interest; and so

[15] Cormac Ó Gráda, *Ireland: A New Economic History, 1780–1939* (Oxford, 1994), 1–23, 69–110.

[16] Massimo Livi-Bacci, *A Concise History of World Population* (Oxford, 1989), 1–2.

[17] Wes Forsythe, 'The Measures and Materiality of Improvement in Ireland', *International Journal of Historical Archaeology*, 17 (2013), 72–93, 72–6.

squaring is best seen as the work of people, like the arch-'improver' Lord George Hill of Gweedore, preoccupied with the question, 'Does it pay?'[18]

•

No known document confirms the year—between the townland being mapped by the Ordnance Survey in 1835 and that map's revision in 1847–50—that Beagh was divided into squared holdings. However, it can be determined with some precision. Beagh was then part of the Marquess of Conyngham's Boylagh estate, itself part of a larger estate that ran to 123,300 acres in Donegal, 27,613 acres in Clare, 7,060 acres in Meath, and 9,737 acres in Kent, England.[19] The Marquess, Francis Nathaniel Conyngham (1797–1876), rarely visited the county, where one critic styled him 'a landlord king of about 40,000 people', and he left the management of his estate, which he inherited in 1832, to an agent who, in turn, marshalled gangs of bailiffs to implement his decisions.[20] Robert Russell, a Scotsman, was agent for Boylagh in these years.[21] Elevated from the lowly position of 'groom', Russell was anathema to many gentry figures resident in Donegal, for whom his having started his career in a stable was an insult that aggravated their antipathy towards his absentee employer whose Whig politics they found objectionable. A haughty manner compounded a tendency to ride roughshod over rules and regulations, and although the manager of one of the most populous estates in the county, he was removed from the commission of the peace for irregularity.[22]

[18] Anon., *Facts from Gweedore, Compiled from the Notes of Lord George Hill: A Facsimile Reprint of the Fifth Edition (1887)*, with an Introduction by E. E. Evans (Belfast, 1971), 9.

[19] Introduction in Sarah Ward-Perkins, ed., 'Collection List No. 53: Conyngham Papers' (Dublin, 2000), vii; available at www.nli.ie.

[20] Quoting from the letter of 'A Tenant' in *LJ*, 27 Nov. 1838; also see another letter from the same correspondent in *LJ*, 25 Dec. 1838, and the letters of 'J. B. Boswell' in *LJ*, 8 Jan., 26 Feb. 1839.

[21] Russell detailed his management of the estate for two parliamentary inquiries some twenty years apart; see *Evidence Taken before Her Majesty's Commissioners of Inquiry into the State of Law and Practice in Respect to the Occupation of Land in Ireland. Part II*, HC 1845 (616), xx. 164–6 (hereafter *Devon Commission*, II); and *Report from the Select Committee of the House of Lords on the Tenure (Ireland) Bill...*, HC 1867 (518), xiv. 86–98. The Devon Commission also heard from some of Conyngham's tenants, notably John O'Donnell of Letterilly (147–50) and James Dunleavy of Mully (150–5), both of whom criticized Russell and his bailiffs, with Dunleavy saying that they had 'no feeling for the people'. In 1845, Thomas Campbell Foster criticized Russell's management in *The Times*, provoking a sharp reaction from the agent. Foster responded, citing Russell's evidence to the Commission; see his *Letters on the Condition of the People of Ireland* (London, 1846), 103–13.

[22] For a snide remark on Russell having been a groom, see CSORP 1858/17,849 Fort Stewart, 1 Oct. 1858, Stewart to Cruise.

The tenants too found him an abrasive, difficult man. In spring 1846 Michael Boyle, a smallholder in Arlands, one of the poorer parts of the Rosses, had the temerity to ask him a question relative to 'the approaching famine': 'Go, Mick', Russell had allegedly replied, pointing at a dead rat, 'and take that rat along with you, and it will relish the *lumpers* for you—that is my remedy to you, Micky, for the famine you complain of.'[23]

In July 1844, Russell appeared before the Devon Commission, a government inquiry into land tenure in Ireland, when it held a session in Donegal Town. Asked about the prevalence of rundale on the estate and the condition of tenants in areas where it operated, he said: 'The condition of the tenants who hold in rundale, in general, is that of great wretchedness; but of late years a new division and squaring has nearly been effected.'[24] The year 1837, he explained, had been a turning point over much of the Boylagh estate. In the late eighteenth and early nineteenth centuries, leases had been given on a 'large portion' of Boylagh for 'three lives', that is, the lives of three of George III's eldest sons—Frederick, Duke of York, George, Prince of Wales, and William, Duke of Clarence. In June 1837, when the last of these men, William, by then himself king, died, these leases—some now involving twenty to thirty households—expired. Those sections of the estate had to be reset, presenting an opportunity to break up the joint tenancies and to move to a system in which, in Russell's terms, 'every man is only accountable for his own portion'. And this resetting of the estate became an occasion for raising rents. Consequently, in 1837–9, the estate had been surveyed and assessed by 'a person in the habit of valuing land', new rents had been set for squared holdings—on average, rents increased by 20 per cent, a boon to the landlord—and tenants had been required to demolish their houses and build anew on the land now assigned to them.[25]

---

[23] See the printed memorial, dated May 1846, to Sir Robert Peel from inhabitants of Templecrone, requesting the removal of Russell as 'under agent or bog bailiff' for 'arbitrary . . . oppressive and illegal acts', in NAI, RLFC 3/1/3,990, reproduced in Marianne Cosgrove, Rena Lohan, and Tom Quinlan, 'Sources in the National Archives for Researching the Great Famine', *Irish Archives* (Spring 1995), 24–44, 42. The background to this memorial includes local resentment of Russell, who had replaced the popular Francis Forster as agent, and Campbell Foster having drawn press attention to the district by contrasting the Whig Conyngham unfavourably with Hill, a Tory, for whom Forster was then working.

[24] *Devon Commission*, II. 164.

[25] *Devon Commission*, II. 165–6. In *LJ*, 26 Feb. 1839, a letter of 'J. B. Boswell', a critic of Conyngham, quotes Russell telling tenants, in Nov. 1838, that the survey of the estate 'is now being finished'. A hand-drawn map of Dawros, Eden, and Ballyhillagh, a few miles north-west of Beagh, survives among the scattered papers of the Conyngham estate; it is dated 1839. See PRONI, D4,493/2. The OS did not classify Ballyhillagh as a townland; it became part of Eden and Drumboghill.

As is clear from Russell's comments, the change was not complete on all parts of the Conyngham estate by 1844. Indeed, on some of the worst land in the Rosses, rundale survived through the 1870s and beyond; there were places, it seems, not worth the bother of squaring. Beagh was not one of them, however. The townland was scarcely isolated, being only two miles from Ardara (pop. 603 in 1841) where there was a post office and a courthouse, a barracks for the Constabulary, and another for the Revenue Police. There was also a Church of Ireland church, a Methodist meeting-house, and a Catholic chapel in the town. The church was at the top of the hill, the meeting house a step beneath it, and until 1832, when a new edifice was erected in the west end of the town, the chapel had been below it, on the Diamond, the widening at the bottom of the hill where Ardara's two streets met. The elevations reflected the worshippers' aggregate position in the social hierarchy while, paradoxically, the chapel's original location, in the centre of the town, anticipated Catholics' coming into consequence. Ardara's bakers and butchers, tanners and joiners, smiths, nailers, and shoemakers also drew considerable traffic, as did the hotel and the town's many (sixteen in 1838) public houses.[26] And so too did the town's fairs on 15 May, 1 August, 1 November, and 22 December.[27] 'Ardara is never without a stranger!', Biddy, a waitress in the hotel, boasted to William Allingham, a young customs man building a reputation as a poet, when he dined there in October 1847.[28]

The road through Beagh, then, was well travelled, not least by the stronger farmers in the Rosbeg peninsula, many of whom were tenants of Conyngham and had Russell's ear. Among them were the Barretts and Porters of Narin, Hamiltons of Eden and Mullyvea, O'Donnells of Summy, Craigs of Kilclooney and Kiltooris, and McNelises and McGlincheys of Sandfield, immediately north of Beagh. In 1835, much of the arable in Sandfield was already divided by permanent walls. Indeed, it is possible that it had been at least partly squared in the 1600s when tracts were assigned to Protestant tenants. However, Sandfield still included expanses of commonage, and it too was let in bulk, in three separate leases, and consequently it was understood to be held in rundale. But it was neater and tidier than Beagh.[29] And so when the push to square

[26] *Return of the Number of Retail Spirit Licences now in Force…*, HC 1837–38 (717), xlvi. 2.

[27] On Ardara's fairs, see McGill, *Ardara*, 66–73.

[28] *William Allingham: A Diary*, ed. H. Allingham and D. Radford (London, 1907), 40.

[29] Walls and ditches that cut across the boundaries of Beagh's newly squared cuts are marked in the 1847–50 revision of the OS; some of those features may have existed at the time of the first survey (1835), but only been included in the revised map due to a change in policy regarding the representation of 'fences', on which see Andrews, *Paper Landscape*,

came in 1837, Beagh and the adjacent townlands of Derryness—the name pinned by the Ordnance Survey on Ranny and Carn[30]—and Tullycleave may have appeared particularly ragged to Russell. In Carn, for instance, there was a gaggle of a dozen houses down by the Cockle Strand; and in Beagh, a knot of four houses at the bottom of Condy's Brae—no doubt, the type of 'ragged looking, windowless hovels' described by Mitchel—through which all traffic to and from Narin and Rosbeg had to pass. In fact, there had been a serious accident here, after the Ardara Fair on 22 December 1837, when the squaring was already being planned. Isaac O'Donnell, a cess collector, and his son had been attacked at the Owenea Bridge. Galloping home to Summy, they rode down two women in Beagh, leaving one of them, a married woman named Catherine Sweeney—presumably, Catherine (1797–1878), wife of Myles Sweeney (1788–1866)—'in danger' for some time.[31] Russell himself would have known that road well, for his own wife, Caroline Barrett—they married in 1839—was a daughter of the rector of Inishkeel, who lived in Narin. Hence, Beagh, being a conspicuous affront to reason, was likely early chosen for reform.

The Ordnance Survey maps of 1835 and 1847–50, the Census of 1841, and property valuations from 1839 and 1855–7 clarify still further when Beagh was squared. The 1835 map shows twenty-four detached buildings in the townland. Some of those buildings may have been barns or byres. However, barns and byres were not yet common in Beagh, with families bringing their cattle into their windowless and, likely, chimneyless houses until the 1860s. For instance, in 1857, when there were fourteen householders in the townland, only three of them possessed what valuators called 'offices'. James Gallagher then had two substantial outhouses and Patrick Kennedy (Bridge) and Connell (*aka* Condy) Gallagher had one each, the latter's a very rudimentary structure. None of those 'offices' was a detached building marked on the 1835 map, and, indeed, one of

106–7, 195–6, 218–19. Still, Sandfield is represented as more 'divided' than Beagh and Carn ('Derryness North') in the 1835 map. On the three leases (£21, £20, and £34) in Sandfield, see VO, FB OL4.2302.

[30] See Prologue to this volume.

[31] On this accident, see OP 1837/7/166 Glenties, 26 Dec. 1837, Rodden to Kennedy; Glenties, 28 Dec. 1837, Rodden to Miller; Glenties, 13 Jan. 1838, Rodden to Miller. The backwash was the burning of hay belonging to Patrick Kennedy of Tullybeg on 12 Jan. Kennedy's brother had been a witness to the attack on O'Donnell and, when summoned to a court hearing, gave 'impartial evidence'. The chief constable who investigated the incident reported that 'from intimidation I fear it will be very difficult to obtain information on the subject'. See OP 1838/7/9 Glenties, 15 Jan. 1838, Rodden to McGregor. In 1836–8, there were at least five attacks upon O'Donnell's cattle. See OP 1838/7/80 Glenties, 21 July 1838, Rodden to McGregor.

Gallagher's offices had only been built since June 1856.[32] Hence, it is likely that most or all of the twenty-four buildings in Beagh in 1835 were houses, which suggests that the squaring had been completed or was nearly completed in 1841, for that year's Census (7 June) returned only nineteen houses in the townland, and a decrease in the number of houses was a feature of the process, with subtenants being cleared and their houses demolished. Moreover, an official valuation of land (but not houses and including no occupiers' names) undertaken in October 1839 indicates that the process cannot then have been far advanced, for it notes that the two leases, in which the entire townland had been held from 1804 until the death of the king in summer 1837, had yet to be replaced and the rent increased.[33] And so the squaring of Beagh can be dated with a high degree of confidence to 1839–41.

The same Ordnance Survey map that, with the Census and various valuations, helps to date the squaring of Beagh greatly facilitated the transformation of Conyngham's entire Boylagh estate, but here, in this little townland, the synergy of state and estate is particularly striking as points marked by Royal Engineers when plotting a line between a tri-angulation station on top of Meenagrillagh and another on Tullycleave became a boundary between new lots. No less striking is the scale of the change. The decline in the number of houses from twenty-four, in 1835, to nineteen, in 1841—the loss of approximately one in five houses—does not reflect the total number demolished, for a comparison of the 1835 OS map with the revised map of 1847–50 indicates that at least ten buildings marked on the original map had, by that later period, been demolished and at least fourteen new buildings erected, all but the school (built in 1844) most likely constructed in 1839–41; see Table 3.1. There were also now walls where there had been none, and land—arable and pasture—that had been 'undivided' was now 'divided'. Where once a man's cattle had grazed commonage in summer and over the stubble of the townland after harvest, his animals now grazed his own 'cut' (*cuid*, portion) and it alone.

Russell had extolled the advantages of the squared system to the Devon Commission in 1844, insisting that 'the people are now becoming more comfortable; the land is better drained and cultivated, and in a few years, when all the new houses are built, I feel assured they will all be more comfortable and wealthier than at present'. Still, he conceded that in some cases he had 'met a great deal of opposition' in resetting townlands.[34] On other estates too, the break-up of the system, before, during, and after the

[32] PB: Beagh, 1855–6; *GV*: Beagh.   [33] VO, FB OL4.2302: Inishkeel No. 2.
[34] *Devon Commission*, II. 164–6.

Table 3.1 Buildings, 1835 and 1847–50; houses, offices, and school, 1855 and 1857: Beagh

Lot	1835	Demolished	Built	1847–50	1855	1857
1	1			1	1 h., 1 o.	1 h., 1 o.
2A	1		1	2	1 h. 1 o.	1 h., 1 o.
2B			2	2	1 h., 1 s.	1 s.
3A	1		2	3	3 h.	
3B	1	1			1 h.	
4	1	1	3	3	1 h.	1 h., 1 o.
5A	3	1		2	1 h.	1 h.
5B						
6	1		1	2	1 h.	1 h.
7A	3	2		1	1 h., 1 o.	1 h., 1 o.
7B						
8	1		1	2	1 h.	1 h.
9	1	1	1	1	1 h.	1 h.
10A	1		1	2	1 h.	1 h.
10B						
11	3	1	1	3	2 h.	2 h.
12						
13	4	3		1	1 h.	2 h.
14	2		1	3	1 h.	1 h.
Total	24	10	14	28	18 h., 3 o., 1 s.	14 h., 4 o., 1 s.

Note: Lot numbers, taken from GV (1857), are given here to assist in locating houses on Maps 3.1 and 3.2. One of the buildings on 2B is Beagh School, built by local subscription in 1844; its brief use as a residence by the first teacher, Charles McCoale, delayed its acceptance as a national school until 1845; see ED1/24/112/1–2. If the number of 'offices' (3) identified in the initial valuation of tenements in July 1855 had been the same in 1847, then there were approximately 24 houses in Beagh during the Famine. According to the Census, there were 19 houses in Beagh in 1841; 22 houses (18 inhabited, 4 uninhabited) in 1851; 18 houses (17 inhabited, 1 uninhabited) in 1861, and 14 houses, all inhabited, in 1871. The Census defined a house as a 'dwelling with a distinct outer door, inhabited by one or more families'; see *Census, 1861*, pt. V, xviii.

Sources: OS Sheet 73 (1835); OS Sheet 73 revised edition (1847–50); PB, 1855–6; GV (1857).

Famine, often provoked violent resistance.[35] Indeed, opposition to out-side authority was often associated with rundale 'villages'. For instance, in some mountainous districts south of Ardara, light-touch estate-management allowed the system to survive intact or in modified forms into the twentieth century, and agents of both the estate and the state found people in these areas to be unusually vexatious. In Laconnell, there were two clusters of houses in the mid-1850s, one consisting of eleven houses, and the other fourteen. A valuator who called at the larger cluster

---

[35] Mac Suibhne, 'Agrarian Improvement', 558–77.

to establish who paid what rent for different portions of land, left in despair. 'I could not get any information from the occupiers of this lot', he wrote in his notebook, 'They are the greatest set of swindlers in the three parishes. I was for two hours trying to get the rents from them and not one word of truth would they tell.'[36]

Whether met with resistance or not, 'squaring' or 'strip[p]ing' townlands was traumatic for the inhabitants. Wee Paddy McGill, born in 1897, grew up around people whose land, in the south of the parish, was only squared in the 1850s. From them, he heard that families crossed the fields from the condemned 'villages' to the 'isolated' houses on their new holdings, 'as if they were crossing the ocean to a foreign land', and down to his own time, people often 'foregathered' on Sunday evenings in the ruins of the old place.[37] Squaring was often divisive too. Hugh Dorian, born in north Donegal in 1834, lived through this transition in his own community; and his community lived with the consequences of it for decades, that is, 'bitter and lasting hatred'. In his telling, squaring was 'beneficial to some and injurious to others'. The first stage of the process was a 'war upon the cottiers'. Agents required that people entitled to *land* under the old joint tenancy first divest themselves of subtenants; in other words, they had to evict them. And then, in the second stage, the tenants themselves formally relinquished possession while their townland was surveyed and 'new cuts' (squared farms) marked out. Here, the bailiff was 'courted': 'One man got his share in the best part of the land, just where he wished it... Some other poor insignificant persons were sent to the uncultivated outskirts, some on the bleak mountain side, and so on...' The squared lots assigned, the confirmed tenants had then to build new dwellings and demolish their old houses, the condition being 'one farm, one smoke'. Sometimes cottiers or subtenants—having nowhere to go—remained *in situ* through the squaring, and then the agent and bailiffs, accompanied by the sheriff and protected by a 'strong guard of police', would evict the unwanted, that is, forcibly remove the people and their possessions from the house, extinguish the fire, and tumble the roof: 'The trained bailiff knew as well where to stick the exterminator's needle as a physician to point to the heart of his sick patient, and so a stroke or two brought down the roof.' Remembering this 'work of removal' in later

---

[36] PB: Laconnell, 1855–6.

[37] McGill, *Ardara*, 78–9. McGill's account concerns townlands on the Murray-Stewart estate, where, in the 1860s, the landlord 'liberally' assisted tenants in the erection of houses with sash windows. See Coulter, *West of Ireland*, 301–14, esp. 302–4. Ua Cnáimhsí, *Idir an Dá Ghaoth*, 55, recalls an old woman telling him that the squaring of Arranmore was an *lá a ba mhó caointe ar an bhaile seo riamh*, the greatest occasion of wailing that was ever in this townland.

years, Dorian contrasted the pitting of tenant against subtenant—the man with his name in the agent's book against a cottier, craftworker, or labourer—with the valorized resistance to landlords in the 1880s; in the earlier time, tenants themselves accepted the act of eviction as an unpalatable but necessary act:

> This was eviction made easy—this was eviction without lamentation— eviction without sympathy—eviction on the plea of giving to other men their rights. The people who had no land to get and from whom nothing was to be gained in the shape of rent being all got rid of in this way without much talk and without much trouble, and no cry of any injustice for the reason that they did not possess anything, and no more thought about them. It was just removing the dead, as if for the benefit of the living.[38]

On the Conyngham estate, the dismantlement of rundale did not everywhere involve the immediate 'war on cottiers' remembered by Dorian: subtenants were in some places let sit. In Beagh, however, some subtenants—the number is estimated in Table 3.2—were almost certainly removed 'as if for the benefit of the living'. Meanwhile, among the tenants proper there was now a sharp awareness of the size and quality of each other's cuts. The *bó bhradach*, thieving cow, had arrived, and petty bickering followed her. Likewise, 'right of way'—to the bog or shore or, from 1845, the school—would, long after, drive people to distraction. More immediately, this great change, with the attendant demolition and erection of houses and making of walls and ditches, involved a loss of conviviality, most especially for women and most especially in the winter. With houses now on separate squared farms, it took greater effort to slip in and out of each other's doors, to share time and knowledge, skills and resources. Life, suddenly, was more atomized, colder, less intimate. Henceforth, more farm and domestic work would be done by individual families labouring alone. *Na comharsain*, the neighbours—the stem, *comhar*, means both 'cooperation' and 'proximity'—had once been literally *béal dorais*, in the mouth of the door; they were now distant, 'divided'. The elderly too must have acutely felt the isolation. And, for them, who had lived longest in the old landscape, change would have been particularly disorienting, for many touchstones of memory and markers of achievement—the house built by so-and-so in such-and-such a time; the house where he was born and she died giving birth to him—were gone.

But, somehow, the shadow of the past could be discerned. For over a century after the great change came over the land, that is, down to the middle decades of the twentieth century, people cherished shards of the old

[38] Dorian, *Outer Edge*, 236–40 ff.

communalism, quietly denying the cold individualism that was central to the new order, and its insidious dissociation of labour and pleasure.[39] The men of the entire townland kibbed their spuds on the one day in spring and on another day they went together to the bog and, in the autumn, a *meitheal*—a work party comprising men from different houses—would assist in bringing in their neighbours' hay. And when death came, all work in the townland would cease, and women and girls from all houses would assemble to assist the bereaved, and a neighbour would be chosen to dig the grave and to help shoulder the coffin. But it was only a shadow, and, in time too, the shadow itself faded to nothing. On a March morning in the 1950s, one man broke a custom of maybe two centuries standing, when, ahead of his neighbours, he kibbed his potatoes alone. A ritual that bound people not simply to the past but to each other and that allowed them, on a spring day, to collectively experience their own survival had been set aside.[40] Tommy Táilliúr saw the emptiness of the future: 'Ah sure', he remarked, 'we'll all have Christmas on the one day.'[41]

Still, Beagh had been different since it was squared in 1839–41—a shift had been made from a system which, to a greater or lesser extent, involved shared risk and shared reward, to one in which individual households, by and large, wrought for themselves. There had been 'another mode of living' here, with its own rhythms and values, and it was gone now.[42] It may have been going for decades, even generations, as the place became increasingly involved in the market, with boundaries becoming more rigid as plots of arable came to be permanently considered the land of particular families. Or, alternatively, it might have been strengthening on the eve of its own extinction as the desperate worked together to make 'the wastes' sustain life. Indeed, both processes may have been simultaneously unfolding, with periodic redistribution continuing on the bogside where the arable was poorer, while divisions were becoming more fixed on the shoreside. But, certainly, from the time of the squaring the mode of living defined by rundale was no more.

•

The scale of the physical shift in 1839–41—the abolition of commonage, erection of walls, and demolition and construction of houses—and the resulting cultural changes should not distract from clear continuities in

---

[39] See Lloyd, 'Indigent Sublime', 62.

[40] Paraphrasing John Berger, *Pig Earth* (New York, 1992 [1979]), xxii.

[41] Recollection of my father, Patsy Sweeney. The 'Reading Room', a clubhouse of sorts established in the 1930s, was abandoned about the same time; see Ch. 10 of this volume.

[42] Lloyd, 'Indigent Sublime', 40.

landholding from the old to the new system. No rent roll survives for Beagh under rundale in the leases, maps, deeds, wills, and correspondence that constitute the papers of the Conyngham estate; in fact, although valuation records indicate that Beagh was held in 'two equal parts' in 1804–37, no rent roll exists for the townland prior to the year ending 1 May 1856.[43] However, in autumn 1834, officials applotted (assessed) Beagh for tithe—a tax payable by all 'occupiers', that is, both tenants *and* subtenants with *land*, for the support of the established church—and in valuing each occupier's share of the townland, rents were recorded. People with houses but no land—*gan talamh gan trá*, without land or strand—were not liable for tithe, and they are not listed in the Applotment Book.[44]

Applotment was not an uncomplicated process. Roger O'Beirne was the commissioner responsible for applotting Inishkeel. In his entry on Beagh, he directed readers to a note on the first page of the Applotment Book: 'The tenancy is joint and undivided, or what is termed, & understood in the Parish, "Rundale", and is let for a Bulk and not for an Acreable Rent; the Standard of Value, as well as all local assessment, is a cow's grass, for which *no satisfactory definition can be supplied...*' (emphasis added).[45] In that note, O'Beirne was asserting (a) that people dealt in the cow's grass (utility) not the acre (area)—a cow's grass of good land would cover a smaller area than a cow's grass of bad land; (b) that a rent was paid for the entire townland, with tenants contributing according to the cow's grass assigned to them (here, he erred for it was technically held in two leases); and, finally, (c) that the townland was 'undivided', meaning not split into discrete and separate (acreable) holdings. Problematically, in the entry for Sandfield, immediately to the north of Beagh, where the arable was already divided by permanent walls yet there remained commonage, O'Beirne also directed attention to that note; and he did the same in his entry on Carn, to the south, which was held in the classic form of rundale, characterized by a cluster of houses, an infield, and an outfield. Hence, for O'Beirne, 'rundale' was shorthand for bulk rent *and* common pasture, with no particular regard for how arable

---

[43] See Ward-Perkins, 'Conyngham Papers'. On the letting of Beagh in 1804–37, see n. 10 of this chapter.

[44] In Nov. 1837, three years after Beagh was applotted for tithe, it was valued for the purpose of setting rates; the resulting document, VO, FB OL4.336, which does not include occupiers' names, distinguishes nine 'lots', for which it supplies acreages; however, these lots have no relationship to acreages assigned to individual occupiers in NAI, TAB Inishkeel, II (1834) or to holdings registered during the general valuation of tenements in 1855–7.

[45] TAB Inishkeel, II. O'Beirne here errs slightly in indicating the entire townland was let in bulk; again, NAI, VO, FB OL4.2302: Inishkeel No. 2, compiled in Oct. 1839, indicates that it was let 'in two equal parts' in 1804–37.

land was divided.[46] Still, for present purposes, Beagh's system of land use can be located midway between the classic form of rundale in Carn and the semi-squared form in Sandfield.

O'Beirne's applotment of Beagh involved sleight of hand worthy of the best trick-o'-the-loop men at country fairs. To assess individual 'occupiers' for tithe, he had first to estimate what their cow's grass would be in acres. However, there being no 'satisfactory definition' (in acres, roods, and perches) of a cow's grass—there can be no simple one, for the area of a cow's grass varied according to the quality of land—when the Irish acres (1 = 1.62 statute acres), which O'Beirne *assigned* to individual occupiers in a particular townland, are converted into statute acres one finds that the sum total sometimes varies significantly from the area of that townland as *measured* by the Ordnance Survey, and the difference can often not be explained by any shift in boundary. In Beagh, the sum of the acreages (converted from Irish to statute) assigned to occupiers falls slightly (10 acres) short of the total number of statute acres (380a. 2r. 18p.) in the townland; hence, in Table 3.2, those acreages are adjusted as a function of their proportion of the total acreage. Being based on O'Beirne's conversion of occupiers' use rights into Irish acres, these acreages are entirely notional. No 'occupier' in Beagh had a holding of acres, roods, and perches; those 'holdings' only existed on paper. Well, indeed, has James C. Scott remarked of the British state's 'projects of legibility'—its efforts at making the human and physical landscape, most especially property in land, intelligible to administrators—that they 'tended to stumble in the hills, where they encountered ecologies and populations that were distinct culturally and linguistically'.[47] Yet in making people accountable for acres, roods, and perches which they did not, in fact, hold, the applotment process was itself quietly wishing the 'divided' world it described into existence—and the wish would soon be fulfilled, for, with slight adjustment, the squaring, in 1839–41, made O'Beirne's tabular representation of Beagh, in autumn 1834, as a place in which individuals had acreable holdings, a reality.

To the extent that the acreages assigned, on paper, to thirteen individuals create a mirage of squared holdings where there was none, they have the capacity to mislead. Still, those acreages—and associated valuations (best represented by tithe) and rents—reveal considerable inequality under rundale. Of thirteen 'occupiers' (people with land) in Beagh, one, John Gallagher, father of James, was responsible for over 20 per cent of the townland's rental. And his rent, at £6 6s. 5½d., was significantly higher than that paid by any of his neighbours. In fact, the next highest rent was

---

46 TAB Inishkeel, II.   47 Scott, 'Production of Legal Identities', 109.

Table 3.2 Occupiers, 1834, and tenants, 1855 and 1857: Beagh

	Autumn 1834					1 May 1855						1857					
Occupiers in TAB (bold)	Notional Acreage	% Acreage	Tithe	% Tithe	% Titheable Rental	Tenants listed in Rent Roll (bold)	GV No.	Acreage	% Acreage	% Val.	% Rental	Tenants per GV (plain text)	GV No.	Acreage	% Acreage	% Val.	% Rental
John Galaher	79.4	20.9	20.8	20.8		James Gallagher		100a. 3r. 03p.	26.5	18.4	17.2	James Gallagher		158a. 1r. 33p.	41.6	33.8	31.4
							2A	34a. 0r. 10p.					2A	34a. 0r. 10p.			
							2B	66a. 1r. 33p.					2B	66a. 1r.33p.			
													3A	5a. 1r. 0p.			
													3B	20a. 0r. 5p.			
													4	32a. 2r. 25p.			
Andrew Galaher	32.8	8.6	8.3	8.5	Condy Gallagher		30a. 1r. 25p.	8.0	6.6	7.3	Condy Gallagher		30a. 1r. 25p.	8.0	6.4	7.2
							7A	6a. 2r. 0p.					7A	6a. 2r. 0p.			
							7B	23a. 3r. 25p.					7B	23a. 2r. 25p.			
Pat McSwine	23.2	6.1	8.3	6.0	Nancy Sweeney and James Gallagher		44a 0r. 35p.	11.6	12.5	11.3	Patrick Sweeney	8	18a. 3r. 30p.	5.0	5.7	5.6
							3A	5a. 1r. 0p.									
							3B	20a. 0r. 5p.									
							8	18a. 3r. 30p.									
James Meeny	17.8	4.7	4.5	4.7													
Alexander Hill	26.1	6.9	7.3	7.3													
James Kennedy and James Kennedy	44.2	11.6	11.1	11.5	James Kennedy		47a. 2r. 0p.	12.5	11.8	11.3	James (Táillúir) Kennedy		47a. 0r. 0p.	12.5	11.5	11.1
James Kennedy	*11.4*	*3.0*	*2.8*	*3.0*		5A	6a. 0r. 35p.				James and Thomas Kennedy	5A	6a. 0r. 35p.			
James Kennedy	32.8	8.6	8.3	8.5	James Kennedy	5B	24a. 3r. 20p.				James and Thomas Kennedy	5B	24a 3r. 20p.			
						6	16a. 1r. 25p.					6	16a. 1r. 25p.			

(continued)

Table 3.2 Continued

Occupiers in TAB (bold)	Autumn 1834				1 May 1855						1857					
	Notional Acreage	% Acreage	% Tithe	% Titheable Rental	Tenants listed in Rent Roll (bold)	GV No.	Acreage	% Acreage	% Val.	% Rental	Tenants per GV (plain text)	GV No.	Acreage	% Acreage	% Val.	% Rental
							16a. 1r. 25p.				James and Thomas Kennedy					
Bryan Kennedy	15.2	4.0	3.8	4.0	Brian Kennedy	1	21a. 3r. 25p.	5.8	8.1	8.3	Patrick Kennedy	1	21a. 3r. 25p.	5.8	8.3	8.2
John McHugh	34.0	8.9	8.7	8.9	James Campbell and John McCue		52a. 1r. 15p.	13.7	17.7	18.8	John McHugh		52a. 1r. 15p.	13.8	17.9	18.5
					John McCue	14	33a. 3r. 30p.	8.9	11.8	n/a	John McHugh	14	33a. 3r. 30p.			11.5
James Campbell	16.5	4.3	4.2	4.3	James Campbell	13	18a. 1r. 25p.	4.8	5.9	n/a	Cornelius and Condy McHugh	13	18a. 1r. 25p.			7.0
Pat Kennedy	48.3	12.7	12.1	12.7	Pat Kennedy		49a. 0r. 25p.	12.9	13.3	13.2	James Pat Kennedy	9	16a. 2r. 0p.	4.3	4.5	4.4
Myles and Owen Sweeny	43.2	11.4	11	11.4	Myles and Owen Sweeney		34a. 2r. 10p.	9.1	11.5	12.6	Myles and Owen Sweeney		34a. 2r. 10p.	9.1	12.1	13.7
Miles Sweeny	21.6	5.7	5.5	5.7		10A	13a. 3r. 30p.				Owen Sweeney	10A	13a. 3r. 30p.			
Owen Sweeny	21.6	5.7	5.5	5.7		10B	2a. 3r. 30p.				Owen Sweeney	10B	2a. 3r. 30p.			
						11	15a. 2r. 30p.				Myles Sweeney	11	15a. 2r. 30p.			
						12	2a. 0r. 0p.				Myles and Owen Sweeney	12	2a. 0r. 0p.			

Note: This table, compiled for the purpose of comparing families' status over time, is complicated by discrepancies between records of state and estate. For instance, Cornelius (Nogher) and Condy McHugh are identified in the Perambulation Book (1855–6), which includes their rents, and in Griffith's Valuation (1857) as holding land directly under Conyngham; however, they are not listed in the 1855–6 or 1859–60 rent rolls as tenants. The valuation records also represent James and Thomas Kennedy as joint-tenants under Conyngham but the rent rolls show only James as a tenant. Conversely, Myles and Owen Sweeney are identified in estate records as joint-tenants but in valuation records they appear as individual occupiers of most patches of land that they held. James and Thomas Kennedy were essentially equal partners, as too were Myles and Owen Sweeney. Patrick Sweeney is listed in the valuation records (1855–6, 1857), but his mother, Nancy, is listed in the rent rolls (1855–6; 1859–60).

Sources: TAB Inishkeel, II [1834]; Conyngham Papers MS 35,394 (2) Rental of the . . . Boylagh Estate, for the Year Ending the 1st of May 1856; Rental of the Boylagh Estate for the Year Ending 1 May 1860; PB: Beagh, 1855–6; GV (1857).

only £3 17s., paid by Pat Kennedy, and the only other rents above £3 were for occupancies returned by the first rent roll (1855–6) as joint tenancies, that is, tenancies involving two members of the same family with separate households: James and James Kennedy (Táilliúr), £3 10s., and Myles and Owen Sweeney, £3 9s. In 1834, the other seven 'occupiers' were all paying less than £3, four of them less than £2. Moreover, if there was inequality under rundale, a comparison of the (notional) acreages, rents, and valuations derived from the Tithe Applotment Book of 1834 with the first rent roll (1855–6) and initial valuation of individual tenements (1855) does not show inequality, between those 'occupying' land, to have increased significantly during the squaring in 1839–41. Rather, that comparison—all the more impressive as it concerns data collected at points over twenty years apart—attests to a determined effort by Russell to allocate squared holdings of a valuation proportionate to *families'* entitlements under rundale, that is, to reproduce existing inequality (between families named in the two leases in which the townland had been held in 1804–37). And that the new holdings of three families—Gallaghers, Táilliúr Kennedys, and Condy Gallaghers—were then in two or three disconnected blocs—a deviation from the principle of squaring—is a further indication of an effort, on the agent's part, to act 'fairly' towards those 'occupiers'.

Russell's effort at reproducing inequality mystifies the nature of change: a tenth share of 100 acres of rough pasture under rundale is not necessarily 10 acres, for there might be sections of different quality. Still, if favour was curried with Russell by particular landholders at the time of the squaring and favour dispensed to them, as Dorian remembered happening in north Donegal, it cannot be discerned in surviving records. In short, of thirteen *occupiers* returned by O'Beirne in 1834, one—Alexander Hill, a well-to-do farmer—was resident two miles away, just outside Ardara. The remaining twelve *resident* landholders represented ten families, and only one of those families—that represented by James Meeny (Ó Maonaigh, Mooney) in 1834—was not represented by a *tenant* in 1855; nor was any connection of Hill then a tenant. However, Meeny's people had once been tenants here, for his surname is one of two names (the other is Kennedy or Kenny) that appear for Beagh on a list of tenants in arrears on Conyngham's Boylagh estate in 1817, the lean year after the 'year without summer', when abnormally low temperatures had adversely affected harvests; the notation suggests that Meeny and Kennedy represented the 'many' tenants holding land under two leases (Beagh East and Beagh West) taken out in 1804.[48] But whether Meeny himself was a tenant or subtenant in 1834 is not known. If he were a subtenant, he was likely

---

[48] Conyngham Papers 35,394 (1) Boylagh: Arrears, May 1817.

holding land under Patrick McSwine: Meeny's name appears immediately after McSwine's in O'Beirne's book, and in 1855, Widow Nancy Sweeney (*aka* McSwine), a tenant, was subletting a house but not land to Widow Bridget Mooney, presumably James's widow. Still, all that can be said with certainty is that between 1817 and 1855 the Meenys/Mooneys ceased to be tenants, and that between 1834 and 1855 they ceased to hold land.

Other than the decline of the Meeny/Mooney family, there was little change in 'occupancy' from the mid-1830s through to 1855. Surprisingly, perhaps, given the difficult years of 1835–7 and 1846–8, only two of the nine families with tenancies in 1855—those represented by Widow Nancy McSwine/Sweeney, and James Gallagher, who had succeeded his father, John—had acreages significantly different to those notional acreages assigned to them by O'Beirne in 1834. The increase in the McSwine/Sweeney acreage, from 23.2 acres (6.1 per cent of the townland) in 1834 to over 44 acres (11.6 per cent) in 1855, may be attributable to the family having assumed direct control of Meeny's cow's grass, reckoned in the tithe applotment process as the equivalent of 17.8 acres (4.7 per cent). But, again, whether James Meeny had been, in 1834, a tenant in his own right or a subtenant of McSwine is not known; nor is it known at what point between 1834 and 1855 the Meeny/Mooney family ceased to hold land, nor, indeed, in what circumstances—it may be that the McSwines/Sweeneys and Meenys/Mooneys intermarried, for instance. As for James Gallagher, in early 1855 his holding comprised 100.7 acres (26.5 per cent of the townland), a significant expansion of the 79.4 acres (20.9 per cent) reckoned for his father in 1834. That expansion might be attributable to the acquisition of Alexander Hill's cow's grass, calculated to have run to 26.1 acres (6.9 per cent) of low-value land in the mid-1830s. However, in this instance, *seanchas*, oral history, explains that increase by Gallagher's acquisition of a specific segment of land 'in the years of the Famine', not from Hill but from a new landholder, that is, one who was not an 'occupier' in 1834, but who subsequently had rented what had hitherto been pasture and attempted to cultivate it. And so, with the possible exception of the McSwine/Sweeney family, who may conceivably have acquired land from another resident tenant (Meeny) in 1839–41, no family with 'cow's grass' under rundale got an edge on other 'occupiers' at the time of the squaring.

Hidden are the poorest. Those most vulnerable in the squaring were subtenants—people like the Meenys/Mooneys, if they had already become subtenants of McSwine by the mid-1830s, when they still held land—and most especially those people *gan talamh gan trá*, as the Meenys/Mooneys certainly became by the mid-1850s, that is, landless people dependent on wages from agricultural or road labour, or craftwork—knitting, sprigging, or tailoring, for example—to pay rent on a house and purchase food. The number of landless households in Beagh in the 1830s can be estimated. Of thirteen 'occupiers' listed in the Tithe Applotment Book, one (Hill) is known not to have been resident, leaving twelve 'occupiers' assumed to have had houses of their own. Yet the map of 1835 shows twenty-four buildings, which, again, were most likely all houses, meaning there may have been as many as twelve landless householders under rundale. Individual census forms do not survive for Beagh in 1841. However, the published return, as mentioned, gives only nineteen houses. If the total number of 'occupiers' (thirteen) remained the same through the squaring in 1839–41—Hill relinquished his cow's grass, but a new resident occupier took land—then it had reduced the number of landless households from about a dozen to about half a dozen. And so, while the squaring had not been preceded by the general 'war on cottiers' described by Dorian, it nonetheless involved the 'removal' of some landless families. And in their removal, and in the rapidity with which custom had been overturned and the place 'divided', those landless people that remained may have glimpsed their fate.

4

James Gallagher

That there had been marked inequality in Beagh under rundale, that the squaring cannot be shown to have involved an immediate increase in inequality between people with cow's grass, and that any 'war on cottiers' was limited not general, should not distract from the scale of the change that came over the place in 1839–41. In applotting Beagh for tithe, Roger O'Beirne had reckoned that over 86 per cent of the townland was 'mountain and bog', that is, the rough pasture of the rundale system.[1] Now there was no commonage at all. Old houses had been demolished and new ones erected, most likely in a single season. There were walls where there had been none, and soon too there would be more marked distinctions between neighbours. Again, that increase in inequality cannot be shown to have resulted from some landholders having gained and others having lost *at the squaring*. Rather, one man, James Gallagher, adapted better to the new order of things, and in a ten-year period, 1845–55, he doubled the acreage that had been allotted to either himself or his father in 1839–41, consolidating a holding in summer 1855, less than a year before McGlynn turned informer, that accounted for over 41 per cent of the townland's acreage, over 33 per cent of its rateable property, and over 31 per cent of the rental. Seven tenancies then accounted for the rest, and three of those tenancies were de facto joint tenancies, with two households belonging to the same extended family under two of them—those of the Táilliúr Kennedys and the Sweeneys (shoreside)—and three under the third, that of the McHughs.

Nowhere in the official file begun by Patrick McGlynn's first letter to Daniel Cruise is mention made of the break-up of rundale; nor is there a word of it in any report of a court hearing. That said, James Gallagher violated codes of behaviour that more properly belonged to the lost rundale world of the 1830s than the squared farms of the 1840s and 1850s in which, as Russell had put it, every man was only accountable for his own portion. For instance, in one hearing that resulted from the

---

[1] TAB Inishkeel, II. OSFNB, Inishkeel, vol. 3, 101, put the 'bog' section at 75%.

schoolmaster turning informer, a defence barrister led McGlynn into a discussion of the subjects of Ribbon meetings. 'The general subjects at those meetings', the schoolmaster was to say, 'were such as taking arms from persons not connected with the society, breaking into their houses and making them pay money for claims that the members had on them; they received complaints that some of the society were badly used by others; *the time of the famine men bought land cheaply, and those persons who sold the land laid in that they should get a higher price, as land had risen in value.*'[2] In alluding to men buying land cheaply at the time of the Famine, McGlynn did not mean that they purchased the title to property. Rather, he was referring to the trade in 'tenant right' or 'good will', that is, the custom—extra-legal but, in Ulster, prevalent—of an 'outgoer' selling his 'right' to his tenancy.

Here, most certainly, McGlynn had James Gallagher in mind. At the time of writing, a story is still told in Beagh of Gallagher acquiring land 'in the time of the Famine' by paying the passage to America of a family named Mulhern—a cost represented by the tellers as far beneath a fair price for their holding. Problematically, no archival record confirms that story, told with an insistent emphasis on the surname Mulhern, the location of the family's holding—just east of the old school, where a house is marked in the Ordnance Survey map as revised in 1847–50 (but not in the 1835 edition)—and the circumstances of their departure. In fact, no known document attests to anybody named Mulhern ever having lived in Beagh nor is there any record of the land associated with the Mulherns ever having been a discrete holding whose occupiers would have been tenants of Conyngham not subtenants with no 'good will' to sell. Conversely, no known document names the first occupier of the house built between 1835, or more likely, 1839–41 and 1847. And if paper records are few and far between, then maps and acreages and valuations and the insistence with which this story is still told in a place where so few other stories are now told of those years, when Beagh literally took shape, may allow the Mulherns to enter history. Strikingly, if the bloc of land numbered 2B in Griffith's Valuation (Figure 4.1), had been three units, not one, at the time of the squaring—two parts the rough pasture of James Gallagher, and one part the Mulherns' arable and pasture—and had two ditches that then cut diagonally across 2B marked their mearing, then it would be clear how James Gallagher's holding increased from just over a notional 79 acres in 1834 to just over 100 acres by 1855: he purchased the good will of a tract of approximately 20 acres associated with the Mulherns.

---

[2] *LStd*, 12 Mar. 1857; emphasis added.

No. and Letters of Reference to Map.	Townlands and Occupiers.	Immediate Lessors.	Description of Tenement.	Area.	Rateable Annual Valuation — Land.	Buildings.	Total Annual Valuation of Rateable Property.
	BEAGH. (Ord. S. 73.)			A. R. P.	£ s. d.	£ s. d.	£ s. d.
1	Patrick Kennedy,	Marquis of Conyngham,	House, office, and land,	21 3 25	2 15 0	0 10 0	3 5 0
2 A a'			House, office, and land,	34 0 10	4 5 0	1 0 0	
— B			Land,	66 1 33	2 0 0	—	
3 A	James Gallagher,	Same,	Land,	5 1 0	1 5 0	—	13 5 0
— B			Land,	20 0 5	1 0 0	—	
4			House, office, and land,	32 2 25	3 0 0	0 15 0	
2 D a	National School-house,	(See Exemptions).					
5 A / 5 A a	James Kennedy,	Marquis of Conyngham,	House and land,	6 0 35	1 10 0	0 5 0	2 5 0
— B / 6 a	Thomas Kennedy,	ham,	House and land,	24 3 20	0 10 0	0 5 0	2 5 0
6			House and land,	16 1 25	2 0 0	—	
7 A	Connell Gallagher,	Same,	House, office, & land,	6 2 0	1 7 0	0 5 0	2 10 0
— B				23 3 25	0 13 0	—	
8	Patrick Sweeny,	Same,	House and land,	18 3 30	2 0 0	0 5 6	2 5 0
9	James Kennedy (Pat),	Same,	House and land,	16 2 0	1 10 0	0 5 0	1 15 0
10 A	Owen Sweeny,	Same,	House and land,	13 3 30	1 8 0	0 7 0	2 0 0
— B				2 3 30	0 5 0	—	
11 a	Myles Sweeny,	Same,	House and land,	15 2 30	1 15 0	0 5 0	2 0 0
— b	Ellen Callaghan,	Myles Sweeny,	House,			0 5 0	0 5 0
12		Myles & Owen Sweeny,	Land,	2 0 0	0 10 0	—	0 10 0
13 a / b	Cornelius M'Hugh, Condy M'Hugh,	Marquis of Conyng- ham,	House and land, House and land,	18 1 25	1 0 0 / 1 0 0	0 5 0 / 0 5 0	1 5 0 / 1 5 0
14	John M'Hugh,	Same,	House and land,	33 3 30	4 0 0	0 10 0	4 10 0
			Total of Rateable Property,	380 2 18	33 18 0	3 7 0	39 5 0
2 D a	. . . . .	Marquis of Conyngham,	Exemptions: National school-house,	—	—	0 15 0	0 15 0
			Total, including Exemptions,	380 2 18	33 18 0	6 2 0	40 0 0

Figure 4.1 Griffith's Valuation, 1857: Beagh

And so, while lacking any paper record that establishes the existence of the Mulherns, this history—pegged down by maps and rents, valuations and acreages, and, most especially, the documented behaviour of Gallagher a few years later—yields here to memory. The Mulherns existed. They lived on a smallholding behind the school, not all of the land later designated as 2B but about 20 acres of it, and James Gallagher purchased their good will in the time of the Famine, and they went to America.

What would have been a *fair* price for the Mulherns' good will in the late 1840s? Immediately before the Famine, John O'Donnell of Letterilly, a well-to-do farmer, estimated that the good will of holdings on the Conyngham estate was fetching outgoing tenants up to twenty years' rent; hence, a man renting a farm at £1 an acre might get £20 an acre. And James Dunleavy of Glenties estimated that outgoing tenants got ten to fifteen years' rent. Dunleavy himself was paying £15 5s. for 15 acres (4 were arable, 11 rough pasture; he described it as 'four cow's grass') in 1844; hence, according to his figures, he might have expected to get from £150 to £230 from an incoming tenant.[3] The higher figure seems about right, for Russell, the land agent, put good will at fifteen to twenty years' rent, 'according to the locality'.[4] These prices were considered high, and

[3] *Devon Commission*, II. 149, 150, 152. [4] *Devon Commission*, II. 164.

Map 4.1: (*c*.1845)

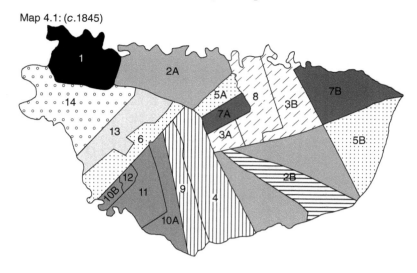

Map 4.2: (*c*.1850)

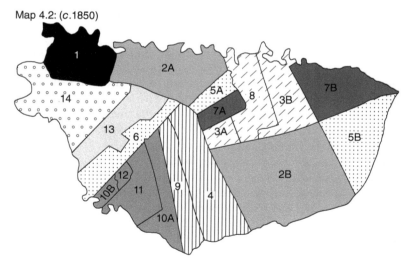

Maps 4.1–4.3 Holdings, 1845–55: Beagh

they were to plummet in the 'bad times', before recovering in the mid-1850s. No representative set of figures for movements in the price per acre of *holdings* has been collated, either at national or regional level; but if their prices tracked the movement of estate prices, for which there are some

Map 4.3: (Late 1855)

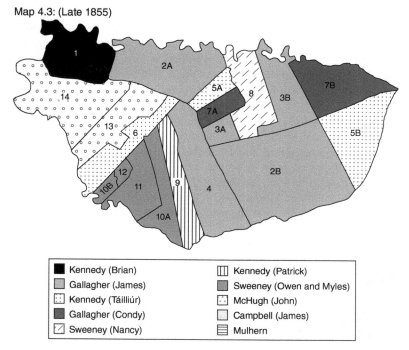

Kennedy (Brian)
Gallagher (James)
Kennedy (Táilliúr)
Gallagher (Condy)
Sweeney (Nancy)

Kennedy (Patrick)
Sweeney (Owen and Myles)
McHugh (John)
Campbell (James)
Mulhern

Maps 4.1–4.3 Continued

figures, then they may have halved in the late 1840s, and then, *c.*1854–5, suddenly attained levels above that paid before the Famine.[5]

The area designated 2B has never been used in the memory of the living (2017) for anything other than foddering cattle or rough grazing for sheep (see Maps 4.1–4.3). It is *scroblach*, scrub, bad land, and in Beagh, where there is no generous field, nothing less giving is known to have been the primary source of a family's subsistence. In a valuator's scribbled notes the lot into which it was absorbed is described as 'heathy and bog pasture—a few acres better'. This 'better' part, the valuator indicated, ran to a mere 2a. 0r. 10p. of the total 66a. 1r. 33p.[6] The entire lot had been part of the old outfield; the 'better' patch had not been broken when the townland was mapped in 1835, and was most likely not brought into cultivation until the overthrow of rundale in 1839–41. Hence, after the labour of

[5] James S. Donnelly, Jr, *The Great Irish Potato Famine* (London, 2001), 164–6; David S. Jones, 'The Great Famine and the Making of the Graziers', in Delaney and Mac Suibhne, *Ireland's Great Famine and Popular Politics*, 142–71, esp. table 5.1.
[6] PB: Beagh, 1855–6.

breaking the land, it can have yielded only six or seven crops of potatoes before the blight came in 1845. And the Mulherns had apparently lived in dreadful conditions. In 1855–7, McGlynn's single-room school, which boasted a window and chimney, was valued at 15s., and most houses in Beagh, lacking windows and chimneys but otherwise similar to the school, at a third of that amount, a mere 5s.; however, the dwelling understood to have once been the Mulherns' was then valued at a mere 2s.—it was a sod-cabin, more a sty than a house. In 1855, a 59-year-old, John McCafferty, was subletting that hut and the 2a. 0r. 10p. of potato ground from James Gallagher. He was paying him £1 in 'black rent'—meaning rent paid by labour—and trying, from that land and, presumably, wage labour for others, to support himself, his wife, Hannah, and at least one adult child, a 25-year-old daughter, Margaret, who helped by sprigging. So poor is the rest of the land in 2B, that the rent on the entire lot—the excuse for a house, the 2a. 0r. 10p. of putatively tillable land, *and* the 64a. 1r. 23p. of bog pasture—would have been approximately £2 in 1855. If the rent had been broadly similar just before the Famine, then the Mulherns' rent—on the potato ground and some 18 acres of inferior ground—would have been approximately £1 7s., and so, in the good times, they might have reasonably expected to get £13 to £26 for their good will; but in the time of the Famine, those prices would have easily halved, to between £6 10s. and £13, *if they could find a buyer*—a critical consideration in any assessment of Gallagher.[7] Hence, the price of the cheapest Atlantic passage for a man, a woman, and a couple of children may not have been an unfair bargain, for in 1845–51 the cost of sailing in steerage from Derry to Quebec, a passage cheaper than to Boston, New York, or Philadelphia, never fell below £2 per adult, and occasionally went as high as £5, with children under 12 generally half-fare. Additional cash would be required for food.[8] For instance, in 1847, the authorities estimated it would cost £10 to send a pauper woman, Anne Jackson of Carrigans, and her two children from Derry to Quebec, after she helped to convict several members of her family of larceny: her passage would cost £3, her children would travel half-fare, and £4 would be needed for provisions and other requisites for the voyage.[9] In short, the Mulherns may have been delighted

[7] Rents and areas (statute acres) are taken from PB: Beagh, 1855–6. McCafferty's age, the name of his wife, and name and age of his daughter are in DCA, BG/92/3/1 Glenties: Registry of Persons Admitted and Discharged, 31 December 1851–66: 3,142, 3,337, 3,429; hereafter, Glenties Workhouse Registry, 1851–66.

[8] Kerby A. Miller, *Emigrants and Exiles: Ireland and the Irish Exodus to North America* (Oxford, 1985), 294–5.

[9] OP 1847/7/210 Newtowncunningham, 25 May 1847, McClintock and Ferguson to Under Secretary; Dunmore, 19 June 1847, McClintock to Under Secretary. She was also to receive £5 on landing in Quebec.

to have a buyer for hard-won land that had ceased to yield sustenance, and, if they were a young couple with two children and Gallagher gave them £10, it might, when fares were cheapest, have got them to America and a second chance at life. They may have left Beagh and its patches of putrid potatoes grateful to the man. Still, in the mid-1850s, when the price of good will had recovered, it may have seemed to others that Gallagher got the land unfairly cheap.

Although the acquisition of the Mulhern holding would be Gallagher's best remembered acquisition, it was neither his last 'take' nor his most impressive, for he subsequently acquired approximately two-thirds of what, at the squaring, had become the second-best 'farm' in Beagh, that is, south-sloping land on the shoreside of the road which was part of the holding of Pat Kennedy. This transaction occurred twelve months before McGlynn informed. Conyngham's rent roll for the year ending 1 May 1856 returns Kennedy as a tenant, paying £5 rent; in other words, he was a tenant a year earlier, in May 1855. However, his name does not appear in government valuation records compiled two months later in July 1855. Rather, those records show his son James Pat Kennedy, a man then married with children, to have been then paying £1 13s. 4d.—exactly one-third of the old rent paid by his father—for a 16a. 2r. 0p. strip of land, while 32a. 2r. 25p. between that strip and the road had now become part of the holding of James Gallagher.[10]

The circumstances in which the greater part of the Kennedy holding was transferred to Gallagher in May–July 1855 were remembered as sordid. Descendants of Pat Kennedy—of whom I am one, by my paternal grandmother—heard from forebears and neighbours that he 'mortgaged' land to Gallagher, that is, put it up as collateral for a loan, and then, being unable to clear the loan, forfeited the land. Kennedy, it is said, was a heavy drinker, the insinuation being that he was a poor credit risk and that Gallagher entered into the arrangement with a view to getting his land.[11] The details of any arrangement between the two men—and Gallagher's expectations—now lie beyond the reach of history. Still, such a scenario accords with his documented involvement with another poor credit risk— Widow Nancy Sweeney. In the same summer months of 1855 that Gallagher absorbed two-thirds of the Kennedy place, he also acquired a substantial portion of Sweeney's holding. The rent roll for the year to May 1856 lists rent of £4 5s. due on a single lot from *both* James Gallagher and

---

[10] PB: Beagh, 1855–6; Conyngham Papers MS 35,394 (2) Rental of the . . . Boylagh Estate, for the Year Ending the 1st of May 1856.
[11] As related by Hughie (Táilliúr) Kennedy (1912–2004).

Widow Sweeney; significant arrears (£2 4s. 2d.) were also owed, but only by Sweeney, suggesting that when she had fallen into distress he had assisted in paying her rent and, in return, got his name in the agent's book. Revealingly, the rent would be paid in full in May 1856—half by Gallagher, half by Sweeney—and Sweeney would clear all but 1s. 2d. of her arrears, yet, thereafter, the agent transferred land that accounted for half (£2 2s. 6d.) of the original rent into Gallagher's tenancy. In fact, while the rent on the land that now passed to Gallagher was the same as that on the land left to the Sweeneys (Nancy was now replaced by her son Patrick as lessee in valuation records, but her name remained on the rent roll), it was not a clean split: the land that Gallagher acquired was in two tracts, one on either side of the portion retained by the Sweeneys, and together they ran to 25a. 1r. 5p. valued at £2 5s. while the Sweeneys' reduced holding was only 18a. 3r. 30p. valued at £2. In other words, they were paying half the old rent for less than half of the old acreage and valuation. As the two families are not believed to have been related, the most obvious interpretation is that by May 1855, the widow was in distress, able to pay only half the rent on her holding, and, with the agent's approval, she had already come to a joint-tenancy-like arrangement with Gallagher. However, in May–July of that year, that is, between the May 'gale' (half-yearly rent day) and Beagh being valued for poor rates, Gallagher purchased the good will of over half of the holding for a sum that enabled the Sweeneys to clear the arrears. And as the Sweeneys were now paying half their old rent for less than half of their old holding but were to be again 1s. 2d. in arrears by May 1856, it is fair to say that they did not get the better part of the bargain. Certainly, if Nancy Sweeney had no other major debts or unexpected expenditure, she had been significantly underpaid: by the mid-1850s, good will was again reaching pre-Famine levels, that is, ten to twenty years' rent, and only a little more than *two* years' rent on the land which was transferred to Gallagher would have both cleared all her arrears and paid the new rent in full.[12]

Importantly, the transfer of some of her land—and some of Kennedy's—to Gallagher involved Robert Russell, for when he was agent, an incoming tenant never paid for good will without first establishing, at his office in Glenties, the state of the outgoer's rent. Any arrears on the land being acquired had to be cleared, from the money being paid to the outgoing tenant, before the new tenant could take possession. Some years later, when explaining the system of good will, Russell remarked that on estates where

[12] Conyngham Papers MS 35,394 (2) Rental of the... Boylagh Estate, for the Year Ending the 1st of May 1856.

there were many 'small tenants', it served as 'a protection to the landlords'; it ensured that they could recover arrears.[13]

Exactly what the Sweeneys received for their good will in Russell's office in Glenties is not known. In all probability, a widow in arrears had other debts too, and other creditors—meal-men, for instance—may not have been as indulgent as the land agent. Furthermore, the Sweeneys, like the Mulherns, may have converted a portion of any money received into a transatlantic passage for a family member. The sale of their good will, then, may have been a choice determined by the necessity of clearing arrears and other debts, and the opportunity of getting a wage earner to America. Certainly, it was a cost-cutting exercise. Formally transferring land to Gallagher in summer 1855, just as the valuation process commenced, ensured that the Sweeneys no longer had to pay poor rates, for henceforth they would not hold land of £4 valuation. And the same was true of the Kennedys. And in slipping below that cut-point, both households also lost the vote for the Board of Guardians. They had disenfranchised themselves to continue living in Beagh; now, besides Gallagher, only one other householder in Beagh (John McHugh) was entitled to vote in those elections. Here, it must be said that I am also a direct descendant, by my paternal grandfather, of Nancy Sweeney.

The land acquired from the Kennedys and Sweeneys—my paternal grandmother's people and my paternal grandfather's—in the year before McGlynn informed, brought Gallagher's own rent from £6 10s. to £12 0s. 6d., approximately one-third of the total rental (£37 15s.) of the townland. He now held 158a. 1r. 3p. of the 380a. 2r. 18p. in Beagh and, in terms of valuation, his holding now accounted for about a third (£11 10s. of £33 18s.) of its rateable land, and about half (£1 15s. of £3 7s.) of its rateable buildings. Now renting a holding valued at over £12, James Gallagher could have registered to vote in Westminster elections. In time, Gallagher would move from a house that he had built *c*.1840–7—replacing his father's house, tucked away behind the Táilliúrs—to one on land acquired from Pat Kennedy. These moves revealed something of the man. His father's house had not been visible from the road and the house that he himself had built, probably in 1839–41, was just off the road, but the new one—the house that had been Patrick McGlynn's—was conspicuously located at the centre of the townland. And in a small place, where small things matter, one now had to pass through James Gallagher's land to travel through Beagh. The only obstacle to hubris,

[13] *Report from the Select Committee of the House of Lords on the Tenure (Ireland) Bill,* 86–98, esp. 90.

that is, the only other people with land on both sides of the road, were the Táilliúr Kennedys. But Gallagher's pride is apparent. On 18 July 1855, when government valuators walked Beagh assessing land and buildings—the first step in the process that culminated in the publication of Griffith's Valuation in 1857—he took an inordinate interest in how his land was registered, insisting that lots acquired at different times be numbered accordingly. 'He wishes to have them published as laid down here, being separate takes', the lead valuator William J. Burke reported to Dublin.[14]

Gallagher's pride can be understood. Although he had started from a position of relative strength—the Gallaghers had been better positioned than their neighbours under rundale—his rise was not a product of any devious gain made at the squaring, in 1839–41, but rather of his having fared better in the divided world created by it. The holding allocated to either John or James Gallagher at the squaring is here understood to have comprised three sections—one, designated 2A in the valuation process of the 1850s, ran to 34a. 2r. 10p., much of it marsh and outcrop but some of it decent arable. The other two sections comprised 46 acres of the 66 acres of poor land behind the school that were later designated 2B, and separating those two plots was the Mulherns' holding. The acquisition of approximately 20 acres from the Mulherns 'at the time of the Famine' brought the entire Gallagher holding up to 100a. 3r. 3p., still a far cry from the near 160 acres—including some of the best land in the townland—which James Gallagher held by late 1855, after he had acquired approximately two-thirds of what had been Kennedy's and half of what had been Sweeney's. In the latter case, Gallagher's name having already appeared in the rent roll for that holding indicates that a formal arrangement, a joint tenancy of sorts, approved by the land agent, preceded the purchase of good will, and, quite possibly, for a period of some years, perhaps, indeed, from the unknown time—before, during, or after the Famine—that Nancy Sweeney lost her husband, Pat. But whenever her troubles began, James Gallagher collected the dividends of the widow's distress in summer 1855.

An individual's aggressive acquisitiveness may have grated with his neighbours, particularly when it extended to hovering over families in trouble. But, as suggested, the Mulherns may have been glad to get money for their good will and to get out to America. Pat Kennedy and Nancy Sweeney too may have been more than happy to divest themselves of large portions of their holdings: most obviously, it allowed them to clear debts

---

[14] PB: Beagh, 1855–6.

and it saved them from paying poor rates. Furthermore, the Kennedys, Sweeneys, and, most especially, the Mulherns may not have had an overly emotional attachment to the particular parcels of which they divested themselves, for again the holdings had only been squared, and those lots assigned to them, in 1839–41; and, in the Mulherns' case, it was only in or after those years that their arable was broken. Ultimately, it was not James Gallagher's sudden supersizing of his holding in 1855 that threatened to bring the Molly Maguires to his door. Rather, it was the *use* he proposed making of it. Sections of what now constituted James Gallagher's expanded holding had been sublet and he resolved to put these people, who, on occasion, he haughtily called 'my tenants', out. Turning land from tillage to pasture, to take advantage of rising prices for cattle and sheep, was one obvious motive for clearing them. So too was a concern about his rate bill. As none of Gallagher's 'tenants' held property valued at £4, he, as the immediate lessor, was responsible for the rates due on their houses and the patch of land on which the McCaffertys kibbed potatoes. But if 'my tenants' were evicted, he was responsible for the rates on nothing but his dwelling, his byres, his land, and the house that he was letting to McGlynn; no rates were levied on unroofed houses.

•

Names can be put to some of the people whom James Gallagher proposed to put out. Those who were householders are listed in a manuscript 'perambulation book', compiled by Burke and his assistants from July 1855, and their names were excised in a revision of the book in 1856. This ledger—a draft of Griffith's Valuation—shows Thomas Brogan, Bridget Mooney, and Owen O'Donnell to have held houses, *but no land*, on the northern side of the bog road, in a field that had been Sweeney's; and, again, John McCafferty had the arable of the old Mulhern holding behind the school. Issues of tenancy and subtenancy may be momentarily set aside. Gallagher intended to get rid of four households in a townland where, in 1855, there were nineteen. In terms of the proportion of families unhoused, it was comparable to what had happened at the squaring, when the number of houses had decreased from at least twenty-four to nineteen.

Brogan, McCafferty, Mooney, and O'Donnell are people of whom there is today no knowledge in Beagh, where, significantly, the Mulherns have, down to the present, been occasionally mentioned. Tenancy, then, mattered, for the longest remembered were tenants, and the soonest forgotten were subtenants. Similarly, there is today no memory of John Fisher, a 17-year-old labourer, who gave his residence as Beagh when he was admitted to Glenties poorhouse with a broken arm on 27 April 1856, perhaps the very week, before the May gale (rent day), when the four households were ejected.[15]

Little is now knowable of these people, beyond the location and valuation of their houses—and, in McCafferty's case alone, his land— and their rent. Thomas Brogan's surname is not particularly common in the parish of Ardara, but no connection can be drawn between this man and any other families in the locality. Nor is there any way to establish a connection with John Brogan who taught in Beagh School in 1857–60. The most that can be said of Brogan is that he seems to have died by the mid-1860s, leaving a widow, Mary.[16] Owen O'Donnell's surname can be connected with the townland over many decades. A man named Mící Mór Ó Dónaill (*fl. c.*1800–*c.*1850), whose house, under the old rundale arrangements, is said to have been on the shoreside of the road, was remembered into the mid-twentieth century as having been of 'gigantic stature (6'5″) and enormous strength'. A notorious rustler of cattle and sheep, it was said that Mící Mór was strong enough to have killed a 2-year-old heifer belonging to Captain Porter of Portnoo, and carried her the four miles home to Beagh.[17] Mící Mór and Owen may not have been related, of course, and even if the latter's people had been in Beagh for many years, they had held no land there in 1834, when Beagh were applotted for tithe. In contrast, Bridget Mooney is presumed to have been the widow of James Meeny who held land there, as tenant or subtenant, in 1834, and whose surname is one of two *tenants* in arrears in Beagh in 1817, when the townland was held in two leases (Beagh East and Beagh West)—an indication, perhaps, that one of the Mooneys had been a person of some standing, a headman of sorts, when those leases were taken out in 1804.[18] And so there was a Mooney renting land in Beagh in 1817, and there was a Mooney still holding land there in 1834, yet the only Mooney household in the place in 1855–6 was headed by a landless widow, Bridget, a subtenant awaiting eviction by James Gallagher.[19]

If there is pity in the removal of families with long connections to a place, there is pity in this instance in their houses, which Gallagher would

[15] Glenties Workhouse Registry, 1851–66: 2,220.   [16] See Ch. 9 in this volume.

[17] NFCM 336: 179–81, story of Mící Mór related by Matt Sweeney, aged 54, to Seán Ó hEochaidh, Apr. 1937. McGill, *Conall's Footsteps*, 188–9, supplies additional details. Also see NFCS 1,048 (Beagh): 58, 'Micky Mór O'Donnell', related by James Kennedy, aged 73, to Matt Sweeney, Dec. 1938.

[18] Conyngham Papers 35,394 (1) Boylagh: Arrears, May 1817.

[19] Bridget Mooney, aged 68, was buried in Ardara in 1858, but there is no way of knowing if she was the widow cleared by Gallagher. See Plot 319, Church of the Holy Family Graveyard, Ardara.

unroof in 1856—to avoid them being subject to rates—and ultimately level, for only Owen O'Donnell's dwelling is marked on the map of 1835. The other three—those of the Brogans, McCaffertys, and Mooneys— were probably built at the time of the squaring in 1839–41. And if these houses had been built on the wreck of custom that was the overthrow of rundale, their roofless walls were also the ruins of poor people's hope, a reminder of the false promise of a world in which every man was only accountable for his own portion. Significantly too, with the exception of the McCaffertys' abode (valued at 2s.), they were, comparatively, decent houses, broadly similar to those of Beagh's other inhabitants. In 1855, Owen O'Donnell's place was valued at 4s., Bridget Mooney's at 5s., and Thomas Brogan's at 6s. In the course of the valuation process, there was some slight adjustment, up and down, in the valuation of houses, but most houses left standing in Beagh in 1857 were valued at 5s. Hence, while these families were more dependent on markets for food than their landholding neighbours, and so more dependent on wage labour or a trade, the material condition of all but the McCaffertys was not very different to that of those around them. All that set the Brogans, Mooneys, and O'Donnells apart was that they held no land, and that their houses were rented not from a distant landlord but from an indebted widow, Nancy Sweeney, and then, after summer 1855, from a man whose coldness was as notorious among them as his pride.

In addition to the houses of Brogan, Mooney, and O'Donnell, and the house and land of McCafferty, James Gallagher was now also letting a house, on land that had been Kennedy's, to Patrick McGlynn, and a garden within the pre-1855 Gallagher holding and a house and garden over the bog road, on what had recently been Nancy Sweeney's, to Patrick and Margaret McNelis. The McNelises were themselves well-to-do people in neighbouring Sandfield, where they had two above average houses and some 66 acres—some of it decent land—held jointly. They were siblings, whose father, Patrick, had come from the neighbouring parish of Glencolumbkille in the decades before the Famine, and established himself as a successful market-focused farmer. The land that the McNelises held in Beagh in 1855–6 must have been taken by themselves or their late father by arrangement with James Gallagher and also, perhaps, Nancy Sweeney. That these arrangements were not renewed in 1856 and that Gallagher proceeded to demolish the house over the bog road probably caused no stir.[20] Simply put, the McNelises were neither resident in Beagh— they were not 'of the place'—nor dependent on that land, and, for all is

[20] PB: Beagh, 1855–6.

known, they may not have wished to take the land or house again. Furthermore, the McNelises were not particularly popular. Patrick McNelis was one of the farmers on whom the Mollies called in 1852, and dictated the price at which he was to sell potatoes; the purchasers would have been landless labourers, cottiers, and craftsmen, and the poorest smallholders whose own stocks would not carry them through the spring.[21] In contrast, the decision to clear the Brogans, McCaffertys, Mooneys, and O'Donnells—people dependent on the likes of the McNelises selling their potatoes at an affordable price—proved massively controversial, and on Sunday 9 March 1856, three weeks before McGlynn first wrote to Cruise, armed Mollies had paid James Gallagher a night visit, and they had warned him that if he evicted 'people' they would come again.[22]

That visit cannot have come as a complete surprise. There had been friction since the previous summer, when Gallagher formally acquired sections of the Kennedy and Sweeney holdings, and with the latter the Brogans, Mooneys, and O'Donnells as subtenants. That October, James Gallagher and Patrick Kennedy had prosecuted 'Nancy Mooney or O'Donnell'—the form suggesting that the Mooneys and O'Donnells may have intermarried—at the Ardara petty sessions for assault and trespass on their land. The case had been dismissed. And then in December, Nancy O'Donnell herself took a case to the same court, alleging that timber stolen from her house had been found on Gallagher's premises. Her case too had been dismissed.[23] One suspects the Brogans, Mooneys, and O'Donnells had already learned their fate—and, indeed, they may been have been anticipating it for some time, as Nancy Sweeney slipped deeper into arrears and became evermore dependent on James Gallagher. Still, Gallagher's decision to turn out John McCafferty, his wife, Hannah, and at least one daughter, Margaret, likely came as a great shock. McCafferty alone of those to be evicted held land from Gallagher and, then aged 59–60, he may have been giving him his 'black rent' for some time. And that scrap of land worked by McCafferty, if it never yielded enough to feed himself and his family, sustained the hope of Margaret marrying somebody with decent land and keeping himself and Hannah from the poorhouse in old age. James Gallagher's decision to evict him blew all those little hopes away.

Something of their loss can be apprehended statistically. John McCafferty had been working two bald acres in 1855–6, when 12–13 per cent of holdings in the Glenties Union comprised less than 5 acres. That percentage had come down only slightly (from 14 per cent) on the eve of the

---

[21] James McNelis, Loughfad, was also a mealmonger; for his prosecution of people, including Patrick Kennedy, Beagh, for non-payment, see IPSCR Ardara: 4 Mar. 1862.
[22] See Ch. 5 in this volume.   [23] IPSCR Ardara: 30 Oct., 18 Dec. 1855.

Famine, and it was to decline over the next few decades, but not catastrophically: 9.9 per cent of holdings (637 of 6,395) in the Union comprised less than 5 acres in 1901. In evicting the McCaffertys, then, Gallagher had relegated them from that poor but relatively secure cohort of survivors into the doomed class of the landless: there were 10.5 per cent more inhabited houses than holdings in the Union in 1851 but only 3.2 per cent more inhabited houses than holdings in 1901, a crude indicator of that group's decline.[24] A man with land could assist non-inheriting children to emigrate, and benefit from remittances;[25] the landless man could often do little for his offspring, and Derry's Bogside was the closest that many of them got to America. There, in the mid-1850s, they were part of what the *Journal*, in 1861, called the city's 'fugitive population', those who had 'flocked in from rural districts after the famine'—and their likes would continue to come into Derry through the 1860s, 1870s, and beyond.[26] There was work there for women, notably, in shirt-factories, but little for the men. Yet there they remained, 'the depressed urbanised surplus of the countryside'[27]—cut off from their past, denied the benefits of progress, 'static vagrants'.[28]

•

One question nags. How did James Gallagher, likely in his mid-thirties in the mid-1840s, manage to expand his holding in 1845–55? That is a question that no historian will ever answer: the man may have won money on the horses. Still, his father, John, had been significantly better off than his neighbours under rundale, and it is known that James had married well, c.1840.[29] His wife, Madge Craig (b. c.1815), belonged to

[24] Percentages were calculated using the numbers of *inhabited* houses in the Glenties Union as given in the 1851 and 1901 Census (7,053; 6,602), and the number of holdings (6,382; 6,395) in *Census of Ireland for the Year 1851, pt. ii, Returns of Agricultural Produce in 1851*, HC 1854 [1714], lvii. 305, and *Census of Ireland 1901, pt. ii.*, HC 1902 [Cd. 1190], cxxix. 305.
[25] The assumption that primogeniture was the norm among the rural poor persists in scholarly works. However, Cormac Ó Gráda, 'Primogeniture and Ultimogeniture in Rural Ireland', *Journal of Interdisciplinary History*, 10/3 (1980), 491–8, long ago pointed to a different reality. Also see Timothy W. Guinnane, *The Vanishing Irish: Households, Migration, and the Rural Economy in Ireland, 1850–1914* (Princeton, 1997), 151–4.
[26] *LJ*, 24 July 1861.
[27] Sean O'Faolain, *Vive Moi! An Autobiography* (London, 1965 [1963]), 145.
[28] Berger, *Pig Earth*, xxiv, on the condition of ex-peasants in twentieth-century shantytowns.
[29] The dates of birth and marriage of James Gallagher and Madge Craig are not known. However, extant sources, and what is known of pre-Famine demography, suggest that James was born in the early 1810s and married c.1840, when men of his class were marrying in their mid- to late twenties. First, James's father, John, was reported to be 70 years of age in 1858, meaning that he was born c.1788, and that he likely married c.1810. Second, James undoubtedly had children in the early 1840s. One of his daughters, Ellen, was

a prominent family, whose head, Manus Craig, had a farm of 235 acres in Kilclooney, about a mile and a half from Beagh. In the mid-1850s, when Manus had been succeeded by a son, Thomas (1817–92), this farm accounted for over half the valuation of land in that townland, and the rates paid on the house and many outhouses—the sign of a cattleman—were just under half the amount due on all buildings in it.[30]

Ostensibly, James Gallagher had much in common with the Craigs. But while Gallagher had pulled himself up during and immediately after the Famine—doubling the acreage that had been assigned to himself or his father at the time of the squaring—they had been people of consequence before the Plantation, and they had emerged from the upheaval of the seventeenth century holding good land and a good area of it, and sending sons to the continent to be educated for the priesthood.[31] The Craigs of Kilclooney were also connected through marriage to well-to-do families across west Donegal, including the Maloneys of Ardara and Carrick, the Boyles of Dooey, the Gallaghers of Castlegoland, and the O'Donnells of Ballinamore, and when, in 1829, with a wink from Daniel O'Connell, the property qualification for the parliamentary franchise was raised from 40s. (£2) to £10, Manus Craig was one of only 73 men in the barony of Boylagh (pop. 1841: 22,120) who applied to register a freehold.[32] Indeed, the family's standing is inscribed on the first Ordnance Survey map, on which the homestead is identified as Craig's Town.

It is unclear where Madge fits into this family. Certainly, Manus was not her father, for her daughter married his son, and so it seems likely that she was a sister of the only other householder of that surname in Downstrands in the mid-1800s—Daniel Craig (1790–1872) of nearby Kiltooris. Daniel too was a large farmer. In the mid-1850s, his holding, like that of James Gallagher in Beagh and Thomas (Manus) Craig in Kilclooney, accounted for half (£19 of £38 15s.) of the valuation of his

reported (GRO) to be 22, when she died in 1865, giving a birthyear of 1843. Another daughter, Mary, was reputed to be 95 when she died in Jan. 1937, suggesting a birthyear of 1841–2; other sources (see Ch. 9) suggest she was born later in the 1840s, but given that she remembered the Famine, the earlier date seems more likely. Finally, one of James's sons, John, gave his age as 50 in his 1901 Census return, but in 1911, he gave it as 69. If the latter age were correct, John would have been born *c*.1842. However, many people exaggerated their age to get the new old age pension; see Cormac Ó Gráda, ' "The Greatest Blessing of All": The Old Age Pension in Ireland', *Past and Present*, 175 (2002), 124–61. On age at marriage before the Famine, see Kevin O'Neill, *Family and Farm in Pre-Famine Ireland: The Parish of Killashandra* (Madison, WI, 1984), 177–86.

[30] Kilclooneymore had been let in 1819 for £25, which, in 1839, valuators considered 'very cheap'; see VO, FB OL4.2302.

[31] Maguire, *Raphoe*, i. 475; ii. 300.

[32] Francis Shovlin, *Narin and Downstrands* (Trafford, 2012), 174–8; for Manus having a vote, see *Strabane Morning Post*, 19 May 1829.

townland—three households (all headed by men named Harkin) accounted for the rest—and he also held land and a herd's house (total valuation £11 10s.) in Drumboghill. And so, irrespective of her position in the family, Madge, being a Craig, doubtless brought a significant dowry to Beagh. Certainly, she brought influence, for her people included some of the most 'respectable' tenants on the Conyngham estate. It is possible, then, that, from the Craigs, Gallagher secured support—loans or gifts or a word with Russell, Conyngham's agent—that facilitated the expansion of his holding. Of course, in the late 1840s, when weaker tenants were falling into arrears, assisting Gallagher to acquire land would have made sense to Russell. Likewise, in the 1850s, when livestock prices were rising, the agent would have preferred to collect rent from a single cattleman—and one connected to a dependable family—than a drunk, like Pat Kennedy, or a widow, like Nancy Sweeney, who had subdivided her holding with people whose capacity to pay her was always precarious.

Still, Gallagher's own initiative may have been as important a factor in his rise as either the Craig connection or the agent's assistance. In a useful local history (1970), schoolmaster P. J. (Wee Paddy) McGill remarked of the later stages of the Famine that 'Meal merchants were setting up in many areas, but money was scarce, and few were able to buy except by *mortgaging* their pieces of land to the "meal man" who was laying the foundations of future wealth and "gentility".'[33] And debt accumulated quickly: in 1844, at the Devon Commission hearing in Donegal Town, when asked what interest rate was charged by 'local usurers', John O'Donnell of Letterilly said that 'in many instances it comes up to 300 per cent', meaning by the time a loan had been repaid. Normal interest rates were probably under 20 per cent—James Dunleavy of Glenties reported Lettermacaward people were paying 4–5s. in the pound (20–5 per cent) which he considered high—but they would have spiked in 1845–8.[34] James Gallagher had corn sacks in his house in March 1856, but there is no evidence that he was a 'meal man'.[35] Still, he was sufficiently better off than his neighbours that they would have looked to him for assistance. Certainly, Widow Sweeney somehow found herself in debt to him. Intriguingly too, the story told in Beagh of one of his other acquisitions—the land obtained from hard-drinking Pat Kennedy in 1855—involved what locally, prior to the 1970s, would have been an uncommon verb, *to mortgage*, which was also used by McGill when discussing meal men. And like those men, Gallagher expanded his holding in hard times.

[33] McGill, *Ardara*, 96, emphasis added.   [34] *Devon Commission*, II. 148, 154.
[35] CRF G/22/1857 Informations of Nancy Gallagher...8 July 1856.

Ultimately, in considering Gallagher's rise, issues of values, understanding, and feeling are crucial. At a time when people married young, his relatively late marriage suggests prudence and thrift. Consequently, while he was physically weak,[36] and so not cut out for agricultural labour, he was ideologically better prepared than his neighbours to be accountable for his own portion when the shift was made from rundale to squared farms. Certainly, his turning out of his 'tenants' in 1856 points to an indifference to custom. And there is additional evidence of a disregard for communal expectation. In early 1856, it was notorious that Gallagher was mistreating his father, John (b. 1788), in part, at least, by denying him money.[37] It is unclear when this mistreatment began, but one can speculate. Across rural Europe, tension between smallholders and their eager-to-inherit sons had been a feature of family life since the Middle Ages. In Ireland, potato-enabled subdivision had dampened that tension in the century before the Famine—a man did not have to give up his land, he could simply give the young fellow a few acres. In Beagh, however, the squaring of the farms marked the beginning of a stricter approach to estate management: the agent may not have immediately prohibited subdivision, but a preference for 'one smoke' on a holding would have been known. Hence, in the Gallagher household, the coincidence of generational strain and the break-up of rundale would have had the potential to cause trouble, for, in 1839–41, when the farms were squared, the soon-to-be married James Gallagher would have been eager to establish himself in his own right, get his father, then 50, to step aside, and let him become the landholder. One scenario, then, is that, in that great change, John ceased to be a tenant, and the young man got his name into the agent's book. James Gallagher's father, in other words, may have been the first person that he 'put out'. At best, within a few years of the squaring, the old man became a lodger in his son's house which was now Madge Craig's.

Whenever the trouble started between father and son, and for whatever reason, James Gallagher's refusal to adequately support the old man broke convention. In 1834 commissioners appointed by the House of Commons to inquire into poverty in Ireland held a series of meetings around the country, at which they discussed labourers' wages, the prevalence of disease, the provision for the ill and infirm, and attitudes to beggars and 'bastards'. This Poor Inquiry held a meeting for the lower section of Inishkeel, which included Beagh. Those who made contributions to it

---

[36] CSORP 1856/16,473 Beigha, 22 Apr. 1856, McGlynn to Cruise.
[37] CRF G/22/1857 Informations of James Gallagher . . . 8 July 1856; Informations of Nancy Gallagher . . . 8 July 1856.

included Robert Russell, the land agent; Daniel Coyle and Daniel Earley, the curate and parish priest of Glenties; Daniel McDevitt, merchant and clerk of the Glenties petty sessions; and Alexander Hill, the commercial farmer who had some cow's grass in Beagh in 1834. Although most were 'gentlemen and clergy', some ordinary people too participated.[38] 'I strive to work as hard as I can', Daniel Wilson, a labourer, was quoted as saying, 'and I cannot see how, after paying rent and taxes, I can save anything.' 'It is hard', said an unnamed 'cottier tenant', 'for a man who is over head and ears in debt to be industrious, for he knows not what to look to.'[39]

Among those ordinary men was a 'small farmer', Patrick McSwine, the form of the surname Mac Suibhne (more commonly anglicized as Sweeney) given one of John Gallagher's neighbours in the Tithe Applotment Book, that is, the man who predeceased his wife, Nancy. Indeed, that Beaghman is the only person with that surname in any of three Applotment Books compiled for the parish of Inishkeel in 1834; if there were other 'McSwines' here they did not hold land. McSwine was an active participant in the meeting: his name, unlike that of Wilson, the labourer, was listed among witnesses when excerpts of evidence were published in a parliamentary report. He is quoted only once, and it was when the 'impotent through age' were being discussed. 'For fear it would be cast up to me', said McSwine, 'I would support my sister, my mother, my father, or even my uncle.'[40]

McSwine's values were those of a world in which a man was his kin's keeper, and, if he was the Beaghman, then his comments may help to explain why his widow was in debt in the wake of the Famine and her holding carrying three subtenants, one of whom was also a widow.[41] Not everybody always lived by those values, of course. And a concern for others' well-being and a concern for others' perceptions of one's conduct did not suddenly disappear, and they are not gone. But certainly, in 1855–6, the values of James Gallagher, who was neglecting his near 70-year-old father, were pre-eminently those of coming times.

---

[38] Niall Ó Ciosáin, *Ireland in Official Print Culture, 1800–1850: A New Reading of the Poor Inquiry* (Oxford, 2014), 51–2 ff., argues that the Inquiry's publication of oral evidence from people of all social classes was 'unusual, even unique' in scale.
[39] *Poor Inquiry*, appendix A, 177.   [40] Ibid. 275.
[41] There had been other houses on the Sweeney lot, including one over the bog road, and another, on Henry's Hill, to the left of the lane down to their post-1839–41 house. Both can be seen in the first OS (1835). The house furthest to the east had been demolished by the time of the OS revision, 1847–50, and the other house had gone by 1855. In that year, a house, constructed *after* 1847, stood on the land over the bog road sublet by the McNelises.

PART III

5

The Name of Informer

On Monday 2 June 1856, Patrick McGlynn wrote his eighth and last letter to Daniel Cruise before giving up the names of the Molly Maguires. He was worried. The letter was long and now, for the first time, the magistrate became 'your worship', as the master spun plans to prevent himself being exposed as an informer. After the first arrests were made, he suggested, he might take some other Ribbonmen into 'some place in Ardara', where the police could be 'hid within hearing'. There, he would 'lead the conversation into such a channel that they would tell all they knew of the connexion those that were taken had with the society and also their own connexion with it. The police could then arrest them.' McGlynn, in this scenario, might then be summoned as a witness and testify as to what he had heard, and, if one of those arrested turned informer, as one or more surely would, he could corroborate their information, but as a witness not an informer. Similarly, he suggested bringing some of the Mollies into his own house to discuss the arrests, adding 'my wife always has a fashion of listening'—a nudge to Cruise to have the pregnant woman take the stand as the prime informer and screen himself.[1]

They were fanciful proposals, not seriously considered by the man who made them. If by 'some place in Ardara' McGlynn meant a public house—and what is known of his trips to the town suggests that he had some drinking shop in mind—he can scarcely have believed that the police might be 'hidden within hearing'. Those establishments were small and spare. The bar room in Teague Breslin's, adjacent to the chapel, was only enlarged in 2002: it was 9'6" by 17'9", and the counter and workspace behind took up about a third of that area. The backroom was 13'6" by 11'2".[2] There was nowhere in Teague's to hide. Moreover, several publicans were Mollies themselves or had Mollies in the family, and those who were not Mollies would risk ruin by conspiring with the Constabulary to ensnare customers. As for McGlynn's pushing his wife

---

[1] CSORP 1856/16,473 Beigha, 2 June 1856, McGlynn to Cruise.
[2] Ground Floor Plan, June 2002; copy supplied by John Breslin, publican and architect.

forward as the informer and his suggestion that he, by force of circumstance, could then appear as a witness, he would have known only too well that the Mollies would not draw a fine distinction between a witness and an informer, nor between a man and his wife, if she testified against them. His proposals, then, were a faint-hearted denial of the glaring reality that he was already an informer and that he needed to get out of Beagh. In truth, McGlynn was coming to accept the empty future that he had made for himself when he first wrote to Cruise on 31 March, and now, in the same letter that began with those far-fetched suggestions, he asked that the government send himself and his family to Australia, or else give him 'some situation in Ireland as good as the one I hold now'. 'I must leave this place should they be taken and I have any hand in committing them', he wrote, '. . . Because Sir the people hate the very name of informer, though I think the action meritorious.'[3]

McGlynn had no illusion about what 'the people' did to informers. Again, in 1850, he had been a teacher or 'monitor' in Letterbrick, Glenfin. In nearby Cloghan, on the night of 16 May 1847, upwards of 100 people headed by a man attired in women's clothes had attacked the house of Patrick Doherty, a schoolmaster cum land agent. They got inside, disarmed him of a gun and two pistols, and then took him outside, where they cut an inch off his tongue.[4] Doherty was an informer and, around Glenfin, the incident would be vividly recounted into the mid-1900s: in 1850, anybody teaching in Letterbrick would have known of it.[5] A severed tongue was but one of the stigmata on the bodies of informers. Cropped ears too reminded people of the golden rule: you have not heard and you never tell. So did rolling an offender in shit and showering him with feathers, and then hunting the ridiculous bird to hear him squawk. And killing informers made the point more emphatically. It is no surprise, then, that in his very first letter to Cruise McGlynn had emphasized that his life would be in 'imminent danger' if he were exposed as an informer or that, in his second letter, he asked to be given 'some arms', a request he would repeat a fortnight later, threatening not to tip off Cruise about the

---

[3] CSORP 1856/16,473 Beigha, 2 June 1856, McGlynn to Cruise.
[4] OP 1847/7/152 Reward poster, dated 4 June 1847. *BH*, 21 May, 28 May 1847. Doherty was himself subsequently prosecuted for posting threatening notices; he was acquitted; see *LJ*, 15 Mar. 1848.
[5] For one anecdote about Doherty, related in 1935 by Dónall Mag Fhloinn, aged 60, An Clochán, to Liam Mac Meanman, see NFCM 169: 11–12. In this account, Doherty was set to testify that he had served processes on tenants scheduled for eviction, but *scoilt na Mollys a theangaidh le é a chur ins an dóigh nach mbeadh sé ábalta mionnú*, the Mollies split his tongue so that he wouldn't be able to swear.

Mollies' plans unless he received a weapon: 'I know I should be well paid
were they taken but it might be to provide for my funeral were I not
prepared for a surprise.'[6]
  Knowing what might be done to him if exposed as an informer, why
had McGlynn contacted Daniel Cruise? Contemporaries believed finances
were a factor. In the only court appearance that McGlynn made in the
case, a barrister got him to acknowledge that he had been in the habit of
getting goods on credit, was in debt to 'several shopkeepers', owed money
to 'three or four persons', and had 'three or four decrees' hanging over
him. He did not know, he admitted, how many times he had been
decreed.[7] Also, McGlynn's rent probably had to be paid within a
few weeks of his writing to Cruise, for he was subletting from James
Gallagher, whose half year's rent, which had effectively doubled with the
acquisition of Pat Kennedy's and Nancy Sweeney's in summer 1855, fell
due on 1 May. Hence, McGlynn likely had a particularly pressing need
for cash when he wrote to Cruise on 31 March. However, if financial
problems contributed to the master's decision to put pen to paper, so did
two additional worries. One was a heightening fear that the Constabulary
might connect him to either a recent or an imminent 'outrage' against
James Gallagher. The other was an acute anxiety that he himself might
be informed upon, and that anxiety stemmed, in large part, from
the fractious politics of the Ardara Mollies as they adjusted to post-
Famine realities.

THE POLITICS OF THE ARDARA MOLLIES

Patrick McGlynn had been an incomplete sort of Molly Maguire. For
sure, he attended meetings, paid for signs and passwords, and passed them
with 'brothers' with whom he drank in Ardara, Glenties, and Donegal.
Likewise, before one of the abandoned raids on James Gallagher, he
carried a weapon out to Beagh for Condy McHugh, and McHugh, a
committeeman, sent him to Downstrands to bring up more men for
that attack. He was privy too to many of the Mollies' secrets, and he
knew who was involved in particular arms raids. But, importantly,
McGlynn himself had never participated in an arms raid or a beating,
which was consistent with Little John Breslin's stipulation, when he made
him a Ribbonman, that schoolmasters would not be involved in 'attacking
parties'. Still, the master's fear of being implicated in an 'outrage' had

become all-consuming in the three weeks before he sent his first letter to Cruise. Again, on the night of Sunday 9 March, there had been a raid on Gallagher's house. A party of about ten men had rapped on the door and when Gallagher's daughter, Nancy, had answered, they had fired a shot and stormed inside. Two or three of them had then taken hold of Gallagher and dragged him to some sacks that were under corn on the floor. The raiders announced that they were from County Cavan, perhaps adding, as was a practice on such occasions, that they had been brought 100 miles by Molly Maguire to do justice or words to that effect. In fact, at least some of them were local men, including Matthew Sweeney of Beagh, who had slunk back against the wall so as not to be recognized, and James Hanlon of Ardara, a publican's son. In the crowded house, the Mollies had asked Gallagher for his wife—Madge Craig, apparently away from home that night, was a particular focus of their resentment—and they had warned him to 'be good to my father and the neighbours and not to dispossess the cottiers or they would come back again'. And lest there be any misunderstanding, they had left a letter behind reiterating the threat.[8] It was a colourful letter, invoking the most radical French revolutionaries of the day and, in addressing Gallagher as 'your royal highness', poking fun at the pretensions of the would-be king of Beagh:

> We, the Red Republican Irishmen, hereby notify to you, James Gallagher, that if you do not forthwith relinquish your idea of dispossessing people, and if you do not treat your father with more kindness, we shall do ourselves the distinguished honour of paying your royal highness another visit.
> We also beg leave to inform you that travelling is expensive between here and county Cavan, so do not bring us again [to] Ardra.
> Sergeant Reilly, Fogabollagh Fencibles[9]

The name appended to the letter was at once mockery of Hugh Reilly, the constable in Ardara, a marker, like the use of legalistic language ('hereby notify', 'forthwith'), of the procedural nature of the visit, and a claim of legitimacy for the Mollies' use of force and the justice of the threatened punishment.[10] 'Fogaballagh Fencibles' was an additional jibe at Reilly: the

---

[8] For the Gallaghers' accounts of the raid, see CRF G/22/1857 Informations of James Gallagher...8 July 1856; Informations of Nancy Gallagher...8 July 1856. James Gallagher's testimony about the attack can be found in press reports of the assizes of Mar. 1857. McGlynn claimed that Hanlon and Sweeney told him of their involvement in the raid; see CSORP 1856/16,473 Mountcharles, 14 June 1856, Further Information of Patrick [Mc]Glynn. McGlynn's servant girl witnessed the Mollies assembling 'behind a fir ditch' near Gallagher's on the night of the attack: see CRF G/22/1857 Informations of Sally Gallagher...8 July 1856.

[9] The letter is reproduced in *Saunder's Newsletter*, 13 Mar. 1857.

[10] Vaughan, *Landlords and Tenants*, 153–6.

Royal Irish Fusiliers, which recruited heavily in his home county of Cavan, were nicknamed the Faugh-a-Ballaghs, from their battle cry, which translates as Clear the Way. Gallagher would later remark that the letter, which he had found the following morning, had been left on 'my dresser'. A dresser was an article of furniture that not all his neighbours would have then possessed and, indeed, one that some Beagh households may not have boasted for another generation.[11] Certainly, in 1856, the McCaffertys scarcely had a dresser in their hut, and so Gallagher's reference to it hints at his sense of himself and the things that he counted important. But wherever it was left, the letter contributed to McGlynn's informing, for he had written it. Matthew Sweeney of Beagh and Jack O'Donnell of Tullycleave had come to him on the evening of the raid to ask him to write it, and he had done so in a disguised hand. In the generation after the Famine, the posting of threatening letters or notices accounted for over half of all offences which the Constabulary classified as 'agrarian outrages', and the 'dark figure' for such missives—the total number of letters and notices, including those never reported to the Constabulary—was doubtless higher than those for other 'agrarian outrages' such as murder and assault, maiming, arson, and theft. And so, in penning that letter, McGlynn had committed what W. E. Vaughan has identified as the 'most common agrarian outrage'.[12]

James Gallagher had not been intimidated. On the night of the raid, when the Mollies had demanded 'as much money as would pay their expenses back to the County of Cavan, or would pay for grog for them', he had replied that he 'had no change'.[13] Then, the following day, he had reported the raid to Constable Reilly, saying, perhaps truthfully, that he did not recognize any of the intruders, and he had given him the letter. And little over a week later, he had publicly demonstrated his determination to face down the Mollies, by letting St Patrick's Day—the date at which agreements were normally struck with cottiers and subtenants— pass without any new arrangements being made with the Brogans, McCaffertys, Mooneys, or O'Donnells. The McCaffertys, the only one of those four families with land, kibbed no potatoes that March, while they tried to determine where and how they would live once Gallagher ejected them.

Gallagher's determination to evict these families called for a response. Soon after St Patrick's Day, McGlynn met with Condy McHugh of Beagh and William Maxwell of Doohill in a 'waste house' of James Fisher's at the

---

[11] CRF G/22/1857 Informations of James Gallagher . . . 8 July 1856.
[12] Vaughan, *Landlords and Tenants*, 142, 150.
[13] CRF G/22/1857 Informations of Nancy Gallagher . . . 8 July 1856.

bottom of Ardara's Front Street; both were committeemen. There they told McGlynn that Gallagher should be attacked, and 'that both he and wife should be taken out and dipped in a hole of water, and that they should be beaten, and the wife more than him', and, that if any money was found in the house, it should be given to Gallagher's father.[14] Now, fear crystallized, for McGlynn knew that Gallagher was 'a man of very delicate constitution', and, if the Mollies did beat him, it was 'as likely as not that they would kill him'.[15] And if they killed him, the letter written on Sunday 9 March would be an object of renewed interest, with the potential to implicate him in murder.

That letter, given to Reilly by Gallagher, was then somewhere in a chain of command that rose from the Ardara barracks to the district headquarters in Glenties to the County Inspector's office in Letterkenny and, finally, to Dublin Castle. Literacy in these years was very much the exception: five years later, the 1861 Census returned only 11.4 per cent of males over 5 years of age in the parishes of Ardara and Glenties, as able to write; the figure for females over 5 was 6.7 per cent.[16] Literacy was also higher among Protestants than Catholics. Hence, the pool of suspects capable of writing that letter and inclined to do so would have been small. Convictions for writing threatening letters were few relative to the number of such letters sent—again, they accounted for over half all reported 'agrarian outrages'—but the offence was considered serious and treated severely by the courts, most especially when the malefactors were schoolmasters responsible for the moral instruction of the young. If charged and convicted, McGlynn might be facing several years' penal servitude. Moreover, conviction had just become easier: a recent act of parliament had made the opinion of 'respectable' men—bankers and land agents, for instance—as to the hand in which letters were written admissible as evidence in court.[17] Compounding matters, McGlynn had not been some 'semi-literate' indulging in a 'solitary vice', as a historian of landlord–tenant relations has depicted those who penned such letters.[18] A fluent writer, he had put pen to paper at the behest of Matthew Sweeney and Jack O'Donnell, most probably in their presence. *Ní scéal rúin é ó chluinfeas triúir é*—It is no secret once known to three—was a wisdom acquired early in life in a district where poaching and smuggling *poitín*

[14] McGlynn's evidence at the assizes, *LJ*, 11 Mar. 1857.
[15] CSORP 1856/16,473 Beigha, 22 Apr. 1856, McGlynn to Cruise.
[16] *Census of Ireland for the Year 1861. Part V. General Report*, HC 1863 [3204-IV], lxi. 314–15.
[17] Vaughan, *Landlords and Tenants*, 153–4.   [18] Ibid. 150.

and tobacco had long been important. And Condy McHugh too knew who had written that letter.

McGlynn's anxiety about being implicated, through the letter, in either the recent raid on Gallagher or the imminent, potentially murderous, attack upon him now dovetailed with his concern that some 'brother' was liable to turn informer. McGlynn variously claimed that he had joined the Mollies out of curiosity, 'through fear more than anything else', and with the intention of informing.[19] He had joined 'solely for their betrayal', he told Cruise in his last nervous letter prior to his arrest, and 'never assisted or counselled violence'.[20] The idea that he joined the Mollies to destroy them is not credible, but there may be some truth in his claim to have joined out of fear. Certainly, there was an element of pressure in the new-man-in-town being made a Ribbonman: again, James Melley, then master of Meentinadea National School, had strongly advised him to join in 1853, after hearing that he had rejected an overture from William Maxwell, the shoemaker who was chairman of the Ardara lodge, and Neil Breslin. Still, it seems more likely that McGlynn joined, and paid for secret signs and passwords, as he believed in the organization, or at least believed that it might do something for him—perhaps, indeed, protect him from his various creditors. However, within two years of joining, he had grown disillusioned with the local leadership, as had other members, albeit for different reasons. In the 'information' which McGlynn gave in Wood Lodge, second only to a detailed description of how he was made a Ribbonman was an account of a meeting that he had attended in Neil O'Donnell's public house in Glenties on St Patrick's Day 1855. The purpose of that meeting was to resolve a dispute in the Ardara lodge. That dispute rose from a challenge to the mastership of Little John Breslin of Doohill by Moses Ward of Brackey and Condy Boyle of Meenagolan, who thought that Breslin was 'not breaking enough of houses [sic]'. The meeting had involved the masters of lodges in Glenties (Neil O'Donnell), Killybegs (Charles Herroran), and Dungloe (Martin Quigley), and a large contingent of Ardara Ribbonmen. The chairman was James Gallagher of Fintown, the west Donegal delegate. Gallagher, judging from McGlynn's account, parried Ward's challenge. Having taken the mood of the meeting and evaluated Ward's base, he had pulled a paper from his pocket, and holding it up, he said it contained the signs and passwords for the ensuing quarter, which he would give to Ward for 10s. The Brackey-man did not have the money that night and, when he failed to raise it over the following week, leadership reverted to Breslin.

[19] *BN*, 12 Mar. 1857; *LSnl*, 13 Mar. 1857.
[20] CSORP 1856/16,473 Beigha, 2 June 1856, McGlynn to Cruise.

McGlynn had little time for Breslin. Less than three weeks after the meeting in O'Donnell's, McGlynn had to undergo the annual oral examination of national teachers, held in 1855 in Donegal Town. There, he had fallen into company with Cormac Gillespie, the teacher in Glencoagh Agricultural School, who he knew to be a 'brother'. Gillespie, who was 'under the influence of drink' and indiscreetly making Ribbon signs, asked him if Little John Breslin was still master in Ardara and how he was coming along. McGlynn replied that he was still master and that he was coming along 'badly', adding that he was taking in the 'worst characters in the country'. (It was an encounter which McGlynn had not remembered when making in his first statement, on 8 June, only describing it in his second statement; his memory had been jogged by Cruise, who had Gillespie in his sights since the previous year.) And on another occasion, James Moore of Loughfad, sometime master for 'the lower end of the parish' (Downstrands), had called at night to McGlynn's house and the two men had spoken of 'the folly' of having 'such a man as John Briesland' as master in Ardara, and they had agreed that he should be put out.[21]

If McGlynn had little time for Breslin, he had less for Moses Ward. In the weeks after the meeting in Glenties, when the militants' challenge was faltering due to lack of funds, he had refused to pay Ward for passwords and signs. With hindsight, Ward's challenge to Breslin can be seen as the high-water mark of opposition around Ardara to the transformation of the Mollies from an organization committed to protecting the rural poor, by acts which the state considered 'outrages', to one more focused on opportunities; in other words, the militants peaked a year before McGlynn informed. But their decline was not immediately apparent. Indeed, but for McGlynn's informing, the militants may have succeeded in regrouping and gaining control of the lodge. Certainly, Ward's faction remained powerful. Notably, at meetings in the backrooms of public houses (Barney Kelly's and John Dorrian's) in 1855–6, they successfully pressed Breslin to sanction arms raids. Among those raids were 'attacks' on the house of John Hill, cess collector and process server, in Monargan Glebe, in which a gun was taken; the house of a man named Scott in Downstrands, when they left with a 'large pistol'; and another on the house of Henry Spence in Garvegort, between Ardara and Kilraine.[22] Spence may have been obnoxious to the Mollies for some time: in late 1853 John Breslin, a quarryman,

[21] CSORP 1856/16,473 Information of Patrick McGlynn...8 June 1856.
[22] CSORP 1856/16,473 Mountcharles, 14 June 1856, Further Information of Patrick Glynn [*sic*], Beagha. Hill was no stranger to such visits; at 2.00 a.m. on 7 May 1846 some fifty men, with their coats turned as a disguise, arrived at his house; they had come, they said, 'to give him a civil advice, not to serve any processes for Lady Anne Murray'; the investigating magistrate reported that 'they spoke in Irish which he understood and

of Liskerraghan had successfully sued him for unpaid wages due for raising slate.[23] And Hill, as a process server, made few friends. Unfortunately, however, no cause is assigned in extant correspondence for the raids on Hill, Scott, or Spence, and notwithstanding Spence's dispute with Breslin and Hill's job, the acquisition of weapons may have been their sole purpose. Moreover, while all three men were Protestants, no obvious sectarian animus moved the Ardara lodge. Indeed, Protestants too had recourse to it: again, an Ardara Ribbon leader, publican Patrick Friel, had been brought out to Meenagrillagh by the Protestant William McCready (and his friend, Alexander Burns, of Tullymore) to intimidate his father-in-law, James Arle, in 1855, and the lodge once proposed to rescue a horse belonging to Jack Boyd, presumably a Protestant, from the Ardara pound.

Crucially, these raids increased tensions in the lodge; or, rather, the weapons taken in the raids did. Guns were routinely passed to committee-men, who would make them available to members as the need arose. For instance, on the night of 1–2 May, when the police were lying in ambush in Beagh, the Mollies actually assembled behind McGlynn's house to attack Gallagher, but separated. (McGlynn, in a letter to Cruise, suggested that they dispersed because the police had been spotted leaving the Ardara Road, and word 'circulated' to that effect, but later claimed that it was on account of there being insufficient Mollies to raid the house.) That night, behind McGlynn's, Condy McHugh had Scott's 'large pistol'. It had been held by Barney Kelly, a publican and committeeman, who gave it to Neil Breslin who, in turn, had given it to McGlynn to bring out to Beagh for McHugh. Meanwhile, Con O'Donnell had a 'small pistol' and James O'Donnell of Tullycleave had Hill's gun; Matthew Sweeney brought a rod to ram it. A few days later, O'Donnell claimed that Hill's gun was 'stolen' from him by some fellow Mollies. Little John Breslin had to convene a special meeting in the backroom of Dorrian's on the fair day (15 May), when five members—Dan Boyle of 'Sand Hill' (perhaps an error for either Sandfield or Dooey), Matthew Sweeney of Beagh, Con O'Donnell and Jack O'Donnell of Tullycleave, and Patrick McNelis, alias White, of Ardara—denied the 'charge'. Breslin eventually got James O'Donnell himself to admit that he had lost the gun.

It is hard to lose a gun, harder still to lose a gun that requires a rod to ram it. Control of weapons was becoming a source of contention as the moderates tried to restrain the militants, and this contention was causing

---

disguised their voices; he saw them distinctly, but swears he did not know any of them'. See OP 1846/7/11,437 Glenties, 9 May 1846, Holmes to Under Secretary.

[23] IPSCR Ardara: 13 Dec. 1853.

unease. In his last letter to Cruise before naming the Mollies, McGlynn remarked that, 'I heard one of them say yesterday, that should he be taken about a gun he had lost (one of their stolen ones) he would swear on the whole lot.' It was an obvious reference to James O'Donnell of Tullycleave. But in the same letter, McGlynn also indicated that it was 'most likely' that, if arrested, the master (later identified in his information as Little John Breslin) would turn informer. And it would soon become apparent that he actually felt Condy McHugh was the most likely to give information. McGlynn, then, was not the only one growing disillusioned, and his own concern that some member of the troubled Society might inform on himself—a concern that had come to preoccupy him since he wrote the threatening letter on 9 March—had probably been incubating for many months, possibly since St Patrick's Night of the previous year, when the depth of the divisions between 'brothers' had become apparent in Neil O'Donnell's in Glenties.

MADGE CRAIG

Here, a puzzle remains. Why did the Mollies harbour such animosity for James Gallagher's wife? At the best of times, belonging to a family whose menfolk served as cess collectors and process servers would not have endeared Madge Craig to all people.[24] More immediately, a close connection, Neil Craig (1831–1909) of Kiltooris—almost certainly her younger brother—had recently killed a man. The killing, as was often the case with rural homicides, resulted from a row at a fair. On the evening of 1 November 1855, Roger O'Donnell of Drumboghill, near Kiltooris, left Ardara fair 'a little tipsy' to walk home. About a mile and a quarter outside the town, that is, in Tullycleave, adjacent to Beagh, Craig, riding his 'entire horse', overtook O'Donnell. An 'entire horse' is a stallion kept for breeding. Typically, fiery, more toned, and powerful than a gelding, and requiring special stabling if brought to town, lest mares excite it, such an animal was a status symbol. As Craig rode by, O'Donnell taunted him, calling, in Irish, 'What have you to say to Nicholson?' The import of the taunt is unclear. It later transpired that the wife of a man named Nicholson—who, being married, was likely a householder—was a 'friend' (relation) of O'Donnell, and that Craig had been 'scolding' with this man

[24] See *Strabane Morning News*, 3 May 1836 (Daniel Craig, Drumboghill), *LSnl*, 2 May 1851 (Thomas Craig, Kilclooneymore); DCA, GJ/1/43 Public Orders, Summer Assizes, 1861 (Thomas Craig, Kilclooneymore).

coming from the fair.[25] Now, Craig took umbrage at O'Donnell's comment and turned back. Without dismounting, the 24-year-old approached O'Donnell, and struck him with his loaded stallion whip. O'Donnell fell. 'The man is killed!', a bystander exclaimed. However, on checking his pulse, people found that 'there was life in him'. O'Donnell was then carried to a house at the side of the road, where he lingered 'insensible' for two days before succumbing.

Craig absconded after striking O'Donnell, and then, fearing a capital charge, he did not surrender when the man died. The Constabulary inserted Craig's description in the *Police Gazette; or, Hue-and-Cry*, a newspaper published every Tuesday and Friday and circulated to barracks across the country. His description first appeared on 9 November and the *Gazette* continued to carry an abbreviated notice for him into the New Year.[26] But there was no trace of Craig. Then, on 29 February, a detective arrested him, with a younger brother, John, aboard a steamer in Cork harbour, as it prepared to embark for London. Bizarrely, the detective had taken Craig to be a man wanted for the sensational murder, by Ribbonmen, of a Cavan landlord, Charlotte Hinds. Brought ashore, John fainted. When he came around, he and his brother were separated, searched, and questioned, and they gave contradictory stories. On Neil, who had given his name as McGlinchey, the detectives found fifteen sovereigns in a leather belt around his person, five sovereigns in his shirt, and eight sovereigns in the waistband of his trousers. On John, they found thirteen sovereigns. A sovereign had a face value of £1, meaning they were carrying over £40, and quizzed as to how they came to have such a considerable sum, both men identified themselves as sons of Donald (*aka* Daniel, Dónal) Craig, who, they said, had given them the gold coins.

The Craigs were remanded in custody, while a sub-constable was sent from Ardara to confirm their identities; the fellows' family, he remarked at the hearing, were 'in pretty comfortable circumstances, and they had always borne a good character'. The brothers were duly returned to Donegal on 5 March, and on 17 March Neil had stood trial for murder at the assizes in Lifford. Defended by Alexander Norman, he had entered a plea of not guilty. The trial had proceeded some length, with several witnesses having testified that Craig had delivered the fatal blow, when Galbraith Hamilton (1803–86) of Eden was called. Gilly, as he was known, was a hard-living middleman, holding a few townlands from the

[25] *GV* returns three Nicholson householders in the parish of Inishkeel—John Nicholson, Derryness (Carn), Michael Nicholson, Rosbeg, and Bridget Nicholson, Narin.
[26] *Police Gazette; or, Hue-And Cry*, 1 Jan. 1856. The issue carrying the full notice was not found.

Marquess of Conyngham; he was also agent for some small estates. Returning home from the fair, he had given O'Donnell, a neighbour, a ride in his car about a quarter of a mile outside the town and he had let him off in Tullycleave. Hamilton now clearly described how Craig had killed O'Donnell. However, he also affirmed that O'Donnell had been drunk; that he and Craig had been 'scolding' all the way from the town; and, crucially, that the deceased had been holding a little rod in his hand when he was struck and that he had called for a stick before falling. He gave Craig a good character too. He had known him 'since he was a child', he said, 'and both his family and himself are quite inoffensive'. And he allowed him the excuse of alcohol: 'I never saw the prisoner in liquor all my life, but I think he was a little under its influence that evening.' At this juncture, the defence attorney proposed that his client would withdraw his plea if the Crown would consent to the charge being reduced to manslaughter. The Crown consented, Craig entered a plea of guilty, the jury convicted him, and the assize judge, Robert Torrens, sentenced him to be imprisoned for twelve months, and kept to hard labour. Strikingly, another man convicted of the manslaughter of his wife at the same assizes got fifteen years' transportation, with the judge delivering a 'very impressive and solemn admonition about the awful crime of which he had been convicted'; he too had committed the offence when intoxicated.[27] Then, as now, sentences for manslaughter varied widely, and the distinction between manslaughter and murder was often lost on the public. And so it must have seemed to many people that O'Donnell's life had been weighed lightly at Lifford. Compounding matters, Torrens, then aged 81, had been one of a number of Irish judges described in parliament the previous year as incapacitated through age or infirmity, and on 29 March, less than two weeks after Craig's trial, he died at his home outside Draperstown, south Derry.[28]

The light sentence passed on O'Donnell's killer on 17 March meant the Craig family would have been the focus of heightened animosity when, 'after St Patrick's Day', Condy McHugh and William Maxwell told Patrick McGlynn in Fisher's waste house that Madge Craig should be beaten worse than her husband. Of course, resentment of the Craigs would have been particularly pointed among the dead man's own people. McGlynn's second statement, sworn when he was in protective custody,

---

[27] For the arrests, see *Dublin Evening Mail*, 3 Mar., 4 Mar. 1856; *Advocate*, 8 Mar. 1856; *Enniskillen Chronicle*, 6 Mar. 1856; *Southern Reporter*, 29 Feb., 6 Mar. 1856; and for the trial, see *BH*, 21 Mar. 1856; *Tyrone Constitution*, 21 Mar. 1856; *Ulsterman*, 21 Mar. 1856.
[28] *LJ*, 2 Apr. 1856.

identified Pat O'Donnell, a son of Roger, as a Molly Maguire, and
described how he had agreed to come out to Beagh for an attack on
Gallagher:

> I know Pat.k O'Donnell[,] son to the man that was killed. One of the nights
> that Golagher's house was to be attacked, Condy McHugh told me to tell all
> that I knew down strands to come up that night. I met Pat.k O'Donell[.]
> I told him that Condy McHugh told him to come to attack Golagher's
> house. He said he would. He said it rather in a hesitating way. I asked him
> again would he certainly come when he said 'when he took stuff from John
> Briesland that he told him he would never ask him to go out in consequence
> of his father being killed'. I said McHugh and I would watch for him when
> they would be attacking the house. He then said he would come.

This young man was not the only person of his surname in the local
Mollies. Also named as members of 'the body' by McGlynn were
Neil O'Donnell, master of the Glenties lodge; James, Jack, and Con
O'Donnell of Tullycleave; and Frank O'Donnell of Ardara, a sometime
chairman of the lodge. None of these men can be shown to have been
connections of the dead man. However, O'Donnell was not a common
surname west of the Owenea, which increases the probability that the
Tullycleave-men were related to the O'Donnells of Downstrands. Significantly too, Jack O'Donnell of Tullycleave had been involved in the
first raid on Gallagher; again, on 9 March, just before Craig's trial, he
had come with Matthew Sweeney to ask McGlynn to write the threatening letter, and he had been in the party that burst into Gallagher's
house and left it on the dresser.

Yet resentment of Madge Craig may have had a deeper source than the
killing of Roger O'Donnell. Her arrival in Beagh had been roughly
coincident with the squaring in 1839–41: her eldest children were born
in the early 1840s. Hence, her neighbours may have associated Madge not
simply with her husband's mistreatment of his father—first, displacing
him as tenant and, latterly, reducing him to 'begging'—but also with the
overthrow of rundale, and all that followed in the 'divided' townland, that
is, her husband's acquisition of the Mulherns' place, his hovering over the
hard-drinking Pat Kennedy and indebted Nancy Sweeney, and, most
recently, his proposed clearance of the Brogans, McCaffertys, Mooneys,
and O'Donnells.[29] And that Madge's own people, the Craigs, had long
since anticipated the spirit of a world in which each man was only

---

[29] Gallagher himself acknowledged that, when the Mollies raided his house on 9 Mar.,
they had warned him 'to be good to my father *and the neighbours* and not to dispossess
the cottiers' (emphasis added), see CRF G/22/1857 Informations of James Gallagher . . .
8 July 1856.

accountable for his own portion can only have sharpened animosity towards this *bean as baile isteach*, blow-in woman. She who had arrived a harbinger of change had become an everyday reminder of futures lost.

DIGGING FOR EVIDENCE

Neither the names of the men arrested in the early hours of Monday 9 June nor those of the men who had named them appeared in the press that month. But the names were known. And at firesides from the Tullies to the Glen of Glenties, and 'Down the Point' (Loughros), 'Downstrands' (Kilclooney to Rosbeg), and 'In Through' (Glencolumbkille), people wondered why one of the McGlynns of Glenties and one of the McHughs of Beagh should have turned informer. Carried by car-men, dealers, and tinkers, the names then became known beyond west Donegal, and a rumour now ran the roads into Derry, Strabane, Omagh, Enniskillen, and Sligo, that Daniel Cruise was in possession of a list of all the members of the organization in the north-west, and men left home, lay low, and made arrangements to leave the country.

Cruise was initially smug. He had two extensive statements from the prime informer, McGlynn, and another corroborating those 'informations' from McHugh. And he himself had heard the rumour that he had an extensive list of members. The arrests, he assured Dublin Castle, would be 'of incalculable advantage to this county as I expect it will completely break up the ribbon system in it'.[30] Senior officials were circumspect, however. On 14 June, Thomas Larcom, the Under Secretary, reviewed Cruise's long report on the investigation and arrests, and his request for permission to support McGlynn. He immediately detected a problem. An effort to arrest Molly Maguires in the act of committing an 'outrage' had turned into something radically different, for McGlynn was now an accomplice turning on his associates and, with a few exceptions, he did not implicate them in anything other than membership of a secret society.

Larcom's response to Cruise was abrupt: 'As no act of outrage appears to have been committed by any of the parties arrested and as both McGlynn and McHugh are in the position of accomplices... no effective prosecution can take place untill corroborative evidence be obtained. To that point, accordingly, Mr Cruise's attention must be directed & he must proceed with great caution & discrimination...' Larcom expressed himself poorly: administering oaths—the focus of McGlynn's first statement—was an 'outrage'. But it was clear what he meant: McGlynn had not shown those involved in the criminal conspiracy to be responsible for any violent act. At this stage, Larcom had not received a copy of McGlynn's second statement, the very taking of which, on 14 June, indicated that Cruise had independently come to grasp that he had not built a strong case. In that second statement, clearly prompted by the magistrate, McGlynn identified several men whom he had seen with weapons, claiming inter alia that Neil Breslin had given him a large pistol to take out to Beagh to Condy McHugh; and he had been present when Breslin got the pistol from 'Barney [Kelly] the publican'. These men could be charged with possession of arms in a proclaimed district. But much of this second statement was tittle-tattle that did little to tighten evidential screws with respect to specific charges: a judge might dismiss many of McGlynn's claims as hearsay.

Cruise was called to Dublin. There, on Friday 20 June, he met with Larcom and Thomas FitzGerald, the crown solicitor for Donegal, to discuss the best course to pursue. Fitzgerald was new to the job, the previous incumbent having died in May,[31] and Cruise remained in Dublin for the next week, working in FitzGerald's office on Fleet Street, to help to prepare several cases for the attorney general and his deputy, the solicitor general, who would advise on how to proceed at the assizes. A day before his arrival, John D. FitzGerald, the attorney general, had carefully reviewed the file on 'the Ribbon case', including McGlynn's second information and that of McHugh. He had written an opinion on it before passing it to John Christian, the solicitor general, who read it on Saturday 21 June.

Cruise received the file with their opinions early the following week. The attorney general was blunt. The case did not have a 'satisfactory appearance'. McGlynn and McHugh were accomplices, and their evidence was subject to the ordinary rule requiring some corroboration of their testimony in respect of the material facts. No books, written passwords, or other documents had been captured, nor were the prisoners taken at any meeting or in the prosecution of any overt act. 'If all with one exception turned approvers', he remarked sniffily, 'the case as against the remaining one would be still without corroboration. . . . The last meeting of the Society at which some of the prisoners were present was on the 17th of March 1855 (15 months since) and it does not appear to have been followed by any overt act, by any crime or outrage traceable to the conspiracy and, against some of the parties named, the whole case seems to

---

[31] *BH*, 16 May 1856.

be that they were present at Fishers' of Ardara and paid 6d. each.' The problem, as the attorney general saw it, was simple: 'It is most desirable indeed to bring the leaders of the Ribbon Society of Donegal within reach of the arm of the law, but an indiscreet and unsuccessful attempt may be productive of much mischief.' As it stood, the prisoners should be released on bail, to stand trial at the assizes now scheduled for mid- to late July, and Cruise should use the interval to 'supply the defects in evidence' and 'test the story told [by McGlynn and McHugh] so as to ascertain its truthfulness'. Christian, the solicitor general, fully concurred that the case was 'wholly without corroboration', and questioned the credibility of the schoolmaster. McGlynn had repeatedly assured Cruise that Mollies would be taken in the commission of an outrage, but on none of the four nights that the Constabulary lay in wait at Gallagher's did any outrage take place. There was not, at present, evidence upon which any of the accused could be put on trial with any prospect of conviction. The prisoners should be bailed, and Cruise, as the attorney general had directed, should build a better case.

By the time he had received this rap on the knuckles, Cruise had got word from Donegal that the prisoners' attorneys intended making an application to the Court of Queen's Bench to have them admitted to bail. Cruise immediately wrote to the governor of Lifford Gaol, asking him to tell the prisoners that he, Cruise, had received government sanction for bail. It was a ruse intended to deny the Mollies the satisfaction of knowing that they were being released against his wishes. Leaving Dublin on 27 June, Cruise went north to Lifford. The informations against the prisoners were to be read to them in the presence of the two informers. For this purpose, the Constabulary hired a car to take McGlynn under escort from Donegal to Lifford Gaol on 28 June. After the statements were read, Cruise swore McGlynn, and told the prisoners, who were now over two weeks in custody, that they could ask him any question they liked. To a man, they said that they had nothing to ask him. McHugh, who had entered the room laughing, refused to take 'the holy evangelists' from Cruise and he made 'signs' to the prisoners indicating that he would not testify against them. When Cruise reminded him that he had sworn to stand over his information in court, McHugh laughed and put out his tongue; 'No matter what I did', he said, 'I will not support it now.'[32] Cruise had lost one informer. His case against all but one man now rested entirely on the uncorroborated statement of an accomplice, Patrick

---

[32] *LSnl*, 13 Mar. 1857.

McGlynn. That man was Cormac Gillespie of Mountcharles, against whom Cruise had additional evidence, a threatening letter. None of the men in custody had their bail ready, but they gave Cruise a list of sureties. Cruise appointed Wednesday 9 July as the day on which he would receive bail in Glenties. He intended continuing onto Lifford that same day to be present when the men were let out, reinforcing the impression that he had no objection to their release. However, on Tuesday 8 July, he received news that gave him grounds to deny bail. Paddy McRoarty of Tievachorky, a man in his mid-fifties, was close to death from the effects of a beating by Molly Maguires at the end of February. If, believing he was dying, McRoarty would now name the men who had beaten him, Cruise might land another blow on the Ribbon Society. But he had little time. The assizes were to open in little over a week.

A DYING DECLARATION

Tievachorky, where Paddy McRoarty lay dying, is midway between Mountcharles and Glenties. The ruins of his house are still there, a few hundred yards off the most travelled road into west Donegal. It is the road along which the Constabulary had marched the men arrested on McGlynn's information on 10 June, when transferring them from Glenties to Lifford via Donegal Town. Indeed, the house was visible from the road, for Tievachorky forms part of the southern slope of Binn Bhán. The mountain rises only to 453 metres, yet it offers clear lines of sight across the highlands of Donegal, Sligo, and North Mayo, and, for that reason, the Royal Engineers had erected a triangulation station on its summit when mapping the district for the Ordnance Survey in the 1830s.

The resulting map was that which Robert Russell's surveyors had used when they began resetting the Conyngham estate in 1837. Like Beagh, Tievachorky was part of that estate, and Paddy McRoarty, like James Gallagher, lived in its best homestead (15s. valuation for the houses and offices), on a holding that accounted for the lion's share of its acreage; it comprised almost half the land (124 of 278 acres), the rest being held by two families. And McRoarty too was a cattleman. The cause ultimately assigned for the attack on McRoarty was his refusal to compensate the owners of sheep and geese that his dog had killed. However, a vacant house on McRoarty's lot in 1855 suggests that he may have recently expanded his holding or that he had recently got rid of a subtenant. Either action might have generated acrimony. So too may the dismantlement of rundale. Here, that process had been accompanied by greater discontinuity in landholding than in Beagh. Notably, nobody named McRoarty had any cow's grass in the then undivided townland when it was applotted for tithe in 1825; and of four families—Kelly, Kenny, Davitt, and Tolan—who did, only the Tolans were still represented there by a householder in the mid-1850s, and two new families, those of McRoarty and James Thomas, had been established.[33] A partial transcription of McRoarty's 1851 Census return—made when his daughter Ellen applied for a pension in 1920—sheds light on this discontinuity. It shows McRoarty's household to have then comprised himself and his wife, Mary (née Breslin), for whom no ages are given in the transcript, eight children—Ellen (b. 1850), Mary (*c.*1836), Bridget (*c.*1848), George (*c.*1840), Kate (*c.*1849), Marg[aret] (*c.*1843), Pat (*c.*1845), and John (*c.*1848)—and 'Nancy Dermmot, half sister'. Nancy is the first listed, but no age is given for her. If 'half-sister' refers to her relationship to the pension applicant, then Paddy's wife had been widowed before her marriage to him in 1831, a date provided in the transcript; and if she had retained possession of her first husband's holding, McRoarty's 'right' to it may well have been contentious, or at least resented by the 'Dermmot' family (possibly a misreading of [Mc]Devitt/Davitt). Alternatively, if 'half sister' refers to Nancy's relationship to Paddy, the householder, then it was his father who had married twice, which, for the same reason, may have been a source of trouble.[34]

Such deeper causes of resentment are nowhere noticed in official correspondence, but McRoarty being an interloper who had prospered at the expense of neighbours would go some way to explaining the viciousness of the attack upon him. Moreover, the 'unmerciful' attack itself hints at the fate which McGlynn had spared James Gallagher, and it gives credence too to the master's own surmise that if the Mollies had beaten the weak Beagh-man that they would likely have killed him.[35] Between 1.00 and 2.00 a.m. on the morning of Wednesday 27 February, a number of men had surrounded McRoarty's house, throwing stones at the doors and windows, front and rear. McRoarty had shouted that if they had anything against him, they would get it and they should not break his house. But the men continued firing stones. At length, he opened the back door. The attackers, who had guns and pistols, now burst inside, knocked him down, and beat him. They then lifted him to his feet, lit candles, and asked if he knew them and if he would know them if he saw them again. McRoarty tried to look at one of them, and was struck with a whip across the head and knocked down a second time. He was then hauled down to 'the room', meaning the bedroom, the most likely place for money or

[33] TAB Inver: Tivehurkey [*sic*]; PB: Tievachorky; *GV*: Tievachorky.
[34] CSF S/7/184 [1851].
[35] CSORP 1856/16,473 Beigha, 22 Apr. 1856, McGlynn to Cruise.

weapons to be concealed. There, the raiders told him that they had been brought twenty miles to his house, and that he should give them £2 to carry them home. At this, one of them said he would not take less than 50s. (£2 10s.). McRoarty opened a press and gave them three notes. By now, he was 'nearly blinded', presumably by blood from head wounds and swollen eyes, and the attackers were 'ill-treating' his wife, demanding to know where their son, a teenager, was hiding. They poked under beds, gave a servant girl a 'punch of a stick' in the stomach, smashed the family's milk vessels, and spilled all their milk. When McRoarty's dog attacked them, they shot it dead, and fired several other shots in the crowded house. 'Your husband is now nearly dead', they told his wife; 'and the son would get as much as he got.' At length, the men found the boy and stretched him on the kitchen floor; his mother threw herself across him to protect him, and it was only the intervention of one of the attackers that prevented the others from inflicting serious harm on the two of them. The house now wrecked and McRoarty severely beaten, the men menacingly told him to be a 'good neighbour' and left. One of them then suddenly appeared at a window, saying that if it were not shut, they would shoot all inside and, after firing more shots, the Mollies slipped away.[36]

A well-to-do cattleman from Tievachorky would have bought and sold animals at fairs and markets in Inver, Mountcharles, and Donegal Town, to the south and east, and in Glenties and Ardara, to the north and west, and so the attack now reverberated across a wide area. Indeed, a century later, when the McRoartys were long gone from Tievachorky, old people could remember hearing from their parents what the priest had said in the chapel in Frosses in the wake of the attack. It had been a terrible thing, he had said, to stand ankle-deep in blood and milk mixed together, and he had asked the people to pray that they never saw the like of it again.[37] McRoarty had been attacked little over a week before the raid on James Gallagher's house when the threatening letter penned by McGlynn had been left on the dresser: the master had got himself deeper into the Mollies at a moment when clerical and Constabulary resolve was stiffening against them.

•

Cruise had taken a statement from McRoarty on Saturday 1 March, three days after the attack. Then, the battered man had insisted that, although

[36] CSORP 1856/18,243 Information of Pat[ric]k McRoarty, Tievachorkey..., 1 Mar. 1856.
[37] See e.g. NFCM 1,579: 423–4 Séamas Mac Amhlaigh, aged 83, Na Saileasaí, May 1962.

candles were lit and the attackers had not concealed their faces, 'they were strangers to me'. Cruise had not believed him. He thought that he knew his attackers, but was afraid to name them. And so on 8 July, he called on McRoarty again, hoping to take a 'dying declaration' from him.

A 'dying declaration' has a precise meaning in law. It is a statement in which a person, believing him or herself to be dying, names the person or persons responsible for his or her apprehended death. Provided that it includes a clear affirmation of the individual's conviction that death is imminent, it makes admissible evidence of a statement that might otherwise be dismissed as hearsay. It is evidence too that juries tend to take seriously, for it comes freighted with the superstitious notion that a person will not risk damnation by telling a grievous lie without an opportunity to confess. If McRoarty would name his attackers for Cruise, his statement would carry great weight in the event that those named were ever brought to trial.

'I am sure I will not recover', McRoarty began, providing the words necessary to make his statement admissible in court; 'I have no expectation I will; I am sure it was the beating and ill usage I got from the [Ribbonmen] the night they came to my house last February that has brought me to this.' The men who caused the Ribbonmen to be brought to his house were Pat Thomas and James Coyle. (Thomas was a neighbour in Tievachorky, a son of James Thomas, and Coyle a publican, in the adjacent townland of Tullinalough.) Manus Byrne of Dubbin had warned him, he said, that the Ribbonmen would come for him because he had not compensated Thomas and Coyle for sheep and geese which, they said, his dog had killed. The two of them had been in Neil O'Donnell's public house in Glenties on the night that he was beaten; Priest Gallagher had seen them leave it. And Neil O'Donnell himself was one of the men who had come to his house that night. 'He had a striped waistcoat on', he now remembered of the publican, 'he beat me very much; there was a man next him who had a whip, he beat me severely with it.' Also there, he said, was Andy O'Donnell, whose mother was a sister of Pat Thomas. O'Donnell had since gone to Scotland. And he thought that 'the two Sweeneys and White from Ardara' were there too, but he was only 'sure' of the O'Donnells. 'The day I swore the informations', he told Cruise, referring to the statement he made three days after the attack, 'I would have told you this and more but I knew they would take my life if I did and I hope God will forgive me for not telling then.' Death was near now. 'I forgive them', he told Cruise, 'as I expect to be forgiven by Almighty God.'

That night, Neil O'Donnell was in Lifford, where he and the other twenty-six prisoners were expecting to be released on bail the following day. The 'dying declaration' that Cruise had taken in Tievachorky now raised the distinct prospect of a murder charge against him, if Paddy McRoarty died. Also among the prisoners in Lifford was a baker, Patrick White (alias McNelis) of Ardara, and Thomas Sweeney of Altnagapple, identified by McGlynn as a committeeman, and his brother John Sweeney and also John Sweeney of Ardara, and Matthew Sweeney of Beagh. McRoarty had not clearly identified which two Sweeneys he had in mind, but his phrasing points to the Altnagapple brothers. Still, McRoarty not having been 'sure' that the Sweeneys and White had been in his house meant that, if he died, additional evidence would be required for the charge against them to be raised to murder.

McRoarty's son was confident that he would recognize the attackers again, and Cruise would have taken 'the boy' to Lifford that night, but his father, convinced he was dying, did not want him to go. 'I am not sure I will be alive tomorrow night', McRoarty told Cruise. Having got what he wanted, the magistrate left Tievachorky determined not to take bail for any of the men in Lifford until young McRoarty had a chance to see them.[38]

EXHUMATION

Paddy McRoarty died on 9 July, the day after making his 'dying declaration' and he was buried in Frosses. Cruise was busy in the days between his death and burial. In Donegal Town, he interviewed McGlynn again, to see if he knew anything of the attack in Tievachorky, and in Glenties and Ardara, he had everybody whose house had been raided by the Mollies brought before him and examined on oath. He got nothing of substance. He had then gone north to Church Hill, near Letterkenny, to preside at the petty sessions. A letter from Dublin was waiting for him on his return to Wood Lodge. It included express instructions from the attorney general, that, in the event of McRoarty dying, a medical man was to attend at a coroner's inquest on his body, that is, a hearing to determine whether or not the deceased had died by natural or unnatural causes. Although there had been a coroner's inquest, no doctor had attended. Consequently, on 17 July, Cruise took Dr Samuel Smyth of Mountcharles and some constables to Frosses. There, he paid two men 4s. to exhume McRoarty's body, and Smyth then performed a post-mortem examination.[39]

---

[38] CSORP 1856/18,243 Dying Declaration of Pat[ric]k McRoarty, 8 July 1856; Donegal, 9 July 1856, Cruise to Larcom.
[39] CSORP 1856/18,243 Donegal, 28 July 1856, Cruise to Larcom.

Coroner's inquests were unpopular, and post-mortems even more so. One was considered an unnecessary intrusion in the grief of the bereaved and the other seen as akin to interference with a corpse. For instance, in nearby Mountcharles, about 11.00 a.m. on 11 March 1858, a bed-ridden woman named Margaret Brogan was left unattended by her daughter, who tied the door of the house on the outside, so that the 80-year-old would not wander. The woman rose about midday and sat by the hearth; her clothes caught fire and she was severely burned, dying several hours later. A constable was unable to prevent the body being removed for burial and the coroner reported that 'the priests and the people were quite opposed to inquests and would not allow them to be held if they could'.[40] In McRoarty's case, the post-mortem was conducted without incident, but the examination was inconclusive. Smyth found that 'that all the leading organs which would cause death by disease were in healthy condition with the exception of the brain which was in a decomposed state'. But he did not say that McRoarty had died as a result of the beating four months earlier. It was, Cruise reported, a 'negative sort of evidence'. McRoarty's widow and son were prepared to testify that he had never recovered from the beating, but when the doctor had not sworn that death had resulted from the beating a jury would be unlikely to capitally convict O'Donnell. Indeed, a judge might very well dismiss the murder charge.[41]

Smyth had only graduated from Glasgow in 1854 and he was still in his mid-twenties. Youth and inexperience might explain his failure to give Cruise the statement he needed. But it is possible too that the young man had shrewdly avoided becoming a key witness in a case that might result in a man being hanged for murder. A few months later, in January 1857, Smyth would marry Isabella Scott, daughter of the Mountcharles post-master.[42] Curiously, her brother, William Scott, had an involvement in the Ribbon case, for he would post bail that summer for Cormac Gillespie, the schoolmaster charged with writing a threatening letter. Mountcharles was a small village, and the doctor and the postmaster's family had nothing to gain by antagonizing their neighbours.

O'Donnell remained in Cruise's sights and the names which McRoarty had mentioned on his deathbed might yet be used to pry information. Time was running out, however. The 'Ribbon Case'—much anticipated since the arrests in June—was to be called at the assizes in a few days' time.

[40] CSORP 1858/12,717 Ballyshannon, 13 Mar. 1858, Crawford to Eglinton. See also the opposition given to a coroner in Killygarvan: CSORP 1858/13,696 Buncrana, 25 Apr. 1858, Considine to Larcom.
[41] CSORP 1856/18,243 Donegal, 12 Aug. 1856, Cruise to Larcom.
[42] GRO, Donegal, Marriages 1857/1/4/591.

Indeed, on 18 July, the day after the post-mortem in Frosses, McGlynn and his family were taken in a car from Donegal to Lifford, so that he would be available to give evidence.[43] O'Donnell was now charged with the murder of McRoarty, and his capital trial added to the list of cases. Still, the possibility of the Glenties publican being convicted had faded with the post-mortem. Also, with McHugh having refused to stand over his statement, the case against the other men was, at best, fragile. Cruise had erred in rushing to arrest the men on the uncorroborated evidence of an accomplice. There was now a strong likelihood that, if brought to trial, all the men named by McGlynn would be acquitted.

[43] CSORP 1856/19,443.

6

Judges and Appearances

As I passed through the titular capital of Donegal the other day, the withered town of Lifford, dead as Herculaneum or Pompeii, I thought it was a significant type of what the exterminators would make of all Ireland if we failed to arrest them. There was the enormous gaol, the stately courthouse, a palace for the police, lodgings for my lords the judges, the messrooms of their worships the grand jury: but not a human creature on the streets, not a pulse of industry—nothing but the grim silent castles of authority and the miserable cabins of the poor. And this is our fate—to have nothing left of this ancient nation, but a herd of miserable peasants, and their hard task masters, if we cannot save ourselves.

Charles Gavan Duffy[1]

It was the state that gave what life it had to Lifford. 'The chief part of the town', a visitor once remarked, 'is composed of the gaol and courthouse. It has no trade, and little market; and is, in fact, but nominally the county town; for although the assizes are held in it, the neighbouring town of Strabane, though in another county, reaps all the benefit of them.'[2] Tellingly, Lifford had only five public houses in 1856, when Ardara had sixteen.[3] Still, the three storeys of black stone that dominated this otherwise inconsequential town loomed large in the minds of people who had never seen the place. From the mid-eighteenth century, judges had come to prefer imprisonment to corporal and capital punishment and transportation when sentencing people for minor offences. And, from the 1830s,

---

[1] From a speech at Ennis, recalling Lifford, through which Duffy had passed en route to a Tenant Right meeting at Letterkenny in Oct. 1850, in *The League of North and South: An Episode in Irish History, 1850–1854* (London, 1886), 95.

[2] Henry D. Inglis, *A Journey throughout Ireland, During the Spring, Summer and Autumn of 1834*, 2 vols. (London, 1834), ii. 188–9. People in north Donegal had long resented Lifford being the county town. Indeed, in 1856, William Hunter (1773–1860), a Letterkenny merchant, circulated a printed letter, protesting at the 'absurdity and the ridiculousness' of key facilities being in 'the very extremity of the county'; see CSORP 1856/16,573.

[3] CSORP 1856/16,476 Lifford, 10 July 1856, Knox and Humphrey to Larcom.

when the Constabulary and petty sessions courts were more efficiently
organized, a spell in the county gaol, erected in 1793 and refurbished in
the early 1820s,[4] became the typical sentence for breaches of the peace
(brawling at fairs), revenue laws (*poitín*-making), and fisheries acts (poaching). Indeed, at least one man arrested on the word of Patrick McGlynn
had recently seen the inside of the place where he was now incarcerated. In
January 1853, William Maxwell, the shoemaker identified by McGlynn as
chairman of the Ardara lodge, had been convicted at the petty sessions of
an assault. The judge had given him the choice of paying a fine of £5 and
costs of 1s. 6d. or doing two months' hard labour: it would have taken a
lot of shoes to make £5 1s. 6d. profit, and so Maxwell had opted for the
custodial sentence. In fact, Maxwell had already served two other sentences in Lifford, both also for assault—two months' hard labour in 1844
and four months' hard labour in 1850. His character was 'indifferent',
Head Constable Thomas Wiley reported to the County Inspector, 'being
much addicted to drunkenness and loose company'. He was 'good when
sober', another report concluded, 'but apt to drink & then quarrelsome'.[5]

The steady flow of petty offenders, like Maxwell, in and out of the
gloomy castellated building meant tall tales of short sentences were
common. Former convicts used to talk of how, for good behaviour in
Lifford, they 'got into "grace" with the turnkeys after some time, and . . .
got to be promoted to be boiler attendants and assistants at the making of
stirabout and having the distribution of it by means of a long handled ladel
[*sic*], also getting light jobs to do about the governor's house'. And they
told yarns too of 'the devices used in getting in pieces of tobacco', or, not
getting the contraband, of how they had been reduced to chewing 'pieces
of leather, the same being taken from inside the heels of their soles, for
the "bacca"'.[6] Lifford was also the stuff of fireside tales about celebrity
prisoners, notably James Napper Tandy, the republican leader who spent
nearly two years there in the early 1800s, and the various hangings at its
entrance. Ironically, in summer 1856, when the men arrested on the
information of Patrick McGlynn were in Lifford, the last prisoner to
have been hanged there was Sam Crummer of Summy, executed in
1847 for the murder of his father. Crummer would have been well
known to many of the Ardara men who had been arrested, and his fate
very much in the mind of Neil O'Donnell now facing trial for murder.

[4] Rowan, *North-West Ulster*, 348–9.
[5] IPSCR Ardara: 11 Jan. 1853; CRF G/22/1857 Glenties, 25 Sept. 1857, Wiley to
Anderson; CRF M/36/1857 Information Required in the Case of the Prisoner [William
Maxwell] . . . 12 Sept. 1857, details the three convictions.
[6] Dorian, *Outer Edge*, 170–1.

In 1856 there were over 400 committals to Lifford, with a daily average prison population of some seventy inmates—sixty men and ten women.[7] Still, in June and July, with the assizes imminent, the number in the gaol would have been greater than usual, with many people in custody awaiting trial. If monotonous, the prison regime was not onerous for these 'untried prisoners'. They did not have to wear a uniform, they were not under the 'rule of silence', that is, forbidden to speak to each other, and they were not required to labour. They were also supposed to be kept apart from the convicts. That rule was not rigorously enforced, but, in this instance, it would have been wise to do so, for among the convicts was Neil Craig of Kiltooris, serving his one-year sentence for the manslaughter of Roger O'Donnell the previous November, and the untried prisoners included three O'Donnells from Tullycleave.

•

To the right of the county gaol was the courthouse. An older (1746), more architecturally accomplished building, its basement had been the gaol down to the 1790s.[8] The assizes, held here twice a year, in spring and summer, had both governmental and legal dimensions. First, the grand jury met and ratified a series of 'presentments', allocating funds for the upkeep of roads and buildings and the employment of officials. Then the assize judge, travelling on a 'circuit' that included Fermanagh, Derry, and Tyrone, would arrive in town with a military escort, and open legal proceedings, in which he presided at civil and criminal trials. Usually lasting several days and sometimes a week or more, the assizes had been occasions for balls, dinners, and meetings of the Donegal Hunt in the eighteenth century. Although less of an event in the 1850s, the assizes were still important dates on the gentry calendar and they brought large numbers of people to town even if, at night, much of the fun was in the taverns and inns of Strabane.

The judge on the north-west circuit that summer was Chief Justice James Henry Monahan. A native of Eyrecourt, County Galway, Monahan, like Cruise, was a Catholic. In fact, they knew each other of old, their paths having crossed when Monahan had been a young barrister working

---

[7] *Thirty-Fifth Report... Prisons of Ireland, 1856*, appendix, 24–31. Typically, the vast majority of inmates, about fifty prisoners, were people who had been summarily convicted at petty sessions for 'minor misdemeanours'; only about ten had been convicted for serious offences by juries at the assizes or quarter sessions, with the remainder being 'dangerous lunatics'.

[8] C. E. B. Brett, *Court Houses and Market Houses of the Province of Ulster* (Belfast, 1973), 60–1; Rowan, *North-West Ulster*, 348.

the Connacht circuit and Cruise a resident magistrate in Mayo. In those years, Monahan, having been called to the bar in 1838, had been establishing himself as one of the most gifted lawyers of his generation. Edward Sugden, the Tory Lord Chancellor of Ireland (1841–6), believed that he had no superior at either the Irish or English bar.[9] And the Whigs agreed: on the collapse of Peel's administration in 1846, Lord John Russell had appointed him solicitor general. He became attorney general the following year, and in 1850 he took a seat in the Court of Common Pleas. His rise had been rapid and, with government then appointing more Catholics to high office, it was unfairly ascribed by Tories to his religion. Radicals, meanwhile, represented Monahan as the 'Castle Catholic' par excellence, suggesting that he overcompensated for his advancement by erring on the side of the Crown; specifically, they accused him, when attorney general in 1848, of having allowed sectarian jury-packing in the 'treason felony' trials of William Smith O'Brien, Thomas Francis Meagher, and John Mitchel.[10]

A reputation for severity meant that Monahan was not a man whom the defence attorneys wanted to see on the bench in Lifford. Still, the loss of McHugh had undermined the prosecution's case, and the twenty-six prisoners and their lawyers were cognizant of that development. The Crown, meanwhile, was considering a postponement. As early as 13 July, John FitzGerald, the attorney general, had suggested that it might be necessary to delay bringing the men to trial so that additional evidence could be found connecting individuals to specific outrages. He did not normally approve of postponements, FitzGerald emphasized, but he was prepared to make an exception, as the case was of such 'great importance to the public' and, 'if properly followed up', it might lead to 'the breaking up of the conspiracy which exists in the district'.[11]

The assizes opened at 10 o'clock on the morning of Tuesday 22 July. Escorted by the High Sheriff, Monahan had entered court wearing a full-bottomed wig and scarlet robes with ermine trim.[12] Five cases were heard that day. None was particularly sensational: an attempt to obtain money under false pretences from the rector of Stranorlar; the sending of a threatening letter to a doctor in the Rosses; an effort to defeat the ends of justice by giving a false name at petty sessions; assault; and perjury and concealment of birth. The following morning, when the case of Cormac

[9] Oliver J. Burke, *Anecdotes of the Connaught Circuit, from its Foundation in 1604 to Close upon the Present Time* (Dublin, 1885), 309–12.
[10] Desmond McCabe, 'James Henry Monahan', in *DIB*.
[11] See FitzGerald's memorandum on CSORP 1856/18,243 Donegal, 9 July 1856, Cruise to Larcom.
[12] Vaughan, *Murder Trials*, 90.

Gillespie for sending a threatening letter was called, his attorney immediately applied for a postponement, on the grounds that sufficient notice of trial had not been given. Monahan acceded to the request, and he granted an application for bail. By now, the Crown had decided to take the advice of the attorney general and apply for a postponement in the other cases. And so, when the 'Ribbon Case' was called, James Major QC asked that the trial be put off. Monahan agreed to the postponement, and, with the consent of the Crown, the men were allowed to stand on bail until the next assizes. Major also asked that the trial of Neil O'Donnell for murdering McRoarty, be postponed to allow fresh evidence to be obtained. O'Donnell's attorney was John McCrossan (1822–64) of Omagh, a ubiquitous defence lawyer on the north-west circuit, who was also acting for the prisoners who had just been bailed. He immediately applied for bail for his client. Monahan said that, having read the information against O'Donnell, it was a case in which bail might be accepted, 'if the amount was sufficient and the securities solvent': 'Let the prisoner give security, himself in £100, and two sureties in £50 each.'

James P. Hamilton (1819–92), another barrister, then sought bail for Condy McHugh. There followed some confusion, with McCrossan saying that he acted for him.

'Has he instructed you?', Monahan asked.

'Not personally, but his brother has been with me', McCrossan replied, referring to either John or Nahor.

'His wife has been with me, my lord', countered Hamilton who lived at Mossvill, about five miles north-west of Beagh. Hamilton would have frequently travelled through the townland en route to and from Ardara, and, a farmer as well as a barrister, he knew several of those involved in the case, most especially James Gallagher.[13] 'I know every man and woman within a ten mile radius of where I live in Donegal, without regard to their station in life', he would boast to a parliamentary inquiry into the Irish jury system in 1874; 'I know their modes of thought and habits.'[14]

'Go to the prisoner now, sir', Monahan directed Hamilton, 'and see what reason he can urge for his discharge.'

Hamilton consulted with McHugh. The judge, meanwhile, asked for his sworn statement. He then gave it to Hamilton, saying 'Read what he has to say for himself in his information.' Hamilton proceeded to read

[13] *Ulsterman*, 28 July 1856. On Hamilton's career, see *Irish Law Times and Solicitor's Journal*, 23 July 1892.

[14] *Report from the Select Committee on Jury System (Ireland)*..., HC 1874 (244), ix, Minutes of Evidence, 5, 12. See too his evidence to *First, Second and Special Reports from the Select Committee of the House of Commons (in 1873) on Juries (Ireland)*, HC 1873 (283), xv, Minutes of Evidence, 63–89.

McHugh's statement, detailing his attendance at various meetings of Ribbonmen.

'Oh!', exclaimed Monahan, feigning surprise, 'He confesses himself guilty of a transportable offence. I'll try him on his own information.'

'There is nothing against him more than the others', objected Hamilton, 'And you have admitted them to bail.'

'Nothing but his own confession, on which I have a good mind to transport him.'

Hamilton persisted, saying that McHugh had sworn his statement under a promise that it would not be used against him. However that might be, the Chief Justice responded, it was proper that, in considering whether to bail McHugh, the court weigh his sworn statement, in which he admitted he was guilty of a transportable offence. He asked the Crown to consider whether it wished McHugh go to trial at the next assizes on his own statement and the evidence of Patrick McGlynn, and he denied bail.[15]

It had been a revealing exchange: in six weeks in custody, McHugh had not been allowed access to an attorney and his young wife and his brother had disagreed on who should represent him, a local Protestant barrister or a Ribbon-favoured Catholic lawyer. And now, in remanding him to the next assizes, Monahan stipulated that he could only consult with Hamilton, the lawyer engaged by his wife, in the presence of the governor of Lifford Gaol.[16]

•

On the last day of the assizes, Daniel Cruise received a warm encomium from the grand jury. Sir James Stewart, its chairman, read him a letter, signed by twenty-two justices of the peace, noticing 'the extraordinary exertions you have made and the trouble you have taken to bring to justice the leading members of the Ribbon Society, a society which strikes at the root of the peace and prosperity of the County generally and must be ruinous to the welfare of those connected with it'.[17] The backslapping was premature. Although the arrest of so many men had undoubtedly discomfited the Ribbon Society, the case against the suspects was poor; indeed, with the exception of Condy McHugh, all the arrested men, including the alleged murderer Neil O'Donnell, were going home. And Cruise had additional bother. In the course of the assizes, priests had been

[15] *BN*, 26 July 1856; *Ulsterman*, 28 July 1856; *LJ*, 30 July 1856; *BH*, 1 Aug. 1856. The *Ulsterman's* article represents Ribbonmen as being 'at war' with their church, and living in terror of an 'impenitent death'.

[16] *LJ*, 30 July 1856.

[17] CSORP 1856/18,243 Lifford, 22 July 1856, Style et al. to Cruise, enclosure in Donegal, 28 July 1856, Cruise to Larcom.

coming to him, wanting 'to know what was to become of the people'. They were concerned not only about the men named by McGlynn, but also about others who, crediting the rumour that Cruise had a list of all the Society's members, were now fearful of arrest. Men were afraid to remain in their houses, the priests were saying. Some men, they said, were about to quit the country. Cruise, for his part, believed that 'the greater part of the people here through fear and intimidation joined this society and are now anxious for a way to get out of it'. The priests, who shared that view, now raised the idea of an amnesty for all local Ribbonmen, not just those arrested on McGlynn's information. Essentially, they were proposing that 'if all the people connected with this society came in and expressed their regret for it, had their names enrolled and took the oath of allegiance to Her Majesty' that they might avoid prosecution.[18]

If it was an extraordinary proposal, it was not entirely without precedent. An amnesty for members of seditious societies had been offered in the late 1790s, when the country was under martial law: then, United Irishmen who surrendered and took the oath of allegiance were released without charge. And more recently, in 1839–40, judges had interpreted the Unlawful Societies (Ireland) Act (1839) to have an element of an amnesty to it, that is, 'to pardon the past as an encouragement to the abandonment of the [unlawful] society for the future': unless the Crown could connect the accused to an offence committed after 1 September 1839, it would not pursue a prosecution for membership of a combination bound by an unlawful oath.[19]

Now, the assizes over, Cruise met privately with Monahan to seek his advice on the priests' proposal. The Chief Justice thought it worth pursuing. Cruise then mentioned·it to the grand jury, and its members 'unanimously' supported the idea. However, when he floated the idea to Dublin Castle, the attorney general vetoed it. He could not approve, he wrote in early August, of people being induced to take the oath of allegiance on the 'false notion that there was a charge against them'. Moreover, if men who took the terms of this amnesty were later 'found to have been ringleaders in the Ribbon Society or engaged as principals in some of the outrages directed by that body, the Crown could not fairly prosecute'. In a well-argued response, Cruise emphasized that the proposal, 'voluntarily made' by the priests, was that men should take the oath of allegiance 'lest they should be suspected of being connected with those

---

[18] CSORP 1856/18,243 Donegal, 28 July 1856, Cruise to Larcom.
[19] The Unlawful Societies Act resulted in the collapse of several trials, including that of the Donegal delegate, Patrick Doherty, a Buncrana publican, 'a meek-looking, well-dressed, middle-aged man ... considered in comfortable circumstances'. See *Morning Register*, 30 July 1840.

societies and to show their determination in future not to sanction them'. He was convinced that 'the great body of the people' had been forced to join 'through fear', and they were now 'really desirous to quit the Ribbon System':

> I am strongly of opinion that the principal part of all the young men in the lower [meaning western] and mountain parts of my district are implicated in the system. The lower classes in this part of the country are generally not a daring but rather a cowardly sort of people. They are all now extremely frightened and I am sure would be glad to take the oath of allegiance as a security to them for protection. The only serious outrages committed are those detailed in my reports; it is not therefore likely that those now against whom we have no charge and who compose those that are desirous to take the oath of allegiance are likely to be implicated in any serious crime that would call forth prosecution.

The attorney general relented, agreeing that 'parties against whom there is no charge' should be encouraged to 'come in and take the oath allegiance'. A record should be kept of all those who availed of the offer, he pointed out, and Cruise should be mindful too that taking the oath could be interpreted as 'condonation of past offences'.[20]

No general confession and absolution ever materialized, however. The initiative does not appear to have been publicly announced, and there was no report of repentant Ribbonmen trooping out to Wood Lodge that autumn. Fear was a factor: anybody who agreed to the arrangement would be suspected of informing. But so too was growing confidence. The release of the men on bail highlighted the weakness of the Crown's case, and with no arrests having been made since mid-June the rumour that Cruise had some master list of Ribbonmen lost credence. Cruise's priority now was building the best possible cases for the spring assizes. His prime target remained Neil O'Donnell, back behind his bar since his release on bail. In early August, Cruise saw Manus Byrne of Dubbin, who, according to McRoarty's dying declaration, had warned him that the Ribbonmen were coming for him. He got to see him only 'with difficulty', suggesting Byrne was avoiding him. 'He distinctly denied having told McRoarty anything about the Ribbonmen', Cruise reported to Dublin, 'and indeed I expected he would as here they are so much afraid at present that I fear they would swear anything sooner than divulge anything they knew relative to the Ribbon System.'[21] McRoarty's wife and son remained ready to testify

[20] CSORP 1856/18,243 Donegal, 28 July 1856, Cruise to Larcom; Donegal, 12 Aug. 1856, Cruise to Larcom, including the attorney general's marginalia dated 5 Aug. and 17 Sept.
[21] CSORP 1856/18,243 Donegal, 28 July 1856, Cruise to Larcom; Donegal, 12 Aug. 1856, Cruise to Larcom, including the attorney general's marginalia dated 5 Aug. and 17 Sept. 1856.

against the publican, but the prospect of O'Donnell standing trial for murder had receded. And the fate of all the other men except Gillespie and McHugh hinged entirely on how a jury weighed the testimony of a self-confessed Ribbonman—Patrick McGlynn.

All those arrested on McGlynn's word were now out on bail bar the informer *manqué* Condy McHugh. On 25 August, his wife sent a 'memorial' to the lord lieutenant, protesting that her husband was 'one of a number of men who were taken off their beds about ten weeks ago' and lodged in the county gaol charged with Ribbon and Whiteboy offences; that all of the others had been released on bail except him; and that his continued detention had left her in 'a most awkward position having no one to mind a small landed property and labourers being very scarce at this season of the year'. In asking that he be released, like 'all the rest', she said that 'any amount of bail your Excellency may suggest will be had without delay'.

'Any amount of bail' was a surprising offer from a poor woman. It suggests, as Cruise suspected, that either money had been raised by those upon whom McHugh had informed to ensure that he did not again change his mind and give the evidence which he had retracted, or that the priests had offered help.[22] It was probably the priests. Again, it had transpired in court that one of McHugh's brothers had instructed John McCrossan, the Omagh lawyer acting for the rest of the alleged Mollies, but that Condy's wife, who had precedence, had engaged a local man, James P. Hamilton, as his attorney. Hamilton, then in his late thirties, would have been on familiar terms with John D. McGarvey, parish priest of Ardara, and Patrick (commonly Pat) Gallagher, parish priest of Glenties, both of whom were, like himself, gentlemen farmers. An advocate of temperance (unlike his uncle, Gilly), Hamilton was investing heavily in improving the house and grounds at Mossvill, and a genial man, who was decent to his tenants, he was popular in the district.[23] Although deeply conservative in politics, this known entity—and accomplished lawyer destined to finish his career as recorder of Cork—would have been more to the priests' taste than their co-religionist McCrossan, a bullish anti-establishment figure.[24]

[22] CSORP 1856/18,409 'The Memorial of Keat McHugh of Beagh near Ardara Co. Donegal', postmarked 25 Aug. 1856.
[23] For obituaries and a report of Hamilton's funeral, see *DJ*, 18, 22, 27 July 1892. And for a motion passed by the Glenties Board of Guardians, recalling his 'genial qualities', see *DJ*, 10 Aug. 1892.
[24] The previous year, McCrossan had come close to prosecution for perverting the course of justice in a Molly Maguire case at Lifford. In Nov. 1854, Mollies had attacked and beaten Patrick McCaye and his wife's grandmother, Hannah O'Donnell, of Dalraghan Beg,

McHugh's wife's name is given in church and state records as Catherine Cannon. Born in Doohill, adjacent to Ardara, in 1837, she was not yet in her twenties and, given her age and that they had as yet no children, the couple can have only recently married. Irish was her preferred language— she raised her eleven children, including the last, Rose, born in 1881, speaking it, and, interestingly, the memorial gives her name as Keat, a rendering of the Irish form (Cáit) of Catherine.[25] She was also illiterate: the memorial had been written for her, almost certainly by Hamilton. The memorial had no effect. Larcom passed it to Thomas FitzGerald, the crown solicitor for Donegal, who sought the opinion of the attorney general; citing 'the importance of the case', he directed that 'any application to admit McHugh to bail should be resisted by the Crown'.[26] Condy was to remain in gaol.

•

After the rulings in Lifford in July 1856, the authorities had to support Patrick McGlynn until he testified in March 1857. The authorities also had to provide for his one-year-old daughter, Anne, and his wife, Catherine, then some five months pregnant. Finding accommodation for the McGlynns proved difficult. Initially, the Constabulary had housed the 'crown witness', with a sub-constable for his protection, in 'private lodgings' in Lifford. However, the county town was the headquarters of the Donegal Militia and, the regiment being then at home, its staff and their families had taken most of the lodging houses in town. Consequently, McGlynn stayed in the police barracks through the autumn, while his wife and child got a room in Patrick McCloskey's lodging house. This arrangement violated Constabulary regulations—crown witnesses were not allowed to bunk for extended periods in barracks—and when, in mid-November, it came to the attention of John Anderson, the County Inspector, he directed that McGlynn and a sub-constable get accommodation out of barracks. Sub-constable John Houlahan was assigned the task of

near Fintown, and stolen three cows, two heifers, and a small sum of money. Hearing that he would be killed if he gave evidence against four men arrested by the Constabulary, McCaye had gone to see their attorney, McCrossan. He had told McCaye that they would be transported if he testified, but not otherwise, and he had assured him that nothing would happen to him if the men got out of gaol. For McCaye's subsequent refusal to identify the prisoners, the collapse of his own trial for perjury, and Cruise's conviction that McCrossan should have been in the dock, see CSORP 1855/6,980 Glenties, 3 Aug. 1855, Cruise to Larcom. Also see *LJ*, 21 Mar., 25 July 1855. And see Ch. 10.

[25] Census, 1901: Beagh.

[26] CSORP 1856/18,409 'The Memorial of Keat McHugh of Beagh near Ardara Co. Donegal', postmarked 25 Aug. 1856; n.d., Thomas Fitzgerald to Larcom: 'County of Donegal: Report: The Queen *v.* Condy McHugh and Several Others', received 22 Sept. 1856.

protecting McGlynn. However, the McCloskeys, who were keeping McGlynn's wife and child, refused to supply a bed for the informer and the sub-constable; nor would they allow them bring a tick (a straw-filled mattress) into the house. The Constabulary was able to get an unoccupied house (without coal and candles) from William Sharkey for 9s. 6d. per month, but initially he would not take in McGlynn's wife and child. Pressed, Sharkey changed his mind and, for 18s. per month, he housed the two men, pregnant woman, and child.

Still, there were problems. Houlahan had to first cover expenses out of his own pocket and then wait to be reimbursed when he submitted receipts. The cost of supporting himself and the McGlynns was liable to run to £4 a month. On 30 November, he asked to be relieved of the duty. The following day, McGlynn wrote Robert Faussett, Constabulary Sub-Inspector in Raphoe, asking that the money allocated for his support not be reduced if Houlahan was recalled to barracks. Faussett forwarded the correspondence to the County Inspector, pointing out that 'we could get nobody in [Raphoe] to receive them'. Anderson, in turn, sent the file to headquarters. There, it was decided that the McGlynns should be moved to the Constabulary depot in Ballybough, north Dublin, where informers were often kept for their own protection. The family left for Dublin when their second child, Mary, born in November, was but a few weeks old.

It was a hard winter and early in the New Year, McGlynn wrote to the Clontarf Constabulary complaining that, on account of 'the extreme severity of the weather, and our insufficiency of clothing we suffer severely from the cold'. He submitted a list of clothes which he and his family required: an overcoat, trousers, out-boots, socks, two shirts, a neckerchief, flannel drawers, and a flannel shirt for himself; shoes and stockings, a petticoat, two chemises, a shawl, and a gown for Catherine and, for Ann, a frock, a petticoat, and two chemises. The authorities costed the clothing at £4 4s. Reviewing the list, Henry Brownrigg, the Deputy Inspector General, remarked that it was not usual to supply 'great coats' to crown witnesses and that 10s. 6d. for Catherine's gown was 'too high'. A revised list, with the cost of his coat and his wife's gown reduced, was accepted and the McGlynns got their new clothes.[27]

ANOTHER DAY IN COURT, MARCH 1857

The postponement of the trials in July and the release of the prisoners on bail—most especially, the release of O'Donnell—had been a public

---

[27] On accommodation and outfitting, see CSORP 1857/6,799.

indication that the Crown did not have strong cases against them. Again, the prosecution was dependent on the word of an accomplice, McGlynn, in all but three cases, those of Neil O'Donnell, the Glenties publican, Cormac Gillespie, the Mountcharles schoolmaster, and Condy McHugh of Beagh, and in none of them was the additional evidence compelling. Given the results of the post-mortem on Paddy McRoarty, his widow's identification of O'Donnell as one of the men who beat him was unlikely to secure a capital conviction. Notwithstanding Monahan's threat to try McHugh on the information that he had sworn and marked, the admissibility of that statement was sure to be contested on the grounds that he had made it on the understanding that it would not be used in evidence against himself. And finally, in Gillespie's case, other than the allegation of an accomplice (McGlynn) that he was a Ribbonman, the Crown was relying on handwriting evidence which, having only recently been ruled admissible in court, a jury might not find convincing.

Gillespie, for his part, decided not to leave matters to chance. On 15 January, one of his bailsmen, William Scott, son of the Mountcharles postmaster, notified the Constabulary that the teacher had left town and was on his way to Derry 'to quit the country by the next vessel'. Forewarned, the police intercepted him in Ballybofey, and returned him to Mountcharles. There, Robert Russell, agent of the Conyngham estate who lived locally, acting as a justice of the peace, accepted bail for him from James McLaughlin, a shopkeeper who had been a pupil of Gillespie in the early 1850s, and Daniel Harkin. It was substantial bail—£100 from himself and £50 from each of the two bailsmen. But on 19 February, Gillespie again absconded. Hearing that he had been seen in Strabane that night, Harkin and McLaughlin notified the authorities. A warrant was issued for his arrest, and by 23 February Gillespie was back in Lifford, where he would remain until the assizes.[28]

•

The assizes opened with the usual bustle and bombast on Thursday 5 March with Richard Pennefather, chief baron of the exchequer, presiding in his scarlet robes and wig. Then aged 86, Pennefather was a judge of great integrity and considered lenient in criminal cases. A Tipperary man, he had practised on the Munster circuit in the early 1800s, when a young Catholic barrister, Daniel O'Connell, had become a friend. He had been widely hailed for his 'upright' conduct in 1829, when presiding at

[28] CSORP 1857/1,587 Donegal, 23 Feb. 1857, Cruise to Larcom; Joint Information of James McLaughlin and Daniel Harkin, both of Mountcharles, 22 Feb. 1857.

the so-called Doneraile Conspiracy trial, he had handed O'Connell a document that had been concealed from him by the prosecutors, and which allowed the defence attorney to completely undermine the credibility of an informer. But notwithstanding his high reputation, Pennefather should no longer have been on the bench, for he had gone blind, and the previous year, his infirmity had been brought up in the House of Commons.[29]

The Crown Court sat at 3 o'clock on Saturday 7 March, and Pennefather proceeded to deliver his 'charge', that is, a statement, directed to the grand jury, on the state of the county as represented by the cases that were to be tried at the assizes. If the men charged with Ribbonism had hoped that he would live up to his reputation for leniency, his remarks disappointed them. He could not congratulate the grand jury on the appearance which the calendar presented, he began. It was 'widely different' from that exhibited in other counties through which he had passed on circuit. Here, in Donegal, there was 'a criminal combination to resist the laws of this happy country, under which we have all enjoyed so much prosperity, and . . . evil-minded persons are still desirous of disturbing the peace for their own abominable purposes'. Such societies, he went on, had existed in other parts of Ireland in 'former times', and they had 'no ostensible purpose except to create terror in the minds of the loyal subjects of the Sovereign, in order to effect their own wicked objects, at first, perhaps, not accompanied with violence, but ultimately resorting to such means to accomplish their purposes'. Alluding to a recent wave of sheep stealing in Gweedore, he deplored the 'flagrant outrages' committed on the property of 'persons coming into this county, to bring into it that civilization which has been practised in other parts of the empire'. It was essential to 'repress' those 'outrages' and to bring to justice those who had attempted to plunge the country into crime and disorder, and those who had violated the laws could rest assured that 'the whole power of the law will be set in motion to repress this crime'. After the list of cases was read, the court adjourned at quarter past five.

At 10 o'clock on Monday morning, Pennefather took his seat on the bench and a jury was impanelled to try James Adamson, a 'respectable looking man', for the rape of Catherine Doherty in Buncrana. Adamson was acquitted, but severely admonished by the judge for 'criminal intercourse' with the 17-year-old. The trial of two men for the highway robbery of £7 0s. 4d. and a watch near Ballybofey followed—one man was acquitted and the other sentenced to fifteen years' transportation—and

---

[29] Patrick Maume, 'Pennefather, Richard', in *DIB*.

then trials for assault, rape, and murder. The jury in the last case had not reached a verdict when the court rose at 6 o'clock, and the following morning the jurors were discharged when they said they were unable to agree a verdict.

On Tuesday 10 March, the Ribbon Case was called. Seventeen men now filed into the dock. They included twelve men from the parish of Ardara: Condy McHugh of Beagh; Big John Breslin of Shanaghan; Con O'Donnell, John (aka Jack) O'Donnell, and Patrick Kennedy, all of Tullycleave; William Maxwell of Doohill; Daniel Herron of Mullinacloy (Snugborough); John Sweeney of either Ardara or Altnagapple; Patrick McNelis (alias White) and James Hanlon of Ardara; Thomas Sweeney, Altnagapple, and Edward Kennedy, Crannogeboy. And there were five men from parishes other than Ardara: Martin Quigley, Dungloe; James Gallagher, Fintown; Neil O'Donnell, Glenties; Cormac Gillespie, Mountcharles; and James Melley, Carrick. Given that twenty-six men had been released on bail at the previous assizes, as many as nine had since got themselves out of the way. Among those 'not amenable' were Neil Breslin, who was said in court to be in America, and Little John Breslin of Doohill, master of the Ardara lodge.[30]

Sixteen of the men were charged on an indictment framed under the Unlawful Societies (Ireland) Act, 1839 (2d and 3d Vic., cap. 76), with membership of an unlawful combination on and since a number of dates, including 17 March 1855, the date of the meeting in Neil O'Donnell's in Glenties. The indictment comprised six counts, relating to communication with each other using secret signs and passwords and with knowingly maintaining intercourse with officers of the society. The seventeenth man, Cormac Gillespie, who had not been at that meeting in O'Donnell's, was arraigned under the same act, and he faced an additional charge of sending a threatening letter.

All seventeen pleaded not guilty. The court then assented to a proposal by James Major QC, again acting for the Crown, that they proceed with the trial of five of the accused—James Gallagher, Cormac Gillespie, Condy McHugh, Big John Breslin, and William Maxwell. Gillespie was the defendant against whom there was the strongest evidence; hence, the decision to try him. Gallagher was a delegate, and McHugh, Breslin, and Maxwell were all committeemen in Ardara. The Crown, it seems, was calculating that these officers of the Society, involved in the communication of its signs and passwords, were the most likely to be convicted. And

---

[30] The account here is based upon *LJ*, 11 Mar. 1857; *LStd*, 12 Mar. 1857; *LSnl*, 13 Mar. 1857; *BN*, 12 Mar. 1857; *BH*, 13 Mar. 1857; *Ulsterman*, 13 Mar. 1857; *Saunder's Newsletter*, 13 Mar. 1857.

Cruise, for his part, must have been hoping that the conviction of ringleaders might cause somebody else to provide information against the men named by McRoarty—Neil O'Donnell and 'the two Sweeneys and White of Ardara'.

Patrick McGlynn was the first witness called by the prosecution. Robert Johnstone, prosecuting, led him through his evidence, essentially getting him to repeat for the court what he had sworn in his two 'informations' the previous June. The schoolmaster spoke confidently. He recalled how, in January 1854, in Hanlon's public house in Ardara, Neil Breslin and William Maxwell had first invited him to join the Ribbon Society, by asking if he knew what was going on, and if he had wished to know:

> I said I did not; two days after I was talking to James Melley, a national schoolmaster, who asked me were not Maxwell and Brisland speaking to me; he said that it was dangerous to refuse and that he became a member through fear; he also said it was better to take the sign, and they would not ask me to break the law any further; the Sunday after, they were coming from mass, and Melley said, he would talk to Maxwell . . .

In response to Johnstone's questions, McGlynn described being initiated into the Society in a ceremony, after Sunday mass, in the backroom of Hanlon's. Present were two of the defendants—Big John Breslin and the shoemaker William Maxwell, chairman of the lodge. Also present that Sunday were the go-between Melley, Neil Breslin, and the master, Little John Breslin of Doohill. After the initiation, which had involved swearing an oath and kissing a Bible or prayer book, he had paid a shilling for signs and passwords and he regularly met with other members, Sunday being the 'general day of meeting'. On St Patrick's Night 1855, he had been present at the meeting in Neil O'Donnell's to consider Moses Ward's challenge to Little John Breslin's mastership of the Ardara lodge; James Gallagher of Fintown, one of the defendants, had presided.

Having had McGlynn testify about the involvement of the various defendants in the distribution of signs and passwords for different quarters, Johnstone moved onto various 'outrages' plotted by the Mollies. He had McGlynn acknowledge writing the threatening letter addressed to James Gallagher of Beagh; he had written it, he said, at the behest of Matthew Sweeney of Beagh and Jack O'Donnell of Tullycleave. The letter was produced in court, and McGlynn identified it. He proceeded to describe how, after St Patrick's Day, he had met with McHugh and Maxwell in a waste house of James Fisher's in Ardara, when it was determined that Gallagher's house was to be raided a second time, and 'that Gallagher and his wife should be taken out and dipped in a hole of water, and that they should be beaten, and the wife more than him; [and] that if any money was got in the house it was to be given to Gallagher's father'. He confirmed that Condy McHugh had been involved in meetings to establish what had happened to a gun taken in a raid on John Hill's house, and reviewed the 'general subjects' discussed at meetings of the lodge.

Alexander Norman QC then rose to cross-examine McGlynn. A Dubliner, then in his mid-forties, Norman had been on the north-west circuit for many years, and at the previous assizes he had made a particularly positive impression on Pennefather when he presented a powerful case contesting the Irish Society's control of the Foyle fishery. He was deeply conservative in politics—indeed, he became legal adviser to the Church of Ireland after its disestablishment—and when he died, in 1870, the *Irish Times* opined that if he had been 'less consistent in his principles, he might have attained a higher position in the profession which he adorned', meaning he might have been appointed to the bench.[31] Norman immediately set to discrediting the schoolmaster. First, he had him acknowledge being dismissed after six months from Letterbrick School, and then say that he did not know why he had been dismissed. He had him admit that he was in debt to different parties, and that there were 'three or four decrees hanging over him', but deny ever saying that he would get 'Government money' for transporting the men whom he had named. The reason he had informed, he said, was because he was afraid that the Ribbonmen would kill Gallagher and that he himself 'might be implicated in the matter'—which suggested his motivation was not entirely altruistic. Norman then concluded his brisk cross-examination by getting the schoolmaster to swear that he did not know whether taking oaths and exchanging passwords was breaking the law.

After a less than impressive performance, McGlynn stood down. The man who had put him in the witness box was then sworn. Cruise testified that McHugh had come to him in the bridewell on 9 June—a statement at variance with his report at the time indicating that he had McHugh brought to him when McGlynn identified him as the man most likely to inform— and he had asked him 'what was to be said against him'. An hour later, Cruise told the court, McHugh had voluntarily made a statement to him. He denied using any threats and when asked if he cautioned him against saying anything that might incriminate himself, replied that 'he had the expectation of being examined as a crown witness . . . the man knew he was criminating himself; the man put his mark to the document'. Major, for the Crown, now prepared to read McHugh's information, but Richard Dowse, for the defence, objected, and a wrangle ensued about its admissibility. Pennefather ruled that it should be admitted.

31 *Irish Times*, 23 Sept. 1870.

James Gallagher of Beagh then took the stand. For Major, he went through the details of the raid on his house in early March 1856, describing how he had been warned not to 'put out' any more of 'my tenants' and confirming that a threatening letter had been left on the dresser. Constable Hugh Reilly was then sworn and, in answer to Major, he confirmed that he had received the threatening letter from Gallagher. He described the letter as a warning to Gallagher that 'if he would not be more kind to his father, and desist ejecting his cottiers', the Molly Maguires would have to pay him a second visit. Major now read the letter with its jibes at the pretensions of his 'highness' Gallagher and the Cavan-man Reilly.

Then came the case of Cormac Gillespie. A *nolle prosequi* having been entered in the charge of belonging to a secret society, he was only tried for sending a threatening letter to Thomas Cassidy of Mountcharles. The key evidence was the similarity between the handwriting in the letter and that in a copybook belonging to Gillespie which the police had seized in a search of his house. A national school inspector, Louis Harkin, testified that, 'in his opinion' the handwriting in the copybook was Gillespie's. However, he would only say that the hand in which the letter was written bore a 'strong resemblance' to Gillespie's 'or the writing of those taught by him'. The letter was 'more in the schoolboy style than Gillespie's; there was bad spelling in it'. He could not swear that Gillespie wrote the letter. James Crosbie, manager of the Provincial Bank in Strabane, was more emphatic. The handwriting, he said, was the same.

The defence had objected vigorously to the use of handwriting evidence, but Pennefather had over-ruled the objections. The defence had then opted to present various documents, written by the prisoner, to the witnesses, which Harkin and Crosbie failed to identify as being in his hand. Pennefather being blind, it was an awkward phase of the proceedings. Indeed, the previous year, when Pennefather's sight had been mentioned in parliament, it was recalled that, at the Fermanagh assizes in 1855, when a case involving the writing of a threatening letter was before him, the accused had cried out, 'My Lord, if you will examine the papers yourself, you will see that they were not written by the same hand!' Pennefather, it had been pointed out in the Commons, could not do so, and, in future cases, if a prisoner appealed against being tried by 'a blind judge', it was hard to know how the appeal could be resisted: lawyers might say a defendant had no legal right to make such an appeal, but public opinion would decide otherwise.[32]

The Crown having rested its case, Alexander Norman then spoke for the defence of Gallagher, McHugh, and Gillespie. After first asserting that

---

[32] Speech of Sir John Shelley, in Hansard, 3rd ser., vol. 140, Vic. 19, c. 766, 14 Feb. 1856.

it was a 'wholesome rule of law' that the evidence of an 'approver' needed to be corroborated, he vigorously attacked McGlynn's credibility. After the 'exhibition' which McGlynn had made of himself in the witness box, he would say little of his character. But if he were a fair specimen of the men to whom the Government, in their wisdom, had entrusted the youth of the country, then he would say let the national system perish and let the people remain in their ignorance. It was a line calculated to appeal to the jury, for there was a lingering resentment of the national schools among members of the Church of Ireland; and surnames, while a fallible indicator of religion, suggest that as many as eleven of the twelve jurors were Protestants. The jury, Norman continued, had seen how 'this man with decrees and debt and difficulty against him' had deceived both the Government and the people, and brought these 'respectable tenants' to the bar of criminal justice, without any corroborative evidence. As for McHugh's statement, the peculiar manner in which it had been obtained prevented it being regarded as corroboration of McGlynn's, and it could be used only against himself. And as for Gillespie, he reminded the jury of the witnesses' failure to identify samples of his writing and conflicting opinions as to the hand in which the threatening letter had been written. Gillespie's case, he said, proved 'the fallacious nature of the test of comparison as regards handwriting', a reference to the recent and contro-versial decision to admit handwriting evidence in court.

Richard Dowse then spoke for Breslin and Maxwell. A native of Dungannon, and then in his mid-thirties, Dowse was known for his acerbic wit.[33] He began by deploring Ribbonism as a 'kind of a social cancer that was destroying the country's vitals', and which, if not repressed, would ultimately destroy it. 'Subversive of social morality and obstructive to the progress of civilization', it was 'one of the greatest evils under which this or any other country could labour.' Dowse then turned on the detestable character of the crown witness:

> [McGlynn] was the lowest of a depraved class, for he had come into that box, to swear away the liberties of these men, and that under the sanctity of an oath, although it was much to be feared he did not greatly respect the sacred act, for he had already committed perjury to the members of the Ribbon Society. Was it on the uncorroborated evidence of that foul, tainted witness, that they were to convict these men? He had not even been arrested—he had come forward voluntarily, and, from the hands in which he had placed himself, he was sure to be rewarded, if not respected. M'Glynn was corrob-orated in no part of his story, excepting that he was a thorough villain; for, although the informer said he supposed he had ceased to be a Ribbonman

[33] C. L. Falkiner, 'Dowse, Richard (1824–1890)', rev. Peter Gray, *DNB*.

when he became a crown witness, he could assure him that the two offices were by no means incompatible. (*Laughter*)

Dowse concluded with what the liberal *Londonderry Standard* described as a 'powerful appeal to the jury to reject the testimony of the perjured witness'.

The case was now nearing its close. The defence called a number of witnesses who testified that Gallagher, Gillespie, McHugh, Breslin, and Maxwell 'bore good characters in their respective neighbourhoods'. Among them were a landlord, a middleman cum agent, a school inspector, a cess collector, and a poor law guardian. Captain James Hamilton, Gallagher's landlord, gave his tenant a good character. Admitting, under cross-examination, that he himself had told a magistrate that he had heard Gallagher was a Ribbonman, he said that he did not 'discharge' (evict) him as 'he could do very little [harm] where he was, in care of a house in the mountains'—an indication, perhaps, that the delegate, like many masters and committeemen, was a publican. Ironically, Hamilton had been one of the justices of the peace who, little more than five years earlier, had lobbied successfully for the proclamation of sections of west Donegal under the Crime and Outrage (Ireland) Act, in order to suppress 'Bastard Ribbonism'. Next came Gilly Hamilton of Eden, who the previous spring had given evidence in the trial of Neil Craig; he was an uncle of Condy McHugh's lawyer. He swore that Gallagher, McHugh, and Maxwell were all men of good character. However, in response to a question from the prosecution, he conceded that he had 'heard it reported that men of otherwise good character belonged to the Ribbon Society'. It was a comment that did little good for the men on trial, but, like Captain Hamilton's evidence, it said much about changing attitudes to the Society. Louis Harkin, the national school inspector, and James Griffith, a cess collector, then gave Gillespie a good character. But the most impressive witness was the poor law guardian—John O'Donnell of Letterilly. Well educated and articulate and connected to the O'Donnells of Glashagh and Ballinamore, O'Donnell, with two brothers priests, was the epitome of Catholic respectability in west Donegal. He now spoke to the good character of both the Ardara chairman, the hard-drinking shoemaker William Maxwell, and the delegate, James Gallagher.

Pennefather charged the jury. Observing that it was not usual to convict prisoners on the uncorroborated evidence of an informer, he said 'the present case was such, and the importance of repressing the spread of secret societies so great, that this might be an instance in which somewhat to infringe on that practice'. He asked the jury to look at 'the facts in their entirety, with reference to the credibility of the witnesses', and reminded them that 'persons connecting themselves with secret societies rendered themselves answerable for any acts which the other members might commit, with or without their knowledge, tending to promote or advance the objects of the association'. The jury then retired and, within three-quarters of an hour, returned with verdicts of guilty.

Before passing sentence on them, Pennefather addressed the five men in the dock:

> the Ribbon confederacy was one which must have a tendency to render life and property insecure. It was a confederacy which was not only dangerous to the public in general, but in the end would tend to the destruction of all those who were engaged in it. The present case showed that the members of these societies had no security among their associates in guilt, as such men could have no principle of consistency; and [I] would earnestly impress these facts on all who are treading on dangerous paths and were at any moment liable to be betrayed into the hands of the law.

Pointing out that transportation for life was the punishment for their offence under the Whiteboy Act, under which they might have been indicted, Pennefather said he would only sentence them to be imprisoned for twenty months, with hard labour. The twelve other men who had come to court were now bailed until the next assizes.[34]

•

The 'Donegal Ribbon Case' was reported in great detail in the press and it was the subject of editorial comment in a number of (mainly Tory) newspapers. The calendars of the various assizes were light that spring; the number charged in the case was impressive, and the accounts of meetings to punish enemies and resolve disputes conjured up images of 'midnight legislators' which had been common in conservative polemic in the years before the Famine. The case, in bringing a menacing Catholic underworld back into view, suggested, in a favourite metaphor of Tories, that the leopard had not changed its spots. Still, it was the self-confessed Ribbonman being a national schoolmaster, and other alleged members of the Society belonging to the same profession, that most animated hostile commentators. On the roll-out of national education in the 1830s, ultra-Protestants had identified the system as part of a wedge, being driven by a combination of Whigs and Irish Catholics, which would one day sunder Church and State in Ireland. Although conservative elements in the Church of Ireland ran a rival system of schools, under the auspices of the Church Education Society, most Protestants had accepted national schools from the outset, and opposition had declined by the mid-1850s. However, national education remained a bugbear of hardliners, and so the involvement of schoolmasters in the Ribbon Society drew much negative comment. For instance, the *Evening Packet*, a flagship of Dublin conservatism, opined that the 'peculiar and serious case' had established that the 'abominable confederacy we had imagined destroyed exists among us': 'We seem to be carried back many years in perusing M'GLIN the approver's account of the lodge-meetings of Ardara.... The government of Donegal was, in fact, centred in HANLON's publichouse at Ardara and the National teachers who did the literary part of the business of this lodge.'

> It is a sad thing to contemplate this Ribbonman's position as a trainer of the youth of the county. What can be expected of our peasantry if they are to be subject to such influences as M'GLIN must have exercised upon his pupils? We would fain hope that his case is a solitary one of Schoolmaster-Ribbonism, but we see no ground for laying that flattering unction to our hearts. There may be others at this moment occupying the position held by the teachers of Donegal in the flourishing days of the Ardara conspiracy.[35]

A predictably more frothing reaction came from William Johnson's *Downshire Protestant*, an Orange newspaper published in Downpatrick. In Johnson's mind, the Ribbon Society was a 'ghastly puppet' of 'Roman Catholic magnates', that had as its end 'the subversion of all government'. Its 'ruffianly legislators—who were executive as well—acted on the assumption that they were very Solons in wisdom, uprightness and justice; and proceeded accordingly to trample underfoot the British Constitution, the rights of individuals, the claims of society, and ... to burn the property, beat the persons, and take the lives of the individuals who happened to incur their sovereign displeasure'. Interestingly, the paper did acknowledge that disputes about land arising from the Famine were prominent among the matters adjudicated by the 'cowardly administrators of a "justice" which both the laws of God and man condemn':

> During the famine, many well-to-do persons, who had contrived to make money while the sun shone and the weather was fair, bought land at an extremely cheap rate; and a class of complaints consisted of applications to make buyers refund the increased value of the property, land having risen considerably in price during the last prosperous years. And thus, if the hapless individual, who had purchased land once, at a time when land was cheap, did not purchase it over again, when land was dear, or, in other words, did not chose to hand over the difference of the two prices, he was liable to be

assailed with threatening letters, liable to have his house ransacked, his person abused, or his life taken.

Still, here too the focus was on the involvement in Ribbonism of men 'employed by the State to train the minds of the rising generation':

> And among this dastardly band of assailants of women and children were schoolmasters—*National* schoolmasters—men paid by Government to instruct the rising minds of Ireland in all things necessary for their own good and advancement in the State, as well as for the maintenance of the majesty and beauty of the Constitution as it stands. The Bible, as teacher, is excluded from our National Schools, and men like these are admitted! Can we laud too highly the practical wisdom that devised all this? Truly, that wisdom was a 'liberal' one—in a strangely perverted sense—which dispensed with the Bible, and took midnight marauders and dastardly assailants of persons and property, by way of a substitute in the sacred office of tuition![36]

It was all a bit overblown. Pennefather, in opening the assizes, had noticed the existence of an 'illegal secret society' in the county and spoken sternly of it, but he had been careful to add that, from the cases before him, 'I am not to infer that your county is in a disturbed or unsatisfactory state as regards crime'.[37] And even the *Evening Packet* had acknowledged that the Ardara case seemed to belong to a different time. Although not apparent to the *Downshire Protestant*, the Ribbon Society was changing, and if it continued to be responsible for occasional 'outrages' in a few counties, it was scarcely a subversive threat. Gilly Hamilton's concession that otherwise respectable men could be Ribbonmen echoes. And so too does James Hamilton's notion that the Ribbon delegate James Gallagher of Fintown could do little harm in a remote mountain district and that he, as his landlord, had no reason to evict him. Ribbonmen did occasionally commit heinous acts, such as the killing of Paddy McRoarty, but much of their activity now involved settling disputes about land and wages, often without violence against people or property. As such, the lodges, as the Tory press contended, were a rival justice system to the courts. Crucially, there were other bodies that dispensed justice. For instance, in 1843–4, parochial branches of the Repeal Association had established 'arbitration courts' across Ireland; indeed, there had been one such court in Ardara which issued summonses on printed forms, capped by a harp beneath the crown, wreathed in shamrock.[38] Those courts ceased to function in most

---

[36] *Downshire Protestant*, 20 Mar. 1857.   [37] *LJ*, 11 Mar. 1857.
[38] In 1844, Thomas Sweeney had summoned Charles Boyle of Ardara and John McGill of Beagh to this court for 'wages due for taylor work': OP 1844/7/8,865 Glenties, 23 May 1844, Holmes to Lucas, enclosing printed summons.

places with the demise of the Association during the Famine, but, by the mid-1850s, 'arbitration courts', which were legal if there was no compulsion to attend, were again in quiet operation across Donegal. Now, however, they derived their authority directly from Catholic clergymen—men viewed with as grave suspicion as Ribbon masters by the tub-thumping *Downshire Protestant*. For example, John Doherty, parish priest of Gweedore, and Hugh McFadden, his counterpart in Cloughaneely, oversaw 'courts of arbitrators' in the early to mid-1850s—these courts, which were controversial due to the priests' denial of sacraments to those who disregarded them, also set the price of kelp and land, much as Ribbon lodges fixed prices.[39] And in Rossguill, as late December 1855, four men were appointed at a meeting in the local chapel 'to do justice'.[40] From a narrow Tory perspective, then, it was perplexing when, in spring and summer 1857, the very priests whom ultra-Protestants represented as a threat to civil liberty worked with the magistracy to 'resolve' the remaining Ribbon cases. But, taking a broader view, two justice systems can be seen to have combined against a third; faced with Molly Maguire who set them both at defiance, Christ and Caesar were now hand in glove.

PRÍOSÚN DUBH LEIFIR

> . . . *Is ag príosún dubh Leifir fuair mé deireadh achan scéil.*
> And at the black gaol of Lifford I got the end of every tale.
>
> *Amhrán Áranna*, The Song of Arranmore[41]

After Baron Pennefather had passed sentence on them, Gallagher, Gillespie, McHugh, Breslin, and Maxwell were taken from the courthouse to the gaol. There, they had their heads shaved, and they were required to strip and bathe, and to don prison uniform. The five men were then removed to the convict section where, under the 'rule of silence', prisoners were prohibited from speaking to each other during the term of their

---

[39] *Destitution*, 246, 352, 361, 366, 370.

[40] In early 1856, the magistrate who investigated the Rossguill courts obtained a letter addressed to a local man by a priest, Tom Daly, who was transferred to Ardara the following summer, instructing him not to bring his case to the petty sessions, but to let it go 'to an arbitration where if you have suffered a wrong it will be remedied. I will look on your conduct—if you proceed [to the petty sessions]—as arising from spite.' Although the magistrate, who complained to the bishop about the court, believed the proceedings involved illegal oaths, the Castle's law adviser could see no evidence of criminal behaviour. See CSORP 1856/11,797.

[41] A traditional song, recounting the *via dolorosa* of a man marched in chains from Dungloe to Lifford.

sentence. Any infringement of rules might now result in solitary confinement in the 'dark cell' or whipping: indeed, two men had been whipped in Lifford in the last months of 1856. The 'hard' or 'punitive' labour to which they had been sentenced was breaking stone and bone in 'stalled sheds' (intended to prevent communication) in one of the prison yards. The regime had been lax over the previous few years, with no great amount of stone provided for the prisoners to break. Unluckily for the new convicts, on the afternoon of 20 September 1856, a draconian prison inspector, on his annual visit, had found that many prisoners in the breaker's yard were 'basking in the sunshine whilst the turnkeys were present'. On further investigation, the inspector established that 'an industrious man was frequently able to break the quantity of stone required of him before breakfast; thus being idle, or comparatively so, for the rest of the day'. 'This is an evil', he noted in his report, 'which ought to be remedied without loss of time.' Consequently, when the five men were convicted in March 1857, 'hard labour prisoners' were breaking stone from morning until lock up, that is, in summer, 7.00 a.m. to 6.00 p.m., and in winter from the earliest light until the latest. In fact, all convicted prisoners had to be employed at something, and ordinary prisoners broke stone from 7.00 a.m. until 4.00 p.m.: 'The sole difference between the hard labour and other prisoners . . . is that the former have a larger quantity of stones to break in the day than the latter.' Convicts did have the option of attending school for three hours a day, where they got instruction in reading, writing, and arithmetic, and some respite from the breaker's yard. Meals were served in a day room, but the governor was under pressure from the inspectors to have the prisoners eat alone in their cells, so as to restrict opportunities for communication. The food was poor. Breakfast every day was 8oz meal and a pint of buttermilk. Dinner four days a week was 4lbs of potatoes and a pint of new milk; twice a week it was 14oz bread and a pint of oatmeal gruel, and once a week 14oz bread and a pint of new milk. The prisoners washed at troughs in the yard. No lights were allowed in cells to which the prisoners would have been confined in winter from 6.00 in the evening to 6.00 in the morning.[42]

The five men had been hard done by.[43] Maxwell, Breslin, and Gallagher had been convicted solely on the evidence of an accomplice, which was

---

[42] *Thirty-Fifth Report . . . Prisons of Ireland, 1856*, appendix, 24–32; *Thirty-Sixth Report of the Inspectors-General on the General State of the Prisons of Ireland, 1857 . . .*, HC 1857–58 (2394), xxx, appendix, 15–19.

[43] Membership of an illegal confederacy was still a transportable offence. However, Westminster had abolished transportation for anything less than fourteen years in 1853, and a bill then before parliament—it got its second reading in May and was enacted in June 1857—completely abolished it as a judicial sentence.

unusual, and the verdicts at Lifford had raised concerns in legal circles. In the wake of the assizes, a letter to the editor of the *Irish Jurist*, citing their cases, pointed out the danger of convictions on the uncorroborated evidence of an informer.[44] Gillespie, meanwhile, had been convicted on handwriting evidence, which had only recently been made admissible in court. And, most controversially, the conviction of McHugh, who had been denied access to an attorney between his arrest and first court appearance, had been secured on the basis of a statement made on the understanding that it would not be used as evidence against himself. James Hamilton, his lawyer, now went to the Court of Criminal Appeal to have his conviction overturned. The court, consisting of five senior judges, including Pennefather, who had presided at the original trial, sat in Dublin on 8 May. After hearing submissions from Pennefather and Hamilton, it retired to consider the arguments. Little over a month later, on 12 June, it reported a majority decision: a statement made by a prisoner with a view to his being examined as a crown witness was inadmissible as evidence against the prisoner. Pennefather was the sole dissentient.[45] McHugh got out of Lifford and came home to Beagh. He had been eleven months in custody, only two as a convict. Breslin, Gallagher, Gillespie, and Maxwell remained in prison, breaking stone, with eighteen months to serve.

---

[44] *Irish Jurist*, 9 (1857), 61–2.
[45] See Reg. *v.* M'Hugh (reported by P. J. McKenna BL) in Edward W. Cox, *Reports of Cases in Criminal Law Argued and Determined in all the Courts of England and Ireland*, 7 [1855–58] (London, 1858), 483–8.

7

The Judge between God and Man

O my God! I am heartily sorry for having offended thee, and I detest
my sins most sincerely, because they displease thee, my God, who art
so deserving of all my love, for thy infinite goodness and most
amiable perfections; and I firmly purpose, by thy holy grace, never
more to offend thee.

'An Act of Contrition', 1846[1]

There had been a moment of light relief in Lifford courthouse in March
1857. Asked what had been discussed at Ribbon meetings, Patrick
McGlynn had run the gamut of what he had seen and heard in the
backrooms of Hanlon's, Dorrian's, and Kelly's. 'The general subjects
under consideration at such meetings', he said, 'were such as taking
arms from persons not connected with the society, breaking into their
houses and making them pay money for claims that their members had on
them; [and] they received complaints from members of the society that
were badly used by others...' He remembered a boy who had left his
master applying at one meeting to have his house attacked to recover
wages. And at another meeting, Neil Breslin had proposed stealing
the priest's sheep because he had not paid his father for a wall he had
erected. Stealing the sheep, Breslin had said, would 'teach him to pay
better'. There had been laughter in the court at the idea of stealing from a
clergyman's 'flock'.[2] But if the Ardara people present laughed, it can have
come as no surprise to hear that John D. McGarvey (c.1796–1888) had
not paid his bill, for the parish priest was notoriously mean. In a history of

---

[1] *The Most Rev. Dr. James Butler's CATECHISM: Revised, Corrected, and Enlarged, by the
Four Roman Catholic Archbishops of IRELAND, as a General Catechism for the Kingdom*
(Dublin, 1846), 6.

[2] *Saunder's Newsletter*, 13 Mar. 1857. The reference to a wall built for the priest may
point to Neil Breslin belonging to the family of a publican-shopkeeper (leather sales, nail
manufactory) whose premises abutted the chapelyard. Intriguingly, work was carried out at
the chapel in 1855–6 and a fine retaining wall separates the chapelyard from the public
house: see PB: Drumbarran [Ardara], 1855–6. However, the surname Breslin is common
around Ardara and, given his farming interests, McGarvey likely needed walls elsewhere.

the diocese of Raphoe, published in 1920 when McGarvey was over thirty years dead, Edward Maguire, himself a priest, took pains to refute claims that 'he battened on an impoverished flock':

> So far from being a man of greed, who tried to squeeze the last pence out of a parishioner's purse, he possessed neither the coaxing arts of avarice nor the methodic habits of business. While it must be admitted that he was by no means generous, he never was known to press any poor person for money, or to threaten the refusal of religious rights or privileges on the score of non-payment of fees.

However, Maguire also told how, in 1841, when McGarvey's younger brother, Christopher, beginning his career as a doctor in Mountcharles, was sued by the executors of his predecessor's will for the value of 'surgical appurtenances' which he had purloined, the priest allowed him to be arrested and hauled off to Lifford before he would pay the 'trifling sum' owed. And he observed too that, later in life, McGarvey, who had never spent a penny of the money ('considerably over £100') collected at his first mass on Rosapenna Strand in 1829, could not be persuaded to leave large sums to his relatives as such gifts would destroy 'their spirit of self-reliance and economy'.[3]

Maguire was here skirting a controversy. When McGarvey died in 1888, he left, in a will dated 1882, almost his entire estate—a 'small farm at Ardara' (estimated value, £2,300) and 'cash invested in deposit receipts amounting to £23,711'; the total, over £26,000, equivalent to several million pounds sterling in 2016—to Michael Logue, then bishop of Raphoe, for religious and charitable uses. He left only £800 to his relatives. Logue, who by the time the will was read, had become Archbishop of Armagh and Primate of All Ireland, had actually thought it best that the 'poor' relatives get no money. He had rejected two wills drawn up by the elderly priest himself, and threatened him with suspension if he did not have a solicitor draft one for him. These details were revealed when a niece of McGarvey contested the will. Her challenge failed, but the disclosures in the probate case did not reflect well on Logue. Still, it was the spectacle of a priest ministering in a mountainy parish being able to amass such wealth that grabbed attention, as fellow priests and acquaintances testified that McGarvey had gone from being very 'economical' to being, in fact, a 'miser'. He had often, the court heard, failed to pay shopkeepers' bills and his bishop had to compel him to clear his 'small accounts'.[4]

---

[3] Maguire, *Raphoe*, ii. 131–3, 193–4. Elsewhere (i. 346), Maguire describes how McGarvey, when a clerical student and employed as an assistant in the seminary in Letterkenny, 'initiated an agitation for the redress of financial grievances of over-worked intermediate assistants, and extorted a substantial salary and bonus from the old Bishop'.
[4] *BN*, 8, 9 June 1888; *FJ*, 8, 9 June 1888.

Ardara had been this 'economical' priest's first appointment. In 1857, when McGlynn took the stand in Lifford, McGarvey had already been twenty-seven years in the parish, twenty-three of them as parish priest. In that time, he had never been a particularly active pastor, appearing more concerned with sheep and cattle than souls. Indeed, by the mid-1850s, he was one of the biggest graziers in the parish, leasing the mountain townlands of Meenagolan (over 800 acres), which he stocked with sheep, and Meenaboll (almost 200 acres), where he had three subtenants, while he lived in considerable comfort on a fine 70-acre farm in Lough Hill; his house and outbuildings were valued at £4 10s. (90s.), considerably higher than the 5s. valuation of a typical smallholder's house.[5] The priest was a noted dealer at fairs and markets, and long after his death, 'no greater compliment could be paid to a cattle man than to say that he was "as good a judge as Fr McGarvey"'.[6]

Whatever attention McGarvey gave his farm, he did not manage the parish well. On his appointment to Ardara, the parish had two chapels, one in the town and another in Mullyvea, about a mile north-west of Beagh. Only about the size of an ordinary countryman's house, but with an arched doorway, the Mullyvea chapel is identified as an 'R.C. Chapel & School Ho[use]' on the OS map of 1835, and into the twentieth century, old people could recall how McGarvey used to ride out to Sandfield and cut across the *Léana* to say mass here.[7] In the mid-eighteenth century, when the main road to Rosbeg ran by the shore, it would have been a convenient place of worship. However, with the new road having been made from Beagh–Kilclooney in the 1770s, and with the expansion of population further inland, Kilclooney had, by McGarvey's time, emerged as a more central location for a new, larger chapel. McGarvey had duly neglected Mullyvea—the building was 'in ruins' when the OS map was revised in 1847–50—yet, as late as 1856, he had not moved to erect a new chapel in Kilclooney, contenting himself with holding services at *scáthláin*, shelters, at various sites around Downstrands. In the mid-1800s, there were other spots in the diocese, generally in poorer and more remote areas, where congregations still assembled in the open. But in a district where there were wealthy Catholic merchants and farmers, it seemed out of joint

[5] *GV*. The Raphoe Diocesan Statutes stipulated that a priest could not hold more than 15 acres without the express approval of his bishop; McGarvey never received this approval but held extensive farms until his death. See *FJ*, 8 June 1888.

[6] McGill, *Conall's Footsteps*, 271.

[7] For accounts of mass in Mullyvea, drawing heavily on *seanchas*, see McGill, *Ardara*, 26–8; McGill, *Conall's Footsteps*, 159–61, 271; Shovlin, *Narin and Downstrands*, 30–1, 90. Maguire, *Raphoe*, i. 281, has McGarvey celebrating mass in Downstrands 'under the blue canopy of heaven, or beneath an improvised shelter, at various convenient locations'.

with the times. In the mid-1830s, the proportion (19.3 per cent) of the parish's Catholics that typically attended Sunday mass, per a return by McGarvey to the Commissioners of Public Instruction, had been significantly lower than in Inishkeel (29.8), where there were modern chapels in both Glenties and Fintown. McGarvey's return only refers to a single mass every Sunday in the town chapel, which suggests that he had omitted a mass said by either himself or a curate in Downstrands. However, even allowing for an omission, the figure was still low. Attendance at mass may well have increased here by the mid-1850s, but McGarvey's failure to build a chapel in Kilclooney almost certainly caused his parish to continue to lag behind Glenties.[8]

After chapel building, schooling was the other great concern of mid-nineteenth-century Irish priests; but it too was of little interest to McGarvey. Although legislation allowing for the establishment of national schools had been in place since 1831—and despite his bishop, Patrick McGettigan, being a supporter of the system—it was only after the appointment of an eager young curate, Daniel O'Donnell, to Ardara in 1840 that a Catholic clergyman applied to the Board of Education to establish national schools in the parish. In five years, O'Donnell was responsible for the establishment of schools at Kilclooney and Crannogeboy in 1840; Laconnell in 1843; Brackey, Crove, Drumboghill, and Lergynasearhagh, all in 1844; and Beagh in 1845 (built in 1844, it was not accepted by the board until 1845). It was the curate not the parish priest who served as manager of these schools, appointing teachers and overseeing their day-to-day operations.[9] Later, in 1847, McGarvey had managerial responsibilities thrust upon him when O'Donnell's successor was suddenly removed from the parish. However, he quickly lessened the burden by ceding control of schools (Crove, Shonagh [Coguish], and Straleel) erected by O'Donnell in mountain townlands beyond the boundary of Ardara to neighbouring parish priests, and he paid little attention to those of which he remained manager. Within a few years, the Board dismissed a number of teachers, inspectors reported others as 'negligent', and two schools were temporarily struck off, Lergynasearhagh

---

[8] *First Report of the Commissioners of Public Instruction, Ireland*, 272a–273a, 280a–281b.

[9] On O'Donnell's departure from Ardara, an address from his parishioners noted his establishment of schools: 'Every portion of this parish felt the influence of your exertions in that respect; and today the wild mountain districts of Boylagh and Banagh have their beautiful national schools; and those infant children who are educated there, when they grow up to manhood, will call down blessings on him who was instrumental in procuring for them the blessings of education.' *Vindicator*, 18 Apr. 1846. The address was signed by William Walker, Thomas Cregg (*aka* Craig, of Kilclooney), and Thomas Mulherin, who presented him with a new car.

in 1851–4 and Laconnell in 1855–6. His disinterest produced some bizarre correspondence with the Board. Informed by the Board in 1855 that he, as manager, had the authority to dismiss John Campbell from Brackey School for negligence, McGarvey, who, in an uncommon moment of concern, had first brought the teacher's 'negligence' to its attention and asked that he be fired, replied that he would be 'willing to overlook Campbell's faults if Comm[issione]rs will do likewise'. On the basis of his original complaint, the Board insisted that Campbell be let go.[10] Similarly, in 1856, after the reopening of Lergynasearhagh, he wrote to the Board, asking if it would sanction the appointment of Patrick Bresland [Breslin] as its master despite 'he having been accused of intemperance and immorality while in charge of Glenties NS'. The Board refused. (Ironically, Breslin was an extraordinary schoolmaster. He had been one of only two 'first class' teachers in Donegal and he had won a prestigious national award for teaching in 1845. However, he had been obliged to resign from Glenties in 1850, when, 'only seven months' after his wife's death, he fathered a child with his servant girl.)[11] And so, in the mid-1850s, when there were fifteen national schools in the predominantly Catholic parish of Ardara, McGarvey was manager of only eight of them, and in one case (Clooney), he shared the responsibility with Knox Barrett, the liberal rector.

A POLITICAL PRIEST

> Blessed is he that considereth the poor and needy.
>
> Psalm 41: 1[12]

If John D. McGarvey was not an overly engaged pastor, Edward Glacken (1806–84), his curate since 1853, might have been expected to compensate. Glacken was a consummate organizer, who had been responsible for building a chapel and schools in other parishes. He was also a politically minded man, who had been active in the Repeal campaign in Donegal in

---

[10] ED 2/59/27: Brackey; ED 2/54/115: Brackey.

[11] ED 2/59/92: Lergynasearhagh; ED 2/13/35: Glenties. Glenties was unfortunate in its choice of schoolmasters: Bresland's successor, Michael Boulger, resigned after only two years in 1852; a 'dissipated and careless' character, he had been accused of translating into English some 'obscene language in Irish' which the larger boys in the class had used before the girls. On one occasion, the manager, Robert Russell, arrived at the school at 12 o'clock to find that Boulger had 'just made his appearance and in a state totally unfit for duty'.

[12] Quoted in a testimonial from the inhabitants of Ardara to Edward Glacken on his removal to Gartan, *Vindicator*, 25 Dec. 1847.

the early 1840s and, latterly, in the early 1850s, prominent on Tenant Right platforms.[13] Moreover, he knew Ardara well, for he had been a curate there in 1845–7. In those years, he had been heavily involved in relief work and a scourge of officials.[14] For instance, on Christmas Eve 1846, he penned a public letter to the lord lieutenant which appeared in the *Vindicator*, Belfast's first Catholic newspaper, deploring 'the systematical shuffling and shifting' of Lieutenant John W. Milward of the Royal Engineers, who as the Inspecting Officer of the Board of Works, was responsible for organizing desperately needed road projects to employ the poor and enable them to purchase food. Milward was pompous and officious—a man possessed by 'the demon of official technicality', according to Glacken—and, at the year's end, he had yet to get the poor working. 'I can't for the life of me', the priest wrote, 'fathom the depth of this contemptible maneuvering of overseers and officers of the Board of Works. Perhaps they have received instructions from headquarters to treat the people thus. Why not tell us then, in plain words, that our poor people must starve, must bite the dust, linger and die, and their fetid carcasses fatten the soil of their unfortunate country.' Glacken had been particularly vexed when, after a meeting in Glenties, Milward had told poor people crowding around his tandem car, that he would have issued tickets for employment on road works if the local relief committee, composed of gentry, clergymen, and merchants, had provided him with lists. The committee, Glacken claimed, had provided lists, and only for the 'influence and exertions' of its members, Glenties would have presented 'a sad spectacle of anarchy and confusion' that evening. His picture of the scene was stark: 'The gloomy despair of some with starvation and death depicted in their emaciated countenances—the firm resolve of others expressed in menacing threats, that they would not die of starvation whilst a four-footed animal roamed at large through our pasture fields—the angry indignation—the open defiance of all law and order—the reckless despair . . . ' And he laid blame for the unfolding catastrophe on government:

---

[13] For Glacken's Repeal politics, see *Evening Packet*, 10 Aug. 1843. In 1850–2, he officiated at Tenant Right meetings in Letterkenny, Strabane, and other towns, and accompanied Campbell Johnston to Lifford to be nominated for the 1852 election. See *FJ*, 30 July 1850, and *The Nation*, 3 Aug. 1850; *Evening Freeman*, 19 July 1852; *Evening Mail*, 28 July 1852. Maguire, *Raphoe*, ii. 131, 152–3, notes that he built a chapel in Glenvar, in north Donegal, and that 'in all the other parishes where he ministered, his name is held in veneration'. Maguire presents his appointment to Ardara, in 1845, as 'reward of his work and resourceful efforts in raising funds'.

[14] Glacken also publicized the district's plight in England's Catholic press; see *Tablet*, 24 July 1847, where he thanks people for donations to the 'starving poor of this parish', and *Tablet*, 28 Aug. 1847, which acknowledges funds sent by the Brotherhood of St Vincent de Paul in London.

Our tale of misery is a short one—our entire population starving—hundreds dying, and many of them dead and in their graves, the untimely victims of starvation. Really these are sad objects to look upon; fit subjects to be insulted and laughed at by the paid servants of the Board of Works. Within the last fortnight, I have conducted to the grave the last remains of eight individuals, victims of disease, brought on by the insufficiency of food; and if a coroner's inquest had been held on their dead bodies, 'death from starvation' would have been the verdict of a conscientious jury. May God in His mercy look down on the poor starving population of Boylagh! We cry for bread, a stone is offered us in return. We supplicate for relief; our supplications are listened to with a cold, calculating, official indifference. Applications are made to the Board of Works to open up lines of road through the destitute districts—we are laughed at by its paid officials, and insulted by the haughty sneers of its officers. How long, O Lord!, will this state of things continue? Until society be revolutionized and life and property be insecure? Until thousands will have been carried away by starvation and death? If it is so, it is upon the shoulders of the government and Board of Works will rest the responsibility.[15]

On his transfer—or, more correctly, his removal—from Ardara to Gartan in late 1847, Glacken had received a warm testimonial from the inhabitants of the parish, who credited his 'judicious humanity' with having 'saved starving hundreds from death'. They noted too that his 'works of mercy and of love' were not confined to his own persuasion, but 'extended wherever the appeal of distress presented itself'.[16] Those words were an allusion to the circumstances of his departure. In July 1847, the *Vindicator* had carried another public letter from Glacken, this time addressed to the Narin Poor Relief Committee. It was a subcommittee of the Inishkeel Relief Committee, the government-approved body that was an official

---

[15] Letter dated Ardara, Christmas Eve 1846, in *Vindicator*, 2 Jan. 1847. Several weeks earlier, *Vindicator*, 25 Nov. 1846, had carried another letter from Glacken, citing the failure of the Board of Works to open road projects as evidence that government was not doing all that it could to relieve distress. He described administering the last rites to the dying and consolation to 'the most patient people on the face of God's earth', and raised the spectre of 'outrage': 'Food, food, and employment to enable them to purchase food, is the burthen of our prayer for the last three months. In the name, then, of humanity and religion—in the name of the God of Charity, we call upon the government to snatch us from instant death. Neglect this appeal, let the ears of our rulers be deaf to our most earnest entreaties, let their hearts be heartened against the loud cry of starving thousands, and all the efforts of the clergy, both Protestant and Catholic—all the influence and exertions of the friends of social order may prove ineffectual to control the violence and outrage of famishing thousands.' For Milward's version of events, see his letters dated 3 and 19 Dec. 1846, in *Correspondence relating to Measures for Relief of Distress in Ireland (Board of Works Series), July 1846–January 1847*, HC 1847 [764], l, 325, 414. And for his perspective on subsequent developments, see *Correspondence from January to March 1847, Relating to the Measures Adopted for the Relief of the Distress in Ireland*, HC 1847 [797], lii. 33, 37, 99–100.

[16] *Vindicator*, 25 Dec. 1847.

conduit for aid; James Ovens, rector of Inishkeel, was secretary of the parent committee and McGarvey was a member.[17] The subcommittee's area was the electoral division of Narin (sometimes Naran), which stretched from the Tullies and Maas west to Rosbeg. At the time of the Famine, this division contained near 4,000 people (1841 pop. 3,712). It came to be seen as too large, and in a rearrangement in 1850, it was divided, with the greater part of it now forming the divisions of Dawros and Maas (combined pop. 1841: 3,601).

In July 1847, when Glacken's letter to the Narin Committee appeared in the *Vindicator*, the country was in the depths of the Famine and descriptions of hunger and disease were losing their capacity to shock. Still, its explicit and oblique allegations about the 'mysterious workings' of the Committee made for extraordinary reading:

> I accuse you of inhumanity in the treatment of the poor; injustice, exclusiveness, and bigotry in the distribution of charities unwisely entrusted to your management.... With charitable funds at your disposal, calculated, under a proper and judicious management, to alleviate for a time the unparalleled destitution in your electoral division, you are looking on with fiendish indifference at hundreds writhing in the last agonies of starvation, without affording them any relief. Whilst the most alarming stage of the famine is yet to be encountered, you positively refused to ration the destitute, who are in the most decided and abject state of destitution, and thus counteract the merciful intentions of government in the outdoor relief act. Whilst fever, famine and emigration are decimating this once happy country, and when the remaining poor who are unable to leave the country—the widow, the orphan, whom age, youth, or infirmity have thrown helpless and destitute at your committee door, the starving, half-dead, half-dying—apply to you for rations, what response meets their cry of distress? They are laughed at in their misery, mocked at in their sufferings, and insultingly told, to 'go to h——ll and get rations'. Oh! God of mercy, look down with compassion on my poor people, who are handed over to the keeping of such men! Monsters in the creation! Christians without a Christian heart—men without the common feelings of humanity! God help the poor people who have to suffer.

---

[17] For Ovens's correspondence, see RLFC 3/2 2/441/41. After the recurrence of blight in 1846, local notables across Ireland had established relief committees to administer aid allocated by the Relief Commission. The Commission expressed a preference for committees comprising two parishes. Here, a single committee was formed for 'Ardara and Inniskeel'. This extensive district lay in two baronies, which created difficulties as the Commission organized matters on a baronial level: Ovens, as secretary, complained of having to keep two sets of accounts. There were also tensions about the location of a meal depot: the Commission chose the Loughros coastguard station, convenient to Ardara, but Ovens pressed the advantages of the station in Portnoo, equidistant from both towns and closest to the impoverished fishing communities around Rosbeg. Ultimately, in Jan. 1847, the committee split on baronial lines.

God help the poor priest who has to witness such indignities, such unparalleled scenes of worse than fiendish barbarity.

Glacken proceeded to explicitly blame the 'starving committee' for 'two deaths from actual starvation, and many from protracted starvation . . . within the past three weeks'. And he threatened further revelations about the 'savage cruelty' of the 'squireens' of Boylagh:

> I am in a capacity to prove, if allowed an opportunity, and I court investigation, that persons have received *meal*, and *rice*, and *breadstuffs*, at your relief store, who had four or five head of cattle, and other means of support, irrespective of your relief; others have some of your charity meal and rice stored up in their houses, whilst the poor are repulsed with ignominy, and told to go home and die—insulted, beaten, and abused like brute beasts—whilst your dependents—cottiers and labourers—are plentifully supplied. Is this distributive justice? I could point to farms labored—out-fields fenced in—houses repaired and furnished—illegitimate children supported—profligate characters maintained with the money, and meal, and rice, and breadstuffs sent by the charitable and humane from all parts of Europe and America to this western portion of Donegal, for the support of its destitute starving inhabitants. I could tell other tales, gentlemen, that would make our common humanity blush—tales which are not fit to be told in the columns of a public newspaper.[18]

The townlands that constituted the Narin electoral division were almost all the property of the Marquess of Conyngham (1797–1876) and Edward Michael Conolly (1786–1849), with the former owning most of the section that became Dawros and the latter, the Tory MP for the county, most of that which became Maas. However, by the 'squireens' of Boylagh, Glacken was pointing at a few tenant gentry families in the area, notably Gilly Hamilton of Eden—the hard-living middleman cum agent who was to testify at the trial of Neil Craig in March 1856 and give evidence as to the good character of Ribbonmen in March 1857—Isaac O'Donnell (d. 1850) of Summy, high constable of the barony of Boylagh and coroner, and the Porters of Lackagh and Ballyiriston. The rector James Ovens was being rebuked too, for he, as secretary, was the link between the Inishkeel Committee, its various subcommittees, and the Relief Commission in Dublin. In fact, Ovens lived in the middle of the Narin Committee's area and he was most likely a member of it as well.[19]

---

[18] The letter dated, 10 July, appeared in *Vindicator*, 17 July 1847. 'The above letter', the editor remarked, 'carries its own comment. If Government does not institute an immediate inquiry into the astounding charges put forward by Father Glacken, we shall be much mistaken indeed.'

[19] Ovens vigorously protested to the lord lieutenant about Glacken's 'wanton attack' on the Committee. See NAI, Distress Papers 1847/D7,923 Inishkeel, 27 Aug. 1847, Ovens to

The area was undoubtedly poor, most especially around Rosbeg, Lackagh (Portnoo), and Maas, where income from fishing had allowed families to subsist on particularly small plots of land. Consequently, the loss of potatoes had been here a very severe blow, and these smallholder- and cottier-fishermen, some seven miles from a market town, suffered terribly in the Famine.[20] Indeed, the decline in population from 1841 to 1851 in Dawros (–17 per cent) and Maas (–28 per cent) was significantly greater than that in the entire Union of Glenties (–6.9 per cent; from 43,144 to 40,159), with the decline in Maas the greatest in any of its electoral divisions. The decline in those two divisions, from a combined total of 3,601 persons in 1841 to 2,832 in 1851, was 769 persons (–21.3 per cent).[21] Three of thirty-four inhabited townlands accounted for over half (464) of that shortfall: Drumboghill (217), Dawros (149), and Maas (98)—the latter two townlands gave their names to the electoral divisions. In these three townlands alone, the number of inhabited houses more than halved from 134 in 1841 to sixty-five in 1851, with the number of closures being particularly high in Drumboghill; there, the number of inhabited houses fell from forty-four to just thirteen. Drumboghill and Dawros were then held, under Conyngham, by Gilly, George, and John Hamilton, who sublet a lot of land to smallholders: in 1834, when it was held in rundale, a tithe applotter had judged it 'impossible' to establish what land was held by either the Hamilton brothers or their 'cottier tenants'.[22] Maas, also on the Conyngham estate, was seven miles from the Hamiltons' main holdings, near their seat at Eden, but it was still within their ambit; none of the brothers is known to have held land in Maas prior to the Famine, but Gilly would be subletting a farm there by the mid-1850s, when he had just under 1,000 acres of mountain pasture in nearby Letterilly, Derk More, and Derk Beg. Other 'squireens' and large farmers doubtless took advantage of the crisis too—at the very least, they let subtenants relinquish land and resort to the poorhouse—but Gilly and his brothers stand out.

The effect of Glacken's letter on the provision of relief in 1847 is unclear; on Friday 3 December, the first week that the Board of Guardians

Clarendon. And for details of a fractious meeting of the Committee, attended by Glacken, on 8 July, two days before he wrote his letter to the *Vindicator*, see Distress Papers 1847/D7,707.

[20] On the higher interest rates charged to fishermen, see *First Report of the Commissioners of Inquiry into the State of the Irish Fisheries: With the Minutes of Evidence and Appendix*, HC 1837 (22), xxii. 69.

[21] The data refer to the Union as defined in 1851.

[22] TAB Inishkeel, II. For George Hamilton's lease, dated 1829, of Drumboghill and Dawros, see PRONI, D1,583/20.

of the Glenties Union offered outdoor relief, Narin—one of thirteen divisions, between Killybegs and Crolly—accounted for 221 of 962 names on its lists, but numbers fluctuated by the week.[23] Irrespective of any effect the letter may have had on relief, it was doubtless a factor in Glacken's removal from the parish at the year's end. Correspondence that might illuminate the thinking of his bishop in removing him is no longer extant, if indeed any ever existed. However, given that Glacken was being promoted to administrator of Gartan, a step to becoming parish priest (a title which he used in the early 1850s), McGettigan cannot have entirely disapproved of his ascription of sectarian partiality to the Committee or, indeed, his shaming of the 'squireens' of Boylagh. Rather, he may have judged that Glacken, having so flagrantly abused local notables, would be less effective in the deepening crisis. His work here was done.

Glacken was no sectarian partisan. Indeed, in Clooney, in the middle of the Narin Committee's area, in 1845, he and Knox Barrett, the Ardara rector (and brother-in-law of Gilly Hamilton), had established a national school under their joint patronage, an uncommon arrangement at a time when, locally and nationally, it was more common for a single clergyman to be sole patron of a school, thus associating it with one church. Tellingly, Ovens, who had only succeeded Barrett's late father (after forty-two years as rector) in winter 1844–5, was not involved in that school which was, in fact, in his parish (Inishkeel) not Barrett's (Ardara), and, being in a townland adjacent to his glebe, only a short walk from his door. Ovens, a Fermanagh-man whose forebears had 'supplied many members to the army and Church', was more of a 'political Protestant' than the liberal and popular Barrett who had been born and reared in the area, and who may well have expected to get his father's place.[24] Tellingly too, Glacken's stand had not alienated Ardara Protestants. The majority of the seventeen 'sincere friends' who signed the testimonial to him were Catholics, among them Thomas Craig of Kilclooney, William Walker of Loughros Point,

[23] Patrick Conaghan, *The Great Famine in South-West Donegal, 1845–50* (Enniscrone, 1997), 211.

[24] From Ovens's obituary in *BN*, 13 Jan. 1872. It notes that he was 'much and deservedly beloved by the people of all denominations and classes of Inniskeel'. Revealingly, perhaps, during the squabble with Glacken, Ovens used the old-fashioned and offensive term 'Romanists' to describe the majority community in the Narin Committee's area to the lord lieutenant. See Distress Papers 1847/D7,923 Inishkeel, 27 Aug. 1847, Ovens to Clarendon. Nevertheless, Ovens did work closely with priests on relief in 1846–7, and after Glacken's first allegations about the management of the Committee's funds— delivered verbally at a meeting on 8 July—McGarvey, his other curate John O'Donnell, and Dan Earley, parish priest of Glenties, all wrote letters to the Committee in which they accepted that Ovens had at all times acted appropriately. For this correspondence, see Distress Papers 1847/D7,707.

and several merchants in Ardara, including John Crumley (1798–1866), who was clerk of the petty sessions. However, the signatories included five prominent Protestants who had been involved with him in relief work: Richard William Nesbitt, owner of the Woodhill estate, and his nephew, James Nesbitt Evans; Richard Pearson, the Methodist minister; Knox Barrett, the rector, and his brother William Barrett, a crown solicitor. Likewise, public officials involved in relief—Thomas Moore, commanding officer of the Coastguard in Loughros; Owen McDermott, Inspector of the Revenue Police; and William McCaul, an officer in the Revenue Police—put their names to it, as did Christopher McGarvey, the local surgeon and brother of the parish priest.[25]

From the perspective of the poor, meanwhile, Glacken left Ardara with his reputation only burnished by his denunciation of the squireens of Boylagh, and, in time, the controversy became a key event in *seanchas* about the Famine. In 1937–8, Con Melley (55) of Tullycleave told his daughter, Theresa (14) of it, mentioning Ovens but omitting the detail that he had been the minister:

> The time of the Famine there was free broth distributed to the poor people. There was a man named Ovens living in Downstrands, and he tried to stop the giving out of the broth. There was a priest named Father Glacan [*sic*] and he told Ovans [*sic*] that he would die of hunger and he having plenty of food. This prophecy came true because ever after that every place that Ovens went he was always eating and some time later he died of hunger and he having plenty of food to eat.[26]

Similarly, in November 1938, 78-year-old Mary Boyle of Tullycleave, told her granddaughter, Philomena Breslin of Summy, a story that she called 'The "Stinting" of the Broth'. In her telling, it is not Ovens who is the villain but a Protestant family, who had charge of a broth house. Complicating matters, these people were named Gallagher, an indication that, at some stage, they had converted from Catholicism.

> There was a Protestant family in Clogher near a little river, and they were in charge of the broth-house, but they did not treat the Catholics properly. This family was named Gallachers [*sic*]. They were to give a canfull [*sic*] of broth to the Catholics every day, but the measure was often stinted. There was a priest living nearby by the name of Father Glacan. The priest reproached the Protestants and they had a mind to kill him. The priest said to himself that

---

[25] *Vindicator*, 25 Dec. 1847. Ovens's name is on a similar address, 'From the Protestant and Roman Catholic Inhabitants of the Parish of Inniskeel' to John O'Donnell, Catholic curate, on his removal from Inishkeel in 1849; see *LJ*, 13 June 1849.

[26] See NFCS 1,048 (Tullymore): 101. Con Melley's father, Edward (b. *c.*1823), who told him other stories of the Famine, was the likely source of the story.

he would make them poor. These people had six cows, and the priest went in one night and he asked the people in Irish did they smell anything? They said that they did not but when they arose in the morning, the six cows were burned in the byre without the byre being burned. They begged his pardon, and they began to become rich by a miracle which he worked, by acknowledging his power.[27]

For Mary Boyle, the story was a rebuke to the Gallaghers of Clogher for the 'stinting of the broth' (and, presumably, their conversion to Protestantism) and it was an explanation too of the prosperity of the family, who, in her time became pillars of Catholic respectability—once they accepted the priest's 'power', they thrived. The destruction of the Gallaghers' cattle may be a Famine-time 'outrage' now lost to history. However, there can be smoke in *seanchas* without fire in history, and the miraculous incineration could be a complete fiction, a way of casting Glacken as a heroic figure, using his 'power' to punish those who had maligned his people.[28] Paradoxically, despite Boyle's focus on partiality against Catholics (which accords with Glacken's complaint in July 1847), her story undermines the easy association of 'Protestant' with 'advantage'. The Gallaghers of Clogher having been converts (not 'proper' Protestants, in the eyes of many), the listener is reminded that some Catholics were markedly better off than some Protestants, and that class differences predated the crisis and persisted after it: while there may have been sectarian partiality in the distribution of the broth, the critical cleavage was between men with six head of cattle and those with empty cans.

•

Given the circumstances of Glacken's removal from Ardara in late 1847, his reappointment to the parish in 1853 was unexpected. However, in Gartan, things had not gone well for the priest and, after an incident that garnered national attention, it was a diminished man who returned to the town. On 8 April 1853, Glacken reported to the Constabulary that two days earlier he had been shot and wounded between Meenadrain crossroads and his house in Tirargus, by a man wearing a flat Jim Crow hat. At the quarter sessions, meeting in Letterkenny on 11 April, the grand jury offered a reward of £400 for the arrest of the gunman—subscriptions at the assizes were expected to bring it to £1,500—and Dublin Castle, already in the process of proclaiming the barony of Kilmacrenan at the time of

[27] NFCS 1,048 (Kilclooney), 273; story told by Mary Boyle (78), Tullycleave, to Philomena Breslin, Summy, 1938.
[28] On the 'heroic priest' and 'drunken priest' in *seanchas*, see Taylor, *Occasions of Faith*, chs. 4–5.

incident, prepared to post additional rewards. Meanwhile, those Dublin newspapers that picked up the story discerned a political motive for the attack in Glacken's prominence in Tenant Right politics, including, the previous year, in the campaign of Patrick Campbell Johnston, who had polled well in the hotly contested general election, but failed to secure a seat.[29]

Daniel Cruise was assigned to investigate. Awkwardly for both the Church and the Castle, it soon transpired that, at the time of the alleged shooting, Glacken had been visibly drunk and several people had seen him fall, and a doctor, who had examined him after the incident, believed that he was suffering from *delirium tremens*, a condition for which he had treated him on two occasions over the previous fifteen months. The local magistrates, who had taken the priest's original claim seriously, now pressed Dublin Castle to prosecute him for a false statement, the eagerness of some of them for a prosecution animated by Glacken being 'remarkable for his extreme liberal and popular opinions'. However, Larcom, the eminently level-headed Under Secretary, wanted to drop the matter, and he readily accepted the law adviser's argument that prosecuting the priest would only embarrass the magistrates who should not have taken a statement from a man in his condition.[30]

Patrick McGettigan, Glacken's bishop, was himself fond of a drink. In 1851 Paul Cullen, archbishop of Dublin, told a friend in the Vatican that McGettigan went through Drogheda 'in a state of intoxication';[31] and the historian Oliver Rafferty, an admirer of the 'indomitable McGettigan', concedes that 'the aged bishop... could be seen drunk in public in his declining years'.[32] In transferring Glacken back to Ardara, where he would be busy, McGettigan may have hoped that this able man would sort himself out. In fact, Glacken did get to grips with his drink problem, but not, it seems, in Ardara. In 1860, he was transferred to Killymard, four years later he resigned, and then, in 1867, he entered Mount Melleray Abbey, a Cistercian monastery to which alcoholics resorted to 'dry out'. There, he took the oblate's vow in 1871, and, as Brother Luke, he served

[29] See *FJ*, 15 Apr. 1853; *Saunder's Newsletter*, 16, 23 Apr. 1853. And for a premature offering by a Catholic publisher, see *Barbarous Attempt on the Life of the Rev. Mr Glacken, Gartan, County Donegal...* (Dublin, 1853).

[30] For a substantial file, including evidence to a magisterial inquiry, see CSORP 1854/ 12,532. *Saunder's Newsletter*, 26 May 1853, includes an account of a meeting, attended by Glacken, at which the magistrates gave the results of their investigation.

[31] Cullen to Propaganda, 28 Sept. 1851, quoted in John H. Whyte, 'The Appointment of Catholic Bishops in Nineteenth-Century Ireland', *Catholic Historical Review*, 48/1 (1962), 12–32; also see Donal Kerr, *'A Nation of Beggars'? Priests, People and Politics in Famine Ireland, 1846–52* (Oxford, 1994), 313.

[32] Oliver Rafferty, *Catholicism in Ulster, 1603–1983: An Interpretative History* (Dublin, 1994), 108, 110.

as 'guest master' for over a decade and 'died the death of saint'. According
to Maguire, the diocesan historian, he had been a 'very remarkable and
gifted curate... one of the best known, most esteemed and gifted of the
Raphoe priesthood'.[33]

THE BISHOP AND THE CURATE

Patrick McGettigan was in his early seventies when Patrick McGlynn
turned informer in 1856. A coadjutor, his nephew Daniel McGettigan,
had been appointed to Raphoe in February of that year, but the bishop
retained tight control of the diocese over which he had presided since
1820. It had been a remarkable episcopacy. The historian Emmet Larkin
has calculated that, on McGettigan's appointment, there had been 'only
24 priests, including himself, to serve 29 parishes which at the time
worked out an incredible priest-to-people ratio of one to more than
5,000'. In fact, the number of clergymen in the diocese was then significantly lower than it had been in 1800 (35), when the priest-to-people ratio
had been 1:2,710. His predecessor, in other words, had not only failed
to increase the number of priests in a period of rapid population growth,
he had let it dwindle. Nevertheless, by 1842, McGettigan had brought
the number of priests up to nearly fifty, and if his diocese still generated
one of the worst priest-to-people ratios in the country (1:3,400), he had
improved it.[34] Thereafter, he greatly increased the number of chapels. In
1834, when, per Larkin's calculations, there were 2.0 Catholic chapels per
parish in Ireland, Raphoe had the lowest number (1.2) of chapels
per parish in the country, approached only by other poor dioceses in the
west; then, with the exception of Achonry, Galway, and Killala, all 1.3,
and neighbouring Clogher, 1.4, in no diocese was the number of chapels
per parish less than 1.6.[35] Nevertheless, McGettigan, helped by the likes of

[33] Maguire, *Raphoe*, ii. 154. On the death of Glacken's sister, *DJ*, 17 June 1927, noted
that the priest, then nearly fifty years dead, was 'still affectionately remembered by the older
generation'.

[34] Emmet Larkin, *The Pastoral Role of the Catholic Church in Pre-Famine Ireland,
1750–1850* (Dublin, 2006), 137–86, 185, 271. K. Theodore Hoppen, *Elections, Politics
and Society in Ireland, 1832–1885* (Oxford, 1984), 205–6, errs when, quoting Cullen, he
argues that McGettigan had taken his diocese 'from a period when it had not a single church
of any substance to one of ample provision'. There had been a considerable number of
chapels built during the episcopacy (1782–1801) of Anthony Coyle, including sixteen, he
calculated in 1788, 'built in the space of a few years'; see his *Collectanea Sacra: or, Pious
Miscellany in Verse and Prose in Six Books*, 2 vols. (Strabane, 1788), i. 2. Among them were
some fine buildings, notably Massmount.

[35] Larkin, *Pastoral Role of the Catholic Church*, 150.

Glacken, added twelve new chapels to the diocese in 1834–46, and a
further fifteen chapels in the 1850s.[36]

Such an accomplished administrator cannot have been unaware of
McGarvey's failings. However, the priest was popular—he shared the
people's interest in cattle and largely left them alone—and, prior to the
1850s, McGettigan had more pressing problems. Also, transferring a
parish priest (as distinct from a curate) who did not want to move was
difficult—as McGettigan would explain to Cruise with regard to John
Doherty of Gweedore in 1857—and so the bishop had tended to send
energetic assistants to Ardara to pick up the slack. Still, McGlynn's turning
informer made it difficult for him to continue to ignore McGarvey's
poor management. Three schoolmasters who had taught in the parish
had been exposed as Molly Maguires. Two of them—McGlynn (Beagh)
and Kennedy (Crannogeboy)—had been hired by McGarvey and worked
under his supervision; the third—Melley, who had since moved to
another parish—had been in a school (Meentinadea) established by a
landlord, further evidence of McGarvey's less than acute interest in
education. Moreover, McGlynn's information had revealed the Ribbon
Society to have other adherents in the middle strata of the Catholic
community, which might have been expected to be most attentive to
Church teaching. Finally, the Mollies had been particularly active in
Downstrands, an area that McGarvey had notoriously neglected. Here,
some townlands were over seven miles from the chapel in the town, yet he
had repeatedly refused to build a second place of worship. Ironically, the
unfortunate Glacken had proposed erecting one at Kilclooney during his
first spell in Ardara in 1845–7, but his efforts had been 'frustrated' by
McGarvey's 'insuperable objection to any expenditure on a large scale'.[37]

After the widely publicized arrests in June 1856, the bishop had acted
quickly, sending another curate, Thomas Daly, to assist McGarvey and
Glacken. Connected to prominent shopkeepers in Ballyshannon, Daly
was in his late twenties. A 'pious and zealous' man, he immediately moved
to provide a chapel-centred alternative to lodge meetings in public houses.
To this end, he established a confraternity in winter 1856–7 which, by
summer 1857, claimed some 1,400 members.[38] Daly also took responsibility for building a second chapel. Before the end of 1856, he had
acquired a site in Kilclooney and commenced fundraising. In June
1857, the *Catholic Telegraph*, noting his efforts, dwelt on the spectacle
of a 'congregation of 2,000 people' assembling every Sunday 'to hear Mass
in the open air, exposed to the inclemency of the weather, without any

[36] Ibid. 185.   [37] Maguire, *Raphoe*, i. 281; ii. 152–3.
[38] Letter of Mission in *Ulsterman*, 13 July 1857.

protection from the storm when it comes'.[39] A simple chapel—a 'handsome and well-equipped building'—would open in June 1864.[40] Few families in the parish were now more than four miles from chapel, and Beagh, where the Mollies had come undone, was two miles north of one chapel, and two miles south of another. There was no excuse for missing mass.[41]

AN SAGART MÓR Ó GALLACHÓIR

When Tom Daly was setting the parish of Ardara to rights in winter 1856–7, Patrick (commonly Pat) Gallagher (1806–66), parish priest of Inishkeel, was engaging with the civil authorities to bring the remaining 'Ribbon cases' to a satisfactory conclusion. Born in Ballynaglack, near Stranorlar, in 1806, Gallagher belonged to the remnants of the pre-Plantation élite. His father, a comfortable farmer, was a direct descendant of the stepfather of Hugh O'Neill, who led the Irish against Elizabeth I in 1594–1603, and the priest carried a strong sense of this genteel background. He was, according to one who knew him, a 'brusque, loud-voiced, independent-looking, aristocratic clergyman, born to rule'. He hunted and he fished—the sports of country squires—and in Inver, where he was appointed curate in 1832, and later in Glenties, where he became parish priest in 1852, he associated with Church of Ireland clergy and gentry.[42] Such associations were by no means unusual: on his reputation-wrecking spree in 1853, Glacken had stopped for a drink with the minister in Dunlewey, and in 1846 Edward Maginn, the coadjutor bishop of Derry, had recommended that the Vatican appoint a 'prudent coadjutor' to assist McGettigan in Raphoe because 'in Protestant society . . . he makes no secret of the secrets of his church or his clergy'.[43] However, Gallagher was particularly comfortable in establishment circles. Chief among his gentry friends was the Marquess of Conyngham, the literal owner of much of west Donegal: the two men supposedly met when fishing on the Eany and Gallagher recommended that the landlord change his fly. He was also on close terms with Alexander Montgomery, rector of Inver, from whom he leased an imposing house and 'the finest farm on

[39] Quoted in McGill, *Ardara*, 28.   [40] Maguire, *Raphoe*, i. 281; ii. 73–4.
[41] Daly took a keen interest in schools in this section of the parish; in 1859, he acknowledged receipt of £2 from Robert Russell, Conyngham's 'kind and benevolent agent', for the 'improvement of Begha [*sic*] School'. See *Ulsterman*, 31 Jan. 1859.
[42] Maguire, *Raphoe*, i. 484–6. For a warm obituary, see *LJ*, 11 July 1866.
[43] Maginn to Cullen, 3 Dec. 1846, quoted in Desmond Bowen, *Paul Cardinal Cullen and the Shaping of Modern Irish Catholicism* (Dublin, 1983), 63.

his estate' at Cloverhill.[44] Later, after his transfer to Inishkeel, he took a substantial house and 184-acre farm from Conyngham at the Wood (Stranaglogh); the house and offices were valued at £4 10s. (90s.) in the mid-1850s, the same valuation as McGarvey's house in Lough Hill, and his farm was valued at £6 (for purposes of comparison, just over half the valuation (£11 10s.) of James Gallagher's slightly smaller holding).[45]

Reflecting the priest's ease in gentry society, and his moral and political bearings, the previous tenants of both the farm at Stranaglogh and that at Cloverhill had been evicted, a detail that would have discouraged many people from taking them, and but for his collar it might have roused the ire of Molly Maguire.[46] Significantly, Gallagher had been vocal in his opposition to the Ribbon Society. He had 'frequently' denounced it from the altar in Glenties and, in June 1856, when the first men were arrested on McGlynn's evidence, he had told them that 'they deserved their fate'— a phrase noted in official correspondence at the time and long remembered locally.[47] However, the priest was no toady, and he had a country squire's disdain for jumped-up functionaries. Hugh McFadden, his curate, used to walk in his canonicals to and from chapel on Sunday and Monday mornings. In January 1859, the curate and parish priest both received notes from a Constabulary sub-inspector, stationed in Glenties, pointing out that it was an offence carrying a £100 fine for a Catholic clergyman to appear in the public street in his 'canonical gown'—in fact, under 10 Geo. IV Cap. 7 (ironically, the Catholic Emancipation Act of 1829), the fine was £50—and hoping that there would be no repetition of it. Gallagher responded tersely, expressing 'grave doubts' about the 'discretion and propriety' of the notes. When the policeman sent a second note, Gallagher witheringly mocked the notion that 'in this wild portion of wild Donegal' a curate being seen 'to have gone to chapel and to have returned from it to his Lodging wearing a canonical gown concealed under his great coat . . . should rouse the vigilant attention of a peace officer', and he promptly complained to the lord lieutenant. Not receiving a reply within a month of his complaint, he published both his correspondence with the sub-inspector and his letter to the lord lieutenant in Denis Holland's *Irishman*. Meanwhile, the opinion of the law adviser had been sought by Dublin Castle. He confirmed that it was an offence, but the attorney general decreed that there should be no prosecution and Gallagher and McFadden received a letter to that effect from Thomas Larcom, who

[44] Maguire, *Raphoe*, i. 484–6.   [45] *GV*.   [46] Maguire, *Raphoe*, i. 485–6.
[47] CSORP 1861/7,273 Report of Crown Solicitor on Crime in Donegal; this report, compiled in 1861, reviews 'the state of Donegal' over the previous five years.

expressed regret that the sub-inspector had not sought direction from his superiors before contacting them. And that letter too duly appeared in the republican *Irishman*.[48]

Intelligent and self-assured, Pat Gallagher was a man with whom Daniel Cruise could do business. He was also an influential figure in the diocese and, in spring 1857, Cruise was eager to strengthen his relationship with McGettigan and his clergy in the hope of isolating John Doherty (1815–81), parish priest of Gweedore, around whom militant clerics were rallying. In Gweedore, rundale had been partly dismantled in the early 1840s, when new 'stripped' cuts were allocated to tenants. However, mountain pasture had de facto been left undivided, and tenants continued to graze their stock there. In 1854, several landlords introduced grazing fees while simultaneously increasing rents. They also leased several thousand acres of mountain pasture to Scottish and English graziers who now stocked the hills with black-faced sheep. Doherty, who had addressed meetings in Letterkenny supporting Campbell Johnston, the Tenant Right candidate, in the 1852 election, was early identified by Cruise as orchestrating opposition to the landlords and graziers. Notably, in spring 1854, he was alleged to have imposed 'fines' on parishioners who paid the grazing fees and to have denied confession to the families of those who refused to pay these fines. Matters escalated sharply in December 1856, when forty men wearing white shirts, and described as Molly Maguires, raided the house of a Scottish shepherd and ordered him to leave the country. Over the next three months, some 618 black-faced sheep were reported missing or destroyed in Gweedore.[49]

Overseen by Cruise, the state response was two-pronged. First, in February 1857, the grand jury levied compensation for the missing sheep off the entire population of Gweedore, with the exception of the Church of Ireland minister. Second, an additional forty constables were deployed in the parish under the Crime and Outrage (Ireland) Act (1847) and the population levied for their cost under the Peace Preservation (Ireland) Act (1856). Doherty, however, was not deterred. In April, he sent a petition to Westminster claiming that the loss of the highland pastures and rent increases had impoverished the people, who would now be left destitute if the 'sheep tax' and 'police tax' were collected. The petition asked that government intervene and either relieve the people or assist them to emigrate; the priest offered to emigrate with them. However, as only three of 2,027 'signatures' were genuine, parliament rejected the petition. Doherty, it transpired, had read the petition at

---

[48] CSORP 1859/2,632; *Irishman*, 26 Mar., 9 Apr. 1859.
[49] Mac Suibhne, 'Agrarian Improvement', 563 ff.

Sunday mass, asked the congregation if he should send it to the Commons, and then signed his parishioners' names.[50]

Convinced that Doherty was fomenting trouble in the parish, Cruise had met with three senior figures in the Catholic hierarchy—Paul Cullen, the reforming archbishop of Dublin; Joseph Dixon, archbishop of Armagh and primate of All Ireland ('Cullen's closest, if rather spineless, ally', according to one historian[51]); and McGettigan. Dixon's response is not known, but Cullen was sympathetic and McGettigan expressed his displeasure at the behaviour of Doherty—and his acolyte James McFadden, a curate in Cloughaneely, who had denied confession to the family of a process server—and he promised to remove him.[52] In mid-June, just before the Lifford assizes in July, McGettigan went to Gweedore, and, outside the chapel, publicly upbraided Doherty and reprimanded the parishioners:

> England has sent out an army to the Crimea, and she has conquered the Russians; she has now sent an army to China, and she has conquered the Chinese; and do you mean to tell me, that you, a small corner of a parish in the County of Donegal, mean to stand up and say you will oppose the law of England?[53]

McGettigan was nobody's fool, however. At a dinner for Campbell Johnston, the Tenant Right candidate defeated in the 1852 election, he had described himself as 'the son of a farmer' who could well remember the rent of his father's farm 'having not only doubled, but trebled and quadrupled'; there was something 'obnoxious', he said, about the 'system of rack-renting'.[54] The farmer's son was not going to back landlords against tenants holding the poorest agricultural land in his diocese. Several days after his appearance in Gweedore, the bishop let it be known that he thought the graziers were killing and hiding sheep to collect compensation. Still, he had given Cruise what he wanted—a promise to remove Doherty—albeit, it was later alleged, as part of a *quid pro quo*, with the magistrate promising that the police and sheep taxes would not be levied once the priest left the parish.[55]

[50] CSORP 1860/15,527 Wood Lodge, 3 Apr. 1857, Cruise to Larcom; *Destitution*, 389.

[51] Hoppen, *Elections*, 192.

[52] See CSORP 1857/5,335 n.p., 20 June 1857, Cruise to Larcom, reviewing his contacts with the bishops and enclosing a note from a landlord, Wybrant Olphert, detailing the denial of sacraments to the process server; the file also includes a policeman's notes on a sermon, delivered in Irish on 7 June, by McFadden; CSORP 1860/15,527 Donegal, 3 Apr. 1857, Cruise to Larcom.

[53] *Destitution*, 355.   [54] *LJ*, 18 Aug. 1852.

[55] Holland, *Landlord in Donegal*, 14; *Destitution*, 355, 371; Mac Suibhne, 'Agrarian Improvement', 580 n. 88. The following spring, the *Londonderry Sentinel* praised McGettigan

In late spring 1857, when Cruise was lobbying McGettigan to remove Doherty, it was politic for him to cut a deal with Pat Gallagher on the men whose cases had been held over at the March assizes, and who were due now back in court in July. Most obviously, treating them leniently would demonstrate to the bishop that he was a reasonable man. However, Cruise had other reasons for wanting to close the now substantial file begun when the first letter from Beagh arrived in Wood Lodge. First, if the verdicts at the spring assizes had vindicated his decision to arrest the men, the convictions had been controversial and another jury might not find McGlynn a credible witness. Indeed, the very behaviour that, from Cruise's perspective, had made the cocky young man a malleable informer—his drinking and running up debts—had allowed the defence to undermine him in the witness box; his dismissal from Letterbrick had also been cast up to him in court. It was best not to push the Crown's luck. Moreover, while the McRoartys remained willing to testify against Neil O'Donnell, no other witness had come forward, and there was now no prospect of the publican being tried for murder.

Quietly, then, between Wood Lodge, Stranaglogh, and Dublin Castle, a deal was put together that would see the men on bail ostensibly shown 'mercy'. It was not uncomplicated mercy. Gallagher was helping Cruise to avoid a scenario that would discredit the authorities—the acquittal of known Mollies arrested in sensational circumstances—as much as he was helping the men on bail to avoid gaol. Indeed, four years later, when the crown solicitor for Donegal, Thomas FitzGerald, recollected the details of the case, he strongly suggested that Gallagher's role had been something other than an advocate for the men out on bail. 'The case', he wrote, 'was right well worked up by Mr Cruise and the other local authorities, and the Reverend P. Gallagher the Parish Priest of Glenties gave the Crown every assistance in his power, and was present in the court when they were arraigned. He had frequently denounced Ribbonism from the Altar and when these men were arrested he [had] told them they deserved their fate.'[56]

•

On Thursday 9 July 1857, nineteen men presented themselves at Lifford courthouse to stand trial for membership of an 'illegal combination'. The

and Gallagher for denying claims, by Doherty and other priests, that the police and sheep taxes had left Gweedore destitute. However, both men publicly supported the committee making that charge, and sent donations to it. For an editorial deploring the *Sentinel*'s reporting, see *LJ*, 7 Apr. 1858.

[56] CSORP 1861/7,273 Crown Solicitor's Report.

men and their supporters had been in town since Monday, the night before the assizes began, waiting for the 'Ribbon Case' to be called.[57] Among them were men who had been bailed, for a second time, at the assizes in March and others who had been bailed in July 1856 but who had failed to appear in spring; the latter included Neil Breslin of Ardara, who, in March, was said to be in America. Now, in the courthouse, Pat Gallagher made a proposition to them: if they would plead guilty and take the oath of allegiance, all charges would be dropped and they would be released on their own bail.

It is unclear if the men had any intimation of this proposal. The appearance of Neil Breslin and others who had not presented themselves in March suggests that they knew something was in the offing. On the other hand, Edward Kennedy, the master of Crannogeboy School, later insisted that he had come to Lifford expecting to be tried. But whether they had known of Gallagher's proposal or not, all nineteen now agreed to it. Their cases were called about 3.30 p.m. The men filed into the dock, completely filling it. The charges against each individual were read and each man in turn pleaded guilty. Then, the crown prosecutor, John George Smyly QC addressed the court. Pointing out that south-west Donegal was now 'perfectly peaceable', he asked that the prisoners be discharged on their own recognizances of £50 to appear when summoned, and to keep the peace for seven years.

Pennefather, the judge who had presided in March, was again on the bench. He assented to the proposal and then addressed the prisoners at some length, making particular mention of 'the efforts of their parish priest . . . to repress Ribbonism'. The Crown, he said, had, in a great measure, been induced to release them 'on the promise of the reverend gentleman that none of those now in the dock would ever have anything to do with an illegal society'. The 'judicious conduct of the Rev. Mr Gallagher', he continued, 'set an example worthy of intimation'. Smyly conveyed Gallagher's thanks to the judge, and the men were free to go. In the weeks after the assizes, they took the oath of allegiance in Wood Lodge and Cruise told them that the attorney general was pleased to pardon them.[58]

•

[57] *BN*, 13 July 1857. The prisoners were John O'Donnell, John Dorrian, Daniel Herran, Condy O'Donnell, Thomas Sweeney, Daniel Gallagher, John Breslin, Patrick Finn, Patrick McNelis, James Hanlon, John Sweeney (1), Neil O'Donnell, John Sweeney (2), James Melley, Patrick Kennedy, Edward Kennedy, Martin Quigley, James Shovlin, and Neil Breslin.

[58] *LJ*, 15 July 1857. Gallagher's obituary in *FJ*, 11 July 1866, noted that assize judges had complimented him on several occasions for settling disputes among his parishioners.

In 1861, the crown solicitor, in reviewing how his office had handled Ribbon investigations, indicated that Pat Gallagher's intervention in the McGlynn case had been made 'with the full concurrence of the Government and of the late Baron Pennefather'.[59] It was nonetheless dramatic, and it was long remembered. Nearly a century later, in 1951, Séamas Mac Amhlaigh (b. 1879), who had been reared behind Cruach Leitreach, in Inishkeel, told a collector from the Irish Folklore Commission how *ins an tseanam, i bhfad ó shoin, anseo in Éirinn, bhí cumann faoi rún ag gabháil nach raibh maith*... (in the old times, long ago, here in Ireland, there was a secret society going that wasn't good). He then vividly described how a member of that society turned informer and how An Sagart Mór Ó Gallchóir, Great Priest Gallagher, intervened in the resulting court case. His account errs on some points. It refers to the informer as a leader of the Mollies, which McGlynn was not; it has the prisoners being lodged in Derry, not Lifford, and then remanded in custody until their trial, when they were, in fact, first released on bail in July 1856; and the story turns on the judge noticing that the priest had not doffed his hat, when Pennefather was notoriously blind. Still, it captures some elements of what happened, not least the priest's initial refusal to help the arrested men, and his telling them that they deserved their fate:

> *An ceann a bhí orthu sa deireadh, creidim go bhfuair sé bríob airgid fá dhéin a n-ainmneacha a thabhairt isteach....* The leader of them, in the end, I believe he took a bribe for giving up their names. As soon as they had their names, they searched for them until they had taken them all prisoner. They were lodged in Derry Gaol, until the day they were to be tried in Lifford. They included young boys and married men, and there was a tough time at home in their absence. There was a priest in Glenties at the time that they used to call An Sagart Mór Ó Gallachubhair, Great Priest Gallagher. They went to him, telling him about their people, and the condition they were in, and the condition they were in at home, and the men down in Derry. And they wanted him to broker some sort of deal and get them out some simple way. 'They are getting', says the priest—he gave them no satisfaction—'they are getting what they deserve.' He gave them no satisfaction.

In Mac Amhlaigh's telling, the distress that the arrests had caused the men's families led Gallagher to reconsider his position. The womenfolk, the priest realized, had been left *gan duine ar bith ina ndiaidh sa bhaile le hobair ar bith a dhéanamh*, without anybody at home to work—the very argument which Condy McHugh's wife made in her unsuccessful petition for his release in August 1856. And so, having resolved to intervene in the case, Gallagher went to Lifford where he had an extraordinary encounter with the judge:

[59] CSORP 1861/7,273 Crown Solicitor's Report on Crime in Donegal.

An lá seo a bhí siad le féacháil i Leithbhearr... The day that they were to
be tried in Lifford—Priest Gallagher knew that they were to be tried
that day, and he was wondering how the cases would go. In his own
mind, there were womenfolk whose husbands were inside and their sons,
and there was nobody at home to do any work and it would be a terrible
pity for me not to do my best for them. He left Glenties and he didn't stop
until he got to Lifford. He spent a while about the town until the judge was
seated. At that time, Priest Gallagher used to wear a big castor hat, and he
used to have used to always a have good *croisín* (crook) too. The courthouse
was full when he entered. He never bothered to put his hand to his castor
hat to remove it. And there, when he went in, was the great judge of the
county. He looked over at him. The judge was a Protestant and says he,
'What sort of man are you? Don't you well know the law?', says he, 'And
that you should not come in here without taking your hat off in front of the
great judge of the county? Don't you know that I am the great judge of the
county?'

'I well knew that', says the priest, 'But what about it? I am as high a judge
as you. As the county judge, you're only a judge between man and man, and
I am a higher judge. I am the judge between God and man.'

'Whatever your business is coming here', says the county judge, 'I am
going to defer to you.'

'Well, it won't be long until I show you that', says the priest.

The judge between man and man (Pennefather) having deferred to the
judge between God and man (Gallagher), the priest went to the men who
were to stand trial, and he slung them out of the courthouse with his
crook, warning them never to get involved in another secret society:

> *Chuir sé a chroisín fá mhuinéal 'ac duine acú, á réir duine agus duine, gur chuir
> sé an fear deirionnach amach ar an dioras...* He put his crook to the neck of
> every man of them, one after the other, until he put the last man of them out
> the door. And when the last of them was coming out the door, he lifted his
> foot and he hit him a great kick up the arse.

'Go on away home now!', he says, 'And don't be in every stupid society
that is got up in the country.'

They came home, and I never heard any one of those men in any other
society in which there was any harm from that day to the day that they died.
Priest Gallagher—God have mercy on him!—was a good priest, and no
judge or law would bother him. He wasn't afraid of the English, and he
fought hard for many people.[60]

---

[60] NFCM 1,203: 475–8. For shorter versions, in 1961 and 1962, see NFCM 1,579:
186–7, 283–4. On the contribution that this material, for all its biases and silences, can
make to mid-nineteenth-century history, see Cormac Ó Gráda, 'Famine Memory', in his
Black '47 and Beyond: The Great Irish Famine in History, Economy, and Memory (Princeton,
1999), 194–225.

The release in July of so many self-confessed Ribbonmen raised the hopes of the four men who had been convicted at the spring assizes. Petitions for their release were soon dispatched to Dublin. In September, Mary Maxwell of Doohill, wife of William, sent a memorial to the lord lieutenant. She explained that the time which he had already served had been 'six months of great hardships' to herself and her three children, who had been entirely dependent on his shoemaking; and she 'respectfully' pointed out that men arrested with her husband had been released in July on their own recognizances on 'bowing submission to the law'. That same month, Catherine Breslin of Shanaghan sent a similar memorial, claiming that the arrest of her 'poor husband', Big John, a 'poor labourer', had caused 'great hardships' to herself and her 'poor children', and in October, Cormac Gillespie petitioned for release, detailing his various medical complaints and warning that the hard labour sentence would be 'the cause of his death or at least be the means of accelerating it'. Dublin Castle canvassed the opinions of the sentencing judge, prison authorities, and, in Maxwell's case, the Constabulary. The prison doctor reported that the health of Gillespie—who had been 'very troublesome' while in custody—would not suffer by continued imprisonment, but that, given his weakly condition, Maxwell should be freed. However, Pennefather was insistent that all three men serve out their sentences. Catherine Breslin persisted, sending two more memorials to the lord lieutenant, one of which included the curious claim that 'her husband was no rebel or member of any illegal society *other than redressing family grievances which the Law could not recognize* and was as loyal a subject to the Crown as any of her Majesty's subjects' (emphasis added). She also sent a note from their parish priest, McGarvey, saying that he had known Breslin since he was a child, that he had always been 'well-conducted' and that he had been convicted 'by mistake', that is, in place of Little John Breslin of Doohill. McGarvey's hastily written note was signed by his curate, Tom Daly, several Ardara merchants, and Gilly Hamilton of Eden. Meanwhile, Patrick Kennedy of Beagh and Teague Fisher of Doohill offered to become Maxwell's sureties in the sum of £200 that he would keep the peace 'for any len[g]th of time': his confinement, they submitted, had reduced his wife and four children (she had claimed three in September) to 'abject misery' and men charged with similar offences had been released on bail. But government was not for turning; all four remained in gaol through winter 1857–8.[61]

[61] CRF G/22/1857; M/36/1857.

ACTS OF CONTRITION

Q. What must we do at confession?
A. We must beg the priest's blessing; say the Confiteor, accuse ourselves of our sins, listen attentively to his instructions, and renew our sorrow when he gives absolution.

Butler's Catechism, 64–5

Pat Gallagher's engagement with the authorities and Tom Daly's pastoral activity in Ardara were part of an increasingly subtle and resolute response by the diocese of Raphoe to the Ribbon Society in the 1850s. At the same time, Daly's confraternity was part of a drive by reforming clerics to bring the Irish Church into line with continental or, more particularly, Roman practice. The most influential reformer was Paul Cullen, archbishop of Dublin. In 1851, Cullen had brought the Redemptorist Order to Ireland. The Redemptorists were renowned on the continent for three-to-four-week 'missions', involving daily confession and mass, theatrical sermons on sin, and symbolic visual displays such as candle-lit processions and Stations of the Cross.[62] If missions were not entirely without precedent in Ireland—the temperance movement had a missionary element—a new religious form was being introduced to Irish Catholicism, and to the extent that it emphasized the necessity of regular communion and confession, it abruptly oriented the laity, particularly the young, towards chapel and, in doing so, it strengthened the priest as moral arbiter, that is, as 'judge between God and man'. Dramatically in missions and, with greater regularity, in chapel, members and prospective members of the Ribbon Society were being confronted with the dangers which their politics posed to their immortal souls, and stricter, more severe priests, like the 'pious and zealous' Daly in Ardara, were coming to set the tone of Catholic society.

In the 1840s and 1850s, Cullen and some of the more ardent reformers suspected the bishop of Raphoe of 'Gallicanism', that is, resistance to direction by the Vatican. McGettigan did sometimes present as an old-style country pastor, yet since the early 1820s, he had been steadily moving his diocese towards more chapel-centred devotion, and when he died in 1861, even Cullen would acknowledge that, starting from a difficult position as regards plant and personnel in 1820, he had transformed Raphoe.[63] In truth, McGettigan had always been a quiet modernizer— he was an enthusiast of temperance societies and national schools—and,

---

[62] Taylor, *Occasions of Faith*, 167–89. [63] Bowen, *Paul Cardinal Cullen*, 62.

willing to innovate, on the Redemptorists' arrival in Ireland, he invited them to hold a mission in Letterkenny, a town with a strong Ribbon element.

This first mission in the diocese ran from 21 November to 14 December 1852, and it proved a learning experience for both the bishop and the Redemptorists.[64] McGettigan had given his house in Letterkenny over to the visitors, confining himself to the parlour. However, things began inauspiciously when the Redemptorists, led by Joseph Prost, an austere Austrian, declined a welcoming glass of punch. There was also friction at the opening of the mission. The Redemptorists had decorated the altar 'in a fashion that had never been seen in Letterkenny', constructed a throne for McGettigan in the sanctuary, and, most remarkably, 'clothed the bishop like a bishop'. To encourage the poor and the young to attend, Prost had insisted that there should be no collection in the chapel. McGettigan had agreed, but loath to let a lucrative opportunity pass, when announcing the mission, he had said that the poor should come to him to receive free tickets: naturally, as Prost noted, many were afraid to do so. And while McGettigan kept his word and held no collection in the chapel, the Redemptorists were annoyed to discover, on the first evening, that he had posted collectors outside the gate, and they were not impressed when a girl fell and hurt herself in the rush to get over the churchyard wall. In his sermon that night, Prost preached on 'the love of Jesus for us in the Holy Sacraments and how our sins and our errors are opposed to his love'. Then he deftly admonished McGettigan, who was sitting on his throne. Addressing the 'wealthy Catholics', 'the better people in the community', he reproached them 'for showing so little love to Jesus' that they would not support the bishop sufficiently, but instead 'forced' him to such an 'abominable' practice as putting collectors at the gate. 'Bring forth your voluntary offerings', he said, 'then the bishop and his priest can allow the poor to come and hear the Word of God and to pray to their God through the Holy Sacraments...' His point made, Prost quickly soothed things over with McGettigan, who had sat 'in a horrified state' through the sermon and hurried home after the service. Prost had caught up with him at the door of his house. 'My lord', he said, 'I am so exhausted, I could

[64] Emmet Larkin and Herman Freudenberger, eds, *A Redemptorist Missionary in Ireland, 1851–1854: Memoirs by Joseph Prost, C.Ss.R.* (Cork, 1998), 60–4. For another memoir of Letterkenny's mission, see 'Le Rapport de Furniss du 26 Juin 1854', in Jean Beco, 'Le Père John Furniss et les missions pour enfants en Grande-Bretagne et en Irlande de 1851 à 1862', *Spicilegium Historicum Congregationis SSmi Redemptoris*, 46 (1998), 367–402. Edward Hosp, 'First Redemptorist Missions in Ireland, According to Father Joseph Prost's Diaries', *Spicilegium Historicum Congregationis SSmi Redemptoris*, 7/2 (1960), 453–85, provides a useful narrative based on Prost's account.

stand a glass of "whiskey" punch.' 'That you shall have', McGettigan had replied. He went into his cellar and returned with a bottle of ten-year-old whiskey. Then, with sugar and hot water, he prepared the punch and, according to Prost, they sat 'in a brotherly way and drank our glass without mentioning one thing about what had happened in the church'.[65]

Thereafter, the mission proved a resounding success, with numbers increasing once the collectors disappeared. Several thousand daily attended confession and mass, which included 'music, lights, [and] incense', then uncommon in services in the diocese, and, in every mass, a hell-fire sermon delivered by one of the Redemptorists, two of whom had the ominously redolent names of Father Furniss and Father Coffin—John Joseph Furniss (1809–65) and Robert Coffin (1819–85). The names did not escape the attention of the Tory press: Prost, quipped the *Londonderry Sentinel*, should be coffined and thrown into a Purgatorial furnace,[66] and Prost remembered the line in a memoir written some twenty years later. The sermons were the daily highpoint, but there were other acts and scenes that deeply impressed participants and observers, including some 800 children assembling at the chapel to receive their first communion in a ceremony lasting three hours. However, for Prost, the mission's signal achievement— 'an especially brilliant success'—was the recantation of members of the Ribbon Society:

> This society could be found all over Ireland and England, but we noticed that it was especially strong around Letterkenny. Our mission made such a strong impression on the members of this society that they came to us in masses and abjured their membership and accepted the Holy Sacraments. Many swore on my mission cross.

At the end of the mission, Prost was able to bring McGettigan the insignia and diploma of a freemason. 'At that point', he recalled, the old man had wept, saying 'I have been a bishop for thirty years, but I have never experienced such a conversion.'[67]

---

[65] McGettigan got gentle revenge on Prost. 'At our departure', the Redemptorist noted in his memoir, 'he gave us no money for the trip.' Prost compared McGettigan to 'a rough Austrian village priest', adding that 'He was able to behave himself, if a little crudely, in polite company, but that is how Pope Gregory XVI and King Louis Phillipe liked to see him.' See Larkin and Freudenberger, *Redemptorist Missionary*, 61–3; Hosp, 'First Redemptorist Missions in Ireland', 470.

[66] *LSnl*, 15 Oct. 1852.

[67] Larkin and Freudenberger, *Redemptorist Missionary*, 64. Also see 'Le Rapport de Furniss du 26 Juin 1854', 394–5. If upbraiding members of 'secret societies' was a feature of missions in these years, Conservatives were not impressed. A leader-writer in the *Irish Times*, 4 Oct. 1859, saw a correlation between missions and Ribbon activity: 'It is remarkable that Ribbonism generally becomes more murderous in connexion with the movements of certain Jesuit priests, or missionaries. The Redemptorist Fathers had made a

The Redemptorists scarcely routed the Ribbonmen in 1852: there were active lodges in and around Letterkenny through the 1850s and, indeed, many years later. Still, this first mission, a protracted exercise in shock and awe, fear and deliverance, demonstrated the Church's readiness to contend with the lodges for the hearts and souls of Catholics, and, if it caused some young fellows to 'abjure' Ribbonism, its success likely stemmed from the Redemptorists' dramatic delivery of their core message—confess and do penance or face eternal damnation, whose torments they described in lurid detail—the emotional charge of which was heightened by their own conspicuous 'holiness', or 'otherworldly severity', as anthropologist Lawrence Taylor phrases it, which set them apart from familiar diocesan priests, men whose weaknesses (like Glacken's alcoholism) and worldliness (like McGarvey's economy) were well known.[68] John Furniss, one of the preachers on that first mission, reported to his superiors that the people's 'pressing earnestness to get to the confessional is so great that they fight for it'.[69] Known as the Children's Apostle, Furniss was an English Catholic, which added to his peculiarity in Ireland. In Letterkenny, he was said to have 'worked wonders with the children and young people', and his sermons were attended 'not only by children but by adolescents up to twenty years of age'.[70] In the course of the mission, he and a colleague went, at McGettigan's request, to Doe about eighteen miles north-west of the town, to preach to children. 'It was winter', Furniss remembered, 'and an extremely wet stormy morning, nevertheless the children came in crowds soaked with the rain. A simple crucifix was held up before them, and at the very sight of it, there was a universal screaming and shouting through the whole church.'[71]

The mission was not simply an exercise in emotion, however. Importantly, the Redemptorists sought to perpetuate its immediate effects through organization. To this end, they established a confraternity, a new institution in the diocese, in Letterkenny and they distributed devotional literature. Much of this literature was intended for children, and the confraternity too was an effort at marshalling the young; many of its members came from parishes around the town, some from up to fifteen miles away, and they were generally aged 10–20 years. Returning to Letterkenny the following September for a special 'Children's Mission',

long stay in and about Limerick. After they had left, it was evident that an impulse had been given, by some means or other, to the Ribbon movement. A sort of fanaticism was observed to exist among the people, which did not exist before.'

[68] Taylor, *Occasions of Faith*, 172–3, 176.
[69] 'Le Rapport de Furniss du 26 Juin 1854', 382.
[70] Hosp, 'First Redemptorist Missions in Ireland', 471.
[71] 'Le Rapport de Furniss du 26 Juin 1854', 382–3.

Furniss found that the numbers in the Letterkenny confraternity had increased from 500 to 1,200:

> They were most admirably organized; all their voices united in singing produced a most wonderful effect. The parish priest told me the Confraternity had made a great change in the physical condition of the children, their dress, etc. He told me the Confraternity had become a spectacle to the whole country, that strangers had travelled from considerable distances simply to see it[,] that the children had an extraordinary affection for their Confraternity, that when they emigrate they say their biggest sorrow is to leave their Confraternity. A gentleman from Letterkenny came here two weeks since and told us that the effects of the mission at Letterkenny, where this Confraternity is founded, are as fresh after a lapse of two years as they were in the first week after the mission.[72]

By then, McGettigan himself had established five confraternities in other parishes, as had six parish priests on their own initiative, and more were to follow over the next few years, including the one established by Daly in Ardara in late 1856.[73] These groups would typically meet in chapel after mass on Sunday—the usual time for lodge meetings, according to McGlynn's account—and conduct a series of religious exercises lasting 'at most an hour and a half'; the exercises often involved the recitation of the Rosary, for which adults were sometimes present. Here, children and adolescents from poor families encountered peers from a higher 'rank' more accustomed to chapel-centred devotion, and, for Furniss, this disciplining of the poorer sorts was one of the confraternity's great benefits: 'it teaches them habits of order in the church, which they are unaccustomed to, keeps them out of bad company, [and] brings the poor into connexion with the better classes'; there were also 'substantial charities' given through the confraternity to 'poor children'.[74]

From the 1850s, then, Catholic children were being more firmly oriented towards chapel and the norms of the 'better classes'. And clerical discourse was becoming more severe with greater emphasis placed on sin and the hitherto neglected sacraments of confession and communion: bluntly, the fear of God was being put into children to fashion chaste and obedient adults. Furniss's *The Sight of Hell* (1855), the tenth in a series of fourteen books for children, was an exemplary text. A short pamphlet, only thirty-two pages in length, it gives a sense of Furniss's mission sermons to 'young people'. It poses a series of childlike questions about Hell, including, 'Where is Hell?' and 'How far is it to Hell?'

---

[72] Ibid. 384–5. Larkin and Freudenberger date the 'Children's Mission' to 25 Sept.–17 Oct. 1853; see *Redemptorist Missionary*, 17.
[73] 'Le Rapport de Furniss du 26 Juin 1854', 384–5.   [74] Ibid. 398–9.

And the answers include vivid descriptions of its sights, sounds, and smells. Here, for instance, is the answer to the 'What are they doing [in Hell]?':

> Perhaps at this moment, seven o'clock in the evening, a child is just going into Hell. Tomorrow evening at seven o'clock, go and knock at the gates of Hell, and ask what the child is doing. The devils will go and look. Then they will come back again and say, the child is burning! Go in a week and ask what the child is doing; you will get the same answer—it is burning! Go in a year and ask; the same answer comes—it is burning! Go in a million of years and ask the same question; the answer is just the same—it is burning! So, if you go for ever and ever, you will always get the same answer—it is burning in the fire![75]

In Furniss's vision, the pains of Hell are suited to the vices that destroyed the sinner's soul. A girl who 'used to walk about the streets at night, and do very wicked things' finds herself condemned to suffer eternity dancing on a red-hot floor.[76] A drunkard cries in perpetuity for water to soothe his burning tongue. And, in such vignettes, the reader glimpses the preacher in full flight at the mission:

> You drunkards, who on Saturday evenings are in the public-house, and on Sundays away from Mass; you drunkards, whose children are hungered and in rags, and go neither to Catechism nor Mass, go down to Hell, and listen to your brother-drunkard crying out for a drop of cold water to cool his burning tongue![77]

The 'pain of loss' was the greatest of Hell's pains, and it was also the most difficult to understand because, unlike all the other pains, there was nothing like it on earth. Curiously, Furniss's evocation of this unearthly pain is explicitly pitched to an Irish child:

> You must know that when a soul has been condemned to hell at the judgment-seat, God lets it see for a moment something of what it has lost. It sees the immense happiness it would have had in heaven with God and his angels and saints. And now it sees that all this blessed happiness is lost—lost by its own fault, lost for ever, lost without hope! Listen to the painful cry of a child which has lost its mother! *Listen to the wailings of the people in Ireland when their sister is leaving them to go to America, and perhaps they will never see her any more.* Then you may think what a wailing there will be when a soul hears these words from God: 'Depart from me for ever.'[78]

With the diocesan clergy now in control of most national schools attended by Catholics and literacy levels rising, there was a growing demand for this

[75] John Furniss, *The Sight of Hell* (Dublin, n.d. [1855]), 25.   [76] Ibid. 20.
[77] Ibid. 22.   [78] Ibid. 16–17 (emphasis added).

type of material. Typically, a couple of hours a week were set aside for 'religious instruction' in national schools. For instance, in the parish of Ardara, the schools of which McGarvey was patron devoted 10 o'clock to 12 o'clock on Saturday to it, generally using a Catholic catechism—there were several available, notably *Butler's Catechism*—and books of English-language prayers, most of which the children's parents would likely never before have heard.[79] The hours devoted to organized religious activity outside the home could accumulate quickly—two hours' catechism on Saturday morning, perhaps an hour for confession on Saturday night, an hour-long mass on Sunday morning, and an hour or longer for a confraternity meeting. Of course, not every child was a member of a confraternity, and not all members were active. Still, the tone of Catholicism was changing, and there was a shift in focus too towards the young, with 'religious instruction'—unlike anything that their parents had received—increasingly being provided to the poor.

It was a coincidence that the Redemptorists should have arrived in Ireland in the decade after the national school system had, to a greater or lesser extent, been put in place, and, for most Catholics, placed under clerical control. Nevertheless, first confession and first communion—after appropriate preparation in national school—becoming life-cycle events for Catholic children owed much to the Order's emphasis on those connected sacraments in its first missions.[80] Certainly, from the Redemptorist-led first communion in Letterkenny in December 1852, a new, soon-to-be annual spectacle became part of popular Catholicism in parishes across the north-west. Indeed, little over a year and a half later, in July 1854, 'upwards of eleven hundred little ones' made their first communion in the same town; all were members of the confraternity.[81] And over the next few years, other parishes followed suit.

Writing of the decades before the Famine, historian S. J. Connolly has suggested that, when it came to sacraments, 'there appears to have been a distinction in popular attitudes and practice between those marking rites of passage and those which lacked this fundamental significance'; hence,

[79] For religious instruction in Ardara's schools in the 1860s, see *Returns of the Names of All the Schools in Connection with the Board of National Education in Ireland, 1862. Part I. Province of Ulster*, HC 1864 (481), xlvii. 124–31. By 1896, in Beagh, the last half hour of every schoolday was devoted to 'catechism and prayers'. See ED 2/53/39: Beagh.

[80] 'Le Rapport de Furniss du 26 Juin 1854', 397–8. Parish priests, according to Furniss, expressed 'delight' at first communion being part of the missions, and some brought children long distances to be prepared for it; without those 'unexampled' events, he wrote in 1854, many children 'might never have gone to the Sacraments'. Among Furniss's publications is a book on teaching catechism, *The Sunday School or Catechism* (Dublin, 1861), which makes mention of his experiences in Ireland.

[81] *FJ*, 29 July 1854.

baptism, marriage, and extreme unction had been important, but not confession and communion and attendance at weekly mass.[82] In effect, the national schools broke down this distinction by making rites of passage of first confession and first communion, which, in turn, contributed to greater observance of those sacraments as those children grew to adulthood. Confirmation, which required examination on the basic tenets of the faith, was another sacrament that had not been held in particularly high regard. Triennial 'confirmation tours' which McGettigan made of his diocese had almost certainly diminished the number of unconfirmed adults by the 1850s: for instance, in August 1845, he confirmed 8,030 *persons* in eleven parishes in south and west Donegal, an increase of more than 4,000 on his previous tour through those parishes; among them were 805 in Inishkeel and 1,007 at Ardara.[83] The schools, however, changed everything: although people of advanced years would continue to come forward to go *fé láimh an eapsaig*, under the bishop's hand, confirmation now became a rite of passage for which children were prepared in their last years as scholars.[84]

•

After the first mission in Letterkenny, the Redemptorists and other missionary orders came to the diocese on a regular basis. Indeed, in 1857, when the McGlynn and Gweedore cases were before the courts, McGettigan brought Furniss and the Redemptorists back to Letterkenny, this time to hold a mission specifically for 'young people' from 17 June to 6 July. 'Each day during the mission', the *Ulsterman* reported, 'did the young boys and females flock from every quarter of the parish to the chapel, and from morning until night were the confessionals crowded by anxious penitents, many of whom, although attending daily, could not be received owing to the immense numbers always around the confessional.' On 2 and 5 July, 1,200 girls and upwards of 900 boys received communion, and on 6 July, McGettigan confirmed 820 *persons* (prepared by the

---

[82] Connolly, *Priests and People*, 91.

[83] *Pilot*, 10 Sept. 1845. Six years later, a report on confirmations in the western and southern parishes of the diocese refers to the bishop having confirmed 'upwards of 700 *children*' (italics added) in Letter and Dungloe. See *FJ*, 12 Sept. 1851; on this tour, McGettigan expressed 'high satisfaction at the knowledge of the Christian doctrine exhibited by those who presented themselves, and the extreme decorum observed at all these places. He also expressed gratification at the large congregations, notwithstanding the decimation of the people for the last few years by destitution and emigration.' For parochial breakdowns of the 6,000 persons confirmed his 1854 tour, see *LJ*, 2 Aug. 1854.

[84] For confirmation day in Ardara in the mid-1860s, see *LJ*, 4, 8 Aug. 1866. Also see *LJ*, 10 Dec. 1884, where the bishop compliments Cloughaneely teachers on their preparation of pupils for confirmation.

Redemptorists). 'Sights of such imposing solemnity', it was said, 'have never been seen in this town, or, perhaps, in Donegal.' At the close of the mission, Furniss addressed the children, telling them that he had come to Letterkenny to save their souls, and that he prayed now, as he was departing from them, that they would not forget the mission nor throw away the graces that God had bestowed on them during it: from the congregation, 'an outburst of grief broke forth, which continued half-an-hour, and which, with difficulty, was suppressed'.[85]

'It is admitted by all', Furniss had written in 1854, 'that the future perseverance of Ireland in the faith depends very much on the children.'[86] Yet while the young remained the prime target of the preachers who led (one could fairly say 'staged') the missions, it is clear that the bishop and his coadjutor and successor directed missionary orders to parishes that gave trouble. In 1866, for instance, the Redemptorists descended on Fanad, a parish long considered unruly, where top of any list of sins to be denounced were *poitín*-making, Ribbonism, Fenianism, feuds between families, and 'bitter and lasting hatred' over the 'grabbing' of land in the Famine.[87]

Ardara, where Ribbonism had been strong, was not to be overlooked. The Oblate Fathers opened the parish's first mission for the 'sanctification of souls' at 11 o'clock on Sunday 28 July 1861 with a high mass, with choir and harmonium accompaniment, followed by solemn benediction. If the Oblates shared the Redemptorists' reservations about collections, McGarvey overcame them: reserved seats were 1s., side galleries 6d., and the floor 2d.[88] The mission ran for a full month, some days bringing numbers to town that can only ever have been exceeded at the great fair of 1 November: 'ten thousand' were said to have received the 'holy body of Christ'. Indeed, there was likely an element of a fair to proceedings, with stalls ('stannins', standings) near the chapel selling rosaries, statues, and 'holy pictures'. The mission itself involved not only thunderous sermons and continuous confessions, but also a large-scale first communion, a massive candle-lit procession, and the erection of a 'mission cross' in the chapelyard. The town was also 'honoured' with a visit from Dan McGettigan, the new bishop, who had only succeeded his uncle in May. A correspondent of the *Catholic Telegraph*, who thanked the bishop for his 'unceasing labours in the confessional', captured the drama of different 'scenes' during the event:

[85] *Ulsterman*, 13 July 1857.
[86] 'Le Rapport de Furniss du 26 Juin 1854', 398. Elsewhere (397), he admits that, 'It is certain that after a mission the greater part of the Parents relapse...'
[87] 'Introduction' in Dorian, *Outer Edge*, 22.   [88] *LJ*, 24 July 1861.

A gratifying sight it was to see 700 children approach the Holy Communion for the first time, and the vast throng who listened to the final discourse and breathed their Baptismal vows again—when more than 4,000 lighted wax candles were borne in their hands—can never, as long as memory lasts, forget that scene; and is it not consoling that the child, as old man, as he kneels by that mission cross, will ever send up from their inmost soul a prayer for the Fathers Fox, Gubbins and Nowlan.

Whether or not it was as fully realized as this enthusiast claimed, the communal catharsis at which the Oblates aimed was clear:

Ah! may the Fathers of Mary Immaculate ever succeed—many a way-worn, forlorn, erring child, lost one, have found the bright path again, and are tonight happier than ever they felt before. Happy, by the hundreds, are the homes they have left behind them in the black regions of Donegal. 'Oh! come again, oh! come again', is the prayer of all, more welcome than before. Oh! may the pure heart of Mary Immaculate ever guide them. Many a troubled heart, and blighted soul calmly rest at their moorings—Faith, Hope and Charity—because of their instruction, council and example.

Ages unborn will tell of the happy results and fruits of this mission.

The Oblates being a Marian order, their 'instruction, council and example' may have had special meaning for girls and women. But it was young males whom the preachers had in their sights:

Sin—the prevailing vices that beset poor humanity—got a deathblow from their incomparable sermons . . . *To the secret societies they doled out destruction, and their unsparing denunciation thereof fills the hearts of all with the fond hope they never can rear their monster heads again.*[89]

It was, indeed, a fond hope.

---

[89] *Catholic Telegraph*, 13 Sept. 1861.

8

Departures and Returns

The Constabulary had brought Patrick McGlynn down from Dublin for the assizes of July 1857. It was the third assizes that he had attended in twelve months. The proceedings abbreviated by Pat Gallagher's intervention, he had not been called to the box. His services no longer required by the Crown, his days in Ireland were now numbered. On 11 July, he was taken from Lifford back to his wife and daughters in Ballybough; he and his escort arrived at 11.00 p.m. 'It is quite impossible with safety to himself or his family', Thomas FitzGerald, the crown solicitor for Donegal, explained to the Chief Secretary, 'that McGlynn could be allowed to reside in any part of this kingdom.' FitzGerald recommended that the family be given a free passage to Australia, together with all necessaries for the voyage, and that, on arrival, Patrick should be paid £40. McGlynn, he noted, had already expressed a desire to go to Australia, where he would be able to resume work as a teacher.

The proposal reached the desk of Thomas Larcom. He had long had intimation of it, for McGlynn had specifically asked to be sent to Australia in a letter to Cruise before he swore his information the previous summer. On 24 July, Larcom approved FitzGerald's proposal, and he instructed the Inspector General to estimate the cost of outfitting the family for the journey. A humane man, Larcom inquired about the age of the children. Anne was 2 years and 1 month, and Mary, 9 months. Within days an itemized list arrived from Ballybough. It included a couple of outfits and two pairs of shoes for each of the four of them. Also on the list were six towels and 12lb of soap. The total cost, including a 10s. box, came to £12 13s. Larcom approved the list and his officials contacted Samuel Ellis of the Emigration Office to book the family's passage to Australia. By 4 August, arrangements had been made, through Gibbs, Bright, & Co., for the McGlynns to sail on the *Carrier Dove* from Liverpool to Melbourne; the cost of their passage, bedding, and all extras (including the £40 which McGlynn was to receive on arrival in 'the colony') ran to £87.

Before noon on Thursday 13 August, the Constabulary brought the family to the Emigration Office at 2 Marlborough Street. McGlynn knew the street. One of its most imposing buildings was the office of the Commissioners of National Education. Its address had been on much of the correspondence that he had received in relation to school matters. Ironically, it was here, at Larcom's suggestion, that Cruise had come in April 1856 to check the authenticity of the first letter he received from Beagh. Later that day, the family sailed for Liverpool. They spent Friday night in the city, presumably in a boarding house near the docks. The *Carrier Dove*, which was to take them to Australia, was a medium-sized American clipper, a swift three-masted sailing ship of a type soon to be made redundant by steel-hulled steamships. She had only been built in Baltimore in 1855, and in a port that saw many elegant vessels, she was widely puffed as 'one of the most beautiful ships afloat' and a 'floating palace'. It was reckoned that in the few weeks that she was docked in Liverpool many 'thousands' had come to see her.[1]

Saturday 15 August was 'a beautiful, fine day', and at 4 o'clock in the afternoon, the *Carrier Dove* left Prince's Dock, and glided down the Mersey. She was carrying 315 passengers; twelve were 'cabin passengers', travelling in first class, with the rest in the intermediate or steerage section. Among the latter were the McGlynns. The family travelled under their own names, suggesting that the authorities judged all trouble to be behind them. Patrick gave his profession as 'miner', an indication that it was newspaper stories of gold finds in Victoria that had first grabbed the indebted schoolmaster's attention. As far as the crew was concerned, the voyage was not very eventful. Indeed, at seventy-nine days, it was a fast passage. The weather was generally good, and on the best days, particularly in the early stages of the voyage, there was singing and dancing on deck, courting, and raffles for soda water. As the weeks passed, boredom set in, and by the time that their sails had caught the strong westerly winds of the 'roaring forties' in the South Atlantic, the passengers did little but play cards, gamble on the distance the ship would run in a day, and grumble about the 'salt junk' (salted meat) and hard bread or the price being charged for drink. The only bad period was the week it took to pass from the South Atlantic to the Indian Ocean. There, off the Cape of Good Hope, it was 'very rough', with the sea 'running mountains high', and the ship 'rolling very heavy'. And on the night of 8 October, in violent seas, Mary, the youngest of McGlynn's daughters, died. Born in protective custody, she was less than a year old. They buried her at sea at 10 o'clock

---

[1] Arthur H. Clark, *The Clipper Ship Era: An Epitome of Famous American and British Clipper Ships, their Owners, Builders, Commanders, and Crews, 1843–1869* (New York, 1910), 253, 362.

in the morning. It was 'very cold, blowing a gale', but towards evening the wind slackened a little.[2]

On 2 November, after over two months at sea, Patrick aged 26, Catherine aged 25, and Anne just over 2 years of age disembarked in Melbourne. Nothing is known of what the McGlynns did next. And yet it would be a surprise if the informer's track, that can be followed so closely in the months when he was conspiring against his neighbours, could not be picked up again. Before his appointment to Beagh, McGlynn had lost a job in Letterbrick for reasons that he did not care to admit and he had also been summoned for debt more times than he could remember. He enjoyed a drink, perhaps too often, and now with a wife and child in a new country, the £40 that he had received on disembarking was unlikely to have lasted long. The master turned miner seemed destined to have another day in court.

Mining, if he ever mined, soon lost its charm. On 31 August 1858, a man named Patrick McGlynn, who had 'been trained and held a school under the National Board of Education in Ireland', obtained a certificate from the St James Training Institution in Melbourne. That October he was appointed to the Church of England School in Beechworth, a gold rush town 177 miles north-west of Melbourne. He seems to have converted to Protestantism, for both the institution that accredited him as a teacher and the school to which he was appointed were attached to the Church of England. McGlynn did well in the school. Following an examination of the pupils in July 1859, an inspector expressed himself 'perfectly satisfied with the progress of the school since Mr McGlynn had been appointed to its management'. Indeed, that same month, at a meeting in the Star Hotel, McGlynn was a prime mover in the establishment of an 'Educational Institute' to watch over the interests of the teachers in the Beechworth area.[3] But he was soon in trouble. In spring 1860, he was declared insolvent, with liabilities of £161 19s. 8d., and assets of only £50 9s. 6d. The cause of his insolvency was the 'pressure of a creditor and various losses, &c'.[4] Then, in February 1862, he was dismissed from the school, with one week's notice. The reasons for his dismissal are unclear, but his supporters in the local press claimed it was to make way for one of the inspector's favourites. McGlynn, it was said,

---

[2] Public Record Office, Victoria, North Melbourne: Inward Overseas Passenger Lists: Passenger List of *Carrier Dove*, 15 Aug. 1857. Details of the voyage are from diaries kept by two passengers, Benjamin Tongue and Charles Bregazzi, www.carrierdove.org; although Bregazzi does not name her, he notes the death and burial at sea of the infant. *Argus* (Melbourne), 3 Nov. 1857, reports the ship's arrival.

[3] *Ovens and Murray Advertiser*, 2 Nov. 1858; 5, 12 July 1859.

[4] *Argus*, 15 Mar. 1860; *Geelong Advertiser*, 17 Mar. 1860.

had already found a post in Sandridge, a suburb of Melbourne.[5] He had
been master of Beechworth for three and a half years, about the length of
time that he had taught in Beagh.

McGlynn was then about 30 years of age; he may well have survived
into the twentieth century. And if he stayed in Victoria, Molly Maguire
haunted him. The anti-grazier activity in Gweedore and Cloughaneely,
which had encouraged Cruise to close the McGlynn case, had abated in
summer 1857. However, the authorities had continued to levy a 'sheep
tax' to compensate graziers for animals reported stolen and a 'police tax' to
pay for additional constables deployed in the area; their collection in
August and September 1857 involved 170–300 constables marching
from house to house. These taxes now drew the attention of tenant
right and nationalist newspapers. Notably, an editorial on ' "Christmas
Times" in Donegal' in the St Stephen's Day edition of *The Nation*
deplored 'how God's creatures are driven to death by the mechanism of
British laws':

> Along the shore of the coast crawl crowds of gaunt spectres, prowling for
> shellfish and scraping the rocks for seaweed, with which to prolong life's span
> another day. Houseless, homeless, shelterless, naked, cold and starving are
> the once happy, virtuous and warm-hearted people of Donegal. Day by day
> they droop and die; and the sheep will soon thrive gloriously on the rank
> verdure on the mounds where they moulder.

The description was less an accurate representation of conditions in
Gweedore than an expression of nationalist indignation at the prominence
given in Tory newspapers to the India Relief Fund, the mayor of London's
campaign to raise money for the 'victims' of the Sepoy Rising. There were
people more deserving of relief, *The Nation* was suggesting, than the
'servants of the East India Company—whose ill-gotten wealth would
pave the land with gold'. Indeed, the editorial, which gave the impression
that the entire county had been reduced to destitution, concluded by
recommending that a relief fund be established for Donegal, to which
nationalists could contribute:

> Who will organize a Relief Fund for the people of Donegal? . . . Let us have
> no more fabricated tales of horror from foreign lands; there is horror
> enough at our own doors. These victims are not a class who were tempted
> by greed of gold or love of plunder to throw themselves like harpies on a
> foreign country to wrest it from its owners and batten on the spoil. These
> are not a people overtaken in a career of iniquitous aggrandisement, by the

---

[5] *The Age* (Melbourne), 14 Feb. 1862.

infuriate vengeance of the victims of their rapacity. No, but peaceful, virtuous followers of GOD's law, who never sought, by robbery or conquest, the substance of their neighbour.[6]

John Doherty, the parish priest removed from Gweedore at Cruise's behest the previous summer, took the hint. On 14 January 1858, he published an Appeal, signed by ten priests, reiterating *The Nation's* allegation that communities had been reduced to 'destitution' by the sheep and police taxes, and were now facing starvation: 'The fine old Celtic race', it lamented, 'is about to be crushed aside to make room for Scotch and English sheep.' Tories grasped that a declaration by so many priests constituted a serious strike against landlords and denounced the Appeal: the *Ballyshannon Herald* dismissed it as 'a device of Popery to replenish its failing coffers'; the *Londonderry Sentinel* dubbed it a defence fund for sheep stealers; and a histrionic contributor to the *Dublin University Magazine* warned that 'in this obscure corner of Ireland a flame is being kindled which will, if unextinguished, spread far and wide, and shake the rights of property if not defy the power of British law'.[7] Meanwhile, liberals and nationalists supported the Appeal. Sympathizers established relief committees in towns throughout Ireland, organized meetings, and made collections. Presbyterian congregations in Derry, Donegal, and west Tyrone, where many ministers advocated for tenant right, made particularly large contributions. So too did Irish emigrants in Britain and America, and the students and staff of seminaries in France and Spain. But the response from Australia was most dramatic. Between 1 June 1858 and 30 June 1860, 'Donegal Relief Funds' in Melbourne and Sydney raised near £6,000, and from 1859 through 1864 that money, supplemented by the governments of New South Wales and Victoria, paid for the passage to Australia of some 1,500 people from north and west Donegal. Some of the immigrants settled into labouring, farming, and service, while others struck out for the goldfields.[8] From 1859, then, Patrick McGlynn would have encountered naggingly familiar names and faces in the mining towns of Victoria, and songs emanating from public houses must have at once warmed and worried him. And perhaps the phrase that sent the greatest chill was that hearty greeting, *Caidé mar 'tá tú?*

---

[6] *The Nation*, 26 Dec. 1857.
[7] *Destitution*, 391–3; *BH*, 23 July 1858; *LSnl*, 30 Apr. 1858; 'The State of Donegal—Gweedore and Cloughaneely', *Dublin University Magazine*, 51 (1858), 731–41, 731.
[8] Mac Suibhne, 'Agrarian Improvement', 568–73.

ORDER RESTORED

The Crown still had a few loose ends to tie up after Patrick McGlynn left for Australia in August 1857. In March 1858, five men appeared at Lifford charged with membership of the Ribbon Society. They were Moses Ward of Brackey, Patrick McConnell, Patrick O'Donnell of Downstrands, James O'Donnell of Tullycleave, and John Sheerin. John George Smyly, the prosecuting barrister, announced that, owing to the exertions of Revd Patrick Gallagher, the prisoners were prepared to plead guilty and, on behalf of the Crown, he asked that they be admitted to bail on their own recognizances. Old Baron Pennefather was again on the bench. He remarked on how, at the last assizes, in summer 1857, he had alluded to Gallagher's 'very proper conduct, which had tended so much to the peace of the district from which the prisoners came. The public were under a deep debt of gratitude to him for the part he had taken, and his conduct clearly shows what good effects are produced by such as he using the influence which they legitimately possess over their people to induce them to abandon wicked pursuits.' He then granted the application for bail.[9]

It was the last court appearance that resulted from McGlynn having turned informer. Later that month, twenty-four 'clergymen, magistrates, poor law guardians and other inhabitants of Glenties Union' submitted a memorial to the lord lieutenant seeking the release of the four men still in custody—James Gallagher, William Maxwell, John Breslin, and Cormac Gillespie. Larcom solicited Cruise's opinion, and he strongly supported their release: the men who had been released on the terms negotiated by Gallagher had been 'very well conducted', he pointed out, 'and the whole district peaceable, not one case being sent from that part of the County Donegal to either the Quarter Sessions or Assizes for the last 18 months'. And so, in early April, the Castle notified the relevant authorities that the four were to be discharged on entering into securities of £25 and two sureties of £10 each. They had each served a year of their twenty-month sentences.[10]

A year of breaking stone would have taken a physical and mental toll. Bad food, poor conditions, and the rule of silence can have done the men no good either, and the financial consequences were considerable. Gallagher was a farmer cum road contractor, and, if he had a family, they

[9] *LJ*, 10 Mar. 1858. The 'Gweedore Sheep Case' dominated press reports of the assizes and the appearance of the 'Ardara Ribbonmen' passed unnoticed in many newspapers.
[10] CRF G/5/1858 Glenties, 27 Mar. 1858, James Quigley to Eglington, enclosing Humble Memorial of the Undersigned Clergymen, Magistrates...; n.p., 1 Apr. 1858, Cruise to Larcom; CSORP 1858/16,218 Dublin Castle, 3 Apr. 1858, Larcom to Cruise.

may have had to hire workers in his absence. But they would have muddled through the year. The wife and children of John Breslin of Shanaghan, a labourer, were heavily dependent on his wages, and they would have been hard-pressed in his absence; the family had lost their smallholding by the time of his release. Similarly, the wife and four children of Maxwell relied heavily on his shoemaking, and he had been in 'delicate' health in prison, suffering from attacks of dropsy (oedema).[11] The future for his wife, Mary, included seven weeks in Glenties poorhouse in January–March 1866 with their 2–3-year-old son, Daniel, when both were suffering with fever; they were described as 'destitute'.[12] She died in 1884, and William remarried in Ardara in 1887; he died there aged about 80 in 1905.[13] As for Cormac Gillespie, he had been having trouble with the Board of Education prior to his arrest. He had been admonished for his 'gross neglect of discipline and order' in April 1855, and inspectors had reported his school to be 'stationary' that September and 'not progressing' in February 1856. His salary had been suspended in June when he was charged with writing the threatening letter, and a few months later, learning that he had earlier been accused of stealing and selling a pistol, the Board of Education decided that, even if acquitted, he should be dismissed on an outstanding allegation that he had falsified school accounts. So he had no hope of reinstatement.[14] He had been in poor health prior to his conviction. His right shoulder had been dislocated when he was a child, and not receiving proper medical attention, he had partly lost the use of his arm; and then, when about 12, after hurting his hand, he had been prone to attacks of erysipelas, a debilitating disease that manifested itself in severe rashes and fevers and a feeling of being unwell. His parents were 'poor people' and he would not have fared well if he had to resort to physical labour to support them.[15] But Gillespie was clever: he soon left for Scotland, where, in 1860, he married an Irish widow, and in 1861 he was teaching English in Glasgow.[16]

[11] CRF M/36/1857 Information Required in the Case of the Prisoner [William Maxwell] . . . 12 Sept. 1857.
[12] Glenties Workhouse Registry, 1851–66: 4,787.
[13] GRO, Glenties, Marriages: 1887/2438289; Deaths: 1905//4772151. On his birthplace, see 1901 Census, Household Return: House 91, Ardara.
[14] ED 2/59/74: Glencoagh (Male).
[15] CRF G/22/1857 Humble Petition of Cormack Gillespie . . . Lifford Gaol, 30 Oct. 1857. For the description of Gillespie's parents, see the letter of William Sinclair, Drumbeg, a landlord, in *Daily Express*, 27 May 1857, complaining of Louis Harkin having given the Ribbonman a good character.
[16] In 1861, Gillespie was living on Piccadilly Street, in Anderston, an Irish section of Glasgow. His occupation was 'Teacher of English'; see NAUK, Census Scotland, 1861 RG09/15.

The men who had taken the deal brokered by Pat Gallagher had varied fortunes. Like Gillespie, the two other schoolmasters—James Melley of Carrick and Edward Kennedy of Crannogeboy—had been suspended when they were arrested, and they were subsequently dismissed. Melley does not appear to have pressed for reinstatement,[17] but Kennedy, who had a young family to support, did. After pleading guilty in July 1857, he immediately wrote to the Board of Education, asking to be reinstated as master of Crannogeboy School. The Board ignored his first letter, and when he wrote again in October, he was told that he would not be reappointed. Kennedy then appealed to the lord lieutenant, Lord Carlisle, pointing out that he had 'spent eleven years of his youthful prime in the education of his fellow countrymen' and that any inspector who had evaluated his work would agree that he had done 'much toward the education of the rising generation'. He had only once broken any law, when 'he permitted himself to be made acquainted with the secrets of a society known by the name of "Molly Maguire", but then discountenanced and abandoned the same'. He had since taken the oath of allegiance, which he understood 'grants to him a Pardonation of this offence, and that, in legal point of view, a pardon restores all competency as well as an immunity for the offence'.

The memorial, clearly drafted by a lawyer, passed from the lord lieutenant's office to Larcom. He replied tersely that the lord lieutenant could not interfere in the matter. There followed a series of letters and memorials from Kennedy—in January, February, and March 1858—pleading for his reinstatement and referring the authorities to school inspectors and to Cruise, but not, interestingly, to the parish priest of Ardara, McGarvey, or Pat Gallagher in Glenties. All his pleas were rebuffed. Finally, in June, Kennedy made one last appeal, mentioning his 'small helpless family' and, with a hint of bitterness, insisting that he had been ready to stand trial in summer 1856 and again in spring 1857 and that if his priest had not told him that he would be discharged if he pleaded guilty, he would have stood trial that summer. Larcom refused to bend: 'His Excellency cannot interfere.'[18] Reflecting the regard in which Kennedy was held—and the ambivalence in local society to the Mollies—Knox Barrett, the Ardara rector, now wrote to the Board, to see if it would consent to him teaching in a school under his management. Barrett, who took a keen interest in education, received a reply saying that, given the circumstances in which

[17] Carrick school had only been approved by the Board four months before Melley's arrest. After his release on bail in July, Charles McNeely, parish priest of Carrick, had written to the Board asking that he be reinstated, as the charges against him had been 'thrown out'; the Board did not accede to the request. See ED 2/59/94: Carrick.

[18] CSORP 1858/15,435 Mountcharles, 7 Dec. 1857, Kennedy to Carlisle; Mountcharles, 28 June 1858, Kennedy to Eglinton.

Kennedy had been dismissed, it would not be possible to sanction his appointment to any national school.[19]

Other men pieced their lives back together. Condy McHugh lived out his life in Beagh, rearing a family of eleven. He stayed out of trouble. He was arrested for drunkenness in Ardara in 1861 and prosecuted for having an unmuzzled dog on the public road in 1868 and for arrears of county cess in 1877. It was all petty stuff. Several others enjoyed considerable prosperity. In Ardara, the Dorrians, Kellys, and Hanlons remained publicans and road contractors; and connections of John Sweeney would soon have a public house in the town too. And in Glenties Neil O'Donnell, the lodge master in 1856, was again getting road contracts in the early 1860s.[20] And it is possible too that he was the Neil O'Donnell who became relieving officer of the Glenties Union in 1867.[21]

Particularly instructive is the career of Martin Quigley, the 21-year-old identified by McGlynn as the master of the Dungloe lodge. Little is known of his family. However, his father, Francie, was fined £12 10s. in November 1851 'for having let a horse and car for hire without a licence authorizing him so to do'. Car hire, like residence in the town, suggests an involvement in trade, perhaps keeping a public house—the business of many 'committeemen' in other towns—and he, like many publicans, was also a road contractor.[22] Although Martin took the deal brokered by Gallagher and entered a plea of guilty to the charge of membership of an illegal combination, at the summer assizes of 1857, by the end of that year he was the 'whip' (driver) of the posting car (taxi) of the Gweedore Hotel. This 'highland' hotel was the showpiece of Lord George Hill, whose estate was then the centre of the 'sheep war' that was soon to garner attention far beyond Ireland. That December, Denis Holland of the *Ulsterman* visited Gweedore, researching articles that castigated both Hill's management of his estate and the administration of justice in the district. Holland learned of Quigley's new job, and took some pleasure in reporting that Daniel Cruise, who had ordered his arrest in June 1856, was among his regular passengers. 'Martin', Holland wrote, 'may be a very proper person to drive a car for a model hotel in Donegal, notwithstanding his past predilections for midnight amusement; and, for aught I know, may be now a model himself of decorum and legality.'

[19] ED 2/59/18: Croneybais [sic]. Edward Kennedy had been the first teacher in Glencoagh, where he was succeeded by Cormac Gillespie, another alleged Ribbonman. See ED 2/13/38: Glencoagh; ED 2/59/74: Glencoagh.

[20] See GJ/1/43 *Public Orders, Summer Assizes, 1861 . . . Lifford* (Londonderry, 1861). James Fisher of Ardara, in whose 'waste house' the Mollies had met, also received road contracts in 1861. Martin Quigley, the Dungloe master, got contracts that year and again in 1867; see GJ/1/20 Amount Asked off County of Donegal Spring Assizes 1867.

[21] *Thoms*, 1868.   [22] *Northern Whig*, 18 Nov. 1851.

But the 'self-convicted' Molly Maguire having walked 'from the dock at Lifford to the driver's seat at Guidore [*sic*]' might 'suggest something peculiar in the notions of morality and legality' in Donegal.[23]

Other aspects of the case might lead to a similar conclusion. Pat Gallagher, the Glenties priest, knew that Neil O'Donnell had a hand in the death of Paddy McRoarty, yet he had kept the publican and his 'brothers' out of gaol. Similarly, Knox Barrett, the Ardara rector, had no apparent qualms about appointing a self-confessed Molly to a school under his care. And among those who gave good characters to Mollies at their sentencing were a national school inspector, two poor law guardians, a cess collector, and a landlord, James Hamilton, who four years earlier, in 1853, had convened the meeting that petitioned successfully for the proclamation of west Donegal to put down 'Bastard Ribbonism'. But, in truth, only those who deal in moral absolutes would find anything peculiar in morality and legality in the district. It was a small place; the combined population of the parishes of Ardara and Glenties was just over 14,000. The character, circumstances, and connections of the men arrested on McGlynn's information were well known in their own communities. So too were their political capabilities, and, in 1856–7, it would have been known that they posed no immediate threat to the social order or political establishment. The alarm about Ribbonism was abating. The Society was increasingly seen as more concerned with rackets than resistance or revolt. Certainly, the Constabulary had given that impression in their assessment of secret combinations in late 1855. Then, the head constables had concluded that the Society was in decline in most districts in Donegal, its members less inclined to commit acts of outrage, but with a considerable influence on a wide range of transactions.[24] Furthermore, if the Constabulary, in late 1855, had judged the Society to be still holding up in the south-west of the county, moderates within the Ardara lodge had earlier that year seen off a challenge by more militant men led by Moses Ward, and, in 1856, McGlynn's informing had disrupted and discredited the organization.

Violence and intimidation were to be deplored by right-thinking people, of course. So too was racketeering. But severe punishment of a large number of young men would only stir trouble. John O'Donnell of Letterilly had political reasons for speaking up on behalf of William Maxwell, the Ardara chairman, and James Gallagher, the delegate: if he had rebuffed their requests for help, it might have cost him votes in elections for the Board of Guardians. And Gilly Hamilton, who spoke

[23] Holland, *Landlord in Donegal*, 98–100.
[24] CSORP 1856/11,368 Donegal, 27 Dec. 1855, Cruise to Larcom; Dublin, 23 Dec. 1855, McGregor to Larcom.

for Gallagher, Maxwell, and McHugh, had less creditable reasons: although a land agent, justice of the peace, and poor law guardian, he was involved in the *poitín* trade which doubtless brought him into contact with Ribbon leaders.[25] Nevertheless, there is no reason to suppose that those two men did not grasp the wisdom of mercy. Meanwhile, Captain James Hamilton, who spoke on behalf of Gallagher, was a young fellow, in his early thirties, still living in the shadow of his father, John, who had formally transferred the Fintown estate to him in 1845, but remained involved in its management. As landlords, father and son had cultivated a paternalistic style, promoting 'improvement', sending letters to tenants explaining their policies, and hosting dances for them. They had been active too in relief efforts during the Famine, getting deep into debt.[26] Making representations on behalf of a Ribbon leader accorded with their paternalism and also with John's religious views: in a book on 'error' published in 1856 he extolled the virtue of bringing the prodigal wanderer home.[27]

•

Martin Quigley, the Ribbon master turned hotel 'whip', married a young Dungloe woman, Annie McCorry (1845–1929) in the early 1860s.[28] Relations with his wife's family deteriorated within a few years of their marriage. In 1868, his father-in-law John McCorry took him to Dungloe petty sessions on a charge of stealing oats, and Quigley, in turn, summoned him for assault. Acquitted of theft, Quigley asked that the prosecution of McCorry be set aside. However, the judge insisted that the case proceed; his father-in-law was convicted and served a month in

[25] See Prologue.

[26] For John Hamilton, *Sixty Years' Experience as an Irish Landlord*, with an Introduction by E. H. White (London, 1894), esp. chs. 4–12, 16–21. On his involvement in relief, see chs. 18–21, and his 'My Transactions in the Famine, '46 etc.', NLI, P3584. *LJ*, 3 Jan. 1849, reported that 'the celebrated Irish piper Paddy Quigley, better-known by the name of Paddy Bawne', had been found dead on the road from Glenties to Fintown on the morning of 22 December. The previous evening he had been scheduled to perform at a 'ball' in Fintown, 'given by James Hamilton, Esq. (landlord of the place) to his tenants'. A coroner's jury found that Quigley 'came by his death from the effects of drinking an over-quantity of intoxicating liquor, and the inclemency of the night'.

[27] John Hamilton, *On Truth and Error: Thoughts, in Prose and Verse, on the Principles of Truth, and the Causes and Effects of Error* (Cambridge, 1856), 426. He had published letters and pamphlets on the poor law and land system and his religious views were 'very broad, closely approximating in his later years, to those of the Society of Friends': see the review of Hamilton's *Sixty Years' Experience*, in *Friends' Intelligencer*, 51/1 (1894), 246. Also see Dermot James, *John Hamilton of Donegal, 1800–1884: This Recklessly Generous Landlord* (Dublin, 1998).

[28] Like other committeemen, and his own father, Quigley got involved in road-contracting; see IPSCR Glenties, 5 Nov. 1869; he was summoned to Glenties petty sessions when a contractor, James Ward of Coolvoy, for whom he was a surety, failed to repair, as contracted, the road between Doohary and Glenleheen.

Lifford.[29] A few years later, in 1875, Quigley, who was then about 40, availed of a scheme of assisted emigration, and sailed with his wife and six children from Belfast for Queensland, Australia.[30] There, he got a grant of 200 acres from the Land Commission, worked as a limeburner, and used to often recall 'his experiences in Ireland'. He died 'an old and respected citizen' of Townsville in 1914, and Annie in 1929.[31]

•

South-west Donegal fell quiet after Pat Gallagher cut the deal with Cruise in 1857. In a confidential assessment of the state of Ireland in 1863, Sir John Henry Brownrigg, Inspector General of the Irish Constabulary, observed of Donegal that Ribbonism existed 'generally throughout the county, except in a less degree in the Glenties and Killybegs districts'. It was a remarkable turn of events, for the Glenties district had been the area where the Society was most active in 1855. But even Downstrands now seemed a place transformed. In February 1858 a barracks had been established at Kilclooney to suppress illicit distillation—the Revenue Police had been abolished in 1857 and their duties absorbed by the Constabulary. Four years later, in March 1862—the year after the parish's first mission— the County Inspector decided that this objective had been attained, and it was closed. Not everybody was pleased. There was a 'Fenian Scare' in 1865–6 when, after the American Civil War (1861–5), rumours abounded that regiments of Union veterans might land in Ireland. In January 1866, at the height of this scare, James Ovens, the rector, complained to Dublin about the 'unprotected state of this very remote part of the County Donegal . . . not a police station nearer than Glenties or Ardara, both of which are distant seven miles'. The authorities dismissed the complaint, with the sub-inspector stationed in Glenties remarking that Downstrands 'has been exceedingly tranquil for a long time, no disturbance has been in it, during the past eighteen months that I have been here, nor can I ascertain when any outrages (if any) occurred before that time'.[32]

---

[29] *LJ*, 11 Jan. 1868.

[30] Queensland State Archives, Registers of Immigrant Ships' Arrival: *Kapunda*, 17 Nov. 1875.

[31] *Townsville Daily Bulletin*, 28 Oct. 1914; *The Worker* (Brisbane), 12 Nov. 1914. Quigley, like McGlynn, had legal troubles in Australia: in the 1890s, he was involved in a dispute with a lime company that, in his telling, grabbed his land and laid tramlines on it; in fact, the company already had tramlines on the land when he successfully applied to the Land Commission for it. Quigley won the case but the decision was controversial, and he was labelled a 'blackmailer' in parliament. See *North Queensland Register*, 18 Nov. 1901; *Telegraph* (Brisbane), 11 Jan. 1902.

[32] CSORP 1866/1,224 Inishkeel, 6 Jan. 1866, Owens to Parkinson-Fortescue; Glenties, 15 Jan. 1866, Fitzgerald to Hill.

A decade is a long time in policing, but others too represented south-west Donegal as tranquil in the mid-1860s. John McGarvey, in his thirty-sixth year in Ardara in 1866, boasted that spring that 'I exerted myself these many years to keep my people from joining any illegal society, and I can safely say there is not a Fenian or a man belonging to any private society in my parish.'[33] It was a hollow boast, and McGarvey must have known it. Indeed, before the year's end, several natives of the parish were among eighteen 'stout, able-bodied men' arrested as suspected Fenians in Belfast on their return from mining towns in Pennsylvania. Francis Shovlin, 24, was from Sandfield; James Shovlin, 20, from Ballymackilduff, Downstrands; and Patrick McNelis, 35, from Ardara; as too may have been 30-year-old John Boyle.

Those particular men—'poor-looking', but carrying considerable sums of money—were soon released, and they may or may not have been Fenians.[34] But certainly, by these years, a few young men in the locality were embracing republicanism and articulating an alternative to the 'faith and fatherland' pieties of the Ribbon Society. After the abortive insurrection of 1867, through until the 1910s, these men—and a younger generation who gathered around them—were less local agents of an active insurgency than members of a republican subculture, critical of the gradualism of mainstream nationalist organizations, in which, paradoxically, some of them were leaders.[35] Pre-eminent among local republicans, from the mid-1860s, was Neil Keeney (1845–1935) of Stormhill, who after 'the dark days of 1867', was active in the Land League of the early 1880s, the United Irish League of the early 1900s, and, in 1917–22, Sinn Féin; he was involved too in the Gaelic League and Gaelic Athletic Association. In the 1890s, when the clerically dominated nationalist movement in Donegal sent an anti-Parnellite to Westminster, Keeney had 'stood unflinchingly by Charles Stewart Parnell, and mourned the death of the leader as if he had been a member of his own family'.[36] And in 1898, when Belfast Gaelic Leaguers held a meeting in Ardara, he had caused a sensation by deploring, in Irish, their naïve notion that the language was 'non-political'; the chairman called him to order, but he was 'loudly applauded' for 'the force of his sentiments'.[37]

---

[33] *FJ*, 14 Mar. 1866.

[34] *Belfast Morning News*, 3 Dec. 1866; *BN*, 3 Dec. 1866; *Irishman*, 8 Dec. 1866. Boyle's homeplace appears as Ardmore in the press, possibly a typographical error.

[35] Other pre-1916 republicans included Edward Melley (b. *c*.1823), Carn; his son Hugh Melley (1869–1938), Tullycleave; James McGrath (1861–1960), Garvegort; John Mór McGill (1855–1936), Áighe; and John McConnell, Brackey (1872–1939). Thomas Gavigan (1860–1950), Kentucky, emigrated to America *c*.1880; an associate of John Devoy, he returned in the 1920s; see *DJ*, 27 Jan. 1950.

[36] *DJ*, 22 Feb. 1935.   [37] *DJ*, 12 Sept. 1898.

Crucially, however, if there was an identifiable republican subculture around Ardara through the last third of the nineteenth century, the Ribbon Society also maintained a clear presence in the area. 'I was counsel for the Ribbonmen of Donegal for years, and I knew them very well', James Hamilton of Eden, who had been attorney for Condy McHugh in 1856–7, told a parliamentary inquiry into the Irish jury system in 1873; and he was in no doubt that the Society still influenced juries.[38] The following year, when giving further evidence, Hamilton spoke at some length about the Society. Distinguishing it from the Orange Order, 'an organisation in sustainment of the law', he described it as 'an organisation to prevent the administration of the law'. 'I could put my finger on a Ribbonman', he said, adding that 'a great number' of 'my Roman Catholic fellow countrymen' sympathized with the Society and 'other societies':

> I know from very intimate knowledge of the counties on my circuit [Cavan, Fermanagh, Tyrone, Donegal, and Derry], especially in counties like Donegal, and counties where the population is scattered, where men are principally engaged in cattle dealing, and where they have to go long distances to fairs, they are most of them under very great alarm[,] if they are men of low position[,] from Ribbon and other societies. Many of them I know from my own knowledge, sympathise with those societies, and they look upon them as a very useful check on what they call landlord oppression, and that kind of thing.[39]

Eight years later, in 1882, a Constabulary assessment of secret societies listed 'a few of the principal Ribbonmen' in the eleven counties where the group was active. Of nineteen men returned for Donegal ('numerous other names can be given') six were in the west of the county—Ferrigal Coll of Carrick, Gweedore, and five men from the Rosses: Shane Gallagher, David Campbell, and Andrew O'Donnell, all of Dungloe; and Peter O'Donnell of Kincasslagh and Anthony Gallagher of Burtonport. All were described as 'farmers', but Andy O'Donnell was also a publican, as too, it seems, was David Campbell.[40]

---

[38] *First, Second and Special Reports . . . (in 1873) on Juries (Ireland)*, 68.

[39] *Report from the Select Committee on Jury System (Ireland) . . .* [1874], 2, 5–6, 9, 12. Hamilton insisted that literacy had boosted disaffection: 'Tons of treasonable rubbish are sent from Dublin every Saturday night, and nothing else is read on Sundays but that.'

[40] NAI, Irish Crimes Records, Crime Branch B134 (1882). In the early 1880s, the Inspector General ordered monthly reports on 'secret societies' in all thirty-two counties. Donegal officers typically reported that no society had been in active operation. However, for a particularly detailed review of the activities of the Ribbon Society in the Rosses, see NAI, Police Reports 3/715/1 [Carton 1] Ballyshannon, 16 Oct. 1882, Davis to Rudge. Davis identifies John Gallagher and John Campbell of Dungloe as 'the two leading Ribbonmen of that division of the county'. He details a night raid on Hugh O'Donnell of Annagry, a bailiff, in Dec. 1880, during which shots were fired and his processes torn up,

No less significantly, in the years between McGlynn being relocated to Australia in 1857 and that report on Ribbonism in 1882, young men emigrating from across west Donegal to north-eastern Pennsylvania moved easily into the American branch of the Ribbon Society, the Ancient Order of Hibernians (AOH). And there, in the mine patches, immigrants from west Donegal, including several from around Ardara, figured prominently in the Molly Maguire troubles of the 1860s and 1870s that were pivotal in the AOH renouncing violence and reaching an accommodation with the Catholic Church, which, in turn, prefigured a rapprochement between the mother society and the Church in Ireland.

MOLLY IN THE MINE PATCH

In Pennsylvania, where the name Ancient Order of Hibernians had been first formally adopted by the Ribbon Society in the late 1830s, Hibernians met in taverns and saloons, much as Ribbonmen met in public houses, and men who 'gained their influence from behind a pine board' were conspicuous among their leaders.[41] Here too, the 'brothers' were not averse to administering rough justice to those who had wronged them. The Molly Maguire troubles that ebbed and flowed for three decades involved resistance to anti-Catholic and anti-Irish discrimination in the nativist rage of the 1850s; opposition to the draft in the Civil War of the early 1860s, when wages were high in the coalfields and poor men did not want to fight the rich men's war; and a determination, from the mid-1860s through the mid-1870s, to maintain wage levels and improve conditions by organizing unions. In the last phase, the Coal and Iron Police, recruited, paid, and run by coal and railroad companies, violently broke strikes and unions. Strikers were evicted, their jobs and houses given to scabs, and 'troublemakers' attacked and killed. For their part, the miners, most especially during the war, engaged in industrial sabotage. Mines were flooded, breakers burned, stores dynamited, and trains derailed. Mine superintendents and foremen, generally of English,

---

and refers to several reports of drilling. Davis also mentions a fight in Lettermacaward in 1881, during which Patrick Tolan, a relative of Gallagher, was killed; the fight involved 'two sections of a secret society'. Finally, he describes how, in early 1882, Daniel O'Donnell of Dungloe and 'several friends' warned John Devaney of Kincasslagh that if he let a house to the Constabulary, he would 'assuredly incur the vengeance of the secret society'. It was well known, he added, that some years earlier, when a party of armed men had surrounded Devaney's house, they had 'so frightened his wife that she died from the shock'. On that incident at Devaney's, see *LJ*, 16 Apr. 1862.

[41] *Minnesotian Herald*, 6 Apr. 1878.

Welsh, or German extraction, were intimidated and killed, and blacklegs and informers in the Irish community were ruthlessly punished.[42]

The dénouement was a series of show trials that began in 1876 and the hanging of twenty men in 1877–9. The first hangings were on 'Black Thursday', 21 June 1877. In Mauch Chunk, Jack Donahue, Edward Kelly, Mike Doyle, and Alec Campbell, all Irishmen, mounted a scaffold specially constructed in the corridor of Carbon County Prison to execute the four of them at once. The mechanism malfunctioned. Watched by over a hundred spectators, it took them, respectively, six, eleven, thirteen, and fifteen minutes to die. They were strangled not hanged. That same day, thirty miles away, in Pottsville, six other men died in pairs in the yard of Schuylkill County Prison. First Jim Boyle and Hugh McGeehan. Then Jim Carroll and Jim Roarty. And, finally, Tom Munley and Tom Duffy. Boyle had been holding an oversize red rose, which he had sniffed as he walked to the gallows. And when the trap was sprung, the red rose fell to the ground.

At least four of the ten hanged that day had emigrated from west Donegal, and at least two were the sons of emigrants from the district. Jim Roarty was a native of Meencorwick, near Crolly, in Gweedore; his wife had no English. Carroll had been born in a mine patch in 1837 to people from Gweedore, and his wife was an O'Donnell from Meenacladdy in the same parish. Alec Campbell, who had arrived in the States in 1868, was from Dungloe; David Campbell whose name appeared on the Constabulary list of 'principal Ribbonmen' in Donegal in 1882 was very possibly a close connection, for his father was named Alec. Duffy, who had been born in Donegal in 1853, was likely from the Rosses, and McGeehan had been born in the Fintown–Ballinamore area of Inishkeel. Finally, Jim Boyle's surname suggests that his immigrant parents had left the Rosses or Inishkeel; he himself had been born in Pennsylvania about 1852.[43]

Among the ten men hanged as Mollies over the next two and a half years were another five men with west Donegal connections. One of them was Tom Fisher (b. 1837), hanged in 1878. Fisher had been born in Inishkeel; in the mid-1850s there were only four Fisher households in that civil parish, all in the Catholic parish of Ardara—one in Carn, adjacent to Beagh; one in Mullyvea and one in Rosbeg, both two to three miles north

[42] In addition to the works of Broehl, Bulik, and Kenny, cited in Chapter 1, note 5, see Anne Flaherty's well-researched www.mythofmollymaguires.blogspot.com (2011–16), which establishes that more executed men were union leaders than had hitherto been known.

[43] Broehl, *Molly Maguires*, 307–39; Kenny, *Making Sense*, 244–76, 297–306; Breandán Mac Suibhne, '"Them Poor Irish Lads" in Pennsylvania', *Dublin Review of Books* (Mar. 2015), online.

of it; and the fourth was in Altnagapple, a few miles south-east of Ardara. Fisher had been brought to the States as a 12-year-old 'about 1850'.[44] Described in the press as 'a man of considerable intellectual force' who had 'impressed himself upon his countrymen as a more than ordinary personage', he owned the Rising Sun tavern in Summit Hill, and he was AOH delegate for Carbon County, that is, he represented thousands of Hibernians at state level. He was also a township tax collector, an elected position, and the press had tipped him to be elected county tax collector. He was a spokesman too for miners: during the Long Strike of 1875, Fisher and a Summit Hill priest had met with the president of the Lehigh Coal and Navigation Company to press the workers' case. At 41 years of age, he went to the gallows alone, the fourteenth of the twenty to die and the first not dispatched in a multiple hanging. At the scaffold, he made a dying declaration, repeating his alibi. On the night that he was alleged to have killed a man, he had 'a few social drinks' with a fellow named Boyle and another named Breslin in Cornelius T. McHugh's saloon in Summit Hill and he then had a few more in the barroom of Jimmy Sweeney's Hotel. And at no stage that night did he converse, 'in English or in Irish', with a Mulhearn or an O'Donnell or leave Summit Hill for Tamaqua. But for the place-names, Fisher might have been talking of Ardara.[45]

Ardara had been home to at least one other man hanged as a Molly in Pennsylvania: Charlie Sharpe was born around 1843 in Cloughboy, Loughros Point. His death sentence was for complicity in the murder in 1863, at the height of the Civil War, of a mine-owner who had informed on Irishmen evading the draft. By the time of his execution, in

---

[44] *GV*: Inishkeel. There were householders named Bradden, a variant form of the surname, only in Brackey, Killasteever, and Laconnell, all in the Catholic parish of Ardara. Owen Fisher (1805–84) and Mary Fisher (1807–87) were likely his parents or close connections; their grave in St Joseph's Cemetery, Summit Hill (pop. 1890: 2,816), identifies each of them as 'a native of Ardara, Co. Donegal, Ireland'. The ages of their Irish-born son Hugh (b. 1845) and US-born son John (b. 1853) resident with them in 1870 and 1880 indicate that they emigrated from Ireland *c.*1845–53; see US Census. An 'interview' with Fisher in *Easton Express*, 27 Mar. 1878, describes him as having arrived 'with his parents' about 1850.

[45] *Carbon Advocate*, 30 Mar. 1878; *Easton Express*, 28 Mar. 1878. Also see the interviews with Sweeney and Mulhearn in *Times* (Philadelphia), 2 Mar. 1878; the article alleges that Sweeney had perjured himself. For Fisher's will, witnessed by J. F. Breslin (1845–92), see Pennsylvania County, District and Probate Courts: Carbon County Wills; probate date 12 Feb. 1878. Breslin's Donegal-born father, Patrick (d. 1869), 'one of the pioneer miners of anthracite coal', settled in Summit Hill in 1824; a carpenter, contractor, and builder, John was also an undertaker. See F. C. Brenckman, *History of Carbon County, Pennsylvania* (Harrisburg, PA, 1913), 397–9.

January 1879, the role of private security agencies in the prosecution of alleged Mollies and the flagrant packing of juries were causing disquiet across the United States. In Sharpe's case, the impression of gross injustice was compounded by the governor of Pennsylvania having telegraphed a stay of execution, to allow for an appeal, that had arrived at the Western Union office in Mauch Chunk as he and Jim McDonnell, nicknamed 'the Hairy Man of Tuscarora', were being prepared for the gallows. The operator raced up the snowy streets to the gaol, forced his way through a crowd gathered outside, and furiously rang the doorbell. The sheriff said that it must be Sharpe's wife, who had left the prison distraught, and he ordered the execution to proceed. When he finally allowed the door to be opened, the now widowed Bridget Sharpe tried to claw his face. The prison in uproar, a white-haired elder brother of McDonnell loudly cursed 'this Pontius Pilate crew... the hounds of hell'. 'It isn't them as is the murderers', he said, pointing to the swaying bodies, 'but the murderers is about us.' 'Yes', added Sharpe's cousin or brother, Peter or John (reports vary), 'There hangs as *dacent* a lad as any. He never thought of doin' wrong, and there he is, murdered. Curses on them as did it.' A priest intervened to prevent them attacking the sheriff's deputy.[46]

Sharpe had been given the customary opportunity to say some 'last words'. He had started reading a prepared statement and stopped, saying he did not have time to finish it. After confirming, with a journalist Edward M. Boyle, that it would be published, he calmly readied himself for execution. Had he continued reading, the door might have been opened to the man from the Western Union. In this dying declaration, which was carried in newspapers across the States, Sharpe protested that he was 'as innocent as the babe unborn'. He was being hanged, he claimed, as he was an Irishman and a Roman Catholic. And it was said in the patches, and heard in Ardara, that on leaving his cell for the last time, he had pressed his hand on the wall and beseeched the Almighty to leave a sign of his innocence. Today, one highlight of the tour of the old prison is seeing a 'handprint' on the wall. But as is the way with apparitions, this mark has also been claimed for at least two other Mollies—Alec Campbell of Dungloe and Tom Fisher of the parish of Ardara.[47]

---

[46] *Harrisburg Telegraph*, 15 Jan. 1879.

[47] Arthur H. Lewis, *Lament for the Molly Maguires* (London, 1964), 273; *Standard Speaker*, 10 July 1974; Korson, *Minstrels*, 251–2, 307–8; Patrick Campbell, *A Molly Maguire Story* (Lawrenceville, 1992), 9.

MARCHING TO RESPECTABILITY

From the AOH's formation in Pennsylvania in the 1830s, the attitude of the Catholic Church to it had varied from diocese to diocese. It was an oath-bound society which, as historian Kevin Kenny points out, was 'sufficient to ensure its condemnation under prevailing doctrine'. It was also well known that it was the Ribbon Society by another name, and that, in Ireland, that organization was illegal. Still, in America, the AOH was a legal mutual aid society and it provided much-needed support to Catholics in a period of severe economic hardship and 'intense nativist hostility'. Consequently, while some bishops and priests took a dim view of it, others were prepared to tolerate, or, indeed, to openly support it. However, the troubles in the mine patches caused support and toleration to give way to opposition, culminating in the bishop of Philadelphia condemning it in 1875 and the bishop of Scranton, whose diocese included the coal region, excommunicating all Hibernians in 1877. In response, the AOH leadership moved to disassociate itself from criminality. In 1876, its annual convention expressed a determination to act in accordance with Church teaching, and the following year, it revised its constitution 'to remove every clause of an objectionable nature so as to make our rules in harmony with the teachings of our Holy Church'; it also disavowed any connection with the Molly Maguires—'that terrible band of misguided men'—and cut all ties with lodges in four coal counties. Finally, in 1878, the convention declared itself willing to submit its rules to the hierarchy for approval, and it introduced a new oath: members now swore to 'keep inviolable all the secrets of this Society of Brethren from all but those I know to be members in good standing, except the Roman Catholic clergy'.[48]

In Donegal, the place that many of the hanged men (and the men who had betrayed them) had left behind, the Ribbon Society had yet to shake its association with 'outrage'; indeed, in 1878, two of three men involved in the sensational assassination of Lord Leitrim in the north of the county were Ribbonmen.[49] Still, 'outrage' had declined from the 1850s, making the Society less menacing, and, from the early to mid-1870s, Ribbonmen in western districts had been taking steady steps towards respectability and putting themselves at the head of 'national' opinion in their districts, by organizing parades on St Patrick's Day. For instance, in Dungloe, in 1878,

---

[48] Kenny, *Making Sense*, 277–80.   [49] Dorian, *Outer Edge*, 25–6, 35–7.

Andrew O'Donnell, a local publican known since the early 1860s to be a Ribbonman, was the 'leader' of a parade involving as many as ten bands:

> From early hour on St. Patrick's morn until 12 o'clock, parties of men of the Upper Rosses, accompanied by their bands, marched in military order from the different districts to Dungloe. After mass, they formed into line in the following order, under the direction of the leader, Mr Andrew O'Donnell. The mounted men in front, numbered upwards of sixty; next the Dungloe band; then came the main body of the procession, carrying ten flags, with the bard Mr James Glacken, who rode a gray horse, led by two pages, who as well as the bard, were tastefully dressed in suits of green. The bard carried a harp, on which he played several national airs, in company with the bands. The procession marched through the town in this order to Roshine, a distance of three miles, when they returned and proceeded to the Little Bridge on the opposite side. After arriving there, they came back by a different route, and marched to the Fair Hill, an eminence in the vicinity commanding a magnificent view for miles of the surrounding scenery. After partaking of refreshments here, the different companies with their bands marched homewards in their respective directions. The procession seemed to be more successful than any hitherto in this place, and sobriety and good conduct were apparent not only with the processionists, but amongst those who were looking on.[50]

These west Donegal parades being first organized in the mid-1870s—one for the Lower Rosses, in Annagry in 1875, and another for the Upper Rosses, in Dungloe in 1876—the bands that were their main attraction likely only formed from 1873, after Westminster passed the Party Processions Repeal Act in 1872, revoking a ban on 'party' walks, including Orange marches, that had been in place since 1850.[51] Most were fife and drum bands, but some were equipped with expensive brass instruments, and the members acquired uniforms and banners with 'national' images and slogans.[52] Some bands' Ribbon connections are clear; for instance, in Dungloe, the brass band of well-known Ribbonman Andy O'Donnell was known as 'the Dungloe Hibernian Band'; and where Ribbon connections are obscure, that 'the men' from different 'districts' wore sashes when they marched behind their band might be taken to denote membership of an

[50] *LJ*, 29 Mar. 1878.
[51] For reminiscences about Dungloe's first parades, see *DJ*, 21 Mar. 1892. On Annagry's first parade, in 1875, see *Nation*, 31 Mar. 1877. Also see *Nation*, 29 Mar. 1879, for a major parade in Gweedore. On the legislative context, see Neil P. Maddox, ' "A Melancholy Record": The Story of the Nineteenth-Century Irish Party Processions Acts', *Irish Jurist*, 39 (2004), 242–73.
[52] On the Dungloe Hibernian banner, see *DJ*, 21 Mar. 1892.

organization that preferred not to speak its name.[53] In the 1880s, agitation for land reform and Home Rule—and increased participation in electoral politics, due to an expansion of the franchise—created numerous other occasions for bands to parade: they marched to election rallies, evictions, and demonstrations on the release of activists from prison. This agitation, in turn, precipitated the formation of new bands and also the erection of halls: Ardara's 'National Band'—later renamed St Conal's Fife and Drum—was established in Brackey in 1885, and halls were erected in Downstrands and Ardara in that same year.[54] Where associated with Ribbon/Hibernian elements, a hall consolidated the group's respectability. But it was those processions to and from chapel on St Patrick's Day that, from the mid-1870s, were crucial in making the lodges acceptable to the men in the parochial houses. In 1892, a Dungloe correspondent of the *Derry Journal*, reflecting on 'the marching on St Patrick's Day' that had begun in the Upper Rosses sixteen years earlier, remarked that, 'One of the most salutary effects of these processions was the establishment of a peaceful union among all classes of people, and doing away with factions.' The men who had initiated the first parades in the area had 'blotted out a stain on its character'.[55] The lodges, in other words, had brought order where, in the correspondent's eyes, there had been none; and in orienting the people towards chapel on this 'national' holiday, they had implicitly accepted that priests had a place in politics.[56]

Major demonstrations elsewhere in Ireland—notably in Derry, after the repeal of the Party Processions Act, on Lady Day (15 August) as well as 17 March—were a model for this 'marching on St Patrick's Day'. So too, however, were St Patrick's Day parades in the US which were familiar to returned emigrants and widely reported in the Irish press. And that, in the States, the AOH had accommodated itself to the Church by 1880, and that it was courted thereafter by Irish political figures, seeking to fund the land and Home Rule agitations—and by Irish priests, raising money for chapels and cathedrals—helped Ribbonmen (many styling themselves Hibernians from the 1870s) to complete their own metamorphosis into

[53] *Nation*, 31 Mar. 1877; *DJ*, 21 Sept. 1885. *Nation*, 31 Mar. 1877, describes 3,000–4,000 participating in the Cloughaneely parade; addressing the crowd, Bryan Sweeney of Dungloe advocated Home Rule. There was a Hibernian Band in Derry by the mid-1860s; see *DEM*, 20 Dec. 1868. See too its participation in a highly political Lady Day (15 Aug.) parade in 1872, *LSnl*, 17 Aug. 1872.

[54] *DJ*, 1 Sept. 1885.   [55] *DJ*, 21 Mar. 1892.

[56] A. C. Murray represents Ribbonism in Westmeath in the late 1860s and early 1870s simply as 'rural gangsterism' bereft of any higher political concern; see 'Agrarian Violence', 72. West Donegal Ribbonmen continued to commit occasional acts of 'outrage' into the 1880s—see n. 40 of this chapter—but their association, from the mid-1870s, with these parades, clearly registers a heightening concern for the 'national cause'.

a lawful mutual aid society with the American name, Ancient Order of Hibernians.[57] In 1904 the Church ceased to list the AOH among societies that Catholics were forbidden to join in Ireland, and Hibernian lodges now sprang up, with remarkable alacrity, in the very places where the Mollies had been active in the 1840s and 1850s and with the same ritual, rhetoric, and symbols. Among those 'new' lodges, whose members saw no irony in describing themselves as part of the 'old movement', was No. 518 in Downstrands; its president, in the early 1900s, was Patrick Moore, one of whose connections, James Moore of Loughfad, had been a master of the Mollies in the 1850s.[58] Tellingly, the 'spacious hall' erected by the National League in 1885, and then called the National Hall, was known both as the Hibernian Hall and as the Parish Hall in the first decade of the twentieth century.[59] So unassailable now was the lodge's leadership of 'national' opinion in Downstrands that it could accommodate the republican minority: in 1910, the 'brethren' commemorated 'The Anniversary of the Manchester Martyrs', three Fenians executed in 1867, with a torchlight procession watched by several hundred spectators, and in January 1912, at the local curate's suggestion, the lodge was happy to have a play, *The Rebel of Inishowen*, by the returned emigrant and later Sinn Féin activist Brian O'Keeney, son of the old Fenian, Neil, staged in its hall.[60]

That hall, close by Kennedys' public house and about 200 yards from the chapel—itself only erected after McGlynn's informing drew attention to McGarvey's neglect of Downstrands—was a new building erected in winter 1911–12. It was 50 by 22 feet, roofed in zinc, 'beautifully wainscoted some four feet high, and cove ceiled with tongue and groove boards'.[61] Canon John Doherty, parish priest of Ardara, chaired the official opening, in September 1912. The platform included two other priests, Michael Gallagher, curate in Kilclooney, and John Byrne, curate in Ardara. Also present were Michael Dunnion of Donegal, county president of the AOH, several other political figures—including Hugh Law, MP for west Donegal—and various local notables, among them P. J. McNelis, owner of Ardara's Nesbitt Arms, and his brother Dr J. J. McNelis of Glenties.

[57] Garvin, *Evolution*, 95–9; A. C. Hepburn, 'Catholic Ulster and Irish Politics: The Ancient Order of Hibernians, 1905–14', in *A Past Apart: Studies in the History of Catholic Belfast, 1850–1950* (Belfast, 1996), 157–73.

[58] On the depiction of the AOH as 'the old movement', see inter alia the speech of Joe Devlin at Glenties in *DJ*, 1 June 1910.

[59] See *DJ*, 13 Feb. 1885; 24 Mar. 1909; 7 Oct. 1910.

[60] The play had already been performed in Ardara, and was later performed in Castlederg. See *DJ*, 28 Nov. 1910, 24 Jan. 1912, 28 Nov. 1913.

[61] *DJ*, 24 Jan. 1912.

Four bands attended, from Downstrands, Ardara, Glenties, and Ballybofey, and 'the proceedings were very enthusiastic'. The best-received speech was that of George Hamilton Johnstone, a major (retired) with the 4th Battalion Royal Inniskilling Fusiliers. Johnstone was the proprietor of Eden, the local 'big house'. His mother, Maria Frances Hamilton, had succeeded her uncle Gilly who had died without a legitimate heir. Major Johnstone, as he was known, was popular locally. His religion and politics, Catholic and nationalist, were those of the majority community, but he mixed easily in Protestant society. He involved himself too in local development, and he had the fondness for fishing and shooting associated with 'the Gillys'. The major had been in blustery good form. Earlier that year, the Liberal government had introduced a Home Rule Bill, and, in Ireland, Unionists had organized a paramilitary force to resist its implementation if, as expected, it was enacted. That summer there had been serious rioting in Belfast and it was feared that violence would widen and escalate. But Johnstone was having none of it. All talk about civil war in Ulster was bluff and nonsense, he said, adding to cheers and laughter, that given three months and a couple of drill sergeants, he would raise a regiment that would wallop the best that ever came out of Belfast.[62]

Few people in the cheering crowd can have known that, on four nights in 1856, Johnstone's stepfather, John Watkins, had taken constables across the bog from Glenties to lie in ambush for the Mollies at James Gallagher's in Beagh. And that the forebears of the McNelis brothers, the hotelier and the doctor on the platform, had once provoked Molly Maguire by overcharging the poor for potatoes was then, in 1912, a matter of no more consequence than the priests' predecessors having condemned the Mollies as evil men. Here, as in Dungloe, there was 'a peaceful union among all classes of people' or, at least, all classes of Catholics, led by their priests, doctors, and lawyers, and men of trade and property—so the crowd cheered for Home Rule, and few people gave much thought to who would rule at home.

---

[62] *DJ*, 20, 23, 25 Sept. 1912.

PART IV

9

The End of Outrage

In Beagh there came, in time, an end to outrage. Here, the events of 1855–7 did not improve relations between James Gallagher and his father, John. On 24 March 1858, almost two years to the day after Patrick McGlynn had first written to Daniel Cruise, John Gallagher of Beagh, a widower, aged 70, whose employment was 'begging', was admitted to Glenties poorhouse. Two years later, in July 1860, Patrick Hanlon, master of the poorhouse, took legal action against James, charging him with 'permitting his father John Gallagher to be relieved in Glenties Union Workhouse, [despite] you being of sufficient ability to support him, & he being a poor person, who through old age and infirmity is unable to support himself'. He was fined £9 13s. 4d., and £1 costs, and ordered to pay 1s. 9d. per week thereafter for his support. There were then only 100 people in the poorhouse, and of them, twenty were 'aged and infirm' adult males. In total, the old man was to spend over eight years in Glenties, dying there on 15 December 1866.[1] James was himself then three years dead, and the poorhouse records do not show his father being discharged to see him buried.[2]

Other Beagh people entered that same institution in those years. In July 1860, Margaret McCafferty, aged 30, and a sprigger, spent four weeks there. Her father, John, had been James Gallagher's 'tenant' on the old Mulhern place. And the following year, 1861, John McCafferty himself was admitted on 20 June and remained there until 1 August.

---

[1] Glenties Workhouse Registry, 1851–66: 2,725, 2,790, 2,861, 3,150. He left the poorhouse on 4 Aug. 1858, but was readmitted four days later; he left again on 5 Dec. only to return on 17 Dec. 1858. There, he remained until 6 July 1860, when he was again out for less than a fortnight; this period coincided with the case taken against his son. After his return on 19 July 1860, he never left Glenties again. On the court case, see IPSCR Ardara: 10 July 1860. On Glenties poorhouse in July 1860, see BG/92/1/24 Glenties Poor Law Union Minute Book, 3 Feb.–3 Aug. 1860, State of the Workhouse for the Week Ending Saturday 7 July 1860. Of one hundred 'inmates', seven were able-bodied adult males, nineteen able-bodied adult females, twenty aged and infirm adult males, and twenty aged and infirm adult females in the poorhouse; the rest (thirty-four) were children and infants.

[2] Plot 140, Church of the Holy Family Graveyard, Ardara.

Then aged 65, he gave his occupation as labourer. He was readmitted on 27 October, and died there two weeks later on 10 November, aged 66. Both McCaffertys had given their residence as Beagh.[3] It may be that some of the old neighbours put them up after they were put out or allowed them to erect a shelter on their land. Alternatively, they may have had no fixed abode in the intervening years, but, when asked at the poorhouse door whence they came, they had answered 'Beagh'. Only this much is certain: if their having once lived on what had been the Mulherns' place was known to those born in the first decades of the twentieth century, they were not much mentioned, for today McCafferty is in Beagh a name unknown.

One suspects that the McCaffertys did remain in the townland, first in somebody else's house, with their creepies the furthest from the fire, and then in some crude hut. Certainly, others of the evicted were still living there years later. For instance, in 1866, Widow Mary Brogan of Beagh prosecuted Charles McHugh of Tullycleave for assault.[4] Moreover, while the number of houses here fell from eighteen, when the valuation process commenced in July 1855, to fourteen, when it was completed in 1857, the 1861 Census returned eighteen houses (seventeen inhabited, one uninhabited); the number would fall again to fourteen houses, all inhabited, by 1871.[5] And as the evicted saw James Gallagher's cattle graze over the ruins of hope, it would be scarcely any wonder if, in succeeding decades, other families did not talk much of what had happened in 1855–7, or, indeed, in the time of the Famine. There was no need to talk when there was nothing that was not known, and less again when talk could cause trouble in a place that had reminders enough of it. At the same time, unrelenting social and cultural erosion made selective amnesia necessary to sustain any sense of community. The majority of the young were leaving, many of those who remained would never marry, and those who did marry did so later in life, with husbands often significantly older than their wives. And census data indicate that, after a long period of stable bilingualism, language shift occurred suddenly around 1880: in Beagh, with the exception of Rose McHugh (b. 1881), youngest daughter of Condy, no child born after that date was reared speaking Irish; here, and across much of south-west Donegal,

---

[3] See Glenties Workhouse Registry, 1851–66: 3,142, 3,337, 3,429. McCafferty was not a common name in the Union, but there is no way of knowing if James McCafferty, a 29-year-old labourer, admitted to Glenties poorhouse with consumption in July 1865, was a relation; his residence was the 'Union at Large'. See Glenties Workhouse Registry, 1851–66: 4,628.

[4] IPSCR Ardara: 13 Feb. 1866.   [5] See Table 3.2 in Chapter 3.

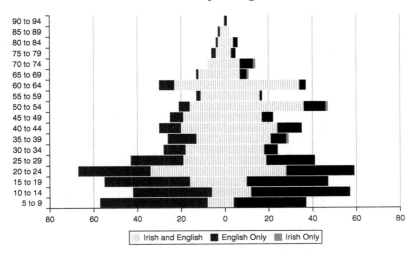

Figure 9.1 Linguistic ability of persons aged 5 or more years, Dawros Electoral Division, 1901

the first generation to pass through national school made English the language of the home (see Figure 9.1).[6]

All was not decline. There would be significant material improvement by the century's end. Particularly important was the erection of byres in the 1860s. In Beagh, where there were only four 'offices' in 1857, there were nineteen 'out-offices and farm-steadings' in 1871. The number increased to thirty-one in 1881 and thirty-eight in 1891, when, judging from breakdowns of outbuildings in the 1901 Census returns, all households had a cowhouse and a calfhouse, most had a piggery, and a few had stables.[7] But it was those first byres erected in the 1860s that mattered most, for they allowed the removal of cattle from the single-roomed houses, and the construction of internal walls then made two rooms where there had been only one. Two small sash-windows were likely added to most houses in that decade and, in those brighter houses, tea went from being a luxury in the 1850s to an everyday necessity by the 1880s; tea cups then began to replace bowls and, by the end of century,

[6] Census, 1901: household returns. On recent scholarship on linguistic change, see Gearóid Ó Tuathaigh, *I mBéal an Bháis: The Great Famine and the Language Shift in Nineteenth-Century Ireland* (Hamden, 2015).

[7] *GV*: Beagh; *Census of Ireland, 1871, Part I, Volume III... Ulster*, HC 1874 [C964], lxxiv. 368–9, and Census of Ireland, 1891, Part I, HC 1894 [C6626], xcii. 368; 'Out-Offices and Farm-steadings Return' (Form B2) in Census, 1901 and 1911.

only five of the townland's twelve houses had just two rooms; the other seven now had three.[8]

Still, for most of those born there from the 1840s, Beagh was a place of diminished possibility. The figures bear repeating—where there had been near 120 people in 1845, there were 60 in 1901. Beagh School moved to a new building in 1894, and the 'new school' closed in 1968. Most children who learned to read and write in Beagh wrote home from America, Scotland, England, New Zealand, Australia, and places now forgotten. At home, in their absence, melancholy rose like damp. Greed and cruel deeds had to be let fade into oblivion. It was hard to remember, and it was best to forget.

But if people find reason to forget, they also find meaning where there is none. Land 'grabbed' was thought ill-gotten, and it was said to bring no luck.[9] 'The property acquired fraudulently in this manner succeeded well for a time with some', Hugh Dorian recalled of Famine-time 'land-grabbing' in north Donegal,

> but such people were not looked upon in the light of being just men, and there was always the foreboding thought that some evil would befall the man or the family, 'not wishing ill to the innocent'. And if evil befell, there was not that general feeling of sympathy which would otherwise be [the case], but rather a whisper would circulate that 'he was one deserving a certain visitation'; 'but it was a pity that the innocent should suffer so, for the crime of his father'; 'his father was not good'; 'he was blamed for turning out Widow So and So'; 'he has all the lands held once by So and So, and never paid a penny for it'; 'got it in the bad times'; 'how could he have luck?'[10]

And so James Gallagher's early death, aged *c*.50, in June 1863, was meaningful. He had not long enjoyed his fine farm. There was consolation in coincidence, a conviction that justice had been done. Two years later, in 1865, the family had more trouble when his daughter Ellen died aged only 22. And others of that generation of Gallaghers had no great 'luck' either. After James's death, his widow Madge Craig managed the holding with her eldest son, John: indeed, she was managing it near twenty years later, in 1882, when Joseph Gallagher of Ballyganny took her to Ardara petty sessions to recover £2 13s. 3d. of unpaid wages, and in March 1883 when she licensed the family dog.[11] It was only in 1888, presumably after Madge's death, that her youngest son, Denis (1853–1918), took a wife, Mary McNelis (1865–1936) of Common. Mary (commonly Mary Phádaí Óig)

---

[8] 'House and Building Return' (Form B1) in Census, 1901 and 1911.
[9] Ó Gráda, 'Famine Memory', 210–12.   [10] Dorian, *Outer Edge*, 229.
[11] IPSCR Ardara: 8 Aug. 1882; she was also summoned for non-payment of cess. NAI, Dog Licence Applications, Ardara, 27 Mar. 1883.

was a daughter of a comfortable farmer, and several of her brothers were schoolmasters. It was a 'good match' and they soon started a family, but, tragically, in February 1900, Denis (commonly Dinny) began to behave strangely. Then, in the first weeks of January 1901, he made several attempts to kill Mary, and she had him committed to the county asylum in Letterkenny. There, doctors diagnosed him with 'mania epileptic', which they judged to be hereditary.[12] It was almost half a century since the events that had precipitated the Mollies' raid on his father, longer since his acquisition of the Mulhern place, and longer still since the squaring of the farms made every man accountable for his own portion. There were people living who had seen it all, but it was a long time ago and the Gallaghers had suffered enough.

TO EXCHANGE THEMSELVES FOR THE FUTURE

> Just as capital is compelled continually to reproduce itself, so its culture is one of unending anticipation. What-is-to-come, what-is-to-be-gained empties what-is. The immigrant proletariat, unable to return home, suffering from being who they were, yearned to become, or for their children to become, American. They saw no hope but to exchange themselves for the future. And although the desperation of this wager was specifically immigrant, the mechanism has become more and more typical of developed capitalism.
>
> John Berger, *About Looking* (New York, 1991 [1980]), 108

John Kennedy (1849–1931) and Dinny Gallagher were about the same age and they were reared in houses less than 100 yards apart.[13] John's short walk to the main road which, as a child he had to cross to get to school, took him through land that his hard-drinking grandfather had transferred to Dinny's father in 1855; the Gallaghers' house was that which Patrick McGlynn had left in a hurry in 1856. Yet notwithstanding all that had passed between their families, John and Dinny were friends. John had Dinny and Mary Phádaí Óig as sponsors (godparents) for his second-born son, Neil, in January 1899, and in 1931, when John drew up a will and put his mark to it (although he could read and write), he had his

---

[12] For the committal of Denis Gallagher, see IPSCR Ardara: 17 Jan. 1901. And for his age and medical condition, see patient no. 3,925 in Census, 1901, Residents of House 1.2 Knocknamona (Letterkenny Rural); Census, 1911, Residents of House 1.2 Knocknamona (Letterkenny Rural). On Mary's death, see *DJ*, 7 Dec. 1936.

[13] John's age was returned as 46 in the 1901 Census but as 62 in 1911. If the age given in 1901 was correct he would have been born *c*.1855; if that in 1911, *c*.1849. The age (82) given for him at death (GRO), in 1931, suggests he was born *c*.1849.

two nearest neighbours witness it. Matt Sweeney (1878–1945), who, in 1903, had succeeded his father Danny (1839–1911) as master of the school, was one and the other was Jim Gallagher (1889–1973), Dinny's eldest son. And John's own children, particularly his heir, Con, had great respect for the Gallaghers.

Both John Kennedy and Dinny Gallagher had succeeded to their families' holdings in the 1880s: John was tenant as early as 1881 and Dinny by the end of the decade, his marriage, in 1888, relegating to the status of lodger an elder brother, John, who had been de facto head of the household; a sister, Madge, became a servant.[14] In contrast, John Kennedy, despite having the holding in his name, took his time to take a wife. When he finally married, about 46 years of age, in 1895, his bride, Annie Boyle (b. 1875) of Tullymore, was twenty-six years his junior.

The mode of living in west Donegal in that decade can be glimpsed in a 'baseline report' on an area roughly coterminous with the parishes of Ardara and Glenties compiled in 1892 by 26-year-old Frederick Gahan (1866–1955), an inspector with the Congested Districts Board (CDB), a new state agency charged with the development of the west of Ireland:

> The houses are almost invariably thatched, some of them being of a very poor description. They have in almost every instance two rooms—one room the day room and room where all the meals are taken and the housework done—the other is generally the bedroom of the women of the house, and is generally much cleaner than the other. Of furniture, there is scarcely any, a couple of chairs or a stool, generally a 'form' on which the basket of potatoes is placed at dinner, sometimes a dresser, a sort of rude bed. The roof of the cabin is always black with smoke, there being no ceiling or upper storey in the great majority of cases. The inner room has generally a boarded floor or a better floor than the outside room. The beds are better, and there are generally pictures round the walls or almanacks. The outside of the house is sometimes whitewashed, but never the interior. The home life is always the same winter and summer, except that in summer the people rise at half-past six or seven instead of eight or nine in winter; in summer there is the farm-work to be done, whereas in winter, the men do nothing, comparatively speaking, to their farms. In summer, the cows are first seen to, and milked; at about eight or nine o'clock they have breakfast. After breakfast the men go out to their farm-work, the women tend cattle or knit, or, if necessary, work along with the men in the fields; at two o'clock, they all come in to dinner. The potatoes, which have been boiling in a large pot, are taken off the fire and put into the skib or basket and placed on the small form above referred

---

[14] *LJ*, 22 June 1877, lists John as one of twenty-three people in Ardara to make a donation for building of a parochial house in neighbouring Carrick and, from 1866 down to 1888, when Dinny married, he usually licensed the Gallaghers' dog.

to; the family gather round and eat them, sometimes alone, sometimes with fish. After dinner, work again till evening, when the cows are milked and they have their suppers. At nine or half-past nine they go to bed; in winter they get up very late—about nine o'clock. The women see to the cows and milk, the men clean out the byres, creel down the turf, and put the cows in at night; perhaps they do a little on their farm in the way of drainage or reclamation, but very seldom. They sit up in the winter gossiping in one another's houses till eleven and twelve o'clock at night. The women are constant workers, and are the sole support almost of all the families in the district. They all knit, down to the tiny children of five and six years of age; they knit in the fields, knit in the houses, knit as they walk along the roads— in fact, unless their hands are otherwise employed, they are always knitting.[15]

Strikingly, the material conditions and associated rhythms of life so well described by Gahan—including features disdained by him—were, in many respects, recent developments, only having emerged since the Famine, but particularly in the 1860s and 1870s, when greater involvement in the livestock economy and the expansion of women's work— sprigging, knitting, and the egg and butter trades—increased smallholders' purchasing power and raised their standards of living and expectations. For instance, in Beagh, it was in the 1860s and 1870s, when John Kennedy and Dinny Gallagher were in their teens and twenties, that the byres were built, and it was these buildings—dismissed in the report on the wider district as 'dirty, badly lighted, and badly built'—that had made possible the houses described by Gahan, that is, two rooms, one with a boarded floor, and it was those same byres, by removing the cattle, that allowed windows and a second chimney to be added.[16] Similarly, while knitting had been prevalent before the Famine, the constant clicking of needles was attributable, at least in part, to a shift in mid-century from women bartering socks with dealers at fairs to a putting out system that allowed firms, notably the McDevitts, to secure large contracts.[17] The egg

<hr/>

[15] Trinity College, Dublin, Congested Districts Baseline Reports: Frederick G. Townsend Gahan, *District of Glenties* (1892), 16. On Gahan, see Brendan O'Donoghue, *The Irish County Surveyors, 1834–1944* (Dublin, 2007), 180.

[16] Gahan, *Glenties*, 4. Notions of privacy changed after the building of the byres, with females now sleeping in a separate room from the males. There were also cultural and, perhaps, even political ramifications. 'If a man's house be neat, clean, and comfortable, it unconsciously tends to elevate his ideas, and increase his self-respect', wrote a Dublin reporter, who visited Ardara in the 1860s, and witnessed the improvements. See Coulter, *West of Ireland*, 304.

[17] In 1864, Daniel McDevitt Jr entered into a partnership with his brother Hugh, the former investing £1,000 and the latter £600, and this firm soon made them the stocking kings of west Donegal; by 1877, the McDevitts were exporting 624,000 pairs of socks and stockings a year (in addition to comforters, guernsey frocks, and other knitted goods). In that year, the firm revealed something of its modus operandi: 'We employ about 1,100

and butter trades too had been transformed in the same period: Gahan describes a great number of little shops—'about one to every two town-lands'—that purchased eggs and butter, 'always' paying with tea, sugar, tobacco, or snuff; these shops, in turn, supplied 'central dealers' in Glenties, Fintown, and Ardara who sent consignments to Derry, for shipping to Glasgow or Liverpool. Potatoes still bulked large in the diet—a family of six was consuming 'about two-stone or a little less daily, say twelve stone weekly' from mid-August to mid-April—but, year-round, people were eating more bread and bacon than in the middle decades of the century. Most conspicuously, a typical household was going through about 1lb of tea and 4lb of sugar per week, in a place where, in the 1850s, those commodities had been rarely tasted—indeed, with an esti-mated annual expenditure of £41 0s. 5d., such a household had a greater outgoing on tea (£5 4s.) than anything—including rent (£2 15s.), taxes (10s.), and livestock (£4 15s.)—except flour (£6 5s.) and meal (£7). Tea, sugar, and tobacco were 'almost forced', as Gahan phrased it, on the women in exchange for knitting and sprigging, eggs and butter, for in those luxuries lay the greatest profits for small dealers. The tea, he remarked, was the 'worst quality' of the Assam variety, and it was not 'drawn' but 'regularly boiled' and 'not considered good unless it [was] almost perfectly black'.[18]

•

The likes of John Kennedy and Dinny Gallagher, people born in the mid-nineteenth century, who lived the life described by Gahan, belonged to what historian Joe Lee has called 'the Land League generation'. This cohort, Lee argued, 'travelled further in historical time than all previous generations in Irish history'.[19] In Beagh, the 'historical time' that it travelled can be measured in rooms added to houses, changes in diet and literacy rates, and new devotional practices and demographic patterns. Indeed, people who remained at home and lived the proverbial three score and ten saw many of the marvels of the Second Industrial Revolution, that extraordinary period of innovation in the half-century prior to the First World War, when new power sources—the internal combustion engine and electric generator—plastics, and new production processes for metals,

---

families (we mean the female portion), and we imagine that each family would number about three, equivalent to 3,300 persons. . . . As a rule, the younger of each family attend school during the day, and assist the others during the evening and at a night, while at home, at knitting.' See Murrough O'Brien, 'The Condition of Small Farmers in Ireland, and their Position with Reference to the Land Question', *Journal of the Statistical and Social Inquiry Society of Ireland*, 7 (1878), 299–310, 306.

[18] Gahan, *Glenties*, 5–6, 14–15.

[19] Joseph Lee, *The Modernisation of Irish Society, 1848–1918* (Dublin, 2008 [1973]), 97.

chemicals, and textiles fashioned a new world. Bicycles went out the Narin Road before the end of the nineteenth century and motorcars and motorcycles in the first decade of the twentieth.[20] In Ardara, pictures moved in the Iona Hall, a wooden structure erected in 1926 by the saddler Patrick Gildea, and that same year the town got electricity;[21] and in Beagh, in the 1930s, there were gramophones—the Kennedys had one carried home from New York—and Pilot radios and Dunlop rubber boots. And yet for all the new things, it is those people born c.1833–66 rearing their own children in a language which had not been their mother tongue—the breaking of a sound barrier with the sudden abandonment of a long-stable bilingualism—that most clearly registers the velocity with which they were moving, the intensity with which they strove to put a distance between their progeny and their past.

That first generation reared in English only—in Beagh, those born from 1880—would itself, in time, see further material and cultural change. Electricity and indoor plumbing were installed in the 1950s; slate replaced thatch and cement covered flagstones.[22] But for all those improvements, the material conditions and basic rhythm of life so well described by Gahan in 1892 persisted into the 1950s; indeed, it was the rhythm of some households into the 1970s, when the click of needles was still a constant and the butter churn not yet put away. And that the mode of living in Beagh in the 1970s—or even the 1950s—was closer to that in the 1890s than the mode of living in that decade was to that in the 1850s—before the byres removed the cattle from the houses—gives some perspective on how far in historical time, as Lee puts it, that people born c.1833–66 had already travelled by the end of the nineteenth century.

Lee's claim for that generation is compelling, yet the name that he put on it seems wrongheaded. Better for it to be named for that which defined it—it was the Famine generation, comprising those people who, in childhood, had most deeply impressed upon them the meaning of an empty pot. In a sensitive study of the making of 'the revolutionary generation'—the people born in the last two decades of the nineteenth century who rejected the half-a-loaf of Home Rule and fought for a Republic—R. F. Foster has argued, that 'The men and women who made the Irish revolution knew that they were different to their parents.'[23]

---

[20] An obituary in *DJ*, 18 Mar. 1955, remembers Denis Boyle, Mullyvea, as 'the first man to own and ride a bicycle in the Downstrands area'; it was a Singer bike, bought 'over half a century ago'.

[21] *DJ*, 8 Jan. 1926. On the Ardara Electric Scheme, which served the town, see *DJ*, 5 Feb. 1926.

[22] On the electrification of Beagh, see *DJ*, 24 Oct. 1952.

[23] R. F. Foster, *Vivid Faces: The Revolutionary Generation in Ireland, 1890–1923* (London, 2014), 1.

It too is a compelling argument, richly elaborated by Foster for the city-centred middle class. And it doubtless holds for the rural poor in places like Beagh, the Tullies, and Downstrands. Still, in that class—not only on the smallholdings of west Donegal but across much of the west of Ireland—it was the fervent wish of the men and women of the Famine generation that their children be different to themselves, that is, that their young, in John Berger's phrase, would not have to suffer for being who they were. And if that wish led many people to deny their children knowledge of who they were—most obviously in opting to rear them only in English—some nonetheless passed to those same children a sharpened sense of belonging to an Irish 'nation' that had endured the deleterious effects of British rule, and that sense of national suffering—deepened by the Famine, demographic decline, and the land and Home Rule agitations of the 1880s—dampened interest in differences between neighbours. In Beagh, the Brogans, McCaffertys, Mooneys, and O'Donnells faded from memory and forgotten altogether were those landless families removed at the squaring: as tenancy had come to define the place, and that sense of national suffering became ramified by experience, their lives had ceased to be 'grievable'.[24] In the end, the only family remembered as having lost house and home in the upheavals of the mid-nineteenth century were the Mulherns—tenants.

JAMES TÁILLIÚR AND THE BOG ROAD GATE

One incident aside, there was no more trouble between the Gallaghers and their neighbours after 1855–7. That incident, in 1904, did not contribute to the ending of outrage at what had happened in the 1840s and 1850s. Again, in the Kennedys' house, where there was reason to resent the Gallaghers, outrage had ended, that is, it had not been passed from those who had seen it all to those who came after them. And in other houses too, for all but the aged, the early death of James Gallagher in 1863 and the extraordinary changes that came over the place in the decades that followed diminished any residual resentment of his family. Graves, it has been said, become neglected once none among the living remembers the faces of the beloved dead. And with the face of that once resented man then remembered by declining numbers, and a place of one-roomed windowless houses (and no tea) difficult for people born after the 1860s to imagine, outrage burned to ashes.

[24] Judith Butler, 'Violence, Politics, Mourning', in *Precarious Life: The Powers of Mourning and Violence* (New York, 2004), 19–49.

Rather than ending outrage, then, the incident in 1904 marked the fact that world had turned. Dinny Gallagher's children were very young when he was committed in 1901, and so his unmarried brother, John, looked after the farm. In 1904, John erected a *fence*—this is how it was described in a court case—across the bog road. His reason for erecting it is not known: it had been a public road since the Ordnance Survey mapped the place in 1835, and it was likely a public road long before then. In truth, calling it a road dignifies what was merely a rutted cart track. Indeed, it was a cart track, with grass growing in the middle of it, down to the 1990s. It is hard now to credit the idea that John was trying to incorporate a few hundred yards of cart track into the Gallaghers' rough pasture, sections of which lay both sides of it. Rather, it seems that the 'fence' was, in fact, a gate and one that served no purpose other than giving himself the satisfaction of knowing that others knew that the Gallaghers had land on both sides of the bog road.[25]

James Táilliúr (1864–1959) was indifferent to such hubris. He knocked down the gate obstructing his access to his own land. John took umbrage, and he summoned James to the petty sessions, suing him for 5s. damages. On the August day when the case was called, the plaintiff brought Hector Wilson and Con Shovlin to testify on his behalf. Shovlin, known as Con Mháire Bháin, was a 19-year-old labourer, living with two siblings and their widowed mother in Sandfield. Wilson, a Scotsman, living in Glenties, had been head bailiff on the Conyngham estate since 1890. An expert on salmon, his main duties included overseeing the lucrative Owenea fishery, not least organizing gangs of waterkeepers to 'watch the river'. It was not a responsibility that won him many friends in the Tullies and Beagh.

Yet times had changed since Russell, the land agent, had facilitated James Gallagher's rise at the expense of his neighbours. Landlordism was dead but not buried. Beginning in 1870 and then, with more effect, from 1881, Westminster had passed a series of land acts, culminating, in the year prior to the row about the fence, in the Land Purchase (Ireland) Act (1903), popularly, the Wyndham Land Act, which provided incentives to landlords to sell their estates and government loans to tenants to enable them to buy their holdings. It was the last nail in the coffin of a failed system; subsequent acts were but spit on the brass plate. Over the next decade, some 200,000 tenants would buy their holdings under the Act.[26]

---

[25] IPSCR Ardara: 9 Aug. 1904.
[26] Fergus Campbell, 'Irish Popular Politics and the Making of the Wyndham Land Act, 1901–1903', *Historical Journal*, 45 (2002), 755–73, includes the estimate of 200,000.

Hector Wilson was yesterday's man—the landlords were going and their retainers with them.

The judges that day were Major General James Richard Knox Tredennick (1843–1928) of Woodhill, owner of the old Nesbitt estate; Alexander Maxwell Hamilton of Mossvill, a gentleman farmer, agent of Lloyds of London at Killybegs, and, from its establishment in 1897, captain of the Ardara Golf Club; and Owen Fallon (1840–1917), a retired District Inspector of the Royal Irish Constabulary (RIC). Tredennick and Hamilton were the sweepings of the Ascendancy. Fallon, an Irish-speaking Mayo man, was a Catholic whose high rank in the RIC and elevation to the commission of the peace (the bench), in 1903, were products of fitful democratization. Revealingly, Fallon, with no connections in the district, was considered better suited than some local Catholic 'gentlemen' to be a petty sessions judge. Fallon, then, was something of a transitional figure, a portent of things to come yet a reminder too of the limits of change.[27]

James Táilliúr called a single witness, a neighbour, Condy Gallagher (1847–1930). The two families had not always been on good terms. Indeed, in late 1889, they had taken each other to the same court, each blaming the other for flooding his land. Condy had allegedly blocked a water pipe; James Kennedy—either James Táilliúr or his father, also James (1823–93)—had supposedly destroyed a ditch, and Condy was said to have assaulted him. The squabble had resulted in four summonses to the petty sessions.[28] But that was fifteen years earlier, and Condy too had land over the bog road, and so he, like the Táilliúrs, was inconvenienced by the fence. Importantly, Condy was old enough to remember 1855, when James Gallagher acquired two sections of Nancy Sweeney's, on the north side of the bog road; and he would have known, as others knew, that the same man had only acquired the Mulherns' place on the south side of the road in the time of the Famine. In other words, whatever Hector Wilson said, James Táilliúr and Condy Gallagher could swear that as far back as they or anybody else in Beagh could remember, people had travelled unobstructed over the bog road. The Gallaghers did not own the road. And when the bench, in an effort to mediate, asked what particular objection James had to the fence, he had an answer, 'It is too heavy for the wains.'[29]

The case was dismissed, yet it was long remembered in Beagh, with some head-shaking at the 'daftness' of putting up a 'gate' on the bog road,

[27] *DJ*, 30 Apr. 1917. *A Return . . . of the Persons Holding the Commission of the Peace*, HC 1905 (118), lxv. 9, returns twenty-six petty sessions magistrates in Donegal—eleven Catholics (42%), eleven Episcopalians, and four Presbyterians. The 1901 Census returned the county's population as over 77.7% Catholic.

[28] IPSCR Ardara: 12 Nov., 10 Dec. 1889.

[29] A sentence ascribed to Kennedy by various people who told me the story of the gate.

and much marvelling at James Táilliúr having 'represented himself' in court. In fact, there was nothing unusual in his having done so. Most ordinary people had no legal representation at the petty sessions. But the significance of the case is clear. The bailiff had been ignored, and when Tredennick rapped his gavel to dismiss the case the landlord-favoured family stood no taller in the town than their neighbours. Such was the way landlordism ended in south-west Donegal, and if James Táilliúr's smashing of the gate or fence or whatever-it-was marked an end, it also served as a new beginning.

The vicissitudes of once favoured families were now a marvel. James Gallagher's first-born child seems to have been Mary (c.1841–1937). She had married Manus (Manus) Craig (c.1831–98) of Kilclooney, a close connection, probably her cousin. The marriage was childless. Manus died in 1898, leaving £295 and a farm, and a few years later, in the early 1900s, Mary—now known as Mary Manus—returned to Beagh. Here, while waiting for a house to be built, she made her home in the one-roomed 'old school' acquired by her brother Dinny when the 'new school' opened in 1894. It was an unexpected turn of events. Her father-in-law (and possibly uncle), Old Manus Craig, had been one of a handful of west Donegal Catholics with a vote in Westminster elections in the 1830s, and as recently as 1892, when her brother-in-law Thomas (Manus) Craig, died aged 75, the mourners at his funeral had included a host of justices of the peace, hoteliers, and publicans, rate collectors, merchants, and poor law guardians. Years later, people remembered it as the biggest funeral that ever went to Kilclooney.[30] Yet Mary Manus—a daughter of a Craig who married a Craig—was living in the old school in 1911.

THOSE WHO SAW IT ALL

Nahor McHugh, born about 1820, was the oldest inhabitant of Beagh on the night that the Census was taken in 1901. He had seen people told to demolish their houses, take up their beds and walk in 1839–41, and those same people, who had survived *ar scáth a chéile*, sheltered by each other, told that henceforth every man would be only accountable for his own portion, that is, that no man was now his brother's keeper. And in that great change, from rundale to squared farms, he had seen as many as half a dozen families whose names were not in the agent's book told that there was no longer a place for them in Beagh. Nahor had seen futures rot

[30] Shovlin, *Narin and Downstrands*, 174–8.

a few years later, and James Gallagher avail of hunger and disease, death, debt, and hardship to acquire the Mulhern place, one half of Nancy Sweeney's, and two-thirds of Pat Kennedy's. He had seen too Patrick McGlynn and his own brother Condy turn informer on friends and neighbours, only for the latter to refuse to testify against them and then, for his original sin (informing on himself), spend almost a year in Lifford. And Nahor had seen James Gallagher clear the Brogans, McCaffertys, Mooneys, and O'Donnells, and let his father go to the poorhouse. All these things he had seen from his late teens to his late thirties, *c.*1838–58. And from those same years, he had seen places first mentioned in Beagh in his youth—Hazleton and Wilkes Barre, Mauch Chunk and Summit Hill—become more vividly imagined at his own fireside than towns in neighbouring counties. Then, from the end of the American Civil War in 1865, the leave-takings had intensified, as his own and others' children left for the mine patches, and he had seen a radical cultural transformation, with children reared in Beagh from 1880 speaking only English which hitherto had not been the language of any house in the place.

Nahor McHugh died in April 1904, a few months before the trouble about the gate, and he was doubtless as keenly mourned in Hazleton, Pennsylvania, as in Beagh, for most of his children were there. Fifteen of the sixty-odd people then living in Beagh were over 54 years of age. The youngest of that cohort had been barefooted schoolchildren in June 1856 when constables arrived on Tommy Maloney's taxi to take the master into protective custody. Several of the eldest—those in their seventies and eighties in 1904—had been married when the constables came, some with children of their own. Among those people was Nahor's sister-in-law, Catherine McHugh, the widow of Condy. And there were people too in the Tullies, Ranny, Carn, Sandfield, and Downstrands who had seen all that had passed in Beagh in 1837–57, or who at the very least remembered Patrick McGlynn and the men whom he had betrayed, and James Gallagher and the families whom he had cleared.

A few of those people survived into the 1920s and 1930s. Indeed, Gallagher's daughter, Mary Manus, the woman who lived for a time in the old school, was reputed to be aged 95 when she died in 1937. She was said to have 'possessed a very retentive memory, and distinctly remembered the Famine years of 1846–47, and clearly recollected the introduction of tea and baker's bread. She could relate many stirring anecdotes of the Land War in the area fifty years ago.'[31] Mary Manus had been in her teens in

---

[31] There is some uncertainty about Mary Manus's birthyear. Her obituary in *Derry People*, 9 Jan. 1937, claims she was 95, suggesting she was born in 1841; the GRO estimates her age as 91, suggesting a birthyear of 1845, while the ages given for her in the 1901

March 1856 when the Mollies burst into her father's house. Others still living in the 1930s had a different perspective on those events.[32] William McNelis was born in Ballymackilduff in 1837, meaning he would have been about the same age as many of the Mollies when, in April 1856, Condy McHugh sent Patrick McGlynn to Loughfad, adjacent to McNelis's homeplace, to ask James Moore to send men to Beagh for another raid on Gallagher. In his later years, McNelis went to live with a nephew in Kentucky, an area on the outskirts of Ardara that took its name from the house of a 'Yankee' who had called it after the place where he had dug coal and made money. He died there in August 1938, aged 101. His obituary represents him as a politically minded man, such as would have had an interest, in his late teens, in the doings of the Mollies, and one too who knew the 'tales and songs', that is, the history, of his place:

> Despite his great age, he was in possession of all his faculties to the end and took a keen interest in current events. He could read the newspaper without the aid of glasses and a short time ago walked ten miles in one day and did not suffer any ill effects. He was extremely fond of potatoes, a diet which, he said, contributed much to his longevity. He never rode in a train, and it was only a few years ago that he had his first trip in a motor car. His store of old Irish tales and songs was unlimited, and he could narrate them in a style all his own that made him one of County Donegal's greatest seanachaidhes. He was actively connected with every movement that had for its object securing Irish freedom. He was prominently associated with the Land League movement and in later years was a strong supporter of Sinn Féin.[33]

In the final years of McNelis's life, his grandniece, Mary Ann McNelis (b. 1924), then a 'scholar' in Tullymore School, transcribed some of his

(52, Kilclooneymore) and 1911 (64, Beagh) census returns would have her born in 1847–9. Following the introduction of the pension, searches were made of the then extant 1841 and 1851 returns to establish the ages of people born before civil registration. Mary Manus (Craig, née Gallagher) applied for her pension in July 1916, consistent with her notion, in 1911, that she was born *c.*1847 and would reach pension age (70) in 1917. Her application was successful; unfortunately, surviving paperwork does not include any additional details from her father's 1851 return. It may have revealed her to be a little older than she had believed, which may explain how she could remember the Famine. See NAI 1851 CSF Cen/S/7/319.

[32] Bridget O'Reilly (née Doherty, b. 1840), widow of the constable who dealt with McGlynn, died in 1938. Her obituary, in *DJ*, 6 July 1938, noted that 'Possessed of a very retentive memory, the late Mrs O'Reilly could recount many interesting anecdotes of her experiences of 80 and 90 years ago. She remembered when labourers worked for as little as four pence per day and when all the provisions that came to Ardara were conveyed from Derry by horse and cart. Widow of the late Sergeant O'Reilly, RIC, she remembered the time when Irish was the spoken language of Cavan and during her visits to that county heard Irish extensively spoken.'
[33] *Ulster Herald*, 20 Aug. 1938.

reminiscences and stories. He recalled how the people of Rosbeg used to make soap from seaweed and sell it to people further inland, and how girls used to sprig around a candle, made from resin, butter, lard, or dripping, that gave a 'very bright pleasant light'. He gave her cures and charms—a fox's tongue could be used to extract a needle—and 'the signs of the weather'. He told her stories of the fairies and ghostly lights seen at the house of a man who cut a finger off a drowned woman to get a gold ring, and how when a cow calved the people used to put a grain of salt into the bottom of a vessel 'so that their neighbours could not take away their butter'. And he remembered that Eoghan Scott of Narin killed Henry Keeney of Killybegs with one box, that Proinsias Mór (Francis McHugh) of Laconnell beat Fr John McNulty (curate in Ardara, 1886–91) in a swimming competition, and that on hearing that six policemen had not been fit to take James Kennedy of Lackagh to the barracks a resident magistrate had remarked that he should have been wearing the belt.[34]

Mary Ann transcribed these stories for a school project, conducted across Ireland at the behest of the Irish Folklore Commission. But interest in such 'yarns' was fading around Ardara. Language shift—people of William McNelis's generation not having spoken their own first language to their children—had raised a cloud of silence between young and old and, that shift occurring over much of the district after three decades of intense social and cultural change, it had produced a generation, that of Mary Ann's parents, careful about appearing old-fashioned or behind the times. Several people born in the mid-1900s corresponded with me on the subject of this book; others discussed it with me. Almost all insisted that, in their youth, the elderly had not made much mention of things that had happened a century earlier. One correspondent, remembering the 1950s, wrote as follows:

> There were quite a number of old people in Beagh when I was young and *all were blessed with good memories*. James Kennedy was the oldest—he died in 1959 aged 94 years. All of the old people gathered every night for the card playing in Jim Kennedy's (James' son who inherited a farm from his aunt Nellie) . . . I was at those card games many times when young but *they never seemed to go into any happenings of the past*.[35]

The notion that the old people were 'blessed with good memories' but did not discuss 'any happenings of the past' may strike the reader as incongruous. Certainly, James Táilliúr, the man unsuccessfully prosecuted in 1904, and whose death in August 1959 is mentioned in that letter, was interested in 'happenings of the past'. His obituary described him as 'one

---

[34] NFCS 1,058: 105–6, 112–15, 121–6, 139–40.
[35] Letter to the author, autumn 2012; emphasis added.

of the oldest and most revered citizens of the parish' and noted that he had been 'a vivacious controversialist' who 'loved to recount many incidences of his young days' and of 'life in the area' long ago.[36] Yet my correspondent remembers well, less with regard to people like James Táilliúr, born in the middle third of the nineteenth century, more the generation that came after them: the past held less fascination for the children of the late nineteenth century.

•

Those people, who, in youth, read the lined faces of those who had seen it all, are gone now. In Beagh, Hughie Táilliúr (b. 1912)—a son of James—was the last of them. A thoughtful, quiet-spoken man, who kept his black hair and himself to himself until the end, he died aged 92 in January 2004. One of a family of ten, Hughie never married. He was the last of his name. Most of his siblings, like most of that generation in Beagh, emigrated. Hughie, like the neighbours he buried, was an exception—he stayed.

My grandfather Néillidh Sweeney (1900–86) was a little older than Hughie Táilliúr. He was a short man, about five and a half foot tall. Thin and almost wiry in frame, his dark hair turned white in middle age (Figure 9.2). He had piercing blue eyes, and the thumb and fingers of his right hand were blackened by nicotine. Never a heavy smoker, he would

Figure 9.2 Annie Kennedy and Néillidh Sweeney, Beagh, *c.*1975

[36] *Derry People*, 29 Aug. 1959. His obituary gives his age at death as 94; *DJ*, 4 Dec. 1953, has him celebrating his ninetieth birthday.

'nick' a half-smoked fag and slip it into his pocket to finish later; and the box was left behind the clock above the Stanley 8 range rather than carried around. Still, he used to cup the untipped Woodbine as if shielding it from a breeze, and the rich tobacco smoke would darken his hand. Nobody smokes like that now, but many of his generation did. He did other things differently too. He got a television in the mid-1970s, and a child was baffled that it was turned on only to watch *The News at 5.45*. On a wet day, he might have watched *Crown Court*, a low-budget afternoon show in which actors played the judge and barristers, the accused and witnesses 'before a jury selected from members of the general public'. But usually he only watched the news. He was witty, though some considered his wit cutting. His mode of transport was a big black bicycle or the bus to get up to the town, and a donkey and cart to bring turf from the bog. His language was English, but peppered with Irish words and phrases. Many of his metaphors belonged to the industry-dazzled culture of his youth. 'There goes a Scotch boat' was the observation when a child farted—an allusion to the steam ships that once plied between Derry and Glasgow. 'I'll tan your arse with a steam shovel!' was the threat for a mischievous boy.

I was that boy, and for me in the 1970s, the Woodbine and the pushbike were an old man's things. My uncle John Joe, my grandfather's eldest son, generally smoked roll-ups; my father and his younger brother James, like most men their age, preferred tipped cigarettes, Major and Benson & Hedges. John Joe and my father drove cars from the mid-1970s. James, when he came home from England in 1978, rode a motorbike, the then ubiquitous Honda 50, which made him cool. Still, when Néillidh Sweeney himself had been in his teens in the 1910s, the Woodbine and the pushbike had set the young apart from their elders. His own father, Seán (1859–1938)—his name is given as John in his census forms, obituary, and will, but occasionally as Shan (*aka* Seán) in a less ponderous dog licence register—had smoked a clay pipe, and probably never threw his leg over a high nelly. Hence, in the 1910s, Néillidh Sweeney was one of those who knew, in R. F. Foster's terms, that he was different to his parents. And he himself was part of Foster's 'revolutionary generation', volunteering for the Irish Republican Army in 1918. His brothers Johnny and Joe, who were then still in Ireland, also volunteered, and half a world away in California, their eldest brother Patrick, who had left Ireland before Néillidh's birth in 1900, was a member of the Citizens' Liberty Committee that oversaw a 'mass meeting' for De Valera in Oakland in July 1919.[37] But crucially, the republicanism

---

[37] *Oakland Tribune*, 19 July 1919; it was a large committee, and his role likely that of a steward.

of those Sweeney boys, born 1881–1900, was not an assertion of their difference to their parents for, in 1917, the founding members of the local Sinn Féin cumann included their father: he, who belonged to the Famine generation, had denied them his own first language but he had gifted them the politics of revolution.[38]

A HOUSE

Néillidh Sweeney was the last of twelve children born to Seán Sweeney and Annie Boyle (*c.*1857–1944) in the house erected at the squaring of the farms in 1839–41.[39] He and his siblings were only the second generation born in it, for their grandfather, Patrick—a son of Nancy Sweeney— would, as a child, have been living in another house, when Conyngham's agent ordained that it was Beagh's time to be squared. Initially, the Sweeneys' place, like most, if not all, houses erected at the squaring, had been only a single-roomed structure and it almost certainly had no windows; it had been the sort of 'windowless hovel' seen by John Mitchel when he passed this way in 1845. But it had changed since then. Here, as on other holdings in the townland, the erection in the 1860s of a range of outhouses—a little smaller than the house itself—was the first and most significant improvement. Those outhouses, comprising a barn, calfhouse, and byre, meant cattle were no longer brought into the living space, which allowed a new internal wall to divide it into two rooms. The main room, entered from the front street, was where meals were prepared and eaten, and the males slept. The 'lower-room', to the left of the doorway, the place where the cattle had been kept, was now sleeping quarters for women. It was here all were born and all waked. Two small sash-windows in the front of the house were likely added around this time; there was also a tiny window, about a foot-square, in the back wall.

In the face of mass migration, the building of the byres had been a commitment to the place and people—somebody would remain to look after the old ones and another generation would call Beagh home. A potato house—pronounced *pré*-house—was added before the century's end, but no hen house; knitting stockings occupied the women more

---

[38] In noticing John (*aka* Seán) Sweeney's death 'at his residence . . . after a rather protracted illness . . . at an advanced age', *DJ*, 7 Jan. 1938, observed that he was 'one of the pioneers of Sinn Féin in South-West Donegal and in later years identified himself with Fianna Fáil'.
[39] The ages given for her in the 1901 and 1911 Census returns would have her born in 1860 or 1857; her age was given as 90 when her death was registered in 1944; see GRO.

than eggs. Nor had the family a piggery, when most (eight out of twelve) of their neighbours did. The Sweeneys, in fact, were among the poorer families in Beagh when Néillidh was born in 1900. The following year's census returned their house as one of four 'third class' habitations in the townland. The other eight, including the house of Dinny Gallagher, the biggest farmer, and Danny Sweeney, the schoolmaster, were 'second class'. But, in truth, if there were differences between neighbours, they were small. To children in all houses, the dismissive 'Go home and bud your supper!'—pick the eyes from the spuds—was wounding into the mid-twentieth century, for down to that late time there was no house in Beagh where there was not at least the memory of days when there was nothing for the main meal other than last year's potatoes.

In Néillidh's childhood, there were more pounds, shillings, and pence than previously in his father's house. By 1911, the addition of a windowed room at the eastern gable—'the upper room'—had elevated the house from 'third class' to 'second class', and there was now a piggery too. The CDB provided small grants for such improvements, and money may have come from that agency. Also, the death in 1904, at 84, of his maternal grandfather, James Boyle of Maolach (*aka* Moolagh), who had returned from the Pennsylvania mine patches in the 1860s, may have occasioned some small bequest to Néillidh's Yankee mother, Annie.[40] However, it was most probably the Sweeneys' own children growing up that made the difference, for the girls could knit more and better, and the boys could leave for Scotland and America. And so the girls knitted and the boys left, and Néillidh grew from boy to man knowing two brothers, Patrick and James, only as dark-suited young fellows in black-framed studio photographs shipped home from Pennsylvania and California. They had been working in Scotland when he was born, and only James is known to have come home before leaving for America when Néillidh was a small child. Something of their personalities he would learn in time from the recollections of others and from the contents of eagle-stamped envelopes. Still, to him, they must have been like off-stage characters in a play—figures of the imagination that occasionally had a tangible effect on the visible. Other siblings too, who left in his later childhood, mid-teens, and early twenties, were soon a blurring of his own and others' memories and what little character shone through letters begun with mantras learned by rote in the eight decades (1863–1942) that first Danny Sweeney and then his

---

[40] James Boyle (1820–1904) had gone to Pennsylvania to mine, most probably in the 1840s, but around the time of the Civil War he had come home to take a farm in Maolach (Tullymore).

son Matt taught in Beagh School: 'I hope this letter finds you in the condition that it leaves me at present . . . '[41]

The mantras were familiar. For first-born males in particular, a passage to America was as good as preordained. Of the twelve children born in the Sweeneys' two-roomed house in 1881–1900, two boys died young—Francis shortly after birth in 1885 and Thomas, aged 3, in 1902—and six of the remaining ten siblings emigrated to America in 1903–22, some after preparatory stints in Scotland. In 1903, James, after several years around Glasgow, went to dig coal in Plymouth, Pennsylvania. It was a family tradition: his mother's father had dug coal in Pennsylvania before him and now James lodged with her brother, James 'Peru' Boyle. Patrick and Annie left, separately, in 1908: Annie went to Plymouth to work in service—and to help her brother James who would die of cancer the following year—and Patrick, then married with a daughter in Scotland, went to Oakland, California, the family's passage paid by a great-aunt who had been brought out to San Francisco before his birth.[42] By 1910, Patrick was a lineman with the telephone company: it was the 1980s before there was a phone in the house where he was reared. Within a few years, he moved to the Pacific Gas and Electric Company, a major employer of Irish emigrants, and then, by 1918, to the San Francisco Oakland Terminal Railway, the streetcar company, where he worked as an electrician.[43] In 1911, Con joined Annie, then in Wilkes Barre, but soon left for the oil fields in the west of the state before making his way out to Patrick in Oakland, where he too got a 'start' with Pacific Gas and Electric. He later moved to the Standard Oil refinery in Richmond, got promoted to assistant foreman, and retired a supervisor after thirty-one years' service in 1949.[44] In 1920, Joe left for New York, where he worked as a grocery clerk in Brooklyn. And, finally, in 1922, Johnny arrived in the States, made his way out to Oakland, lodged for a while with Con, and found work as a labourer. He drank and, in the 1940s, he lost contact with Con,

[41] Danny Sweeney's obituary, in *DJ*, 18 Jan. 1911, noted that many of his pupils held 'lucrative positions both at home and across the sea'. Certainly, some former pupils prospered, notably Danny's son Patrick, who became a wealthy merchant in America; one of Patrick's sons, John Lincoln, became curator of the Poetry Room in Harvard and another, James Johnson, became director of the Guggenheim Museum. However, most Beagh 'scholars' graduated to the working class of Britain and America.
[42] The great-aunt was Jennie Lough (b. 1865), a native of Laconnell. As a child in the mid-1870s she had been brought out to California, where family members had gone decades earlier to mine. She had worked as a chambermaid and a nurse, and never married.
[43] NARA, US Draft Registration Cards, 1917–18: Oakland City 1: Patrick B. Sweeney, 12 Sept. 1918; US Federal Census, 1930: California, Alameda County, Oakland City, District 1–22, Sheet 13B, 75–82.
[44] NARA, US Draft Registration Cards, 1917–18: Oakland City 1: Cornelius Sweeney, 5 June 1917; *Oakland Tribune*, 27 Apr. 1969.

who had been fond of him, and with home. And so of the six Sweeneys to reach the States, James died young and Johnny was lost; and only two of the other four ever came home, both to stay—Annie after three years in 1911, and Joe after thirteen years in 1933. That was the place the Famine had made—four out of ten children who grew to adulthood were in their teens or twenties when they stood on their father's floor for the last time.

Néillidh, as the youngest of the Sweeney boys, may have been early picked to stay. Certainly, after Joe and Johnny left in the early 1920s, he had little option but to remain at home. His father was then in his sixties; he died in 1937, aged about 78. Joe's return in 1933 came too late for Néillidh. America was in the depths of the Great Depression; there was mass unemployment in Britain. There was nowhere to go. And so Néillidh stayed in Beagh and Joe purchased a farm in Gortnacart. The land, at least, was their own. The Marquess of Conyngham had moved to divest himself of his west Donegal estates, including the 'Downstrands Estate', which included Beagh, shortly after the passage of the Wyndham Land Act. However, the smallholders objected to his retention of 'sporting and fishing rights', which delayed sections of the estate being vested in the Land Commission until 1931.[45] Seán Sweeney, who belonged to the Famine generation, had lived to see the back of the landlords—and their 'dog-men and keepers' who 'trampled' on the people—and men of his own stamp in power in Dublin, or so he thought.[46]

A PRETTY WEDDING

A pretty wedding was solemnised with Nuptial mass in Kilclooney Church on Monday morning, the contracting parties being Mr Neil Sweeney, youngest son of the late Mr John Sweeney and Mrs Annie Sweeney, Beagh, Ardara, and Miss Annie Kennedy, second daughter of the late Mr John Kennedy and Mrs A. Kennedy, Beagh. Mr Patrick Shovlin, Meenaleck, a nephew of the bridegroom was the best man, and Miss Mary Kennedy, sister of the bride, was bridesmaid. The marriage ceremony was performed by Rev. T. M'Ginley, C.C.

The bridegroom is well-known in Irish-Ireland circles, and has been one of the treasurers of the Ardara Fianna Fáil Cumann since its formation. The bride is a highly cultured and charming young

---

[45] *DJ*, 15 Mar. 1905.
[46] Paraphrasing James Moore of Narin, who, at the inaugural meeting of the Downstrands branch of the United Irish League, declared, 'on behalf of the people', that 'when the landlords went they wanted them gone bag and baggage, and not to have dog-men and keepers trampling upon them'. *DJ*, 1 Mar. 1907.

lady who is held in high esteem. The happy cauple [*sic*] have been
the recipients of many messages of congratulation.

Derry Journal, 25 January 1939

In January 1939, a year after his father's death, Néillidh Sweeney married
Annie Kennedy (1907–79) of Beagh, and he brought her down to live in
the then 100-year-old house. He was 38, she was 31; living with them
were his 82-year-old mother Annie and 50-year-old sister Mary. Between
1941 and 1953, Annie bore six children in that house, one of whom died
at birth. The house, as I remember it in the 1970s, took shape in the early
1950s. First, the 'upper room' that had been added behind the fireplace in
the first decade of the century was divided into two. Three rooms became
four. The roof was slated, cement was poured over flagstones, and a
Stanley 8 range was fitted in the main fireplace. The old sash-windows
were replaced with larger casement ones, the exterior was pebbledashed,
and an extension built at the back. It comprised a small bathroom with a
flush toilet, a tiny scullery, the width of its Belfast sink and scarcely twice
its width in length, and a small bedroom entered through the kitchen:
Annie had hoped to keep 'visitors', but they never came in any numbers so
it was little more than a storeroom. The kitchen and upper room were
plastered and painted, but still in the 1970s the lower room was white-
washed and children put to bed there would poke holes in the bubbled
lime, watched by the faces in those photographs shipped home from the
States a lifetime earlier.

The Kennedys and their connections had been none too pleased when
Annie married Néillidh Sweeney. Indeed, her uncle Peter Boyle of Tullymore
threw off his coat and declared that it was over his dead body that any
Kennedy would marry a Sweeney. Their objections were likely partly
personal. Again, Néillidh had a sharp wit. Certainly, they were partly
political. The Kennedys supported the Treaty in 1922, but the Sweeneys
had opposed it, and later Néillidh, like other frustrated IRA-men, had
become a footsoldier for Fianna Fáil. There was also an element of
tuppence ha'penny looking down on tuppence in the Kennedys' displeasure. Excluding the house, land, and stock, Seán Sweeney, Néillidh's
father, left £39 when he died in January 1938. John Kennedy died in
1931, and his will dispersed well over twice that amount (£107 2s.), while
his widow, Annie, who received only £5 in her husband's will, left £207
13s. 3d. when she died in 1945.[47] Seán Sweeney had likely helped his son

---

[47] NAI, Calendar of Grants of Probate Wills: CS/HC/PO/4/95/9134 (John Sweeney,
d. 1838); CS/HC/PO/4/92/4963 (John Kennedy, d. 1931); CS/HC/PO/4/99/5661
(Annie Kennedy, d. 1946).

Joe to buy the farm in Gortnacart when he came home from Brooklyn in 1933, but the difference in the legacies is striking, not least as the Kennedys had a little less land than the Sweeneys, 16 acres compared to 18. However, it would be fair to say that they had less bad land, and that their place was neater and tidier, more of a 'farm'. A small orchard and some well-tended fuchsia bushes that, into the 2000s, sheltered the Kennedys' house, seemed less aspirations to gentility than remnants of it. However, the house itself was not a remnant; it had been built at the squaring in 1839–41. Snugly nestled on a height facing south, it had a good well conveniently located behind it. In contrast, the Sweeneys' house was down in a hollow, at some distance from a well that was prone to running dry. The Sweeneys may have drawn a short straw at the time of the squaring or, if the Kennedys had been in Beagh longer than the Sweeneys, they may have had claims to the better land on the shoreside. And so, in the Kennedys' displeasure, in 1939, at one of their people marrying a Sweeney, there was likely something personal, there was certainly something political and something social, and there was, perhaps, something too not of their time, an older condescension. Or maybe it was just that on fair days in Ardara, Néillidh's father had been known to trail his coat home to Beagh and challenge any man in the Tullies to stand on it.

I remember four of the Kennedys, all children of John Kennedy: my grandmother, Annie; her bachelor brother Con, who inherited the home-place; a sister Mamie, who married but separated and lived with Con; and another brother Joe, who after a spell in America, came home, married, and worked as a farm labourer on a rich estate in Beauparc, County Meath. Joe was a gentle, humble man. Con was stern and strong and far from humble. Mamie was a bit contrary. She used to mark the date on which she purchased batteries for a portable transistor radio, and when a set expired quicker than the previous one she complained to the vendor, Thomas Boyle of the Greenhouse. Annie was busy—always knitting or crocheting—and, in a quiet way, cultured. All four carried themselves with a concern for propriety not associated with the Sweeneys.

Joe died in 1978, Annie in 1979, Con in 1988, and Mamie in 1993. They were the last of that Kennedy line in Beagh. And those who now remember the Kennedys at all would be more conscious of the political differences between themselves and the Sweeneys than any social or cultural distinctions, that is, one family 'was Fine Gael' and the other 'was Fianna Fáil'. For his part, Néillidh Sweeney's relationship with Fianna Fáil and, more especially, the anaemic southern state was ambiguous. In 1979 when his eldest grandchild, John Sweeney, joined what the old man still called the Free State Army, the family fretted about how he would react to one of his own in an outfit that he had opposed in the 1920s. But a half-century contradiction left no space for recrimination. After all, from when it first took power in Dublin in 1932, Fianna Fáil had been in government for all but three brief periods—1948–51, 1954–7, and 1973–7. And so, when his grandson arrived in uniform, he got up from the chair by the range, and shook the young soldier's hand. By then, the Six Counties—his preferred term for Northern Ireland—had been a site of carnage for a decade, and Fianna Fáil's failure to adopt a more assertive position on 'the North' had disappointed him. 'It isn't the party we founded', he once conceded. He still voted for Fianna Fáil, however, as too did one of his sons with an exuberance—'Up Devy and bog your man!'—that hid a brief dalliance with the party's dissidents, the one-drum band that was Neil Blaney's Independent Fianna Fáil. But Néillidh's enthusiasm for it was gone: in the course of the 1970s, he had accepted that, when it came to those things that mattered to him, there was little difference between Fianna Fáil and Fine Gael.

As infants, my grandparents were bounced on the knees of those who had seen the squaring of the cuts, the potatoes rotting, the departure of the Mulherns, and James Gallagher clearing the Brogans, McCaffertys, Mooneys, and O'Donnells, much as their own grandchildren, born from the mid-1960s through to the mid-1980s, were cradled by people who saw homesteads raided by the Black and Tans in 1920–1, and again by Free Staters in 1922–3, and later too. And what they heard from those who lived through those mid-nineteenth-century changes and from those who came after them—and what they thought of what they heard—might deepen this history, not least as each of them was the grandchild of a man who became tenant of a much reduced holding in 1855. To reiterate, Néillidh Sweeney was a great-grandson of Widow Nancy Sweeney, who transferred half of her holding to James Gallagher and was succeeded by her son Patrick. And Annie Kennedy was a great-granddaughter of hard-drinking Pat Kennedy who transferred two-thirds of his land to Gallagher in that same season, and surrendered the tenancy to his son James Pat. And they, whose marriage, in 1939, joined those two families, lived out their lives alongside the descendants of James Gallagher.

But little is now known of what my grandparents heard. Their two surviving children—my father and my aunt—remember their parents talking of McGlynn, but recall no connection being made between the master turning informer and Gallagher turning out subtenants. Indeed, they had never heard the names Brogan, McCafferty, Mooney, and O'Donnell associated with Beagh, other than vaguely remembered yarns about the doings of Mící Mór Ó Dónaill (O'Donnell), the pre-Famine rustler. Nor had they heard of Gallagher having had subtenants. Conversely, Néillidh Sweeney did speak of Gallagher having got land 'in the time of the Famine' from a family named Mulhern whose passage he paid to America. As intimated, the Mulherns having been tenants proper (not subtenants) may have fixed them in memory and secured them a mention in oral history. Likewise, that their arable was only broken in 1839–41 and that it was the first of Gallagher's acquisitions may have given that transaction and their departure salience. So too may the very fact of their departure. Not having lingered in the place, as some families cleared in 1856 had done, they needed to be summoned up, their story told. More surprisingly, neither my father nor my aunt had ever heard their father mention that James Gallagher had acquired any part of the Sweeney holding, and if they had heard a whisper, from neighbours, that one of the Kennedys—their mother's people—had 'mortgaged' land to Gallagher to get money for whiskey, they had no idea that it comprised two-thirds of his holding. And yet when presented with the details for the Kennedy and the Sweeney holdings their response was not disbelief. The oft-told story of the Mulherns had established James Gallagher as a grasping, unsympathetic character, as too had stories of his father going to the poorhouse. Still, there was surprise at the proportion of the holdings lost and also at the possibility that those whom he cleared—'people', 'neighbours' (the Mollies), 'cottiers' (McGlynn, Gallagher), 'my tenants' (Gallagher)—may, in the first instance, have been engaged by Nancy Sweeney or her late husband Pat.

The Kennedys and Sweeneys had buried their losses. The Kennedys had done so quickly and completely, as evidenced by the friendship of John and Dinny. The Sweeneys did it less completely for they kept green the memory of the Mulherns, and it would be disingenuous now not to acknowledge that my grandfather and his neighbour Dinny Gallagher (1896–1988) were not close. There was not any animosity between them, more a distance. It may have had social bases. Possessed of more and better land, and rearing more and better cattle, Dinny Gallagher was the first man in Beagh to slate his house and the first to have a son, John, become a priest attached to the diocese of Raphoe, and another son Denis was the first to have a car—all things that mattered in their time. There was also the politics of their own time: the Gallaghers, like the Kennedys, had favoured the pro-Treaty party in the great divide of 1922, and they read the *Irish Independent*. My grandfather was closer to the Táilliúrs, who took his own view of things and read the *Irish Press*. (Indeed, he would caution his children against referring to them as the Táilliúrs, tailors, and to use their proper surname, Kennedy; the origin of the nickname is obscure— there is a notion that their house may have been a stopping place for journeymen tailors, as none of the family had pursued that trade which many people, even those possessed of nothing but a few rock-strewn acres, considered only a step above that of travelling tinsmith.[48]) Néillidh Sweeney's cronies were all like the Táilliúrs—people who had taken the Republican side in 1922. And reinforcing the impression that it was in that fatal year that a greater distance grew between the Sweeneys and the Gallaghers, when Néillidh's brother Joe had gone to America—in 1920, two years before the Split—he went, in the first instance, not to a family member but to a friend in Richmond, Queens. That friend was Johnny Gallagher, the elder brother of Dinny. But, of course, there was personality too—Wee Néillidh Sweeney was a dapper, quick-witted countryman, Big Dinny Gallagher more the stolid farmer.

No historian can read the souls of the dead.[49] It may be that, for my grandfather, things that happened in the 1850s were the substrates of that less than warm relationship, for the place was small and the people who had lost were his own. But like many of his generation Néillidh Sweeney had no great interest in the time before his time. Hence, stories of land acquired cheap 'in the time of the Famine' and the son that let his father go to the poorhouse—and, indeed, the story of a gate erected on the bog road—may have been told less to mark the Gallaghers of the mid-twentieth century as somehow different to their neighbours than to teach something of human nature, to give some rules to live by. And the rules are clear: one has a duty to those who reared you, one should not be proud or boastful, and one should never take advantage of the weak. Crucially too, that distance between Néillidh Sweeney and Dinny Gallagher was not great. At one point in the mid-1960s, there may have been as few as twenty-five people in Beagh, most of them elderly; certainly, there can have been no more than thirty, down from near 120 in the time of the Famine, and from sixty around 1900. And into the early 1970s, it seemed that a day might yet come when it would fall to someone among the living to close the last house in Beagh. This sore night hath trifled former knowings: Néillidh and Dinny were neighbours.

In their middle age, in the 1940s and 1950s, the neighbours' need for each other grew more acute. In those years, the men of Beagh would congregate on winter nights in a tumbledown old house that they called the Reading Room. Comprising a kitchen and a 'room'—the roof of which had fallen in—it had been the home of Jim Chondaí (b. 1874), a

---

[48] Celine Sweeney Cooke, 'Peter Nagher McHugh's Wake', *Dearcadh, 2004–05* (2004), 80, discusses the nickname.

[49] Jonathan Lear, *Radical Hope: Ethics in the Face of Cultural Devastation* (Cambridge, 2006), 104.

son of Condy McHugh, the informer *manqué* convicted on his own statement in 1857. Sometime in the 1930s, when Jim, in his sixties, became ill and went to live with a relation, he let local men use the place as a sort of clubhouse. The 'members' agreed to each provide a cartload of turf and they paid Matt Sweeney, the schoolmaster, a shilling to purchase paraffin for the lamp. A 'caretaker' was appointed to open and lock the door, and to have the fire lit when the men started to arrive about 7 o'clock in the evening. Some nights there could be twenty or more men present. No women attended, and, if children were tolerated for a while, 'when the messing and sod throwing began they soon got the chase'. At the table, a few men would play cards—twenty-five or pontoon, sometimes poker or nap—and the rest would sit around, smoke, and chat until midnight. 'The topics of conversation were endless', according to one poignant memoir, ' . . . local and national news, the weather forecast, jokes, gossip, auld yarns, and plenty of lies!' The politics of their own time had been bitter and divisive enough and, across the parish, the passing of 'the last of the name' and the closing of houses regularly gave people reason to wonder who would remain after themselves. Better now not to dwell on things that their people had done to each other in the far off long ago.

The Reading Room survived into the 1950s. It was, in that time of little hope, an ideal place to gather: 'The men weren't interfering with anybody trying to do housework or put children to bed. They could smoke, spit, gamble, and make noise without the women of the house giving out!'[50] And so when Néillidh was out on long winter nights, Annie was at home with the children and the elderly, needles clicking away until bedtime. A forward-looking woman, the past was of even less interest to her than it was to him and she saw no future in Beagh. In 1952, the death of her sister-in-law Mary was an opportunity to take the young family to England. But Néillidh was then in his fifties, and he baulked. The notion of opening a little shop in Ardara came to nothing. And so the best for which Annie could then hope was that her children would do what she had not done, and leave. Still, in the 1970s, she took quiet satisfaction in the big-windowed modern houses of her son John Joe in Tullymore and daughter Ann in Tullybeg. And towards the end of the decade, there was joy in the return of her youngest son, James, from the building sites of London with his wife and daughter, to live with herself and Néillidh in Beagh. Molloy's knitwear factory and Gallagher's bakery were giving

---

[50] Áine Nic Giolla Dé, 'The Reading Room', *Dearcadh: The Ardara View* (2009–10), 53. *DJ*, 4 Dec. 1953, makes mention of Beagh's 'local card room'.

employment in Ardara. Fish factories were hiring in Killybegs, and there was work with Bord na Móna in Kilraine. Here, for the first time since the Famine, the young had the choice of living at home. That, at least, is the story that we now tell ourselves. But it may be that in the return of James from England, and in the return of John Joe before him, my grandmother was quietly disappointed.

10

Dangerous Memories

Seaton Milligan, a Belfast draper, visited Ardara in 1890, and his encounter with a local man may provide a rear view of the contention within the Ribbon Society in the mid-1850s that was the prelude to Patrick McGlynn turning informer. Interested in history, Milligan wanted to see the *ráth* or fort, above Doohill, from which the town takes its name. A 'very active old man', who lived adjacent to the fort, was happy to show it to him. Milligan later recalled:

> He was able to get over the ditches as nimbly as I could, and seemed to be possessed of an excellent constitution. In answer to my inquiries, he informed me his name was John Breslin, that he was a linen weaver by trade, and had worked for 60 years on the same loom, and was then 86 years old. The loom itself bore evidence of the truth of his statement, as the seat was almost worn through by friction, and brightly polished from constant use. His dwelling, which I visited, consisted of one apartment, about 16 feet by 12; his loom and bed occupied one side of it, and opposite was the door and window; underneath the latter was a table, and two chairs, the total remaining furniture of the house. A hole in the roof without any chimney brace allowed an exit for the smoke. He never had toothache or any other ache, he never lost a tooth, and bids fair to reach the hundred. He is married to his second wife, a woman 20 years his junior, has no family, is still living as I write (May, 1892), and has now attained 88 years. He writes to London and Dublin for orders for his towels, and seems to have formed a connexion who buy all he produces. I attribute this man's good health and entire freedom from pain and ache to his good constitution, his active life, and to the conditions under which he lives. His house is situated on very high ground, underneath the old Rath, and the large opening in the unceiled roof ventilates the place so perfectly that he breathes a perfectly pure atmosphere, both day and night.[1]

This man (b. *c.*1804) was known locally as John the Towel, and it is possible that he and Little John Breslin of Doohill, master of the Ardara

---

[1] Seaton F. Milligan, 'Some Recent Cases of Remarkable Longevity', *Journal of the Royal Society of Antiquaries of Ireland*, 22 (1892), 224–36, 234.

lodge in the mid-1850s, were one and the same person.[2] And if they were the same person, then the master of the lodge, here revealed as enterprising and individualistic, stands in even starker contrast to Moses Ward of Brackey and Condy Boyle of Meenagolan than he did on that St Patrick's Night in 1855, in Neil O'Donnell's in Glenties, when they had the men but not the money to depose him as master. But whether or not the master of the lodge was the towel man, Little John Breslin, being from Doohill, was essentially from the town of Ardara (a mid-eighteenth-century creation), while Ward and Boyle were from mountain-shadowed townlands a few miles south of it. The challengers, in other words, were rooted in the most securely Irish-speaking section of the parish where, in the 1850s, rundale sustained notions of the relationship of a family to their neighbours that were different to those which had long prevailed around the town.

But there is no simple opposition here of tradition and modernity. Moses Ward (1826–1912) was still living when Milligan met John the Towel. Ward had jumped bail after his release in summer 1856, only to appear at the assizes in spring 1858, when he pleaded guilty to member-ship of the Ribbon Society and was released on the terms that Pat Gallagher had negotiated the previous summer. In the early 1860s, Ward had married Bridget Gavigan and settled on a smallholding in Killasteever, adjacent to Brackey. A mason by trade, he harvested and sold seaweed in his later years. It was tough, seasonal work, from which he made no fortune. In 1907, when he was still working with his son, he was getting 10d. for a creel of seaweed. The price is known as in that year, when he was over 80, he took a case against a neighbour, Pat Cunningham, claiming that he had refused to pay 15s. due for thirty creels; the case was dismissed. As it happens, he himself had appeared as a defendant in the same court on several occasions over the previous half-century—charged with trespass (and cutting and carrying away a stick) on the land of Condy Conaghan in Edergole in 1861; for non-payment of county cess in 1878; being drunk on the street of Ardara in February 1888; and for non-payment of seed rate in 1890 and 1891, an offence that may have been part of an organized campaign.[3]

None of these charges concerned a matter of any consequence. Many ordinary decent people were charged with similar infractions. But Moses Ward was an extraordinary individual. Unusually for any person born in

[2] McGill, *Conall's Footsteps*, 206–7, identifies the man described by Milligan as John the Towel.
[3] IPSCR Ardara: 12 Nov. 1861, 9 Apr. 1878; 13 Apr. 1888; 14 Feb. 1893; 9 Aug. 1898; 14 May 1907.

his community before the Famine, he could read and write, and literacy was more unusual still for Catholics. In Killasteever (pop. 1901: 23, all Catholics), only one of eight other persons over 30 could read and write in 1901. In the electoral division of Glengesh (pop. 1901: 1,368), of which Killasteever was a part, there were then 218 people still living who had been born before the Famine, that is, who were 56 years of age or older. Of these people, 182 were Catholics, and, of them, 139 could neither read nor write; of the remaining forty-three, eighteen could read only, and twenty-five (13.7 per cent) could read and write—a sharp contrast with the proportion (twenty-four of thirty-six; 66 per cent) of Protestants in the same age bracket (aged 56 or older) returned as reading and writing.[4] No less unusually, while himself a precocious literate, Ward had not dis-avowed his own cultural background. His children, born in the 1860s and 1870s, grew up speaking both Irish and English, at a time when many people who had attained a high competency in the new language often raised their children with it alone. Moses Ward, then, can be said to represent an alternate modernity, one in which the achievement of the new (literacy and, indeed, fluency in English) did not necessarily have to involve the abandonment of the old and the particular. And there, in pointing to a future different to that brought into view by the Famine, may lie the radicalism of his challenge to Little John Breslin of Doohill: in other words, there may have been more to Ward—and the majority of Ardara Mollies who sided with him in 1855—than 'breaking houses' and a reaction to loss. The critic David Lloyd's admonishment echoes: 'we should not allow ourselves to imagine that the dead, because their own ways of living were destroyed along with them, were incapable of tracing in their own practices the transformable forms of another life'.[5] And there is no reason now to assume that the Mollies did not prevent more usurious interest rates from being charged, more land 'grabbed', and still more people cleared. After all, the authorities' alarm in the early 1850s suggests that they were making a difference, which is how they were remembered.

No great joy lit Moses Ward's final years. None of his eight children married locally; most emigrated. When he died, aged 86, in 1912, the Ribbon Society, which he had most likely joined in the late 1840s, had completed its transformation into the AOH, and it was in many places a de facto branch network of the Irish Parliamentary Party; it was

---

[4] Calculated from Census 1901: Household Returns, Glengesh DED; of thirty-six Protestants (56+), only seven could not read, and only five could read only.
[5] Lloyd, 'Indigent Sublime', 39–72, 72.

respectable and it was important to the powerful. Indeed, in Ardara and Downstrands where lodges had clerical approval, 'the Hibs' seemed part confraternity and part political machine. Their rhetoric was of 'faith and fatherland', their banners depicted saints and priests, and they marched on St Patrick's Day and Assumption Day. It is not known if Ward had any truck with the Society in the decades after his arrest. If he had, it had never materially improved his life. He died in a third-class house with a bachelor son, Charles, and a spinster daughter, Mary. The rest of his children were either dead or in America. Even before his death, there had been local rumblings against the Party–Church–'Hib' axis, and in the tectonic shift that followed the 1916 Rising, it was, in many places, the poorer, less respectable people who abandoned the half-a-loaf of Home Rule for republican separatism. Across west Donegal, disputes over access to halls and marching bands' instruments punctuated the years between the Rising and the Tan War, and there were violent clashes between the two factions through the 'troubles'. Indeed, as early as December 1918 Anthony Herron of Lacklea, a 45-year-old Hibernian, died from a gunshot wound inflicted in a fracas after an election rally in Glenties.[6] Friction between the pro-Treaty right-wing Hibs and left-wing Republicans continued to spark into the middle decades of the century, flaring in 1933–4, when the AOH became indistinguishable from the Blueshirts, a group appropriately dubbed 'imitation Nazis' by their opponents.[7]

In that decade, collectors from the Irish Folklore Commission were calling at houses across west Donegal and, in the glow of Tilley lamps and turf fires, recording songs and stories. It was part of a national effort, unprecedented in size and ambition, to document the oral culture of what was perceived to be a traditional agrarian society on the eve of its demise. Now, in places not unlike Ward's in Killasteever, old men chortled over what their fathers and grandfathers had done in the mid-nineteenth century. So too did some younger men: in 1936 Johnny Timoney (*c*.40) of Mín an tSamhaidh told of hearing from his father how a man named Kennedy from 'near Narin' (probably the Kennedys of Kilclooney, publicans and dealers) had informed on a *poitín*-maker named Porter, resulting in a hefty fine and the destruction of a still. Kennedy used to cart goods to Derry market, and once when he was carrying a load of butter out Bealach na gCreach, the Mollies came on him; Porter being a Protestant, Timoney explained that two Catholics had been working for him. The Mollies killed Kennedy's horse, smashed

[6] Briody, *Glenties and Inniskeel*, 165.
[7] Mac Suibhne, 'Soggarth Aroon', 176–83. For 'imitation Nazis', see the once popular song 'The North-west Tirconaill Boys', in *DJ*, 23 Mar. 1934.

his cart, and carried off the *botannaí* ('butts': firkins, wooden containers). *Tá mé ag fágáilt,* finished Timoney, *gur h-itheadh mórán don im a bhí ann an-chómgharach thart fá na dorsacha againn.* (I make out that much of that butter was eaten *very* close to our doors.[8]) And yet another, more ambivalent note was often struck, namely, that the Mollies somehow 'went bad' or went too far or that violence became an end in itself. Interviewed by collector Seán Ó hEochaidh in winter 1961, Séamas Mac Amhlaigh (b. 1879), who had been reared in the mountains north of Glenties, made an analogy with internecine bloodletting that year in the Congo: 'the good and bad was in this society. They didn't want anybody to be taking advantage of the poor by overcharging. Even some of the shopkeepers were afraid of them and they daren't charge a penny over the market price... For all these reasons, at the start a whole lot of people had a certain amount of respect for them. In the end they became cruel and they did things like what is going on in Africa today...'[9]

It may be that this notion that the Mollies 'went bad' can be traced to the mid-1850s when hard men, like Breslin, became somewhat more respectable, and restrained more militant figures, like Ward, from acts of 'outrage', that is, to a time when a leadership decided that what had been done was not to be disavowed but ideally not to be done again.

Ambivalence is ever the end of outrage.

THE LIVING AND THE DEAD

There was an old man lived up here in Sean-mhín. He was born and brought up in Mín an Ghrubaigh, and his name was Jack Ward. He was telling me a lot of stories about [the Mollies]. He told me that he was only sixteen years of age when he joined up with them. The first case that he was out on was in an elderly woman's house in the townland of Dearrachán on this side of Fintown. There was some other party that thought she got the place just not according to their liking. So the Mollies came this night, and Jack told me that he was there and the job that he got to do was to hold the candle for them to give them light. They went in there, he says, and they caught this woman and threw her across the *bac* [hob] and she fell on the floor, and the other party on the other side picked her up and threw her

---

[8] NFCM 185: 445, 475–6, as related by Johnny Timoney (40), Mín an tSamhaidh, to Liam Mac Meanman in Apr. 1936; he heard it from his father, James (b. *c.*1849). Micí Mac Meanman (68), a native of An Ghlaisigh Mhór, interviewed by the same collector in Apr. 1936, also discussed the theft of butter on this road; see NFCM 185: 363, 376.
[9] NFCM 1,579: 177–95, quoted in Broehl, *Molly Maguires*, 30–1.

Figure 10.1 Séamas Mac Amhlaigh, Na Saileasaí, 1956; courtesy of National Folklore Collection

back, and they kept throwing her around like this till they killed the woman. They did not leave a sound bone in her body. He was telling me a lot of things about them, if I could remember them now.

> Séamas Mac Amhlaigh, 82, native of
> Meenaleenaghan, winter 1961[10]

Seán Ó hEochaidh had interviewed Séamas Mac Amhlaigh (Figure 10.1) on several occasions prior to that meeting in 1961: indeed, ten years earlier, in 1951, it had been Mac Amhlaigh who first told him of 'the Judge between God and Man'. However, on those occasions the Mollies had been just one of many subjects in the man's history of his community. Now, Ó hEochaidh had come specifically to get information on the Mollies. That spring, an

---

[10] NFCM 1,579; 184–5. The woman was Hannah O'Donnell, Dalraghan Beg, and the attack took place in 1854; see Ch. 6 in this volume. For another case in which a woman was beaten in the same area, see OP 1850/7/195 Lough Finn, 27 Apr. 1850, Hamilton to Under Secretary, with enclosures, and *LJ*, 24 July 1850. Curiously, men named John (aka Jack) Ward were charged but not convicted in both cases. In neither case was the woman killed.

American professor, Wayne G. Broehl of Dartmouth College, had arrived in Dublin to research a book on the Molly Maguires in Pennsylvania. Interested in the Irish backgrounds of the hanged men and the activities of the Mollies in Ireland, he contacted Séamas Ó Duilearga, the head of the Irish Folklore Commission. Ó Duilearga, in turn, put him in contact with Ó hEochaidh, who got an article published in the *Derry Journal* in May, asking readers with stories of the Mollies to write to himself or Broehl, then in University College Dublin. Meanwhile, he worked his own network of old-timers in north and west Donegal, and he subsequently compiled a file of their stories that he dispatched to Dublin.[11]

Ó hEochaidh's network had thrown up a good deal of information about the Mollies in Donegal. Some of his respondents—the oldest, like Mac Amhlaigh, born in the 1870s, the youngest around 1900—were able to give details of 'outrages' committed a generation before their birth. For instance, Mac Amhlaigh told, again, of the Judge between God and Man, the killing of Paddy McRoarty—he recalled seeing his daughter when she was an old woman—and also the savage beating of a widow near Fintown; he had known one of her attackers, then a 16-year-old, as an old man. Like Mac Amhlaigh, the other respondents associated the Mollies with fixing prices on potatoes and oatmeal, and they told how those who dared sell above their stipulated price risked night raids in which they would be stripped and carded or their skin scraped with sharp stones. Potato-dealers and meal-men, several said, were in dread of the Mollies. There was a consensus too that they had done some good, but gone bad, with some respondents speaking, disapprovingly, of how they had intervened in disputes within families. In Fanad, Hannraí Ó Sídheail of Ballyhooriskey talked about Paddy Carr from the same townland having been badly beaten by the Mollies when he denied his brother use of a currach. That beating, Ó Sídheail said, finished the Mollies in Fanad; the parish priest had cursed them from the altar, and Ó Sídheail's father, who heard the sermon, had said there was never one like it before or since. Similarly, Donnchadh Mór Mac Gabhann, a 76-year-old, from Keeldrum, Cloughaneely, expressed great sympathy for enterprising men who ran foul of the Mollies. He mentioned Séamas Mac Géidigh of Magheraroarty—*Fear maith cneasta a bhí ann agus oibridhe fír chomh maith agus a bhí sa pharróiste seo*, a decent man, as hardworking as any man in the parish,

[11] NFCM 1,579: 174–232, includes the article from *DJ*, 19 May 1961, a letter to Ó Duilearga, transcriptions of the interviews, and extracts from letters by schoolmasters Pádraig Mac an Ghoill and Pádraig Ua Cnáimhsí. Ua Cnáimhsí subsequently wrote an essay that mentions his grandmother Anna Ní Chnáimhsí (1842–1931) having been present when the Mollies raided her father's house in Cloghglass, dragged the dresser around, beat him, and set the price of potatoes. See *Idir an Dá Ghaoth*, 154–60.

who always had good cattle and oats and potatoes in spring when others had none—being carded for selling a prize cow above the Mollies' price; one of the McCaffertys of Dunlewey being raided and *an duine bocht*, the poor fellow, savagely beaten for having taken too high a price for a lamb; and, most outrageously, in the teller's mind, Mícheál Ó Maoilchiaráin from Gortahork getting the same treatment for paying the Colls of Creeslough, well-known dealers, a higher price than the Mollies had set for meal and potatoes—one of the Colls was beaten too, but the carding of the purchaser seemed unfair as he had not known of the Mollies' price.[12]

Strikingly, while those old people had much information and a relatively consistent interpretation of the Mollies' activities in Ireland, most said nothing of Pennsylvania. Their silence on that score may have been a function of Ó hEochaidh's questions, that is, he may have asked more of their doings in Ireland, for certainly, in the communities where he worked, the local origins of some of those hanged were well known.[13] Indeed, Broehl, when he came north, met, through Ó hEochaidh, with connections of Hugh McGeehan in the Fintown/Ballinamore area: they told him that he had written home, protesting his innocence and asking the family to pray for him, and that at the hour that he mounted the gallows in Pennsylvania, the sky blackened, as if by eclipse, over his homeplace.[14] But, still, in that file which Ó hEochaidh sent to Dublin, it was only in material from Ardara that there was any attempt at illuminating local involvements in the turmoil in the coalfields. Here, Ó hEochaidh had contacted Wee Paddy McGill, a close contemporary and friend, who, as a schoolmaster, was a step above the smallholders who were his usual interlocutors.[15] Wee Paddy met with Broehl when he came down from Dublin, and he promised to get him additional information on one of the hanged men, Charlie Sharpe, about whom he had heard stories 'hundreds of times' in his youth. His efforts were not altogether successful. A few weeks after meeting Broehl, he wrote in exasperation to Ó hEochaidh:

B'as Pointe Luachrois cinnte Charlie Sharpe.... Charlie Sharpe was most definitely from Loughros Point. I often heard the old people talking of

---

[12] Ibid. Ó hEochaidh's conservative politics may have been a factor in his respondents' representing the Mollies as having done some good but gone bad (a depiction that mirrors conservatives' portrayal of the IRA of 1919–22); contrast, for instance, the more favourable view of the Mollies in stories collected by Liam Mac Meanman in the 1930s; see n. 8 of this chapter.

[13] For instance, Campbell, *Molly Maguire Story*, 9–10, recalls hearing in the 1940s of the hanging of his great-uncle, Alec Campbell.

[14] Broehl, *Molly Maguires*, 339.

[15] On Wee Paddy, see Eugenia Shanklin, *Donegal's Changing Traditions: An Ethnographic Study* (New York, 1985), 147–50.

him. When my father went to Pennsylvania in 1882, he was a great topic of conversation and he saw the prison where [the Mollies] were held before they were hanged. I got no information of any kind since that American professor was here with me. I spent all Sunday evening in Cloughboy among [Charlie Sharpe's] relatives and I had nothing to show for it. Some of them never heard of him. It is not twenty years since an old Yankee, Dan Dhónaill Bhig (who spent his life drinking around Mauch Chunk) died, and he had detailed knowledge of the whole case. He always used to say that Sharpe wasn't guilty, nor many of the others either.

McGill signed off, promising Ó hEochaidh that he would spend another evening down the Point. And he added a postscript: Tommy Mulhearn, of Crannogeboy, had told him that 'the informer Mulhearn'—Charlie Mulhearn, a key figure in the Pennsylvania trials—was also from Loughros Point.[16] The Point is a small place, five miles long, and nowhere more than a mile wide. And Charlie Mulhearn's evidence had helped to hang four men, including Tom Fisher, also from the parish of Ardara, and Alec Campbell of Dungloe.

In truth, and belying the impression created by the rich materials collected from great storytellers by the Irish Folklore Commission, a certain reticence about the past, such as McGill had encountered down the Point, was widespread in west Donegal in the 1960s. Here, the living had been walking away from their dead since the time of the Famine. They had been doing so literally through mass migration, and they had been doing so figuratively through cultural change. And the dying knew it. In 1936, Ó hEochaidh, then only finding his feet as a folklore collector, had come to Ardara with an ediphone, a cumbersome phonographic machine, to record old-timers. There, on a frosty November night, Wee Paddy McGill—the same schoolmaster whom he would ask to dredge up information for Broehl in 1961—had brought him out to Áighe, two miles south of the town, where he introduced him to two elderly women, Róise Nic an Ghoill, aged 72, and her sister, Máire, ten years her senior, who sang songs and told stories that they had heard in childhood from *na seandaoine*, the old people. The McGills are remarkable people, Ó hEochaidh wrote in his diary; they all have songs and they think everybody else should have too.[17] Over the next few years, Ó hEochaidh returned several times to record Máire and Róise, particularly the latter, who had the better voice (Figure 10.2). And on one visit, in July 1937,

---

[16] NFCM 1,579: 225–6, 229. Other informers, such as Frank McHugh, son of a Mahanoy City hotelier, and Cornelius (C. T.) McHugh, a Summit Hill bar-owner, may also have had local connections.
[17] For his diary entries on their earliest encounters, see NFCM 421: 265–73.

Figure 10.2 Róise Nic an Ghoill, Áighe, *c.*1937; courtesy of National Folklore Collection

Róise related some poignant anecdotes of singers dying, lamenting that their songs would die with them:

> *Tháinig Séamas 'ac a Ghoill isteach anseo oidhche amháin agus ní raibh astoigh ach triúir nó ceathrar...* Séamas McGill came in one night, when there was only three or four of us here—myself and a brother of mine and another neighbour man—and he started to sing—Irish songs—and he sang from night fall until it was the time of the long sleep ['second sleep'?], and when he was going, 'Well', says he, 'I am away, and I am dying', says he, 'and all that is upsetting me', says he, 'is that I am leaving nobody behind me who will have my songs.' Four days after that, he was dead. He never went visiting again.... Máthair Phádaí John Thaidhg, when she was dying, the neighbours gathered in the evening she died and she sang a song for the family, and when she had sung the song, she said was afraid that her family had none of her songs, and that is all that was bothering her as she lay dying. The last song she sang was *Connlach Glas an Fhóghmhair.*[18]

[18] NFCM 365: 380–2, Róise Nic an Ghoill, 73, Áighe, 10 July 1937.

Máthair Phádaí John Thaidhg. The mother of Paddy, son of John, son of Teague. Time and the decline of the old naming system have done their work. Nobody can today identify Pádaí John Thaidhg, and so his mother cannot be fixed in time.[19] One can only guess that she was of a generation prior to that of Róise Nic an Ghoill, born in 1864, who told her story, and that she died in the first decades of the twentieth century. *Connlach Glas an Fhómhair*, the song she sang on her deathbed, is a love song, its sexual yearning serrated by political longing. Addressing a *cáilín donn*, a brown-haired girl, the singer describes her crossing the green stubble of the infield where oats have just been harvested and cattle will now graze. She is beautiful—red cheeked, with tight curls—and she is utterly beyond him, belonging to a higher rank in society. She wears shoes, and she has a stately walk, and farmers with tall ricks in their haggards—Protestants, perhaps—are wooing her. His only hope is that the King of Spain's fleet will descend on Ireland. Then, he would scatter all challengers, and he and his *cáilín donn* would buy cattle at fairs and drive them across the Gweebarra.

It would be convenient, if poor history, to have the reference to the King of Spain precisely date the song to the 1730s or early 1740s, the last decades when deliverance was expected from that quarter. But certainly, *Connlach Glas an Fhómhair* comes out of the time before potatoes had fully displaced oatmeal in the diet, when *buailteachas*, booleying, was still a feature of the land system. In that time, a century before the Great Famine, the young men and women of Beagh had, with people from the Tullies and Dowras, driven their cattle away from their corn after May Day, up to Croaghubrid, Doobin, and Meenagosoge. Then, in autumn, they would bring the herds down to the lowlands to graze the stubble, and the great cattle fair of Magheramore, two miles north-west of Beagh if one went by the *Léana*, marked the end of the year.

Here, potatoes had only replaced oatmeal as the staple diet in the latter half of the eighteenth century. The decline of booleying was associated with that transition and also with a more rigorous approach to estate management that involved mountain townlands—and marginal places like Beagh—being settled and cultivated; potatoes would grow where grain would not. It was associated too with the development of towns like Ardara and Glenties and also the coach-stop hamlets of Fintown, Doohary, and Dungloe—watering holes for men and horses and not much else. Around Ardara, the last redoubts of booleying were in the mountains in the south of the parish, part of the Murray

---

[19] There were McTeagues in Áighe; Ó hEochaidh may have erred in transcribing máthair Phádaí John Mac T[h]aidhg, the mother of Paddy John McTeague.

Stewart estate, where it continued into the 1870s. But in some places in the district, the practice may not have made it into the nineteenth century.

Connlach Glas an Fhómhair, then, belongs to a world that had been doubtless mourned in the decades before the Famine by old people who had grown up eating more *arán coirce*, oat bread, and *brachán*, stirabout, than they tasted in their later years, that is, people whose youthful summers had been spent in the mountains. The potato-based economy had been little more than a century in the making, when the blight came, and it survived little more than a century after it. The grain- and cattle-based economy that had preceded it had existed from time immemorial. Its demise was epochal. And so, paradoxically, while *Connlach Glas an Fhómhair* was sung by a woman grieving for all that would die with her, the song itself, as a production of a prior mode of living to that which she lamented, attests to continuity through times of great change. All had never been lost—not in the transition from oats to potatoes, nor the ending of booleying, nor the squaring of the farms. But *máthair Phádaí John Thaidhg* had seen the demographic collapse and cultural derangement that had followed the Famine, and the pitching of her people into the global economy. She had seen enough to know that a time was coming in which there would be no remembrance of former things. And Róise Nic an Ghoill, who, in 1937, remembered what that woman had sung on her deathbed, knew it too.

•

Seán Ó hEochaidh was right: Róise Nic an Ghoill of Áighe was an exceptional person. And so too, in Beagh, were Mary Manus and James Táilliúr, for, when they were old, in the middle decades of the twentieth century, few people sang with the dying or set creepies before the fire at *oíche Shamhna*. And fewer still had much time for 'dangerous memories of suffering'.[20] Acts of betrayal had made the people and the place. Poor people had connived in the removal of poorer neighbours at the squaring. James Gallagher had broken faith with the aged father whom he had left to beg and the subtenants whom he cleared. Patrick McGlynn had betrayed the Mollies and the smallholders, spriggers, and labourers who had looked to them for protection; and, as Moses Ward saw things in 1855, the Mollies themselves had betrayed the poor by not 'breaking' more houses. But, in truth, it had been a time of great betrayal, when the poor themselves dismissed as worthless much that had been dear to their

---

[20] Caputo, 'No Tear Shall be Lost', 108–15; the phrase is Johann Baptist Metz's.

dead. To be sure, the poor had been learning too. They had acquired better English and become literate; they had improved their houses, hygiene, and health, accepted new notions of respectability, and adopted different ways of worshipping their God and more effective means of resisting the landlords and the state. But it is betrayal that transfixes. And by the middle decades of the twentieth century, the great betrayal was near complete, and outrage had long since ended.

Epilogue

> OWEN . . . a man long dead, long forgotten, his name 'eroded' beyond recognition, whose trivial little story nobody in the parish remembers.
> YOLLAND Except you.
> OWEN I've left here.
> YOLLAND You remember it.
>
> Brian Friel, *Translations* (1980), II.i

Beagh was the beginning, and it shall be the end. Like any other place, it has been home to some imponderables. One is an adamant insistence by people of the same surname that they are not related. In 1857, when Patrick McGlynn left for Melbourne, eight extended families held land in Beagh directly from the Marquess of Conyngham; and those eight families would own that same land in the middle decades of the twentieth century. Among the eight were two Sweeney families whose descendants today deny any connection to each other. There were also three Kennedy families and two Gallagher families who always insisted on their separate and distinct lineages.

In this place of short men, my granduncle Con Kennedy (Figure E.1) was uncommonly tall at about six foot, and, in youth, he was fit. In the 1920s, Francis Watson was the fishery inspector in Ardara. An accomplished athlete, he used to go out with his bailiffs to 'watch the river' and 'hunt' poachers, and he is remembered to have said that the greatest insult which he ever received was Con Kennedy of Beagh, when being pursued with a net, turning and running back towards him to retrieve a shoe that he had dropped.

Something of Con's character can be glimpsed in his father's will (emphasis added):

> On the 3rd of Jany in the year of our Lord 1931, I John Kennedy, Beagh do make this my last will and testament:
>
> I bequeath to my wife the upper room & £5.
>
> *The house, land & stock to my son Con, with the provision that he is not to act the part of boss over the other members of the family.*

Figure E.1 Con Kennedy of Beagh, *c*.1980

I leave £30 to Annie, £20 to Mary and £20 to Joe.

I leave £2 for Masses for the repose of my own soul.

I leave £2 for Masses for the repose of the souls of my father, mother, brothers & sisters.

I leave 1/– to my son Patk. and 1/– to my son Neil both of whom are at present in America.[1]

Con, then, was bossy, and he was stubborn too. There was a right way and a wrong way to do things. Con's way was the right way. And he had no time for 'ignorance'. One Sunday in the 1970s, when the bus struggled up the hill-head in Ardara after mass, he remarked to nobody in particular that the 'internal combustion engine' was a wonderful thing, and he was duly appalled when a travelling companion sniffed, 'It isn't worth a damn without the diesel.'

No one now remembers Con mentioning anything of what had happened in Beagh in the mid-1850s, a half-century before his birth. Still, genealogy—he might have said 'breed'—mattered to him, and he had the bearing of one who knew that he came of people of more substance than he enjoyed. In the chemist's shop in Ardara in the 1960s, he was once mistaken for one of the Táilliúr Kennedys. When the innocent chemist

---

[1] Document in possession of the author.

responded to his abrupt denial with 'But are you not related?', Con retorted in the English-clad Irish spoken by that generation, 'Not one drop's blood!' The joke was on the indignant one. The Táilliúrs had more and better land than Con Kennedy's people since his great-grandfather, Pat, 'mortgaged' the best part of the second-best 'cut' in Beagh to James Gallagher to get money for whiskey. That is what the Táilliúrs knew, and the records of state and estate—rates and rents, the paper trail of the poor—confirm that in 1855, Con's grandfather, James Pat, succeeded the old man as tenant of a much reduced holding.

The state only started trying to record all Irish births, deaths, and marriages in 1864, and if Ardara's 'economical' priest, John D. McGarvey, ever systematically recorded baptisms, funerals, and marriages before 1867, no register now survives that would allow the accepted notion that families with the same surname are not related to be traced any further back in time. And, of course, records could only carry it so far—at some point, all are related. But, here, fact lies beyond the horizon of history, and some facts do not need to be known. On a summer's day in the early 1970s, the same Con Kennedy squeezed his long frame into the back of a tiny grey car beside three small children. Seat-belts—not compulsory for drivers in the 'South' of Ireland until 1979—were then an added extra, and a child's car seat a puzzling contraption seen only in mail-order catalogues (Figure E.2).

'Adam and Eve and Nip Me went over the bridge to bathe. Adam and Eve were drowned, who was saved?'

The boy who answered received a sharp pinch from calloused fingers. It was an old catch—as old as some mummers' rhymes.[2] And the lesson was valuable in that place in the 1970s. The wise contemplate the consequence of putting words on what they know, and sometimes the shrewd say nothing at all.

The shrewd may say that the boy should have known better than to make a history of the homeplace. *Níl coir san fhocal nach ndeirtear* (There is no harm in the word not spoken) was an adage between the Tullies and Downstrands when the events described in this book took place, and it is not bereft of wisdom. An English historian has compared his method to that of a policeman looking for clues.[3] An Italian historian has reflected on how his weighing and considering evidence compares to the method of a

---

[2] Iona Opie and Peter Opie, *The Lore and Language of Schoolchildren*, with an Introduction by Marina Warner (New York, 2001 [1959]), 58–61.
[3] Robin W. Winks, ed., *The Historian as Detective: Essays on Evidence* (New York, 1969), xiii–xxiii.

Figure E.2 The author and siblings, Fionnuala and Ciarán, Beagh, 1972

judge.[4] And a historian of rural Ireland accepts that he risks comparison to that most reviled figure in the criminal justice process—the informer, somebody like Patrick McGlynn.

But a history has been made of the homeplace, and central to it is James Gallagher. *Translations* (1980), Brian Friel's great play about language and politics, loss, learning, and betrayal, is set in the same time and place.[5] Redcoat engineers are mapping south-west Donegal. A local fellow, a schoolmaster's son, who does not live there anymore, is working with

[4] Carlo Ginzburg, *The Judge and the Historian: Marginal Notes on a Late-Twentieth-Century Miscarriage of Justice* (London and New York, 1999), 12–18.

[5] On *Translations*, see Seamus Deane, 'Introduction', in Brian Friel, *Selected Plays: Irish Drama Selections, 6* (Gerrards Cross, 1984), 11–22, 21–2, since republished in Brian Friel, *Plays 1* (London, 2001).

them to elucidate place-names. And he scoffs at having to explain how a well came to be named after 'a man long dead, long forgotten, his name "eroded" beyond recognition, whose trivial little story nobody in the parish remembers'.[6] James Gallagher had not been entirely 'forgotten' before the making of this history; after all, I heard of him before I read of him in a magistrate's file in a state archive and before I pored over his rates and rentals, and those of his neighbours. His 'trivial little story' was known to me. Still, the story that I heard had been so 'eroded' that it did not include some crucial facts. It was the magistrate's file and press reports of a resulting court case, not some fireside story, that revealed Gallagher's decision to clear his subtenants to have precipitated the Mollies' raid on his house on 9 March 1856; the threatening letter left on his dresser that night had explicitly warned 'your royal highness' to 'relinquish your idea of dispossessing people'. It was those same archival sources that established that, when Gallagher did not heed that warning, the prospect that he would be beaten to death was a factor in McGlynn's decision to write to Daniel Cruise and turn informer. And it was a government land valuation that identified the dispossessed as Brogans, Mooneys, McCaffertys, and O'Donnells. Significantly too, so eroded was the story in my time, that while I had heard that Gallagher purchased land, in sordid circumstances, from tenants—the Mulherns 'in the time of the Famine' and hard-drinking Pat Kennedy (but not, for some reason, indebted Widow Sweeney)—nobody ever made mention to me of the man having got rid of those four families.

This history has offered an explanation of that omission: the people cleared were subtenants, and the stories that I heard were told by the descendants of tenants, people with their names in the agent's book. They and their forebears had been chosen to remain in the place, when their siblings left. The chosen ones—among the Sweeneys, my grandfather (b. 1900) back at least to his grandfather (b. *c.*1830), and as many generations among the Kennedys—were beneficiaries of emigration, for they got the homeplace. But they were tied to the homeplace too, obligated to remain there and to look after elderly parents while the prodigals disported themselves in the bright cities of America, Scotland, England, and Australia. And many of them resented it, quietly cursing the bog and the potato patch, the rain and the reproach of neighbours that were their fate. In autumn 1936, Brian Ó Baoill, 77, of Mín an Chearrbhaigh, in the hills south of Ardara, raked over the ashes of his life with Seán Ó hEochaidh:

[6] *Translations*, II.i.

Tá mé suas le ceithre scór bliadhan . . . I am coming up on eighty years of age
and in my early years . . . yerrah, I didn't see much worldly pleasure in my
early years, just trying to live as best I could. I had few of my own people
around. I only had my mother, and, indeed, I had it tough in my early years,
and I would have to pity my mother trying to do the best for me, and when
I was able to fend for myself I had to look after her. I decided to leave my
mother, but there was no way to leave her by herself, and I used often have a
thought of going away and leaving this place. But then, I used to think that
the neighbours would cast it up to me, and I would bring ill-luck on myself,
for leaving her by herself.[7]

Other people did get away. In the 1910s Barney McNelis (b. 1881) of
Kilgole, outside Ardara, got up one morning, and he went to the bog with a
creel and *sleán* or turfspade. And there he took a bundle with his Sunday suit
and good shoes from the creel and he walked to Glenties, to get a train to
Stranorlar, connecting to Strabane and Derry, where he took ship to
Glasgow, and then to New Zealand. Nobody at home had known he was
leaving. They said that he must have wanted to avoid any upset in the house.
Perhaps he did, but Barney McNelis left Kilgole like a runaway slave.

The elderly, indeed, sometimes went to extraordinary lengths to keep the
chosen one at home. In 1908, one of the Táilliúrs, Patrick, in America sent a
son, Tommy, born in Pennsylvania in 1891, back to Beagh to live with his
sister Nelly and her husband William Gallagher; they had married late, in
spring 1896, when she was in her mid-forties and her husband ten years her
senior. The marriage had been childless, and Tommy would have been
expected to get the place after them.[8] Over a century later, in 2015, in Long
Island, New York, two of Tommy's surviving children (b. 1920s and 1930s)
remembered him saying that Nelly had told him that his by then widowed
mother in Philadelphia had died. It was a lie, a cruel delusion only broken
on a day in 1914 when Nelly was out and the postman arrived with a letter
addressed to the young fellow, then in his early twenties. It was from his
mother, asking why he never wrote. Nelly had been destroying letters from
America in hopes of keeping him in Ireland. Tommy left for Philadelphia.
In 1920, he came back to marry Con Kennedy's sister Sarah. But they saw
no future for themselves in Beagh, and in 1923 with an 11-month-old son,
Patrick, they returned to the States, and settled in Brooklyn.[9]

Such was the place in which the 'trivial little story'—the smallholder-
transmitted memory that was received in my own time—preserved details

[7] NFCM 233: 4,283–4.
[8] GRO, Marriages, Glenties 1896/2/117. Thomas's passport application (1920) indicates that he had been in Ireland in 1908–14; see NARA, Passport Applications, 1906–25.
[9] GRO, Marriages, Glenties 1921/2/84, and for their return to the States, see the
manifest of the *Columbia* departing Derry, 5 Mar. 1923.

of Gallagher's unseemly *purchase* of land from *tenants* but nothing of his *clearance* of *subtenants*. And, for the same reason as those details were preserved, the story told of how the man with most land in Beagh let his father go to the poorhouse. That letter left on Gallagher's dresser in March 1856, warning him against dispossessing people, had also advised him to treat his father with more kindness. And, in time, when the dispossessed were forgotten, his neglect of his elderly parent became his greatest sin. He had not done what they who told his 'trivial little story' did; he had not shouldered his burden. And there lay a great irony—a man who had thrived in the place made by the squaring of the farms in 1839–41 had not been 'accountable for his own portion', the redolent phrase of the land agent who had overseen that 'new division'.

Irony gets other twists too. In the dark time before the squaring, when so little can be known of Beagh, only a single sentence uttered by any person from the townland can be said to have been put down on paper. It is that sole direct quotation from Nancy Sweeney's husband Patrick (his surname then rendered McSwine) when he testified to the Poor Inquiry in the 1830s. 'For fear it would be cast up to me', he said, 'I would support my sister, my mother, my father, or even my uncle.'[10]

James Gallagher had broken that old rule, yet he had only done the complementary reverse of what those who told his 'trivial little story' did themselves. He had simply done to a prior generation, to his father, what every smallholder did to his own generation and the one coming after him, that is, to his siblings and his children. Gallagher apprehended the logic which others here, until the last few decades, have denied: if every man is only accountable for his own portion, then every 'sentimental veil' must, in time, be torn from the family.[11]

The scholar John O'Donovan, who settled the forms of place-names in south-west Donegal for the Ordnance Survey, was the model for the character in Friel's *Translations* who resists having to tell a 'trivial little story'. 'Tradition', O'Donovan himself once observed, 'scarcely ever remembers more than six generations...'[12] Six or more generations have now passed through some of the houses built at the time of the squaring. Making a history of the homeplace was never an exercise in

---

[10] See Ch. 4 in this volume.
[11] Karl Marx and Frederich Engels, *The Communist Manifesto*, with an Introduction by A. J. P. Taylor (Harmondsworth, 1985), 82.
[12] John O'Donovan, ed., *Annals of the Kingdom of Ireland, by the Four Masters, from the Earliest Period to the Year 1616* (2nd edn, Dublin, 1856), 2421. In glossing *le h-anamanna na seacht sinsear a d'fhág tú*, for the souls of the seven generations before you, lexicographer Pádraig Ua Duinnín, remarked that 'seven generations, about 210 years' was considered a 'measurable ancestral period'. Quoted in Fox, *Tory Islanders*, 31.

casting up the doings of the long dead to the living, and, indeed, the history that has been made only underscores the absurdity of calling anybody to account for their ancestors. Each of the eight families who held land as tenants in Beagh in 1857 had benefited from the clearance of half-a-dozen families when the place was squared less than twenty years earlier. Then, from the Famine the eldest children in every house early understood that their mother would one day stand in the door and throw the tongs after them—a charm performed when somebody was setting off on a long journey—and that one of their younger brothers, often the youngest, would get their father's holding. And later, after tenants had become owners and there was a need for things to be done legally, they knew too that when the day came for the old man to sit down to make his last will and testament his only thought of them would be to bequeath them a shilling, so that they, like Con Kennedy's elder brothers in America, could not dispute what had been determined at their birth. Those people who broke the pattern and remained at home with no prospect of inheriting, led quiet, celibate lives, and every decade, when the census was taken, the truth was told on state paper—a brother was their master, and they were 'labourers' or 'servants' in his house.

Beagh is different now. In the early 1990s my uncle John Joe Sweeney complimented Danny Sweeney—no relation, not one drop's blood—on the fine house that his son Myles was building. 'It is a monster!', Danny said, according to John Joe, who told things well: 'It is too big. Houses these days are too big, and nobody living in them. Way back, houses had only two rooms. But if you went out in the morning, you could count the wains coming out the door to go to school—one, two, three . . . maybe ten. And if you went inside you would find a man and a woman and some auld hoor cocked up in the corner.'

That was Beagh, through the early 1900s—a place made in the time of the Famine, when its people's relationship to each other and their dead gained new definition, and they found their place in the wide, wide world.

The End

Appendix: Digital Resources

Manuscript sources accessible, in whole or in part, online are identified in the Select Bibliography. Two of three Tithe Applotment Books for Inishkeel in the National Archives of Ireland were microfilmed in the 1970s, and can now be accessed at www.nationalarchives.ie. Not microfilmed, due to an oversight, was the volume that includes data on Beagh; the original documents must be examined in Dublin. The National Archives is currently putting materials from the Valuation Office online. Among them are Field Books used by valuators in Inishkeel in 1837–9. However, the Valuation Office's more useful Perambulation Book, 1855–7, has yet to appear online. The first edition (1835) of Ordnance Survey sheet 73 can be accessed at www.osi.ie. The revised map (1847–50) was marked up in 1855–7 by the valuators who produced Griffith's Valuation (1857); that marked-up map and valuation data are available at www.askaboutireland.ie. The civil register of births, deaths, and marriages can be accessed at www. irishgenealogy.ie and, for the parish of Ardara, some Catholic baptisms and marriages can be accessed at www.nli.ie.

Select Bibliography

MANUSCRIPT MATERIAL

Asterisked materials are available online; see Appendix.

Donegal County Archive, Lifford
Ballyshannon Poor Law Union Records
Glenties Poor Law Union Minute Books
Glenties Poor Law Union Registry
Grand Jury Road Presentments

General Register's Office
Birth, Deaths, and Marriages*

National Archives of Ireland
Calendar of Grants of Probate Wills
Census of Ireland: Household Returns, 1901, 1911*; Census Search Forms*
Chief Secretary's Office Registered Papers
Convict Reference Files
Distress Papers
Education Department Files
Irish Crime Records
Irish Petty Sessions Court Records*
Dog Licence Applications*
Official Papers
Ordnance Survey Field Name Books
Ordnance Survey Progress Reports
Outrage Papers
State of the Country Papers
Tithe Applotment Books*
Valuation Office, Field Books, 1837–9*
Valuation Office, Perambulation Books, 1855–6

National Library of Ireland
Catholic Parish Registers:*
    Ardara: Baptism, 1869–77, 1878–80
    Ardara: Marriages, 1867–75
Conyngham Papers
Larcom Papers

Trinity College Dublin
Congested Districts Boards, Baseline Reports

University College, Dublin
National Folklore Collection: Main Collection; Schools Collection*

Valuation Office
See National Archives of Ireland

OFFICIAL PUBLICATIONS

Return of the Constabulary Police of Ireland..., HC 1829 (131), xxii

First Report of the Commissioners of Public Instruction, Ireland, HC 1835 (45), xxxiii

Poor Inquiry (Ireland): Appendix (A) and Supplement, HC 1835 (369), xxxii

Poor Inquiry (Ireland): Appendix (D)..., HC 1836 (36), xxxi

First Report of the Commissioners of Inquiry into the State of the Irish Fisheries: With the Minutes of Evidence and Appendix, HC 1837 (22), xxii

Second Report of Geo. Nicholls, Esq.... on Poor Laws, Ireland, HC 1837–38 (91), xxxviii

Return of the Number of Retail Spirit Licences now in Force..., HC 1837–38 (717), xlvi

Evidence Taken before Her Majesty's Commissioners of Inquiry into the State of Law and Practice in Respect to the Occupation of Land in Ireland. Part II, HC 1845 (616), xx

Fourth Annual Report of the Commissioners of Public Works, in re the Fisheries of Ireland, HC 1846 (713), xxii

Correspondence relating to Measures for Relief of Distress in Ireland (Board of Works Series), July 1846–January 1847, HC 1847 [764], l

Correspondence from January to March 1847, Relating to the Measures Adopted for the Relief of the Distress in Ireland, HC 1847 [797], lii

Returns of Agricultural Produce in Ireland, in the Year 1847, HC 1847–48 [923], lvii

Twenty-Eighth Report of the Inspectors-General on the General State of the Prisons of Ireland, 1849; with Appendices, HC 1850 [1229], xxix

Census of Ireland for the Year 1851, pt. ii, Returns of Agricultural Produce in 1851, HC 1854 [1589], lvii

Select Committee of the House of Lords Appointed to Consider the Consequences of Extending the Functions of the Constabulary in Ireland to the Suppression or Prevention of Illicit Distillation, HC 1854 (53), x

Report from the Select Committee of the House of Lords, Appointed to Inquire into the Practical Working of the System of National Education in Ireland..., HC 1854 (525), xv

Twenty-Second Report of the Commissioners of National Education in Ireland, (for the Year 1855), with Appendices, HC 1856 [2142–I], xxvii

Thirty-Fifth Report of the Inspectors-General on the General State of the Prisons of Ireland, 1856, HC 1857 Session 2 (2236), xvii

Thirty-Sixth Report of the Inspectors-General on the General State of the Prisons of Ireland, 1857..., HC 1857–58 (2394), xxx

Report from the Select Committee on Destitution (Gweedore and Cloughaneely)..., HC 1857–58 (412), xiii

Twenty-Third Report of the Commissioners of National Education in Ireland, (for the Year 1856), with Appendices, Vol. I, HC 1858 (2304-I), xx

Return of the Several Counties and Districts, and Baronies of Counties, in Ireland, Proclaimed under the Provisions of the Crime and Outrage Act..., HC 1860 (195), lvii

A Return 'of the Outrages Specially Reported by the Constabulary as Committed within the Barony of Kilmacrenan, County Donegal, during the Last Ten Years', HC 1861 (404), lii

Returns of the Names of All the Schools in Connection with the Board of National Education in Ireland, 1862. Part I. Province of Ulster, HC 1864 (481), xlvii

Report from the Select Committee of the House of Lords on the Tenure (Ireland) Bill..., HC 1867 (518), xiv

First, Second and Special Reports from the Select Committee of the House of Commons (in 1873) on Juries (Ireland), HC 1873 (283), xv

Report from the Select Committee on Jury System (Ireland)..., HC 1874 (244), ix

Royal Irish Constabulary. Evidence taken before the Committee of Inquiry, 1901. With Appendix, HC 1902 (Cd. 1094), xlii

A Return... of the Persons Holding the Commission of the Peace, HC 1905 (118), lxv

NEWSPAPERS

America
Hazleton Plain Speaker (PA)
Oakland Tribune (CA)
Carbon Advocate (PA)

Australia
The Age (Melbourne)
Argus (Melbourne)
Ovens and Murray Advertiser
Townsville Daily Bulletin

Ireland
Ballyshannon Herald
Freeman's Journal
Irishman
London-Derry Journal (*Derry Journal* from 1880)
Londonderry Sentinel
Londonderry Standard
Ulsterman
Vindicator

OTHER CONTEMPORARY WORKS

Anon., *Facts from Gweedore, Compiled from the Notes of Lord George Hill: A Facsimile Reprint of the Fifth Edition (1887)*, with an Introduction by E. E. Evans (Belfast, 1971)

Coulter, Henry, *The West of Ireland: Its Existing Condition, and Prospects* (Dublin, 1862)

Day, Angélique, and Patrick Williams, eds., *Ordnance Survey Memoirs of Ireland*, xxxix. *Parishes of County Donegal II, 1835–6: Mid, West and South Donegal* (Belfast and Dublin, 1997)

Dorian, Hugh, *The Outer Edge of Ulster: A Memoir of Social Life in Nineteenth-Century Donegal*, ed. Breandán Mac Suibhne and David Dickson (Dublin, 2000)

Furniss, John, *The Sight of Hell* (Dublin, n.d. [1855])

Griffith, Richard, *General Valuation of Rateable Property... Union of Glenties* (Dublin, 1857)

Holland, Denis, *The Landlord in Donegal: Pictures from the Wilds* (Belfast, n.d. [1858])

Larkin, Emmet, and Herman Freudenberger, eds, *A Redemptorist Missionary in Ireland, 1851–1854: Memoirs by Joseph Prost, C.Ss.R.* (Cork, 1998)

O'Donovan, John, et al., *Ordnance Survey Letters, Donegal*, ed. Michael Herity, with a preface by Brian Friel (Dublin, 2000)

Ó Muirgheasa, Énrí, eag., *Dhá Chéad de Cheoltaibh Uladh* (Baile Átha Cliath, 1934)

LATER WORKS

Andrews, J. H., *A Paper Landscape: The Ordnance Survey in Nineteenth-Century Ireland* (Oxford, 1975)

Berger, John, *About Looking* (New York, 1991 [1980])

Berger, John, *Pig Earth* (New York, 1992 [1979])

Bourke, Austin, *'The Visitation of God'? The Potato and the Great Irish Famine* (Dublin, 1993)

Broehl, Jr, Wayne G., *The Molly Maguires* (Cambridge, MA, 1964)

Bulik, Mark, *The Sons of Molly Maguire: The Irish Roots of America's First Labor War* (New York, 2015)

Clark, Samuel, *Social Origins of the Irish Land War* (Princeton, 1979)

Conaghan, Patrick, *The Great Famine in South-West Donegal, 1845–50* (Enniscrone, 1997)

Connolly, S. J., *Priests and People in Pre-Famine Ireland, 1780–1845* (Dublin, 1982)

Delaney, Enda, and Breandán Mac Suibhne, eds, *Ireland's Great Famine and Popular Politics* (New York, 2016)

Donnelly, Jr, James, and Kerby A. Miller, eds, *Irish Popular Culture, 1650–1850* (Dublin, 1998)

Dowling, Martin J., *Tenant Right and Agrarian Society in Ulster, 1600–1870* (Dublin, 1999)

Feldman, Allen, and Éamonn O'Doherty, *The Northern Fiddler: Music and Musicians of Donegal and Tyrone* (Belfast, 1979)

Forsythe, Wes, 'The Measures and Materiality of Improvement in Ireland', *International Journal of Historical Archaeology*, 17 (2013), 72–93

Foster, R. F., *Vivid Faces: The Revolutionary Generation in Ireland, 1890–1923* (London, 2014)

Fox, Robin, *The Tory Islanders: A People on the Celtic Fringe* (Cambridge, 1978)

Friel, Brian, *Translations* (London, 1980)

Garvin, Tom, *The Evolution of Irish Nationalist Politics* (Dublin, 1981)

Garvin, Tom, 'Defenders, Ribbonmen and Others: Underground Political Networks in Pre-Famine Ireland', *Past and Present*, 96 (1982), 133–55

Ginzburg, Carlo, *The Judge and the Historian: Marginal Notes on a Late-Twentieth-Century Miscarriage of Justice*, tr. Anthony Shugar (London and New York, 1999)

Guinnane, Timothy W., *The Vanishing Irish: Households, Migration, and the Rural Economy in Ireland, 1850–1914* (Princeton, 1997)

Hoppen, K. T., *Elections, Politics and Society in Ireland, 1832–1885* (Oxford, 1984)

Joyce, Patrick, 'The Journey West', *Field Day Review*, 10 (2014), 62–93

Kenny, Kevin, *Making Sense of the Molly Maguires* (Oxford, 1998)

Kerr, Donal, *'A Nation of Beggars'? Priests, People and Politics in Famine Ireland, 1846–52* (Oxford, 1994)

Korson, George, *Minstrels of the Mine Patch: Songs and Stories of the Anthracite Industry* (Hatboro, 1964 [1938])

Larkin, Emmet, *The Pastoral Role of the Catholic Church in Pre-Famine Ireland, 1750–1850* (Dublin, 2006)

Lee, Joseph, *The Modernisation of Irish Society, 1848–1918* (Dublin, 2008 [1973])

Lloyd, David, *Irish Times: Temporalities of Modernity* (Dublin, 2008)

Lloyd, David, *Irish Culture and Colonial Modernity, 1800–2000: The Transformation of Oral Space* (Cambridge, 2011)

McGill, Lochlann, *In Conall's Footsteps* (Dingle, 1992)

McGill, P. J., *A History of the Parish of Ardara* (Ballyshannon, 1970)

Maguire, Edward, *A History of the Diocese of Raphoe*, 2 vols. (Dublin, 1920)

Miller, David W., 'Landscape and Religious Practice: A Study of Mass Attendance in Pre-Famine Ireland', *Éire-Ireland*, 40/1–2 (2005), 90–106

Miller, Kerby A., *Emigrants and Exiles: Ireland and the Irish Exodus to North America* (Oxford, 1985)

Miller, Kerby A., and Brian Gurrin, 'The Derry Watershed: Its Religious and Political Demography, 1622–1911', *Field Day Review*, 9 (2013), 38–53

Mokyr, Joel, *Why Ireland Starved: A Quantitative and Analytical History of the Irish Economy, 1800–1850* (Abingdon, 1983)

Muir, Edwin, and Guido Ruiggero, eds, *Microhistory and the Lost Peoples of Europe* (Baltimore, 1991)

Murray, A. C., 'Agrarian Violence and Nationalism in Nineteenth-Century Ireland: The Myth of Ribbonism', *Irish Economic and Social History*, 13 (1986), 56–73

Nally, David P., *Human Encumbrances: Political Violence and the Great Irish Famine* (Notre Dame, IN, 2011)

Nolan, William, Liam Ronayne, and Mairéad Dunlevy, eds, *Donegal: History and Society* (Dublin, 1995)

Ó Cadhla, Stiofán, *Civilizing Ireland: Ordnance Survey, 1824–1842: Ethnography, Cartography, Translation* (Dublin, 2007)

Ó Gráda, Cormac, *Ireland Before and After the Famine: Explorations in Irish Economic History* (Manchester, 1988)

Ó Gráda, Cormac, *An Drochshaol: Béaloideas agus Amhráin* (Baile Átha Cliath, 1994)

Ó Gráda, Cormac, *Ireland: A New Economic History, 1780–1939* (Oxford, 1994)

Ó Gráda, Cormac, ed., *Famine 150* (Ballsbridge, 1997)

Ó Gráda, Cormac, *Black '47 and Beyond: The Great Irish Famine* (Princeton, 1999)

Ó Gráda, Cormac, *Ireland's Great Famine: Interdisciplinary Perspectives* (Dublin, 2006)

Ó Gráda, Cormac, *Famine: A Short History* (Princeton, 2009)

Ó Gráda, Cormac, *Eating People is Wrong and Other Essays on Famine, its Past and its Future* (Princeton, 2015)

Póirtéir, Cathal, ed., *Glórtha ón Ghorta: Béaloideas na Gaeilge agus an Gorta Mór* (Baile Átha Cliath, 1996)

Scally, Robert James, *The End of Hidden Ireland: Rebellion, Famine and Emigration* (Oxford, 1995)

Scott, James C., *Seeing Like a State: How Certain Schemes to Improve the Human Condition have Failed* (New Haven, 1998)

Scott, James C., *Decoding Subaltern Politics: Ideology, Disguise, and Resistance in Agrarian Politics* (New York, 2013)

Shovlin, Francis, *Narin and Downstrands* (Trafford, 2012)

Taylor, Lawrence J., *Occasions of Faith: An Anthropology of Irish Catholics* (Dublin, 1995)

Vaughan, W. E., *Sin, Sheep and Scotsmen: John George Adair and the Derryveagh Evictions, 1861* (Belfast, 1983)

Vaughan, W. E., *Landlords and Tenants in Mid-Victorian Ireland* (Oxford, 1994)

Vaughan, W. E., *Murder Trials in Ireland, 1836–1914* (Dublin, 2009)

Whelehan, Niall, 'Labour and Agrarian Violence in the Irish Midlands', *Saothar*, 37 (2012), 5–17

Index

Achonry, diocese 193
Adamson, James 165
Africa 66–7, 275
Áighe 227 n. 35, 279–82
alcohol 1, 5, 6, 10, 32, 54, 113, 123, 141,
    155, 205–6, 216, 225 n. 26, 245,
    265, 266, 279, 287
  clergy 9, 11, 12, 191–2, 195, 205–6,
    207, 209, 212
  emigrants 64, 229, 231, 261–2, 279
  fairs and festivals 1, 9, 10, 11, 12,
    138, 140
  illicit distillation 5, 10–11, 28 n. 17, 30,
    49, 75, 76, 134–5, 154, 212, 225,
    226, 274–5
  Mollies 30, 40, 54, 60, 75, 129, 131,
    136, 154, 171, 199, 217, 223, 225,
    231, 272, 274–5; see also Revenue
    Police; publicans and public houses
  policing 10, 30, 49, 62, 74 n. 62, 154
Allingham, William, poet 92
Altnagapple 43 n. 59, 148–9, 166, 230–1
America 60, 216
  aid from 187, 219
  Civil War 226–7, 229, 231, 254, 260
    n. 40
  emigration to 7–8, 24 n. 5, 64–5, 66,
    108–9, 112–13, 115, 116, 121,
    166, 200, 209, 229–32, 233–6,
    245, 254, 261–2, 263–4, 266, 267,
    274, 276–7, 278–9, 286, 289, 290,
    292
  letters to and from 48, 245, 261, 263;
    see also Ancient Order of
    Hibernians, California, New York,
    Pennsylvania
  return from 7, 64–7, 226–7, 262, 264,
    278–9, 290
Ancient Order of Hibernians:
  Ireland 233–7, 273–4
  United States 65, 66, 229–32, 233, 235–6
Anderson, John 30, 162–3
Anglo-Irish Treaty 263, 266, 274
Annagry 228 n. 40, 234
Antrim, county 24, 29, 67; see also Belfast
Ardara, parish 2–3, 4–5, 8, 25, 27, 48,
    49–50, 53, 54, 73, 118, 161,
    179–83, 184–6, 189–93, 194, 195,
    204, 208, 211, 227, 262, 271

arbitration courts 11, 174–5
churches and chapels 3, 92, 181–2
culture 255–7, 271–3
economy 246–50, 255 n. 32, 268–9,
    271–2
literacy 134
politics 262–4, 273–5
population 12, 224
republicanism 227–8
Ribbonmen, Mollies, and
    Hibernians 40–1, 42–5, 47,
    131–8, 141, 143–4, 148–9, 154,
    166–75, 212–13, 220–5, 230–2,
    235, 236–7, 273–4
schools 37, 182–3, 194, 210
Ardara, town 2, 3, 4, 11, 14, 18, 22, 23,
    24, 30, 32, 33–6, 38, 40, 44, 50,
    54, 55, 57, 64, 81, 88, 95, 103,
    122, 139, 148–9, 157, 162, 200,
    203, 227, 255
  amenities 92
  barracks 12, 28, 41–2, 134, 226
  churches and chapels 3, 92
  establishment 6, 9
  fair 6, 10, 92, 93, 138, 147, 264
  golf club 252
  petty sessions 74 n. 61, 120, 223,
    240–1, 244–5, 250–3, 272
  population 31
  public houses 39, 43, 50, 74, 92, 129,
    153
Ardkeenan, Roscommon 31
Ardnamona 61–2
Arlands 91
Arle, James 73–4, 137
Armagh 29, 67
  archbishops 180, 198
  arms 27–8, 34, 43 n. 58, 47, 50–1, 55, 59,
    60, 62, 63, 66–7, 73, 74 n. 62, 75,
    132, 143, 146, 191, 221, 228 n.
    40, 274
    McGlynn requests 33, 36, 130–1
    raids 25–6, 108, 130, 131, 136–7,
        146–7, 168, 179
    tensions in Ardara lodge over 137–8,
        168
army, British 25, 59, 60, 155, 189, 198,
    252
  Black and Tans 265, 274